The Status of Women in Classical Economic
Thought

The Status of Women in Classical Economic Thought

Edited by

Robert Dimand and Chris Nyland

Edward Elgar
Cheltenham, UK • Northampton, MA, USA

Published by
Edward Elgar Publishing Limited
Glensanda House
Montpellier Parade
Cheltenham
Glos GL50 1UA
UK

Edward Elgar Publishing, Inc.
136 West Street
Suite 202
Northampton
Massachusetts 01060
USA

A catalogue record for this book
is available from the British Library

Library of Congress Cataloguing in Publication Data

The status of women in classical economic thought / edited by Chris Nyland and Robert Dimand.
    p. cm.
  Includes bibliographical references and index.
    1. Women—Economic conditions. 2. Women—Social conditions. 3. Sex
  role—Economic aspects. 4. Classical school of economics. 5.
  Economics—History. I. Nyland, Chris. II. Dimand, Robert W. (Robert William)

HQ1381.S73 2003
305.42—dc22

                                                                        2003061747

ISBN 1 84064 478 8

Printed and bound in Great Britain by MPG Books Ltd, Bodmin, Cornwall

Contents

List of Contributors   vii
Acknowledgements   ix

1. Gender Relations and Classical Economics – The   1
    Evolution of a Tradition
    Chris Nyland and Robert Dimand

2. Poulain de la Barre and the Rationalist Analysis of the   21
    Status of Women
    Chris Nyland

3. John Locke, Equality of Rights and Diversity of   40
    Attributes
    Chris Nyland

4. Biology and Environment: Montesquieu's Relativist   63
    Analysis of Gender Behaviour
    Chris Nyland

5. Adam Smith, Stage Theory and the Status of Women   86
    Chris Nyland

6. Women's Progress and 'the End of History'   108
    Chris Nyland

7. Condorcet and Equality of the Sexes: One of Many   127
    Fronts for a Great Fighter for Liberty of the Eighteenth
    Century
    Peter Groenewegen

8. Cultivating Sympathy: Sophie Condorcet's Letters on   142
    Sympathy
    Evelyn L. Forget

9.   'Let There be no Distinction Between the Sexes':   165
      Jeremy Bentham on the Status of Women
      Annie L. Cot

10.   An Eighteenth-Century English Feminist Response to   194
      Political Economy: Priscilla Wakefield's *Reflections*
      (1798)
      Robert Dimand

11.   The Market for Virtue: Jean-Baptiste Say on Women in   206
      the Economy and Society
      Evelyn L. Forget

12.   Women in Nassau Senior's Economic Thought   224
      Robert Dimand

13.   William Thompson and Anna Doyle Wheeler: A   241
      Marriage of Minds on Jeremy Bentham's Doorstep
      Chris Nyland and Tom Heenan

14.   Taking Harriet Martineau's Economics Seriously   262
      David M. Levy

15.   John Stuart Mill, Harriet Taylor and French Social   285
      Theory
      Evelyn L. Forget

      Index   311

Contributors

Annie L. Cot, Professor, Groupe de Recherches en Epistemologie et Socio-Economie (GRESE), University of Paris I Panthéon-Sorbonne, France, has published extensively about Bentham and utilitarianism. She is a member of the executive committee of the History of Economics Society, and has served as President of the Association Charles Gide Pour l'Etude de la Pensée Economique.

Robert Dimand, Chancellor's Chair for Research Excellence, Department of Economics, Brock University, St. Catharines, Ontario, Canada, is the author of *The Origins of the Keynesian Revolution* (Edward Elgar and Stanford University Press, 1988), co-author (with M. A. Dimand) of *A History of Game Theory*, Vol. 1 (Routledge, 1996), co-editor (with M. A. Dimand and E. L. Forget) of *Women of Value: Feminist Essays on the History of Economics* (Edward Elgar, 1995) and *A Biographical Dictionary of Women Economists* (Edward Elgar, 2000), and editor of *The Origins of Macroeconomics* (Routledge, 2002).

Evelyn L. Forget, Professor of Economics in the Department of Community Health Services, Faculty of Medicine, University of Manitoba, Winnipeg, Canada, is the author of *The Social Economics of Jean-Baptiste Say* (Routledge, 1999) and co-editor (with S. Peart) of *Reflections on the Classical Canon in Economics: Essays in Honour of Samuel Hollander* (Routledge, 2001), (with R. Lobdell) of *The Peasant in Economic Thought* (Edward Elgar, 1995) and (with R.W. Dimand and M.A. Dimand) of *Women of Value: Feminist Essays on the History of Economics* (Edward Elgar, 1995) and *A Biographical Dictionary of Women Economists* (Edward Elgar, 2000).

Peter Groenewegen is Emeritus Professor of Economics, University of Sydney, Australia. He has published extensively on Alfred Marshall and in many other areas of economic thought. Of his great number of publications, the more recent include *Classics and Moderns in Economics, Vol. 1: Essays on Nineteenth- and Twentieth-Century Economic Thought* (Routledge 2003), *A Concise History of Economic Thought: From Mercantilism to Monetarism* (Palgrave Macmillan Eighteenth-century Economics 2003) (with G. Vaggi) and *Becaria and Smith and their Contemporaries* (Routledge 2002).

Thomas Heenan, Post-Doctoral Fellow in the Management Department, Monash University, Melbourne, Australia. He has published in the field of political biography and is currently researching a volume on progressive Taylorism and the Cold War together with Chris Nyland.

David M. Levy, Associate Professor of Economics, George Mason University, Fairfax, Virginia, USA, is the author of *How the Dismal Science Got Its Name: Classical Economics and the Ur-Text of Racial Politics* (University of Michigan Press, 2001), and of *The Economic Ideas of Ordinary People: From Preferences to Trade* (Routledge, 1992).

Chris Nyland, Professor of Management, Monash University, Melbourne, Australia, is the author of *Reduced Worktime and the Management of Production* (Cambridge University Press), *The Webbs, Fabianism and Feminism* (Avebury Series in Philosophy 1999), and co-editor of *Malaysian Business in the New Era* (Edward Elgar 2001) (with Russell Smyth, Wendy Smith and Marika Vicziany).

Acknowledgements

The editors would like to thank the publishers of the *History of Political Economy,* the *Journal of the History of Economic* Thought and *Feminist Economics* for permission to reproduce the articles listed below.

Forget, Evelyn L. 1997. 'The Market For Virtue: Jean-Baptiste Say on Women and the Family', *Feminist Economics*, 3 (1).

Forget, Evelyn L. 2001. 'Cultivating Sympathy. Sophie Condorcet's Letters on Sympathy', *Journal of the History of Economic Thought*. 23(3).

Nyland, Chris 1993. 'John Locke and the Social Position of Women', *History of Political Economy*, 25 (1).

Nyland, Chris 1993. 'Adam Smith, Stage Theory, and the Status of Women', *History of Political Economy,* Vol 25 (4).

Nyland, Chris 1993. 'Poulain de la Barre and the Rationalist Analysis of the Status of Women' History of Economics Review, Issue 19.

Nyland, Chris 1997. 'Biology and Environment: Montesquieu's Relativist Analysis of Gender Behaviour', *History of Political Economy,* 29 (3).

The editors would also like to thank Miriam Lang and Lyn Vinton for their kind and extremely efficient assistance in the processing of this volume. Their efforts and commitment are deeply appreciated.

Chris Nyland would like to dedicate his contribution to the production of this work to Morgan.

1.   Gender Relations and Classical Economics – The Evolution of a Tradition

Chris Nyland and Robert Dimand

The classical political economists gave more attention to the economic and social status of women, and commonly did so with a great deal more insight, than is generally recognized.   John Stuart Mill is remembered as an outstanding liberal feminist for *On the Subjection of Women* and for his Parliamentary support for the enfranchisement of women.   Harriet Hardy Taylor Mill is recognized increasingly as his intellectual partner, while his father, James Mill, is remembered for his cursory dismissal of women's suffrage in his *Essay on Government*, which provoked an eloquent response from William Thompson and Anna Doyle Wheeler.   These exceptions aside, however, the classical economists are generally held to have focused on the activities of men in markets (to the neglect of women's status), the sphere of household production and women's employment outside the home.   It is generally believed that even economists who discussed the principles of population accorded women little role as makers of choices.   Leading feminist explorations of the history of political and social thought about women (Agonito 1977; Okin 1979; Clark and Lange 1979; Kandal 1988; Shanley and Pateman 1991) cover only one classical economist, John Stuart Mill, and he is considered as a liberal theorist of political liberty rather than being viewed in the context of classical economics (Kennedy and Mendus 1987, in which Jane Rendall writes about Adam Smith, is an exception).

As the essays in this volume show, the focus of classical economics was not nearly as limited to the activities of one gender as conventional wisdom has supposed.   The fact that those who have adhered to this convention have been in error is due in part to the classicals' tendency to often publish their contributions in obscure outlets.   Adam Smith, for example, in a lengthy and conjectural history, expounded on how and why the status of women had evolved across four historic stages of economic development.   Had this conjectural history appeared in *The Wealth of Nations*, it would have attracted widespread notice. However, it appeared in Smith's *Lectures on Jurisprudence,* which was not rediscovered until more than a century after his death. Similarly, Jeremy Bentham's incisive thoughts on relations between the sexes, like his thoughts on so many other matters, were scattered across assorted publications and manuscripts, lessening their impact.

This volume has twin goals. It challenges the conventional wisdom by showing that the classical economists did concern themselves with gender analysis. But in so doing, it also makes the point that the classical tradition developed, over time, a sophisticated response to the question, why is it that in all human societies women have suffered a lower status than that enjoyed by men? The classicals' answer to this question emerged as part of an evolutionary process, in which many writers made independent contributions that collectively amounted to an explanation comprising three key elements. First, it was held that human beings are born with certain inalienable rights, the nature of which is common to both men and women. Secondly, the sexes differ biologically in a number of fundamental ways, but most importantly in their respective capacity to give birth and their relative muscular strength. Thirdly, while the biological differences between the sexes are a constant, the social significance of these forms of human diversity is a variable, dependent on the material and ideological character of the community in which men and women reside. The classical tradition came to hold that these factors went a long way towards explaining why it is that men have been the dominant sex in virtually all societies across both historical time and geographic space.

In suggesting that the development of the classical economists' position on gender status was evolutionary, it is not being argued that its refinement was a unilinear process that carried thought to ever higher stages of clarity and sophistication. The classicals' explanation for gender status, though not echoing it, reflected the intellectual and social needs of the dominant forces prevailing within the environment in which their ideas developed. As these needs were shaped and reshaped, in response to changes in the economic and cultural environment, this transformation was reflected in the explanation for gender status offered by the classicals. The most important manifestation of this process was the manner in which the classical school responded to the question, is it possible for societies to progress to a stage where gender equality is achieved? Implicitly and explicitly – when their dreams of what humans might attain soared to their greatest height – the answer to this question tended increasingly to be in the affirmative. But this trend continued only for as long as an affirmative response served the intellectual needs of a significant part of the body politic. When this aspect of the social environment was transformed and an affirmative answer came to be perceived as decidedly undesirable, a negative reply came to dominance within the classical tradition, and remained unchallenged until a new audience emerged willing and indeed eager to push for an affirmative answer.

If unilinear and unending progress is not implied by the use of the term 'evolution', what is implied is that there was transformation over time, and this change was the sum of a number of smaller steps. Further, it is accepted that the contributions made by individual scholars were commonly a consequence of the pursuit of goals concerned only marginally with explaining why it is that men and women have invariably stood in relation to each other as superordinate and subordinate.

This initial chapter provides an overview of the text, traces the evolution of the classical economists' contribution to the analysis of gender status, and introduces the individual chapters. The story begins in the late seventeenth century, when European liberals' hostility to regal absolutism induced them to begin constructing an argument that would specify what are the 'rights of man', by which the liberals normally meant the rights of men. But in developing their case for political and social justice a number of individuals, such as François Poulain de la Barre, were led to consider the status of women. In chapter two, Nyland examines de la Barre's contribution to the emergent gender literature (see also Steinbrügge 1995 for de la Barre's central role in the *querelle des femmes*). A Cartesian, de la Barre pioneered the rationalist analysis of the status of women. As Nyland notes, during the late seventeenth century, de la Barre was not alone in questioning the all but universally accepted belief that women's innate capacities explained their subordinate social status. Nyland insists, however, that de la Barre stands out from his contemporaries, and deserves recognition for his significant contribution to the economic analysis of gender status. He was the first scholar to apply the deductive method of analysis to the study of women's social position. Further, Nyland suggests de la Barre's utilisation of deductivism enabled him to pioneer the application of conjectural history to the analysis of gender relations, and to highlight the extent to which prejudice and context shaped both popular and scientific understanding of the biological differences between the sexes. In short, Nyland argues that de la Barre directed his peers to the fact that gender status is a product of biology, discrimination and a variable environment.

But in acknowledging de la Barre's contribution, Nyland notes that the Frenchman's use of deductivism caused him to succumb to the trap of hypostatizaion, whereby abstractions that are created for the purpose of analysis come to be understood as material reality. De la Barre allowed his abstraction – or fiction – that women differ biologically from men only in their capacity to reproduce to become an unquestioned reality in his mind. Though this enabled him to highlight the extent to which discrimination and misogyny shaped gender status, it also caused de la Barre to embrace a form of idealism that stretched the notion of discrimination beyond sustainable limits. Sadly, this far from rare fault still prevails in much modern gender analysis.

In chapter three, Nyland focuses on the contribution of John Locke. Nyland shows that Locke added the components of contract, labour productivity and property to the classical economists' explanation for gender status. As with de la Barre, Locke took up gender analysis to further what he considered a wider if not necessarily more significant issue. With de la Barre, the motivating factor behind his exploration of gender relations was a desire to highlight the significance of Cartesian deductivism. He considered that he could make a significant contribution to, and broaden the acceptance of, Decartes' ideas if he could show that the orthodox wisdom that held that men are naturally superior to women was subject to challenge. Locke, by contrast, was prompted to consider gender relations by his desire to justify armed opposition to regal absolutism.

Locke denied that the monarchy had inherited its right to rule from God through Adam. In questioning the divine right of Kings, Locke was aware that he had to ease the fears of those men concerned that casting doubt on this concept would weaken political stability, property rights and the authority of the husband and father. Consequently, Locke advanced an explanation for male seniority that rejected the theological claim that men's superior position was divine in origin. Instead, he put forward the secular argument that men's dominance in the family and wider society was a consequence of their greater capacity to produce material wealth. Given the subsequent influence of Locke's ideas, this secularization of the gender debate was a significant contribution to gender analysis. It also contributed to the struggle of women against the binds of a theological determinism, which had had condemned them to eternal subservience to men. While it is true that Locke did provide a new justification for male domination, he conceded that women were born with rights equal to those of men, and thus acknowledged that gender equality was possible if ways could be found to enhance women's capacity to accumulate wealth and thereby increase their power to gain from contract.

Both de la Barre and Locke confined their analysis to abstract levels, as did their peers Hugo Grotius and Samuel Pufendorf, who made important, though lesser known, contributions to the gender debate. By contrast, Nyland shows in chapter four that Montesquieu's primary contribution to the development of the economics of gender was his systematic study of how diverse patterns of behaviour emerged from the interaction between human biology and the social/physical environment. While his work was far from flattering to women, Montesquieu did nevertheless emphasize and popularize amongst intellectuals the fact that environmental context is a variable of major significance in gender relations. In adopting this position, Montesqieu focused on gender relations as situated in specific contexts. In so doing, he appears to have been influenced by de la Barre's sensitivity to the significance of cultural and social diversity. However, he went beyond de la Barre, being more systematic in his analysis of the role and significance of the physical, economic and cultural environments. His conclusions regarding gender relations were often flawed. Nevertheless, even where this was the case, he adhered rigorously to the true method of the sociology of knowledge. By so doing, Montesquieu offered an explanation for why the relative status of men and women differed across cultures. He also revealed that many of the aspects of gender relations that were traditionally viewed as natural were in fact determined by social context. Consequently, he was able to show convincingly that while it is true many biological differences between the sexes are common to all human societies, the social significance of these differences is most decidedly a variable. For Montesquieu, this latter factor explained why it was that though the women of bourgeois England, aristocratic France and despotic Turkey were all subjected to gender subordination the form and extent of this oppression differed markedly across these societies.

The significance of Montesquieu's contribution was that he focused gender analysts' attention on men and women situated in real world contexts. As a result, he was able to explain both how and why gender status might diverge across geographic space. Adam Smith extended on Montesquieu's work by melding his relativist understanding of gender relations with a theory of social evolution. As Nyland shows in chapter five, Smith, having read Montesquieu, broke with the abstracted tradition. Instead, he embraced Montesquieu's environmentalism, and in so doing explained how gender relations might be transformed not only across space, but also across time. For Smith, it was the changing manner by which populations *attained* and *defended* the material wherewithal required for human survival that was the primary factor in explaining the status enjoyed respectively by women and men in any given society and at different historical periods.

Unlike Montesquieu, who disparaged the intellect and spirit of women, Smith followed Locke in contending that the innate differences between women and men are purely physical. This was in keeping with Smith's position that differences among people – such as those between a philosopher and a street porter – primarily reflected the social and cultural influences of upbringing and experience. Otherwise, there were few innate differences between humans. As the growth of trade and manufacturing corroded militarism, Smith held that differences in physical strength would become less important, as would the interference of fecundity with women's ability to serve as warriors or hunters. Rejecting biological, cultural and economic determinism, Smith held the relativist view that although biological differences are a constant, the social importance of such differences depends on both the geographic and historical context. Hence the development of commerce and industry would improve women's social position by lowering the standing of warriors, and by providing women with more opportunities to accumulate property. In his *Lectures* Smith took into account cultural lags, recognizing the persistence of earlier influences such as the lingering glamour of the aristocracy. But in the long run he held that economic development naturally tended to promote increased equality between the sexes.

By accepting that communities progressed through specific and clearly defined socio-economic stages, Smith was able to explain, with an unprecedented degree of rigour, why gender relations tended to change over time. In his hands gendered stage theory was a progressive argument, implying that the development process naturally tended to enhance the status of women. Although he never published the argument, it was disseminated widely because the notion of gender evolution was taken up and published by others, the most notable of whom was John Millar, who attended Smith's lectures in 1752–1753, and then became his colleague at the University of Glasgow.

In Smith's hands, the stages argument was both progressive and supportive of women, but in the hands of gender conservatives like Millar and his contemporaries Antoine Thomas and William Alexander, it was given a very different spin. These men were not attracted to the idea of unending progress towards gender equality. While Smith's *Lectures*, with their historical vision of economic development inducing continued improvement in the social and economic status of women, languished unpublished for more than a century, works from these more conservative writers on gendered stage theory were published in the late eighteenth century. Millar's *The Distinction of Ranks in Society* and Thomas' *Essay on the Character, The Manners, and the Understanding of Women, in Different Ages* appeared in 1771, and were followed by Alexander's *History of Women* in 1779, all attracting considerable attention.

As Nyland shows in chapter six, Millar initially followed Smith's stages analysis. However, fearful of where the forward march of progress might lead, Millar broke with Smith and called for a halt to women's forward march arguing that if this was not halted women would become slaves to the pleasures of both the mind and body. In making his case, Millar sought to exploit men's fear of women's sexuality, the woman of property's fear that she might lose her wealth, and the fears of both sexes that the family would be undermined should women advance their situation and status beyond what had already been attained. This position was supported by Thomas and Alexander, as was Millar's claim that though men such as themselves were sufficiently strong-willed to bear the burden of increasing wealth without being corrupted, this was not an attribute available to weaker-willed women.

In chapters seven and eight, Groenewegen and Forget explore the work of Nicholas Condorcet and his wife, Sophie de Grouchy. Both were influenced by the notion that gender relations tended to evolve over time. However, unlike Millar and his fellow gender conservatives, Condorcet and de Grouchy enthusiastically embraced the idea that unending progress would lead to gender equality. Deciding which of these two classical scholars ought to appear first in this book was difficult. De Grouchy made her primary contribution to gender economics some years after her husband's death. Nevertheless, there can be little doubt that her feminism drew Condorcet to consider gender status. Arguably, therefore, discussion of her work should appear before that of her husband's. However, she has been placed after Condorcet, as her contribution added an important dimension to gender analysis that was not apparent in the work of Condorcet, Smith or Montesquieu, for De Grouchy explicitly recognized that the needs and concerns of working-class women were not identical to those of other women.

Simone de Beauvoir in *The Second Sex* (1972, p. 139) observed that in the history of the debate on women's status in France it was Mercier, almost alone, who 'waxed indignant at the misery of working women, and thus opened the fundamental question of feminine labour'. Forget's chapter reveals that de Grouchy was amongst the small number of late eighteenth-century French intellectuals who shared Mercier's concern about the welfare of women workers. Moreover, Forget shows that de Grouchy did not merely wax indignant over the sufferings of working-class women. Like her contemporary Mary Wollstonecraft, de Grouchy drew on Smith's *Theory of Moral Sentiments* to design policies that could alleviate the common and specific forms of distress experienced by women of the working class. As a consequence, she raised the important question of the role the state should play in shaping the interaction of class and gender relations, an issue that still continues to divide scholars, policy makers and activists concerned about gender status.

During the French Revolution the fact that women might belong not only to divergent, but also hostile, classes became apparent in the markets of Paris. Amidst the revolutionary fervour, class antagonism surfaced, centred on the debate over whether the price of bread should be regulated by the state or the market forces of supply and demand. The women who sold bread wanted food prices set by the market, because this increased their capacity to accumulate wealth and status, even if it disadvantaged working-class women and men. By contrast, working-class women insisted that the state must set a maximum price that would be charged by the bakers. These women were desperately aware that their well-being and the little status they enjoyed were vitally dependent on their capacity to access this basic human requirement. When the Revolution entered its most explosive and democratic stage from 1791, it was the Parisian working women of the market districts who organized in the *Societé Patriotique et de Bienfaisance des Amies de la Verité,* and allied with the *sans-culotte* movement, to lambast and terrify both the middle-class men who dominated the political assemblies, and their wives who held sway in the salons (Fraisse and Perrot 1993, p. 20). That the regulation of food prices should become a focal point of class conflict during the Revolution was a critical stage in the gender debate. It was important for it highlighted the fact that while women's sex rendered them as one, they were in many ways concomitantly divided by class, and revealed that class privilege and solidarity can outweigh sex in the determination of allegiance, consciousness and status.

Both Condorcet and de Grouchy voiced the hopes of those who thought progress towards human perfectibility would lead to gender equality. But the policy reforms advocated by Condorcet, focusing as they did on equal access to political life and education, reflected the limits of the progressive demands of the middle class. In contrast, de Grouchy, by raising the issue of income distribution and labour market regulation, helped advance gender analysis beyond the needs and desires of the dominant classes and her husband's noble but more limited aims.

In his discussion of Condorcet's contribution to gender analysis, Groenewegen observes that Smith's notion of progress and the evolving nature of gender relations is applauded in Condorcet's work. Liberty was sacrosanct to Condorcet and at the core of his social goals. With true and complete liberty, he argued, humanity would progress to the point where it could achieve the perfection of which it is most capable. From the time he bonded with de Grouchy, gender equality became a critical aspect in his understanding of the requirements for humanity's progression to perfection. Motivated by this belief, Condorcet campaigned for social reforms that would counter both men's abuse of their physical strength and the discriminatory practices they had institutionalized to ensure they remained the dominant sex. As Condorcet observed in 1790: 'Either no individual of the human species has genuine rights, or all have the same rights; and he who votes against the rights of another, whatever that person's religion, colour, or sex, thereby forgoes his own rights' (cited in Sledziewski 1993, p. 41).

As far as Condorcet was concerned, both women and men should be accorded equal access to the franchise and education. Given the historical context of the early years of the French Revolution, his contribution was radical and, indeed, decidedly revolutionary. But it was de Grouchy, writing four years after her husband's death, whose ideas and reform proposals more effectively captured the new class factor that had been injected into practical gender economics with the active involvement of the poor in the French Revolution after 1790.

De Grouchy's contribution to the gender debate appeared in a series of eight essays, which she published in 1798 together with a translation of Smith's *Theory of Moral Sentiments*. Forget emphasizes that while Smith articulated a theory of 'sentiment', which held that this factor formed the basis of all human interaction, de Grouchy utilized this notion not only to interpret the social world, but also to promote reforms that could further human progress. She saw in the notion of sympathy the basis for practical action that would change the world by concomitantly transforming gender, race and class relations.

Smith had remarked in his *Lectures on Jurisprudence* that 'the laws of most countries being made by men, generally, are very severe on the women, who can have no remedy for this oppression'. But though he remarked on this, Smith did not devote himself to ending either this legal oppression or women's lack of political representation. In contrast to Smith's detached observations, de Grouchy was an activist reformer, campaigning for women's rights to the franchise and an education, who saw a very positive role for government in furthering both equality and democracy. But the reforms she proposed were shaped not only by her feminism but also by her intense hostility to income inequality. This invariably influenced her approach to the ways in which education and social institutions might be reconstructed to nurture sympathy in society. Voicing her commitment to environmentalism, which she shared with many other Enlightenment scholars, de Grouchy insisted that 'nature is less powerful than human institutions in shaping human action'. Hence, she considered it was possible to transform behaviour by reforming human institutions and laws. But unlike most Enlightenment scholars who tackled this issue, she paid great attention to how institutions and laws might be shaped to eliminate economic inequality. She believed that as it stood the law was primarily responsible for preventing humanity from realizing its full potential. To rectify this, she urged the adoption of policies that would prompt individuals and communities to favour general over personal interests. In particular, she called for legal and institutional changes that would enable the women and men of the urban working class to participate effectively in all aspects of political and social life.

In stating her case for economic equality, de Grouchy insisted that progress in this area would assist the promotion of gender equality. She noted that most marriages were founded on property rather than love, and believed that this foundation encouraged spouses to behave badly. The difficulties created by this arrangement were compounded by the existence of a class sufficiently wealthy, and with enough loose time, to make seduction an occupation. De Grouchy recommended institutional reforms that reduced wealth and social inequality, thereby assisting women to not only overcome the sources of their despair, but also to generally enhance their status and well-being. Hers was a major contribution to the economics of gender debate. Class position and allegiances remain to this day important aspects in the struggles for human rights and equality. This is true, not least, in the struggle for gender equality. Combining class and gender within the debate raised new reform possibilities, suggesting it was possible for all women, not only those from the economic and cultural elite, to gain from gender emancipation. But it was a combination that conservatives could and did exploit to induce confusion and disarray amongst women. By pointing out that reformers such as de Grouchy wanted to advance both class and gender equality, the gender conservatives sought to make women of wealth and privilege aware that while further progress towards human equality might advance their status as women, it was possible that it might concomitantly threaten their class position.

Before the poor and women became active participants in the French Revolution there was no clear dominant position amongst those who participated in the gender debate. However, once women and workers made their masters and mistresses aware of the democratic possibilities implicit in the notion of human rights, a wave of conservativism and indeed reaction swept through European intellectual circles, heavily influencing the gender debate. Sledziewski (1993) has argued that the French Revolution was the 'turning point' which shifted the struggle for the 'pseudo-democracy' of the 'rights of man' onto one for true democracy, in which equal importance was apportioned to the rights of woman. Though this is a valid observation, Sledziewski fails to acknowledge that for a great many the new struggle was, equally, for class as well as gender rights.

Amongst the conservatives who stepped forward to arm intellectually those who feared and opposed further progress towards social equality was Thomas Malthus. In his *Essay on Population* Malthus turned on French and English radicals, advancing what he claimed to be a 'scientific' explanation for gender relations. Malthus maintained that both gender and class inequalities were natural, and that the status of middle–class women in contemporary England was the best that the female sex could ever hope to attain. Malthus was part of a movement that embraced gender conservatism in early nineteenth-century Europe, a movement which is explored by Cot and Dimand in chapters nine and ten respectively. They reveal how the commitment to a progressive view of gender which had strengthened during the eighteenth century waned once the middle classes lost their enthusiasm for radical social change. Cot explores the work of Jeremy Bentham, showing that more than a decade before Wollstonecraft's *Vindication of the Rights of Woman* he began developing a radical view of gender relations. Like Smith in his *Lectures*, Bentham attributed the oppressed legal position of women to the fact 'that legislators seem all to have been of the male sex'. He objected to legal power in marriage residing with the partner possessing the greater physical strength. According to Cot, Bentham considered that marriage under existing English law was based on a combination of muscular capacity and legal oppression, and constituted nothing less than a form of slavery. In terms of conjectural history, Bentham accepted that marriage represented progress in the condition of humanity in general and women in particular, a view in keeping with the stages theory advocated by Smith, Millar and Anderson. However, the institution of marriage had a double character. Historically, it provided protection for women, but it also had the potential to subject them to tyranny.

In objecting to this situation, Bentham noted that English common law called equally upon women and men 'in apprehending vagrants and quelling riots', excluding women only from 'those political rights which may be exercised without labour or hazard'. He was aware that in his *Encyclopaedia Britannica* article on 'Government', James Mill remarked that women did not require political representation, since their interests were involved with those of their fathers or husbands, and dismissed Mill's comment as 'heresy'. In a manuscript note on Mill's article, Bentham declared that such exclusion 'plac[ed] all females under the absolute domination of all males'. He forthrightly concluded: 'Reasons for the exclusion: none'.

In *An Introduction to the Principles of Morals and Legislation*, in which he came nearest to a systematic exposition of his utilitarian doctrine, Bentham recalled that Aristotle had divided humanity into two species, freemen and slaves. The former had the luck to be born free, and *vice versa*. No reason was required – other than it being an accident of birth – as it was simply 'so'. To Bentham, prejudice against women was based on the same sort of groundless prejudice and, as with similar prejudices against slaves, children, homosexuals and religious minorities, it was contrary to the principle of the greatest happiness of the greatest number. But Bentham's insights were scattered in pamphlets, incomplete tracts and treatises and a disorderly mass of manuscripts. He did not publish his critical note on his friend and sometime amanuensis, James Mill, and Bentham's views on gender had little public impact, which may have been indicative of the middle class's growing opposition to radical change. His lack of influence on gender issues is also likely to have stemmed from Bentham's own shortcomings. While he critiqued and decried key aspects of the social construction men had established to preserve their dominance, Bentham, from the early 1790s, was not always there on the day. As Cot shows, while Bentham continued to argue for the principle that women should be enfranchised and allowed to be members of parliament, he voiced his disapproval when in 1791 these possibilities were raised as practical and immediate demands in Revolutionary France. Rather than stepping forward in support of the principle, he echoed the likes of Talleyrand who, in September 1791, declared that while 'in principle' it was impossible to deny that 'half the human race [was] excluded by the other from participation in government', in practice the enfranchisement of women was an unacceptable demand.

The conservatism and reaction that shaped intellectual thought across Europe in the aftermath of the Revolution is also reflected in Dimand's discussion of Priscilla Wakefield's *Reflection on the Present Condition of the Female Sex* in chapter ten. As Dimand explains, Wakefield's contribution to the gender debate broke with the radicalism that had characterized the writings of Wollstonecraft and de Grouchy. While the latter two had focused on women's freedoms,

Wakefield emphasized women's responsibilities. The reforms she proposed were modest and consciously designed to maintain the class structure of British womanhood. Wakefield contended that women should be provided with educational and employment opportunities that would not only enable them to be productive, but also allow them to sustain their class position should they have the misfortune to be without independent means or the support of another. Smith occasionally distinguished between productive labour that creates tangible goods and unproductive labour which yields services. Elsewhere, and more in keeping with his general approach, Smith noted that productive labour is hired out of capital to create a product that is sold to replenish capital with a profit. In contrast, Smith added, unproductive labour is hired out of revenue and does not create a product for sale, however useful or necessary such labour might be. He classified as unproductive labour the armed forces, government bureaucracy, royal court and clergy, along with domestic service. Thus, according to Smith's criteria, household production for direct consumption and reproduction (that is child rearing, cooking, cleaning, candle making, the mending or making of clothes) was unproductive labour. Though reproduction, like national defence, was useful and necessary, it did not directly create a commodity or contribute to capital accumulation.

Smith's failure to consider women's domestic contribution in terms of its 'productiveness' contrasted with the opinions of French scholars. Lieselotte Steinbrügge (1995, pp. 25–28) remarks that although productive activities were seen as strictly male in Diderot and d'Alembert's *Encyclopédie*, they produced many articles on the female body, with emphasis placed on childbirth and breast-feeding. Steinbrügge attributes this to the Physiocratic influence on the Encyclopedists and 'the great ideological significance that the propagation of the mother role held within physiocratic discourse'. Unaware of the substantial growth of the French population in the eighteenth century, and 'haunted by the great mortality crises of the past', the Physiocrats and Encyclopedists addressed their pro-natalist alarms to women, limiting the role of the latter to reproduction. Such an emphasis on growing population as a source of national wealth is more characteristic of Mirabeau the elder in *L'Ami des Hommes* – written before Quesnay converted him to Physiocracy – than of later Physiocratic writings. Wakefield did not draw on this French school of thought. Instead, she added a feminist twist to Smith's concept of productive labour to put a case for women's careers outside the home. In so doing she focused on Smith's assertion that 'every individual is a burthen upon the society to which he belongs, who does not contribute his share of productive labour for the good of the whole'. Wakefield criticized Smith for not explicitly extending this argument to women, and for not demanding that women be given the training and education they need should they lose the support of others. Since women are included in the human species, she added, 'their sex cannot free them from the claim of the public for their proportion of usefulness'.

Dimand shows that Wakefield (1798) also made effective use of the writings of Sir Josiah Child and Sir Frederick Morton Eden to advance a proto-feminist programme (see also Sutherland 1995). However, in the wake of the revolutionary upheavals in France, her moderate pleas on behalf of women were not well received in Europe. What the reading public of the time wanted was exemplified in the work of Hannah More. Her tracts were designed explicitly to keep the poor of England from revolting, as had their peers in France, or lobbying for social reform. This was a notion she also applied to women, arguing that, as with the poor, if women were given a proper moral upbringing, reform of their social or legal status would not be needed.

The extent to which gender conservatism came to characterize the classical school of economics in the early years of the nineteenth century is further detailed in chapters eleven and twelve. Forget and Dimand respectively show how two very influential analysts of the period, Jean-Baptiste Say and Nassau Senior, further embedded the new conservatism in English and French economics. Forget documents how Say, writing as a republican in the later years of the French Revolution, campaigned for social and political stability at the expense of women's economic and social independence. Forget explains how a patriarchal analysis of gender coexisted with, and reinforced, a popular justification of market economics in Say's most influential writings. Though he discussed household labour, women's employment and women's poverty outside the household at greater length than most economists of his time, his analysis was shaped by the problem of poverty amongst independent women. These were women who worked outside the home on wages that were lower than men's. He held that women's wages were lower because a man's wage had to provide for his own subsistence, as well as that of his wife and two children, at the socially required level, while a woman only had to fend for herself, and because so many unattached women were seeking work.

Say concluded that the preservation of the family, and women's place within it, was vital if the supply of women to the market was to be restrained. Where the family failed to provide for the needs of women, he accepted that there was a role for the state and community. But his proposed solution reflected his fixation on familial relations. He recommended the establishment of secular convents that would protect the virginity of women and prepare them for marriage and, if necessary, for the labour market. As Say considered it unwise to have both sexes working alongside each other, he also suggested that certain occupations should be set aside for women. Wakefield had suggested gender segregation in the workforce, but from a very different point of view. She supported the productive employment of women outside the household, while Say considered it a lamentable necessity, which must be minimized by strengthening the traditional family unit. This strengthening required an identical governance structure in both firms and families. Each needed to be ruled by their respective natural authorities, these being the entrepreneur and father. While Say did not extend the analogy from the household to the economy as a whole, because he believed the latter did not need direction from a central authority, he insisted that in both families and firms the interests of all were best served by a division of labour in which the father or entrepreneur directed and others obeyed.

In chapter twelve Dimand suggests that Say's conservatism was matched by that of the first professor of political economy at an English university, Nassau Senior. Dimand notes that Senior's views were important; as an applied economist, fervent Whig and Oxford don, he exercised a stronger and more direct influence on public policy than did purer theorists such as Ricardo, Torrens or the Mills. Women appeared rarely in Senior's Oxford lectures. For example, in his lectures on population, he mentioned women only once, suggesting they have a say in deciding whether or not to marry. Furthermore, his only mention of paid employment for women concerned the marriage of a singer to a famous playwright and parliamentarian, it being presumed the latter would not allow his wife to continue singing for money. Women did fleetingly appear in Senior's work as consumers who were prone to irrational choices and who, along with the working classes and Irish, were incapable of making rational decisions for the future.

The absence of paid employment of women from Senior's Oxford lectures contrasts with his *Letters on the Factory Act*, in which he engaged in a vigorous defence of the conditions under which thousands of young girls and women worked in the cotton and textile mills of Manchester. Women also figured prominently in the *Poor Law Report* of 1834, which Senior wrote with Bentham's literary secretary, Edwin Chadwick. Opportunistically, in this work women are now depicted as rational beings who, unless deprived of any legal claim for financial support from the parish ratepayers or the putative fathers, will deliberately produce bastards for financial gain. Sadly, the *Poor Law Report* had a greater immediate impact on policy than the other works discussed in this book.

But while Senior, Malthus and Say shaped classical economics' contribution to the gender debate during the first three decades of the nineteenth century, hope that perhaps women's progress had not yet reached the limits of which it was capable was rekindling in Europe. By the 1820s a new body of young economists was emerging who sought to promote human liberty and gender equality. As the last three chapters of this collection show, by the 1820s the questions that had been posed in the markets of Paris during the French Revolution, were once again becoming significant within the gender debate. Gender analysts and reformers sought out the areas of human diversity that might advance gender relations and further equality between men and women. Proponents of what would become known as the 'equal rights' position insisted that the only important diversity was male versus female, and that men and women should always receive equal treatment. But others considered this to be a decidedly inadequate position. Focusing solely on sexual differences, the latter observed, often masked issues of greater importance to the status of individuals and of specific groupings than the nature of their gender.

In chapter 13 Nyland and Heenan explore the Irish contribution of William Thompson and Anna Wheeler. They show that Thompson and Wheeler's work drew on a variety of sources, from the French rationalists' optimism about the onward march of progress to the varying collectivisms of Saint Simon and Robert Owen, and onto Ricardo's labour theory of value. But it was Bentham's Utilitarianism, with its call for happiness to be distributed amongst the greater number, which provided the philosophical basis for Thompson and Wheeler's work. Thompson has long been regarded as a radical Utilitarian critic of capitalism. However, his socialist philosophy involved commitments to both class and gender equality. As Dooley has shown (1996, 1997), Thompson's embrace of those socially and economically disadvantaged was all-encompassing. Though his commitment to gender equality predated his friendship with Wheeler, she added a feminist dimension to his work that was informed both by her experience as a subordinated wife and her lengthy activism within the socialist movement. Together, they queried whether true Utilitarianism could be achieved under capitalism, given that within capitalism status is derived primarily from one's capacity to accumulate wealth.

For his part, Thompson focused on the role of labour time. He argued that in a bourgeois society labour was not only the source of value, as Ricardo had observed, but also the primary source of status. Within capitalist societies status is derived primarily from one's capacity to contribute to, and engage in, wealth accumulation. Because labour's productive capacity was largely determined by physical strength, women, being the physically weaker sex, were less able to compete on equal terms with men in the creation of value by selling their labour time within the market place; hence they were less capable of participating in the accumulation process. Women also had the added burden of being childbearers and nurturers in a society which considered these activities unproductive, because they did not contribute directly to profit generation or the accumulation of wealth.

In order to advance gender equality, Thompson and Wheeler suggested the establishment of a society in which the capacity to contribute to wealth accumulation is less prized than it is within capitalism, and wherein status is derived from one's ability to generate use rather than exchange values. In this progressive society, labourers would primarily produce for use within the communities in which they resided. Furthermore, men and women of all classes would be involved in the production process, and women's reproductive activity would be recognized as a form of use value creation and accorded the same significance as the creation of values outside the home. In making these suggestions, Thompson and Wheeler carried the debate on the economics of gender analysis beyond the political limits of liberalism.

But this was not their only significant contribution to the debate. Committed to progress and Smith's notion of social evolution, they also identified in the Industrial Revolution's increasing mechanization a vehicle that could in time overcome men's physical advantage in the workplace. Indeed, they saw in mechanization an instrument that could render irrelevant men's physical strength as far as the generation of value is concerned. According to Thompson and Wheeler, if the trend towards mechanization was situated in societies that valued reproduction as highly as all other forms of use value creation, then for the first time in human history true equality of the sexes could be realized.

In Chapter 14 Levy examines the work of Harriet Martineau, generally regarded as a popularizer of classical political economy who presented women as rational agents (Polkinghorn 1993; Bodkin 1999b) and a pioneer of comparative sociology. She was also a woman with a sharp eye for the economic condition of her sex. As an 'equal rights' feminist, she denounced the Factory Acts which had sought to protect working class women from their employers (Baer 1978; Yates 1985). In exploring Martineau's thoughts on slavery, Levy argues that she was in fact a significant theorist in her own right, and not merely a popularizer of others' ideas. Further, Levy shows that while she may not have accepted that the women who worked in the factories were particularly vulnerable to exploitation, and so in need of a level of legal protection that differed from men of their class, she was acutely aware that women and men who were subjected to enslavement suffered very different experiences. Martineau exposed the vulnerability of enslaved women in the Southern United States. More specifically, she revealed that white male slave owners used their freewheeling legal entitlements to sexually and abusively exploit negro women. In so doing Martineau insisted that these men not only treated their slaves abominably, but also put their own wives at risk. Ironically, in raising this issue, and calling for legislation to end the right of slave owners to sexually exploit their female slaves, Martineau highlighted the paucity of arguments that suggested that the circumstances in which men and women laboured was an irrelevancy and that both sexes must receive equal treatment before the law and within their places of work.

In the concluding chapter Forget explores the work of John Stuart Mill and Harriet Hardy Taylor Mill. Partners in life and, to a lesser extent, on the page, they accepted Smith and Condorcet's belief that though male domination stemmed from men's greater physical strength and freedom from fecundity, social and economic development had the potential to transform and limit the significance of men's physical superiority, enabling women, as equally rational beings, to participate fully in decision-making. Though this position is evident in both their individual and joint works, their contributions to the gender debate differed in a number of ways. Disentangling these differences from amongst their relative contributions – at least in their joint writings – has generated over a century of controversial debate.

Caine (1992) and Pujol (1998) consider Harriet Taylor Mill the more 'radical' feminist of the two. In support, they note that she envisaged the eventual disappearance of the contractual basis for marriage, while J.S. Mill suggested that young married women would generally, though not always, gravitate towards child care rather than paid employment after marriage. Forget questions this contention. Indeed, by relating Mill's work to French social theory, Forget suggests that it is an anachronism. She also observes that Harriet can only be justifiably considered the more radical of the two partners if the word 'radical' is unidimensionally defined, which is inappropriate for a multidimensional debate such as that concerning the relative standing of the sexes. As Forget details, throughout Mill's writings on women he linked socialism to women's emancipation. In his 1831 work *The Enfranchisement of Women,* Mill considered the possibility of abolishing capitalist production and reconstituting the family. But in so doing he did not imagine that many women might question their assignment to household production. Taylor, in contrast, challenged the latter assumption. In so doing, however, she assumed that capitalism was an unchanging constant. Given their contrasting positions, the criteria for determining which Mill was more radical depend on the measure employed, which is not necessarily self-evident. As Forget suggests: 'radical is far too simple an adjective to capture the nature of the debate to which Taylor and Mill were contributing'.

The validity of Forget's argument is highlighted if the respective perspectives of Mill and Taylor are contextualized within the industrial debates of the period. In considering the question of whether women's free entry into the labour market should be supported even if this would drive down wages to the point where the total family wage was 'but little increased', Taylor defiantly responded in the affirmative. This perspective was echoed by Mill in his and Taylor's joint discussion of the Factory Acts, which appeared in *Principles of Political Economy.* But as Forget explains, Mill was not comfortable with this position. As a socialist who was sensitive to the condition of the poor, Mill feared that women's entry into the labour market would mean that for the typical working class family, 'twice as much labour [would be] required to earn the same living as before'. Given that this would result in the family having less labour to utilize in household production, Mill feared that such a development 'would be clearly undesirable from a social perspective'.

It would appear that Mill, but not Taylor, appreciated the complexity of issues associated with women's entry into the labour market, and saw that gender analysis could not, or at least should not, be deemed a unidimensional problem. With the further expansion of the Factory Acts and the rise of the welfare state, the question of whether the gender debate should centre solely on 'equal rights' or be informed by issues such as class and race would become of fundamental importance in the development of the economics of gender status. But here we must leave the classicals and such questions, for with Mill's last contribution to gender analysis we have reached 1869, and shortly ahead we can see Marx and Jevons.

REFERENCES

Agonito, Rosemary (1977), *History of Ideas on Women: A Source Book*, New York: Perigee.

Baer, Judith A. (1978), *The Chains of Protection: The Judicial Response to Women's Labor Legislation*, Westport, CT: Greenwood.

Beauvoir, Simone de (1972), *The Second Sex*, Harmondsworth: Penguin.

Bodkin, Ronald G. (1999a), 'Women's Agency in Classical Economic Thought: Adam Smith, Harriet Taylor Mill, and J. S. Mill', *Feminist Economics*, **5** (1): 45–60.

Bodkin, Ronald G. (1999b), 'The Issue of Female Agency in Classical Economic Thought: Jane Marcet, Harriet Martineau, and the Men', *Gender Issues*, **17** (4): 62–73.

Caine, Barbara (1992), *Victorian Feminists*, New York: Oxford University Press.

Clark, Lorenne and Lynda Lange, (eds) (1979), *The Sexism of Social and Political Theory: Women and Reproduction from Plato to Nietzsche*, Toronto: University of Toronto Press.

Fraisse, Genevieve and Michelle Perrot (eds) (1993), *Emerging Feminism from Revolution to World War*, Cambridge, Mass.: Belknap Press of Harvard University Press.

Gelbart, Nina Rattner (1987), *Feminine and Opposition Journalism in Old Regime France: Le Journal des Dames, 1759–1778*, Berkeley: University of California Press.

Groenewegen, Peter, ed. (1994), *Feminism and Political Economy in Victorian England*, Aldershot, UK, and Brookfield, US: Edward Elgar.

Kandal, Terry R. (1988), *The Woman Question in Classical Sociological Theory*, Gainesville, FL: University Presses of Florida.

Kennedy, Ellen and Susan Mendus (eds) (1987), *Women in Western Political Philosophy, Kant to Nietzsche*, Brighton: Wheatsheaf Books.

Okin, Susan Moller (1979), *Women in Western Political Thought*, Princeton, NJ: Princeton University Press.

Polkinghorn, Bette (1993), *Jane Marcet: An Uncommon Woman*, Aldermaston, UK: Forestwood Publications.

Pujol, Michèle A. (1998), *Feminism and Anti-Feminism in Early Economic Thought*, with a new preface by Janet Seiz, Cheltenham, UK, and Northampton, MA: Edward Elgar.

Shanley, Mary Lyndon and Carole Pateman (eds) (1991), *Feminist Interpretations and Political Theory*, University Park, PA: Pennsylvania State University Press.

Sledziewski, Elizabeth (1993), 'Revolution as turning Point', in Genevieve Fraisse and Michelle Perrot (eds), *Emerging Feminism from Revolution to World War*, Cambridge, Mass.: Belknap Press of Harvard University Press.

Steinbrügge, Lieselotte (1995), *The Moral Sex: Woman's Nature in the French Enlightenment*, trans. Pamela E. Selwyn, New York and Oxford: Oxford University Press.

Sutherland, Kathryn (1995), 'Adam Smith's Master Narrative: Women and the Wealth of Nations', in Stephen Copley and Kathryn Sutherland (eds), *Adam Smith's Wealth of Nations: New Interdisciplinary Essays*, Manchester, UK: Manchester University Press.

Wakefield, Priscilla (1798), *Reflections on the Present Condition of the Female Sex*,

New York: Garland Press 1974.

Yates, Gayle Graham, (ed.) (1985), *Harriet Martineau on Women*, New Brunswick, NJ: Rutgers University Press.

2.   Poulain de la Barre and the Rationalist Analysis of the Status of Women

Chris Nyland

In the second half of the seventeenth century, European liberals began constructing a theoretical foundation for what they believed were the 'rights of man'. By this phrase was normally meant the rights of men. In developing their case for political and social justice, however, a number of these individuals gave consideration to the status of women. This chapter examines the writings of François Poulain de La Barre, an early contributor to this aspect of the debate on human rights. It is suggested that Poulain deserves a place in the history of economic thought because of the pioneering manner in which he applied the deductive method of analysis to the study of women's social position. He also deserves recognition by economists because his utilization of deductivism enabled him to advance a number of important insights regarding the economics of women's status. Most importantly, he was able to highlight the fact that the claim that women are men's social subordinates, because they are naturally less productive, was in many cases merely a product of prejudice. He was also able to challenge the assertion that the biological differences between the sexes fixed forever the relative economic and social status of men and women. These contributions, it is concluded, justify his recognition as a pioneer both in the methodology of economics and in the development of the economics of gender and discrimination.

POULAIN DE LA BARRE

Poulain was born in Paris in 1647. He studied theology at the Sorbonne, an institution then dominated by the scholastic tradition. While a student, he joined a Cartesian study circle and was converted to the merits of Descartes' philosophy and methodology. After graduating he worked as a Catholic priest, but in 1688 converted to Calvinism and was compelled consequently to leave France for Geneva, where he remained until the end of his life in 1723.[1]

Amongst his numerous publications, Poulain wrote three books dealing with the status of women. These were *The Equality of the Sexes* (1673), *Dialogues on the Education of Women* (1674) and *The Superiority of Men, Against the Equality of the Sexes* (1675). The first work is widely regarded as the most significant of the three.

The scholastics, against whom Poulain rebelled, argued that women's inferior place in society was a consequence of God having decreed that wives must be the servants of their husbands. That this was God's desire, it was asserted, was proven both by Scripture and by the fact that females were less rational than were males. It was also noted that women's inferiority was attested to by such notable authorities as Plato and Aristotle. At the Sorbonne the scholastics sought to inculcate pupils with these ideas. Poulain reported that the latter tended to be highly contemptuous of women as a result.

> When I was a scholastic, I considered [females] scholastically, that is to say, as monsters, as beings inferior to men, because Aristotle and some theologians whom I had read, considered them so (Poulain 1674, pp. 327, 331-334).

The depiction of women promoted by the scholastics was occasionally challenged by feminists. However, these critics of orthodoxy tended to confine their criticisms to disputing the meaning of Scripture, cataloguing the intellectual and moral virtues of women and pointing to examples of individual females who gave the lie to the claim that women were incapable of wisdom or leadership (Kelly 1982; Armogathe 1985, p. 18). Moreover, as Schiebinger (1989, pp. 165-170) has observed, the critics invariably employed traditional forms of argument and did not challenge orthodox tools of analysis. Methodologically, Poulain's work is distinguished from this critical literature by the fact that he based his contribution on the scientific method of Descartes. By so doing Poulain was able to develop an alternative explanation for women's status which foreshadowed much twentieth-century discrimination theory. His argument asserted that apart from their reproductive attributes, there were no substantive natural differences between the sexes. Consequently, any divergence in the social position and productive capacities of men and women must be the product of social conditioning.

RENE DESCARTES

Descartes' contribution to the development of economics has been analysed by Mini (1974). The latter has highlighted the extent to which Descartes' methodology, with its reliance on axioms derived purely in the mind, the building of deductive superstructures upon these axioms and the tendency to hypostatize concepts has been a prominent characteristic of much economic analysis through the history of political economy.

Shaken by the collapse of such apparent truths as the immovable earth, Descartes rejected the proposition that knowledge of the material universe could be founded on the word of authorities or the use of the senses. He argued that the pursuit of knowledge must be based on the power of the human mind to derive axioms that our intuition tells us must be a true depiction of reality. These axioms are the raw materials of Cartesian analysis and deduction is the force which links concepts and carries them forward to a proof. Where the deductive process is halted by barriers which logic cannot overcome, Descartes argued that we can do no better than imagine some combination of factors which might give rise to the phenomenon we wish to explain. In other words, such obstacles are to be mastered by using 'rational fictions' and, once overcome, the process of deduction is to continue (Pribram 1983, pp. 57–58).

The work of the many social analysts who were influenced by Descartes tended to primarily reflect this influence in that they accepted that deduction based upon a few simple principles could explain the most complicated phenomena. Cartesian social analysts invariably began by laying down propositions which they believed to be axiomatic. These axioms commonly related to some claimed aspect of human nature. Appropriate theorems were then derived deductively from the axioms, the process being aided by the use of rational conjecture. The end result aimed for was a conclusion which was credible on the basis of the available evidence.

Whether Descartes believed his methodology produced a coincidence of thinking and being is not clear. What is clear is that this is what his followers believed was the result. His method tended to lead Cartesians to hypostatize their psychic creations, that is, what they merely derived in the mind they subsequently came to presume was real. Where this hypostatization occurred, the result was all too often the very opposite of that which Descartes sought to achieve.

> Descartes, the man who aspired to put human knowledge on a secure and firm basis, actually succeeded in encouraging the most unrestrained flights of the imagination. Thought turned megalomaniac in that it claimed to explain wider and wider aspects of reality starting from the narrowest basis. His obsessive doubting led to the most naive theorizing, his ingenious critique of knowledge to the most ingenuous constructs, all ending in tautology (Mini 1974, p. 23).

Mini has also observed that this is the methodology that underpins neo-classical and Keynesian, though not Keynes', economics. It was also the methodology that Poulain utilized in his analysis of the status of women. As regards women's place in society, a critical element in Descartes' metaphysics was his defining of matter and mind in a manner which meant they were totally separated. He depicted the mind as a spiritual substance which is not to be identified with the matter that constitutes the body. Consequently, the mind can have no sexual characteristics. This perspective left Descartes' followers with only one option with respect to the natural attributes of the sexes.

> They could claim that women were superior or inferior to men only if their bodies could be shown to be superior or inferior to those of men in some specified respect (Clarke 1990, p. 10).

It was not possible for Cartesians to gain guidance from Descartes as to whether or not this was the case. In his writings on the human body and its functions, the only differences in the sexes Descartes identified explicitly were those relating to the reproductive system (Descartes 1985, 1985a). As a result Cartesians were left free to believe almost whatever they wished about the respective natural attributes of men and women.

THE ORIGIN OF WOMEN'S SUBORDINATION

Poulain chose to challenge the belief that women's innate capacities explained their subordinate social status. He insisted that, at least in his own world, where women had difficulty matching men's achievements this was invariably a consequence of their social conditioning.

> If one finds that there is some fault or impediment in some women at present, or even that they do not all consider important things in the same way as men do – something which however is inconsistent with our experience – that should be explained completely in terms of the external conditions of their sex and the education which they receive, which includes the ignorance in which they are left, the prejudices and errors they are taught, the example which they get from other women, and all the mannerisms to which propriety, restraint, reserve, subjection and timidity reduce them (Poulain 1990, p. 121).

The women's question was taken up by Poulain because he wished to highlight the value of Descartes' methodology. He reasoned that refuting an assumption so widely accepted as was the claim that women were innately inferior to men would encourage scholars to recognize the need to reject beliefs based only on appearances or the word of authorities (Poulain 1990, pp. 45–46). Poulain began his analysis by discussing the origin of women's social subordination. In so doing he first responded to the scholastics' claim that scripture made it clear that God had decreed women were the natural subordinates of men.

In *The Equality of the Sexes*, he sought to avoid this issue by dismissing readings of the *Bible* which suggested it was God's will that wives should be the servants of their husbands.   He asserted simply that if one read Scripture correctly it became clear that it had nothing definite to say as regards the natural equality of the sexes (Poulain 1990, p. 44). Subsequently, however, Poulain accepted that, given the influence of the scholastics, he could not so easily avoid their reading of Scripture. As a result, in *The Superiority of Men* he challenged their interpretation of the *Bible*. His reply is not particularly illuminating, seldom rising above the opposing arguments. One aspect of his case that is interesting, however, is his interpretation of the 'curse' God supposedly pronounced against Eve at the time of the Fall. This was an important issue for liberal reformers because one of the primary arguments advanced by those who supported the absolutist state was that the King derived his power from Adam, whom God had supposedly made absolute ruler of the world when he decreed that Eve would be the latter's subordinate. To suggest that Eve shared Adam's right to rule both in and outside Paradise was hence to undermine regal absolutism in the present world. Poulain brings much casuistry to bear upon the words of the curse in order to deny the notion that God's words should be interpreted as meaning that Eve was the servant of Adam. Why Poulain's stress on this point is of interest, in terms of the development of political economy, is because John Locke was to subsequently advance a similar interpretation of the curse in developing his secular and economic explanation for women's status (Nyland 1993).

Having denied that the origin of women's subordination was divine in character, Poulain realized that he had to provide an alternative explanation of how it was that men had been able to obtain a position of dominance in all known societies.[2]   It was not sufficient to claim that men had attained their dominant status by discriminating against women. Such an assertion begged the question of how men had acquired the ability to discriminate. What Poulain had to develop was an explanation for how it could be that 'external' conditions were created that enabled men to discriminate against women; that is he sought to explain how it was that men always managed to attain a position where they could discriminate. Poulain's means of dealing with this difficulty was to undertake an exercise in what he termed 'historical conjecture' in which he sought to construct a rational argument which could explain how men, who had no natural advantages save their freedom from childbirth, might manage to attain a position of dominance in all cultures.

To develop his argument, Poulain first formulated a principle, the validity of which he considered was indisputable. Utilizing deduction, he then built upon this axiomatic foundation a conjectural explanation of how men might originally have obtained their dominant status. His axiom was that human beings will impose their will upon others given the opportunity and chance to benefit by so doing (Poulain 1990, p. 54). Poulain believed that the truth of this claim was confirmed beyond doubt by the most casual observation of humanity. Taking the axiom as given, he deduced that, at some time in the past, men must have utilized their freedom from childbirth as a weapon to subordinate women in order that they might enhance their own well-being. Liberty from childbirth was capable of being transformed into a means of suppression because this freedom favoured men over women in that it provided the former with greater opportunity to undertake muscle-building exercise. Poulain believed men's consequent greater physical strength was an attribute which males could and did utilize to impose their will upon females.

In suggesting how men might have attained their position of dominance, Poulain did not utilize the historical record. Rather, he situated his analysis in a hypothetical primitive world in which there was no government and human beings enjoyed an abundance of material resources. It was assumed that in this environment while women remained unencumbered by children they would have worked equally with men in the undertaking of productive activities.

> I imagine that men were like children, that any advantages they had were more like those one finds in a child's game; both men and women were simple and innocent then, and they spent their time equally on the cultivation of the earth or in hunting just as savages do still. Men participated in their way and so likewise did women; whoever did best was most esteemed by all the others (Poulain 1990, p. 54).

However, women's ability to match men's contribution in the production of economic goods would have been undermined by their role in reproduction.

> The inconveniences of pregnancy and its consequences diminished the strength of women for periods of time and hindered them from working as they had before, so that the help of their husbands became absolutely necessary, and even more so when they had children (Poulain 1990, p. 55).

The respective roles of the sexes in reproduction, moreover, would have compelled women to remain at home in order to care for their children. Consequently, a division of labour would have been created which reflected these basic needs with women taking 'care of the home while the men, who were more free and robust, took care of things outside the home' (Poulain 1990, p. 55).

Poulain deduced that women's economic dependence on men that was thus produced would not have provided males with any greater esteem while the economic resources available to the family remained abundant. In an environment of economic abundance Poulain could conceive of no rational reason why the sexual division of labour should lead men to gain a position of dominance over women. The factor which he assumed must have undermined this egalitarian situation was population growth. This 'rational fiction' was a critical assumption, for its adoption enabled Poulain to transform his hypothetical world of peace and economic abundance into one of conflict and scarcity. As per capita resources became scarce, both the value accorded the means of subsistence and the attributes and goods required to attain the material needs for survival would have tended to be enhanced. This development would in turn have heightened the propensity for humans to exploit others where they could gain materially by so doing. Conflict would consequently have been generated in both the home and the wider society. Within the family, individuals would have manifested a greater inclination to use physical force as a means of ensuring they attained what they believed was their rightful share of the family's property. In such a situation women's strength disadvantage and their fecundity-induced economic dependence would have become both more important and more noticeable.

A factor of even greater importance that would have transformed the social significance of women's dependence on men, Poulain deduced, would have been the tendency for population growth to induce conflict between communities. He suggested that once competition for the available economic resources reached the stage where communities were compelled to fight for the right to utilize these resources, we have the beginnings of warfare, slavery and the social subordination of women.

> [The propertyless] seeing themselves completely without any property, they looked for ways of acquiring some. Since there was no way of doing this except by taking some from others, they seized whatever property was nearest to them and, in order to protect their new acquisitions, they also seized the proprietor to whom the goods belonged (Poulain 1990, pp. 55–56).

Why these developments would have especially disadvantaged women, Poulain deduced, was because women's reproductive activities would have rendered them less capable of being warriors than were men. As intercommunal struggle over resources became common, this relative disadvantage would have become of great social significance. Women would have become reliant on the warriors for their immediate physical security, their freedom from slavery and their ability to attain their subsistence. Moreover, not being involved actively in conquest and the defence of the community, women would have been accorded a lesser say in the government of society. From here it would have been an easy step for men to convince themselves that women did not have the intellectual or spiritual capacity to rule. Indeed, they would have found it easy to believe that, apart from the ability to give birth, women's capacities were generally inferior to those of men.

Such a strong preference for one sex over the other resulted in the women being even less esteemed than before; since they were far removed from war and carnage by their natural disposition and their duties, they were considered to be incapable of contributing to the protection of kingdoms except by helping to populate them (Poulain 1990, p. 57).

In time, this prejudice would have become so ingrained in custom and law that even women would have accepted that the natural inferiority of females was a self-evident truth.

Poulain's conjectural reconstruction has a number of attributes that are significant in terms of the development of economic theory and methodology. His argument suggested that where economic resources are available in abundance the differing natural attributes of the sexes will be an irrelevancy as regards the respective status of men and women. In communities where resources are in short supply, on the other hand, these differences will tend to become of major significance in the shaping of gender relations.

For political economy, the importance of Poulain's argument lies in the emphasis it places on both the economic environment and the extent to which changes in the availability of the wherewithal of life can transform the social importance of natural differences between the sexes. His analysis can justifiably be considered a stages theory of economic development based on a mechanism of population pressure impacting on subsistence. It is interesting to note in this regard that in his work Poulain identified the four basic economic stages that Meek (1976) has shown were subsequently to play a critical part in the history of political economy. In his conjectural history he assumed that early human societies attained their subsistence either by hunting or by agriculture. Later in *The Equality of the Sexes* he discusses in detail the place of women in societies characterised by the commercial mode of subsistence, and in *The Superiority of Men* he identified pasturage as a fourth basic stage of development (Poulain 1675, part II, p. 109).

The economic element in Poulain's exercise in historical conjecture has been missed by the philosophers and feminists who have studied his work. These analysts have tended to accept that Poulain believed the origin of the subordination of women was based on a political rather an economic foundation. In short, it has been suggested that Poulain believed women's role in the family had no natural foundation and that the origin of the sexual division of labour was merely a product of men's political power within the family. Likewise it has been suggested that Poulain believed the decision to create the state was primarily a political act. What this interpretation of Poulain's analysis fails to recognize is that his explanation for both the origin of men's power in the family and the creation of the state were founded on a base which was biological and economic in character. In short, as has been shown, the causal direction was recognized to be from economics to politics, that is from the material to the cultural.

Poulain's awareness of the extent to which changes in the economic context can transform women's social position was unique in the seventeenth century. Indeed, his economic relativism was not to begin to be replicated by other analysts of women's status until Montesquieu systematically developed this notion in his magnificent book *The Spirit of the Laws* in the mid–eighteenth century.

A second aspect of Poulain's 'history' of the origin of male domination that deserves recognition by the analyst of economic thought is the extent to which it constituted an early example of 'conjectural or theoretical history'. Dugald Stewart has observed, in his *Account of the Life and Writings of Adam Smith*, that Smith utilized this form of enquiry to a 'peculiar degree' in all his different works (Stewart 1980, p. 292). When explaining what was meant by conjectural history Stewart observed that when analysts compare the achievements of modern society with those of primitive communities they are invariably led to wonder about the steps taken to bring about such a momentous transition. He observed that history provides few clues as regards the transitionary process because many of its constituent important steps must necessarily unfold long before humans learn to write. Confronted with a want of direct evidence it is necessary to replace fact by conjecture.

> In this want of direct evidence, we are under a necessity of supplying the place of fact by conjecture; and when we are unable to ascertain how men have actually conducted themselves upon particular occasions, of considering in what manner they are likely to have proceeded, from the principles of their nature, and the circumstances of their external situation. In examining the history of mankind, as well as in examining the phenomena of the material world, when we cannot trace the process by which an event has been produced, it is often of importance to be able to show how it may have been produced by natural causes (Stewart 1980, p. 293).

Writing in 1793, Stewart asserted that this form of history was 'entirely of modern origin'. By modern he appears to have meant the second half of the eighteenth century. As Poulain's conjectured history of men's rise to domination over women was published in the early 1670s the latter's contribution must surely challenge this assertion.

Finally in assessing the value of Poulain's suggested origin of male domination it should be noted that his work deserves recognition as a contribution to the development of economic deductivism. Klein has observed that early eighteenth-century French theorists have not received the acknowledgment they deserve for being forerunners in the development of the methodology of the deductivist tradition within economics (Klein 1985, p. 51). Precisely because he did adopt this method of analysis, Poulain was able to transcend the methodological and ideological boundaries that had previously constrained feminist critics of the schoolmen. Given that he did so in the late seventeenth century, Poulain surely deserves to be accorded the same acknowledgment Klein grants to the economic deductivists of the early eighteenth century.

THE HYPOSTATIZATION OF WOMEN

Poulain's utilization of deductivism to demonstrate how men's freedom from fecundity might enable the male sex to attain a position of dominance over women should be perceived as an early example of the creative capacity of this method of analysis. However, it should also be recognized as an example of the dangers inherent in a methodology which is not founded on axioms derived empirically from the material world. Assuming that the only natural difference in the respective attributes of men and women was a freedom from childbirth, then analysing the relations that would exist between these abstractions in an imaginary economic context was a valid method of analysis. At least, it was such as long as Poulain sought merely to suggest a possible means by which men's freedom from childbirth might have enabled them to obtain a superior social position. What was not valid was his decision to accept as given that there is an equality in the natural attributes of the sexes when seeking to explain women's status in modern, commercial societies. When undertaking this latter aspect of his argument, Poulain succumbed to the danger inherent in the abstracted rationalism of Descartes. He did not merely assume that the sexes were equal in terms of their natural attributes in order to undertake a thought experiment for the case of argument; he accepted that this was the case in reality. In short, he hypostatized the beings who were his psychic creation and took what was merely a product of his mind as being a true depiction of the material world.

Amongst the natural attributes that Poulain maintained were identical in both sexes were the mental and muscular capacities of males and females. The former claim he justified on the grounds that the minds of both sexes are supposedly identical and the mind is separate from the body. The latter assertion that he did not bother to support with evidence despite the fact that such an assertion does not find justification in Cartesianism. It needs to be added that this claim does not find justification in modern empiricism either. While empirical research has found no difference in the mental capacities of the sexes capable of explaining the relative status of the sexes, it has provided strong support for the belief that men have a large, natural muscular-strength advantage. Women have, on average, only two-thirds the strength of equally trained men. Moreover, in those areas of the body important for the use of tools and weapons there is very little overlap between the strongest women and the weakest men.[3]

Poulain's denial that men had any natural relative advantage apart from their freedom from fecundity led him to adopt an extreme form of cultural determinism when explaining the social position of women in modern, commercial nations. He accepted that in such societies, women's role in reproduction could not by itself explain men's superior social position. Reproductive attributes being accepted as the only natural difference between the sexes, Poulain deduced that it followed that women's subordinate status must be a manifestation of the prevalence of ideas, laws and customs left over from the warrior stage of human development. In short, Poulain claimed that belief in men's natural superiority was a social determinant so powerful it was capable of maintaining the dominance of males even after the material element which had originally enabled men to obtain this dominance had been superseded as a consequence of the development of the means by which humanity attained its means of subsistence.

Poulain's avocation of this idealist perspective constituted a major shift in his economics. More specifically it constituted a shift in the respective weighting and causal direction his analysis gave to material influences and to ideas. In his conjectural history of the origin of male domination, explanatory emphasis was placed on the relative abundance of the material wherewithal of life and on women's innate attributes.   Increasing population reduced the per capita economic resources available to the population, and the consequent conflict over the means of subsistence induced changes in the skills required for survival and people's ideas regarding women's capacities and their status.   In other words, changes in the economic environment induced corresponding changes in society's received notions regarding women's capacities and their natural relationship to men. In this analysis economic factors are clearly perceived as being the prime determinant.   In the modern world, however, the causal direction of Poulain's argument is reversed. It is no longer material factors which determine women's abilities and status.   Rather, it is ideas and the customs associated with these ideas that are seen as being the prime determinants shaping women's abilities and their economic and social position within society. All non-cultural factors are considered to be irrelevant and hence it is concluded that it is ideas that determine women's place in the material world.

Poulain provides no justification for this reversal in the causal direction his economics accorded material and cultural factors. He was aware, however, that his explanation for the origin of women's social subordination did contain one critical element that was difficult to avoid. In his reconstruction of how men might have attained their position of dominance, he had acknowledged that men's greater physical strength would have influenced the sexual division of labour in primitive societies. Given this concession, he needed to refute any suggestion that men's greater capacity to undertake manual activities might be the critical material determinant underpinning their continued dominance of women in modern economies.

Poulain chose to evade rather than confront this problem. His means of so doing were twofold. First, he structured his argument in a manner which situated his hypostatized women in a hypothetical, middle-class world in which the economic advantage men enjoyed as a consequence of their greater physical strength was ignored. He did this by confining his comparison of the capabilities of men and women to intellectual and moral activities. Thus he focused his discussion on emphazising the fact that, given an equal opportunity to attain the required skills, women could match men in the occupations of lawyer, academic, historian, administrator, politician and so on. In so doing he pointedly avoided the respective abilities of the sexes to undertake those manual occupations where physical strength was a critical factor determining the productivity of labour. For example, when assessing women's ability to be soldiers he restricted his comments to a consideration of their potential to act as generals and ignored the question of whether they could match men in physical combat. By situating his hypostatized women in an imaginary world, where physical strength was an irrelevancy, Poulain was able to deduce that the difference in the muscular capacities of the sexes could not possibly be a contributing factor explaining women's status.

Poulain's second device for obtaining acceptance of his argument was an appeal to the class prejudices of the intellectual elite for whom he wrote. He asserted that physical strength tends to be accompanied by low intelligence and is primarily an attribute of the labouring classes and hence could hardly be a source of social status.

> [I]t is not physical strength which should distinguish men. Otherwise beasts would be better than men and, among men, those who are more robust would be regarded more highly. Indeed it is known from experience that those who have a lot of strength are rarely fit for anything else except manual work, and that those who have less physical strength usually have more brains. It is, therefore, useless to rely so much on bodily make-up rather than on the mind in order to explain the differences which can be seen between the two sexes (Poulain 1990, pp. 117–118).

Poulain's failure to consider the status implications of the differing muscular capacities of the sexes deleted from his analysis a human attribute that significantly affected the material wellbeing of the overwhelming majority of the population of the pre-industrial, agricultural society in which he lived. The importance of physical strength lay in the fact that muscular capacity greatly influenced the productivity of manual labour and hence the income of most families. Being a determinant of labour productivity, the muscular strength of the labourer was also a factor of interest to those property owners who purchased labour-power. This was because strength greatly influenced the magnitude of the potential economic surplus that could be extracted from employees and tenants. In short, for most people in Poulain's pre-industrial world, status and material rewards were greatly dependent on how effectively individuals could labour at tasks which required muscular strength. This meant that most adult males had a relative advantage in an area of economic life that was a fundamental source of status and material wellbeing. This was a fact that Poulain chose to ignore in order to highlight the oppressive discrimination and prejudice women were compelled to endure. His decision to do so marks the point where he abandoned science for polemics, embracing an idealist perspective which anticipated developments in much twentieth-century analysis of gender relations.

Much modern economic analysis of women's status is characterized by the assumption that women's social position is a function of their conditioning, the discrimination they experience and the choices they make as regards the accumulation of skills. The difference in the physical strength of men and women is seldom perceived as being a factor contributing to the relative status of men and women or even as being an issue of relevance to the division of labour. This is despite the fact that where analysts have undertaken empirical studies of the link between physically demanding work and job segregation, they have produced results which suggest that the strength factor may still be of significance in important sectors of economic life.

In the United States, for example, the Committee on Occupational Classification and Analysis matched the 12,999 job titles in the *Dictionary of Occupational Titles* to the 591 three-digit occupational categories designed for the 1970 census. They then compared the attribute scores with wages and female representation by occupation. It was found:

> The only job attribute variable that has a high correlation with female representation in an occupation is the physical demands index; jobs requiring greater physical demands are concentrated in male-dominated occupations (Raisian, Welch and Finis 1988, p. 187).

The notion that the difference in the muscular capacities of the sexes is an economic irrelevancy has become so ingrained in the modern literature that many analysts fail to accord the strength issue any explanatory significance even when analysing male–female relations in pre-industrial society. A measure of the prevalence of this perspective is the fact that none of the modern analysts who have studied Poulain's work have questioned his failure to give any serious consideration to the extent to which physical strength influenced relations between the men and women of his society. Nor have any of these analysts challenged his assertion that differences in the physical strength of the sexes are purely a product of social conditioning. Indeed, Armogathe has suggested that Poulain's assertion that the difference in the physical strength of the sexes is purely a product of the respective degree of exercise undertaken by men and women was one of the newest and most exciting of his ideas. It is an idea, moreover, that she appears to believe is completely valid (Armogathe 1985, p. 21).

Fraisse (1985, p. 30) has correctly observed of Poulain's contribution to the study of the status of women that: 'Today alone his text corresponds with our times'. By this she means that it is only in recent decades that his pioneering ideas regarding the rights of women are coming to be fully accepted. Her comment, however, also applies to his analysis of the cause of women's subordination in the modern world. It is only over the last quarter century that the singular emphasis he placed on cultural influences has come to have any significant degree of acceptance. Prior to the 1960s feminist economists generally accepted that the strength differential was necessarily an important variable in any viable explanation of women's status (Goldin, 1990). However, from the 1960s a new understanding came to prominence that was rooted in a misreading of J.S. Mill. It has been suggested by Fraisse (1985, p. 39) that Poulain can be described as the J.S. Mill of the seventeenth century. Any such conclusion, though, is unwarranted. While Mill believed it was not possible to know precisely the nature of women's innate capacities, his idealism was limited by the fact that he accepted that one area where men did have a relative economic advantage was the 'physical one of bodily strength' (Mill 1989, p. 184). It is also of interest to note that, like Poulain, Mill emphasized the greater muscular strength of men when explaining the origin of male social dominance.

> [T]he adoption of this system of [sex] inequality never was the result of deliberation, or forethought, or any social ideas, or any notion whatever of what conduced to the benefit of humanity or the good order of society. It arose simply from the fact that from the very earliest twilight of human society, every woman (owing to the value attached to her by men, combined with her inferiority in muscular strength) was found in a state of bondage to some man (Mill 1989, p. 123).

CONCLUSION

In assessing a scholar's place in the history of economic thought two primary criteria ought to be considered. The first relates to the quality of the contribution and considers to what extent the individual presented new techniques of analysis, new concepts or new propositions. The second criterion relates to the influence exerted by the scholar's work on his or her contemporaries and successors (Groenewegen 1983, p. 585).

Of the first of these criteria, it should be noted that the systematic and secular manner by which Poulain challenged the arguments and prejudices of the schoolmen was without precedent in the study of women's status. Indeed, so unique was his work it can be concluded that Rosso's (1977, p. 60) belief that he provided the first ever 'rational explanation for the inferior condition in which women were held in relation to men' is not an unreasonable assessment. His use of economic deductivism and conjectural history to explain the origin of women's subordination partly fulfils the first aspect of the originality criterion in that the use of these tools certainly amounted to the utilization of new techniques of analysis. His notion that changes in the economic environment can transform the material value that societies place on specific human attributes and his application of the notion of stages of economic development moves further towards fulfilling the criterion. Finally, his proposition that women's capacities and society's understanding of these capacities was severely limited by the prejudice and restricted access to resources women were compelled to endure, while not entirely new, was advanced with an unprecedented degree of rigour.

As regards the second criterion, the most comprehensive of the studies of Poulain's influence is that provided by Stock (1961). She reports that his writings on the status of women enjoyed a degree of immediate success but that this was short-lived. However, in 1690 a new edition of his works was published and this appears to have had a more substantial and long-lasting impact on both popular discussion and the published literature. As far as economics is concerned the two most important individuals whom Poulain appears to have influenced were Montesquieu and Rousseau. The former read *The Equality of the Sexes* and made much of this work, considering it a 'truly philosophical' contribution to the study of women's status.

Not the least of the many aspects of Poulain's work that would have attracted Montesquieu would have been its relativism. This appears not only in *The Equality of the Sexes* but also in *The Education of Women*. In this latter work Poulain (1674, p. 71) points out that standards of correct behaviour vary in different countries and in different centuries while in *The Equality of the Sexes* he suggests grounds for why this should occur.

> Different effects are produced on individuals by exercise, changes in temperature, food and environment. So with whole nations: manners, customs, and laws are the result of such conditions as geographical position (latitude, proximity to the sea), physical features (mountains, rivers, forests, configuration of the terrain), fertility of

the soil, and opportunity for trade with neighbouring countries (Stock 1961, p. 201).

These were general causes shaping ideas, customs and laws which would very much have appealed to Montesquieu. Indeed, they include many of the factors he was to emphasize to powerful effect in his own contribution to the economic analysis of the status of women.

The case that Stock was able to compile regarding Poulain's influence on Rousseau was circumstantial in character. It focused primarily on common acquaintances in Geneva and on textual similarities in the work of the two men. Of these latter, particular note is taken of the similarity of their ideas regarding the effect of the development of the arts and sciences on human progress and the origin of economic and social inequality. It is also observed that Rousseau utilised the technique of historical conjecture in a manner similar to that of Poulain. Further, he utilized this technique, as did Poulain, to suggest that humanity had once lived in an idyllic 'Golden Age' that had now been lost and replaced by the 'Iron Age of Servitude'. Finally, it was noted that Rousseau was acquainted intimately with the literature relating to the debate on the status of women. In the years preceding his writing of his two *Discours* he was employed by Mme Dupin. At the time of his employment she was gathering material for a book in defence of women and had undertaken extensive research on the subject. One of Rousseau's duties was to search out and note the necessary documents. It is highly probable, therefore, that he would have been aware of Poulain's work, and this possibility is further heightened by the fact that Montesquieu was a very close friend of Mme Dupin.

The evidence that Stock amassed as regards Poulain's influence is certainly convincing. This is true even of her claim that Montesquieu and Rousseau were influenced by Poulain. The latter is not sufficient to justify an unqualified endorsement of Armogathe's (1985, p. 24) claim that Poulain provided Montesquieu with his inspiration for *The Persian Letters* or the assertion advanced by Fraisse (1985, p. 29) that Poulain was 'the secret power which appears to have influenced Montesquieu and Rousseau'. Nevertheless, the evidence is sufficient for one to conclude that Poulain was certainly a significant influence helping to shape the debate on the status of women that took place in eighteenth-century France. It can be concluded, therefore, that Poulain also meets the second criterion analysts should utilize when seeking to assess the value of a scholar's ideas. The fact that the economic element in Poulain's work has not previously been recognized is not because there is little economic content. Rather, it is because those who have analysed his work have not been economists, and because historians of economic thought have given little attention to the history of the economic analysis of the status of women.

REFERENCES

Adams, Robert M. (1975), 'Where Do Our Ideas Come From? – Descartes vs. Locke' in Stephen P. Stich (ed.), *Innate Ideas*, University of California Press, pp. 71–87.

Armogathe, Daniel (1985), 'De l'égalité des Deux Sexes, La Belle Question', *Corpus*, **1** (1), 17–26.

Badinter, Elisabeth (1985), 'Ne Portons pas trop Loin la Difference des Sexes...', *Corpus*, **1**, 13–15.

Bayle, Pierre (1984), *The Dictionary Historical and Critical of Mr Peter Bayle*, B. Feldman and R. Richardson (eds), New York: Garland Publishing.

Bishop, P., K. Cureton and M. Collins (1987), 'Sex Difference in Muscular Strength in Equally Trained Men and Women', *Ergonomics*, **30** (4), 675–687.

Celentano, E. J. and L. Noy (1981), *Development of Occupational Physical Selection Standards Canadian Forces Trades: Performance Considerations*, Ontario: Department of National Defence.

Clarke, Desmond M. (1990), 'Introduction' in Desmond M. Clarke (ed.) Francois Poulain de la Barre, *The Equality of the Sexes*, Manchester: Manchester University Press.

Coontz, Stephanie and Peta Henderson (1986), *Women's Work, Men's Property: The Origins of Gender and Class*, London: Verso.

Cumming, David C. and Robert W. Rebar (1983), 'Exercise and Reproductive Function in Women', *American Journal of Industrial Medicine*, **4** (2), 113–125.

Descartes, René (1985), 'Treatise on Man' in John Cottingham, Robert Stoothoff and Dugald Murdoch (eds), *The Philosophical Writings of Descartes*, Cambridge: Cambridge University Press, pp. 99–108.

Descartes, René (1985a), 'Descriptions of the Human Body and of all its Functions' in John Cottingham, Robert Stoothoff and Dugald Murdoch (eds), *The Philosophical Writings of Descartes*, Cambridge: Cambridge University Press, pp. 313–324.

Firestone, Shulamith (1970), *The Dialectic of Sex*, New York: Bantam Books.

Fraisse, Genevieve (1985), 'Poulain de la Barre, ou le Procès des Préjugés', *Corpus*, **1**, 27–42.

Frisch, Rose E. (1987), 'Body Fat, Menarche, Fitness and Fertility', *Human Reproduction*, **2** (6), 521–533.

Goldin, Claudia (1990), *Understanding the Gender Gap. An Economic History of American Women*, Oxford: Oxford University Press.

Groenewegen, Peter (1983), 'Turgot's Place in the History of Economic Thought: A Bicentenary Estimate', *History of Political Economy*, **15** (4), 585–616.

Hine, Ellen McNiven (1973), 'The Woman Question in early Eighteenth-Century French Literature: The Influence of Francois Poulain de La Barre', *Studies on Voltaire and the Eighteenth Century*, **116**, 65–79.

Kelly, Joan (1982), 'Early Feminist Theory and the *Querelles des Femmes*, 1400-1789', *Journal of Women in Culture and Society*, **8** (1), 4–28.

Klein, Daniel (1985), 'Deductive Economic Methodology in the French Enlightenment: Condillac and Destutt de Tracy', *History of Political Economy*, **17** (1), 51–71.

Laqueur, Thomas (1990), *Making Sex. Body and Gender from the Greeks to Freud*, Cambridge Massachussetts: Harvard University Press.

Laubach, L. L. (1976), 'Comparative Muscular Strength of Men and Women: A Review of the Literature', *Aviation, Space and Environmental Medicine*, May, pp. 534–542.

Lemons, J. S. (1973), *The Woman Citizen; Social Feminism in the 1920s*, Urbana: University of Illinois Press.

Magne, Bernard (1968), 'Une Source De La Lettre Persane XXXIII?', *Revue d'Histoire Littéraire de la France*, Mai–Août, pp. 407–414.

Magne, Bernard (1964), *Le Féminisme de Poullain de la Barre, Origine et Signification*, Unpublished Ph.D Thesis, University of Toulouse.

Meek, Ronald L. (1976), *Social Science and the Ignoble Savage*, Cambridge: Cambridge University Press.

Mill, J. S. (1989), 'The Subjection of Women' in Stefan Collini (ed.), *John Stuart Mill On Liberty and Other Writings*, Cambridge: Cambridge University Press. pp. 117–218.

Mini, Piero V. (1974), *Philosophy and Economics: The Origins and Development of Economic Theory*, Gainesville: University Presses of Florida.

Nyland, Chris (1993), 'John Locke and the Social Position of Women', *History of Political Economy*, Summer.

Nyland, Chris (1993a), 'Adam Smith, Stage Theory and the Status of Women', *History of Political Economy*, Winter.

Nyland, Chris and Diana Kelly (1992), 'Beatrice Webb and the National Standard for Manual Handling', *The Journal of Industrial Relations*, **34** (2), 307–334.

Perry, Ruth (1985), 'Radical Doubt and the Liberation of Women' *Eighteenth-Century Studies*, **18** (4), 472–493.

Poulain de la Barre, François [1990] (1673) *The Equality of the Sexes* (translated and edited by Desmond M. Clarke), Manchester: Manchester University Press.

Poulain de la Barre, François (1674), *De l'Education des Dames*, Paris: Jean du Puis.

Poulain de la Barre, François (1675), *De l'Excellence des Hommes Contre*, Paris: Jean du Puis.

Pribram, Karl (1983), *A History of Economic Reasoning*, Baltimore: Johns Hopkins University Press.

Raisian, J., Michael P. Welch and R. Finis (1988), 'Implementing Comparable Worth' in G. Mangum and P. Philips (eds), *Three Worlds of Labor Economics*, New York: Sharpe, pp. 183–200.

Richards, S. A. (1914), *Feminist Writers of the Seventeenth Century*, London: David Nutt.

Rosso, Jeannette G. (1977), *Montesquieu et la Féminité*, Pise: Libreria Goliardica Editrice.

Schiebinger, Londa L. (1989), *The Mind has no Sex? Women in the Origins of Modern Science*, Cambridge, Massachusetts: Harvard University Press.

Seidel, Michael A. (1974), 'Poulain de La Barre's The Woman as Good as the Man', *Journal of the History of Ideas*, **35** (3), 499-508.

Sophia, A Person of Quality (1739), *Woman Not Inferior to Man*, London: Brentham Press.

Stewart, Dugald (1980), 'Account of the Life and Writings of Adam Smith, L.L.D.' in I. S. Ross (ed.) *Adam Smith Essays on Philosophical Subjects*, Oxford: Clarendon Press, pp. 269–352.

Stock, Marie Louise (1961), *Poullain de la Barre: A Seventeenth-Century Feminist*, Unpublished Ph.D. Thesis, Columbia University.

Thomas, Antoine (1781), *An Essay on the Character, the Manners and the Understanding of Women in Different Ages*, London: J. Dodsley.

NOTES

1. For details of Poulain's life see, Marie Stock (1961) *Poullain de la Barre: A Seventeenth Century Feminist*, unpublished Ph.D. thesis, Columbia University.
2. That male dominance is a universal phenomenon is challenged occasionally on the grounds that there have existed societies where male rule is not obvious. However, as the anthropologists Coontz and Henderson (1986, p. 26) have observed, these exceptions invariably 'come from relatively isolated simple societies' and hence cannot be accepted as significant exceptions.
3. In a review of nine studies reporting static and dynamic muscle strength measurements, Laubach (1976) reported mean sex differences as follows: women were (a) 55.8 per cent as strong as males in upper extremity strength; (b) 71.9 per cent as strong in lower extremity strength; (c) 63.8 per cent as strong in trunk strength; and (d) 68.6 per cent as strong in dynamic strength. It is true there is some crossover, that is, some women are stronger than some men. However, the magnitude of this overlap is not great. Celentano and Noy (1981) have calculated that in a number of the areas of the body critical to the use of tools and weapons, 5th percentile strength values for males exceed the 95th percentile values for females. The extent to which the measured differences in muscular strength are a result of socialisation has also been tested. Bishop *et al.* (1987) compared the physical strength of male and female collegiate swimmers with identical long-term training histories. Swimmers were chosen because the training is the same for males and females, begins at a young age, is year-round and involves all-over body activity. A comparison group of non–athletes was also tested. It was found that mean strength differences between sexes were 51.5 per cent for swimmers, and 64.4 per cent for non-athletes, indicating that while differential socialization does enhance this sex difference it is a minor determinant compared to biological factors.

3. John Locke, Equality of Rights and Diversity of Attributes

Chris Nyland

In the history of economic thought, John Locke is recognized as a major contributor to the establishment of the philosophical foundations upon which the general principles of political economy were subsequently constructed. He is also acknowledged as having made direct contributions to the development of economics in the area of both monetary and property theory (Vaughn 1980, Mitchell 1986). The purpose of this paper is to show that Locke should also be given credit for pioneering research into the economics of the social position of women.

Locke developed his analysis of gender relations as a consequence of his involvement in the liberal critique of regal absolutism and the divine rights of the monarchy. This point is critical, for as Ashcraft (1986) has shown, to comprehend Locke's work it is vital that its social context be understood. Because of the importance of this element in Locke's work it is necessary to specify in some detail the environment in which he made his contribution.

The seventeenth-century liberals who opposed regal absolutism argued that the foundation of regency was not divine will. Rather, it was the 'social contract' that existed between the regent and the people. This fundamental covenant supposedly gave monarchs authority to rule only so long as they used their power to protect the people's interests. It had supposedly been forged while the population remained in a state of nature, this being a stage in the development of human society in which there existed no government. In such a society people existed in a God-given state of equality, owning the world in common with all who were rational, and being free of any natural domination by any other. A rational individual was one who had the capacity to comprehend natural law. This was the highest form of law, being that which prevailed irrespective of the existence of government and which must exist if the world is to be compatible with the will of God (Grotius 1925, pp. 38–39; Schochet 1975).

The absolutists denied these claims, replying that there was no social contract and that no matter how regents behaved, their wishes could not be questioned because their powers were divine in origin. In support of these claims they advanced an argument which was a mixture of physiology and scripture. Physiologically, it was argued, God's commitment to regal absolutism was proven by the fact that humans were created in a form which meant they came into the world as beings who were subject to their parents, and as the absolutists' reading of the relationship between Adam and Eve led them to believe God had decreed that husbands had the right to expect obedience from their wives, it followed that the father was the senior parent within the family. Thus children owed their primary allegiance to their fathers. Paternal authority was therefore natural and divine in origin, in that subordination of wife to husband was decreed by God and subordination of child to father was grounded in a nature which God had created. As all individuals were born and remained forever subordinate to their fathers, it followed there could never have been a time when people were totally free. Hence, they could never have forged a free covenant of government. The true foundation of states, therefore, could not be any unconstrained consensual agreement between people and Regent. Rather, it was the God-given paternal power that existed within the family. The people of a nation were no more than the members of an extended family, the head of which was entitled to all the rights due to husband and father within the home (Schochet 1975).

Of the works of absolutist authors, Robert Filmer's *Patriarcha, or the Natural Power of Kings* was particularly influential in England (Filmer 1969). Filmer's primary contribution to absolutist theory was to note that consent theorists could not provide an adequate explanation for how the supposed meeting which forged the social contract could have been held. He argued that if all people in the state of nature had owned the world in common, then all should have partaken in the original decision to divide the world into separate states. The only way this could have been done was if everyone had met and agreed to take this step. But such a meeting was physically impossible. It followed, therefore, that it had never been held and that the claim that there existed an original covenant of government to which all mankind had freely consented was farcical. Filmer added that if this was the case then the consent theorists had no other explanation for the origin of government, authority and private property than the fact that some individuals had in the past usurped the divine rights of others. Therefore, consent theory was a licence for the free use of force and for anarchy (Filmer 1969, p. 267).

Filmer's work was published as part of the absolutists' attempt to win control of parliament. To do so they needed to gain the support of a property-enfranchised, male electorate. This fact is important for understanding why those opposed to absolutism went to great effort both to deny that they had no defence for private property and to discuss the social status of women. It was necessary to debate the first issue in order to disabuse those who feared that to break the link between regent and God would undermine the sanctity of private property. The second topic had to be dealt with because of the need to placate the fears of those men who suspected that breaking this link would undermine the power of husbands. This second issue was especially difficult because one of the means the consent theorists utilized to undermine divine rule was to deny that Adam had ever enjoyed absolute regency of the world. They argued that a rational reading of the Bible showed that Adam had not enjoyed the powers of an absolute ruler because his regency had been shared by Eve. This point was critical because, if it were sustained, it seriously undermined the very foundations of absolutist theory. It meant the regent could not have inherited his supposed divine powers from Adam, as was claimed. The problem, however, was that it followed that if Eve had not been subject to Adam's absolute authority, then husbands could not have inherited any divine right to rule their wives. Such a suggestion had the potential to be politically disastrous in a society in which virtually all men accepted that they had the right to be treated as absolute regents within their own homes. Certainly, telling men that there was no moral or theological foundation to this claim was unlikely to be a positive factor attracting these individuals to the political alliance the consent theorists were attempting to construct.

To reply to Filmer's challenge in a manner which would help build this alliance, the critics of absolutism needed to refute his scriptural evidence while justifying natural equality, men's authority within the home and the disproportionate distribution of the world's wealth. All this, moreover, needed to be undertaken without the requirement that all of humanity had once held a meeting and freely decided these arrangements. It was the challenge of constructing an argument that could simultaneously deal with these difficulties that Locke chose to take up. Because these issues were so integrated, comprehending the nature of Locke's account of women's social position requires an understanding of his contribution as a whole. Only with this overall picture is it possible to grasp Locke's views regarding the nature of women and their relations with men.

LOCKE AND THE DIVINE ORIGIN OF REGAL POWER

In his reply to Filmer, Locke sought to deny the divine origin of regal power and state absolutism. He also strove to disabuse those men who feared that to accept that political power was founded in the will of the people would leave no substantive justification for private property or for political and household authority. Locke began by criticising the claim that the powers of the regent were divine in origin and absolute in extent. He did so by engaging in a scriptural analysis of Filmer's work. By undertaking this exegetic endeavour he was able to argue convincingly that the claim that God had given sole regency of the world to Adam was based on a selective and literal, rather than a comprehensive and rational, reading of scripture.

Locke observed that the *Bible* utilizes the word 'them' when stating to whom dominion of the earth was initially given. As utilized, this word could either refer to Adam and Eve together or it could be a reference to all members of the human race. Locke (1969, pp. 25–26) acknowledged that there was ambiguity here. However, he insisted that what was not ambiguous was the plurality of the term 'them'. To whomever ownership of the world was given, the use of this word made clear that it was not given to Adam alone. Moreover, Locke added, the significance of the plurality of the original grant of dominion could not be dismissed by claiming that Eve was Adam's subject. Even were she a subordinate (a claim he did not accept), this would not mean that Adam's powers were absolute. The 'Bible' explained that Eve '... was not so subjected to him as to hinder her dominion over the creatures, or property in them' (Locke 1969, p. 26). Thus, Eve had a degree of power in her own right and Adam's powers were not absolute.

Locke made explicit his belief that Adam had no divine right to dominate Eve when dealing with the claim that, at the time of the Fall, God decreed that henceforth Eve would be subject to Adam's rule. He noted that when Adam and Eve were being driven from Paradise both were being punished, and therefore it was unlikely that God would have chosen this moment to elevate Adam to absolute ruler of the world. It was true that Eve was subjected to greater punishment than was Adam because she had been an agent in his temptation as well as sinning herself, and that this greater punishment gave Adam a 'superiority' over Eve. However, Locke denied that what Adam accidentally obtained by being subjected to a lesser punishment than Eve was a divine right to rule over her. He insisted that rationality made it clear that when God said to Eve, 'I will greatly multiply thy sorrow and thy conception; in sorrow thou shalt bring forth children, and thy desire shall be to thy husband, and he shall rule over thee' (cited by Locke 1969, p. 37), he was not granting Adam any authority over Eve. Rather, God was foretelling what was going to be the fate of Eve, and of women, outside of Paradise. Locke was insistent on this point. He acknowledged that Adam attained a superiority over Eve at the time of the Fall but he insisted that God had not made Eve Adam's subordinate. Rather, Adam obtained some form of material advantage as a result of the greater disadvantages that were imposed on Eve. In short, he gained a capacity to rule but he did not thereby gain a right to rule over her:

> God, in this text, gives not, that I see, any authority to Adam over Eve, or to men over their wives, but only foretells what should be the woman's lot, how by this

providence he would order it so that she should be subject to her husband, as we see that generally the laws of mankind and customs of nations have ordered it so (Locke 1969, p. 37).

Having made this point, Locke immediately reassured his readers that husbands would normally be the senior marriage partner. Male seniority within marriage, even if not justified by right of inheritance from Adam, was to be expected because there existed 'a foundation in nature for it'. This natural basis was the fact that the relative disadvantage women attained when being driven from Paradise rendered them the 'weaker sex'. It was this fact, Locke observed, that ensured that in the vast majority of cases men were able to attain a superior position in their relations with women. That he believed men's superior social position was based on this natural foundation Locke reaffirmed when discussing how disputes between husband and wife over common family problems would normally tend to be resolved. He argued that in most cases ultimate decision-making power in the family would accrue to the husband because of his greater natural abilities and strengths:

> But the husband and wife, though they have but one common concern, yet having different understandings, will unavoidably sometimes have different wills too; it therefore being necessary that the last determination – that is, the rule – should be placed somewhere, it naturally falls to the man's share, as the abler and stronger (Locke 1969, p. 161).

Fundamental to Locke's explanation and justification for women's subordination to men, then, was the claim that males have greater innate abilities and strengths than women. Hence, he believed men's superior status was not ultimately based on any social arrangement such as the separation of home and civil society, as has been argued by Fox-Genovese (1977). Rather, it was established on this 'foundation in nature'. Locke (1969, p. 37) agrees that 'the laws of mankind and customs of nations have ordered' that wives should be subject to their husbands. However, he does not locate the fundamental cause of women's subordination in these social constructs. Laws and customs merely reinforce the underlying innate advantage upon which men's superior social position is based.

In his reply to Filmer, Locke failed to specify in what ways he regarded women as being weaker than men. Most observers have taken him to be referring to physical abilities rather than mental strengths (Clark 1979). This interpretation would appear to be justified given that he denied there was any difference between the minds of males and females as regards their capacity to comprehend truth. He believed the mental capacities of the two sexes to be so alike that there was no reason why both should not receive an identical programme of education. The only difference between the respective curricula he advocated for boys and girls related to the latter's greater desire to protect their complexions (Locke 1968, pp. 344–346). Locke's acceptance of women's high intelligence and his support for the education of females was recognized by his contemporaries.   An anonymous female admirer of Locke's ideas acknowledged as much in 1696 in a work titled *An Essay in Defence of the Female Sex* (Anonymous 1970, p. 61). The author of this work, of which Locke owned a copy, was one of the first scholars to realize the significance for women of Locke's sensationalist psychology and the emphasis this psychology necessarily placed upon education.   The point was, of course, that if humans were born with minds that were blank sheets, then it was unjustifiable to assume that there existed an innate feminine mind.   Even less was it justifiable to assume that the natural capacity of women's minds was less than that of men's.

Locke's knowledge of the capacities of women would also have been influenced by the relationship he maintained with the feminist Damaris Masham.   The Locke–Damaris friendship began in 1681 and continued until Locke's death in 1704.   It led to his taking up residence in the Masham household for the last fourteen years of his life. Cranston (1957, p. 215) reports that Masham was 'closer to Locke than any other human being'. Their intimacy is indicated by the fact that she was reading to him when he died and it was she who closed his eyes for the last time.   Masham has been described by Laslett (1953, p. 536) as 'the first bluestocking of them all'. Locke described her thus:

> The lady herself is so much occupied with study and reflection on theological and philosophical matters, that you could find few men with whom you might associate with greater profit and pleasure. Her judgement is singularly keen, and I know few men capable of discussing with such insight the most abstruse subjects, such as are beyond the grasp, I do not say of women, but even most educated men, and of resolving the difficulties they present (Locke 1979, p. 237).

During the fourteen years that they shared the same house, these two scholars worked together on a daily basis (Bourne 1969, p. 284).   When Locke's epistemology was criticized by John Norris and the Tory Mary Astell, they replied by publishing anonymously *A Discourse Concerning the Love of God.* This work was widely accepted at the time as being the product of Masham and Locke's collaboration (Perry 1986, pp. 86–96).   Shortly after Locke's death, Masham published a further tract which had been written during their period of collaboration. This book, *Occasional Thoughts in Reference to a Vertuous or Christian Life*, has been aptly described by Smith (1916, p. 113) as a 'feminized' version of Locke's *Thoughts on Education*. In the work, Masham castigated those parents who failed to educate their daughters, and denounced the arrogance of men who considered an educated woman to be unacceptable as a wife. She insisted women have a right and a duty to become educated and reported that this was also the perspective of Locke (Masham 1705, p. 196).

Moreover, she asserted, there was no reason why this education should be any less broad than that available to men:

> Now in the pursuit of that Pleasure which the exercise and improvement of the understanding gives, I see no Reason why it should not be thought that all Science lyes as open to a Lady as to a Man (Masham 1705, pp. 227–228).

Masham's *Occasional Thoughts* differed from most other late seventeenth-century tracts supporting female education. The feminists of the period generally argued that women should be educated so they could better serve the needs of their husbands (Stone 1977, pp. 344–345; Kinnaird 1979). Masham, conversely, argued women needed to be educated so they could join men in the pursuit of truth and in the attainment of the rationality required to defend their belief in God. Only thus could they take responsibility for their own souls. She also insisted women needed to be educated so they could effectively undertake the education of their children (Ballard 1985, pp. 332–338, pp. 421–425). The emphasis Masham placed on this last need replicated the argument advanced by Fenelon in his 1687 work *Education of Girls* (Hearnshaw 1931, pp. 77–79), a copy of which, Harrison and Laslett (1971, p. 134) report, was owned by Locke.

While he accepted that women could match men intellectually, Locke did not believe the innate capacities of the sexes were equal in all spheres. Being a medical practitioner, he was well versed in the literature regarding women's physiology (Dewhurst 1984). One aspect of this literature he accepted as valid was the claim that women have less innate muscular capacity than men. This hypothesis, it should be noted, has been confirmed by modern empirical research. In a review of nine studies examining static and dynamic muscle strength measurements, Laubach (1976) reported mean sex differences as follows: women were (a) 55.8 per cent as strong as males in upper extremity strength; (b) 71.9 per cent as strong in lower extremity strength; (c) 63.8 per cent as strong in trunk strength; and (d) 68.6 per cent as strong in dynamic strength. It is true that these figures are averages and that there is some crossover; that is, some females are stronger than some males. However, in certain parts of the body which are critical to the use of tools and weapons, the magnitude of this crossover is not great. Celatano and Noy (1981) have calculated that less than 5 per cent of women have strengths greater than the weakest 5 per cent of men in the areas of shoulder flexion, elbow flexion, trunk flexion and grip strength.

Because of their lesser physical strength, Locke advised women that lifting heavy weights was a form of labour which 'belongs not to their sex', it being a danger for them to undertake such activities (Locke 1954, pp. 95–98). This is not to suggest he believed women incapable of muscular activities. They were weaker, not weak. Indeed, because he accepted that at times they had to endure muscular effort, Locke suggested that girls' physical constitution should be sustained by a diet, and an exercise programme, similar to that provided to boys (Locke 1968, pp. 344–345).

Acceptance of the belief that Locke was referring only to women's physical strength when he described them as the weaker sex would appear then to be warranted. That he chose to emphasize muscular capacity as a factor explaining husbands' seniority has caused him to become the subject of criticism. It has been suggested that he thus justifies the rule of 'beasts' and implies that husbands have the right to use violence against their wives (Clark 1979, p. 19; Shanley 1982, p. 94). However, such a charge indicates a failure to understand Locke's argument. It is true he argued that men have the right to insist their marriage partners pay heed to their greater strength. This is not, however, because men may justifiably use their physical power to compel their wives to consent to their will. Locke (1969, pp. 121, 124) insisted that no one has the right to force another human being to do their bidding. Rather, the reason why men's greater strength is important is that it is a property of some significant utility. Consequently, as with all other resources that either partner brings to marriage, men may require that, to the extent that their greater strength is of value, it should be taken into consideration in the determination of the provisions of the marriage contract. Greater strength is a property which belongs to the man and the benefits of which belong to him. If wives wish to share the material rewards this capacity enables them to generate, Locke considered it reasonable that men ask a price for this concession. Equally, he insisted that a woman had the right to require that a prospective husband take note of those attributes she brings to the relationship (Derringh 1980, p. 117).

LOCKE'S THEORY OF PROPERTY

To comprehend Locke's argument regarding the respective status of husband and wife, it is necessary to understand his theory of the origin of private property, his justification for the uneven distribution of property within society and his understanding of the relationship that normally exists between property-owning partners. He argued that by the term 'property' he meant all use-values, be they corporeal or spiritual. He is explicit on this point, insisting that 'By property I must be understood here, as in other places, to mean that property which men have in their persons as well as goods' (Locke 1969, p. 210). The use-values within an individual's person to which he refers in particular are their life, liberty and capacity to labour. For Locke, the common feature of these non-physical use-values, and of goods, is that their existence is critical to the preservation of human life, none being necessarily more so than another. As the taking of human life is prohibited by natural law, it follows that the arbitrary expropriation of any of these forms of property threatens life and hence infringes this form of law. Indeed, some types of property are so critical to the preservation of life that individuals cannot contract to give them away even if they so wish. Thus, people cannot sell themselves into slavery, for to be a slave would be to lose one's personal freedom from arbitrary power, and this form of freedom is 'so necessary to and closely joined with a man's preservation that he cannot part with it but by what forfeits his preservation and life together' (Locke 1969, p. 132).

The existence of this natural law restriction on the nature of contracts was a critical point for Locke. Its existence meant that the people, when forging the original covenant which created the state, could not have granted to any person the powers claimed by the Monarch. The natural law command that people preserve human life and liberty meant that they had never had total power over their own lives. As they did not possess this degree of power, it followed that they could never have given it to another:

> [F]or a man not having the power of his own life cannot by compact or his own consent enslave himself to any one, nor put himself under the absolute arbitrary power of another to take away his life when he pleases. Nobody can give more power than he has himself; and he that cannot take away his own life cannot give another power over it (Locke 1969, p. 132).

Therefore individual liberty is a form of private property, as is the capacity to labour. The latter is so because it is a product of the individual's inalienable person. Where these forms of property are melded with natural resources, moreover, these too necessarily become private property because they become part of the individual's essence (Locke 1969, pp. 142–143). Having thus given justification to private property, Locke proceeded to justify its uneven distribution amongst the population. He argued that, while he believed all rational members of the human race were equal by nature, he did not mean by this that people are equal in all respects:

> Though I have said ... 'that all men by nature are equal', I cannot be supposed to understand all sorts of equality. Age or virtue may give men a just precedency; excellency of parts and merit may place others above the common level; birth may subject some, and alliance or benefits others, to pay an observance to those whom nature, gratitude, or other respects may have made it due; and yet all this consists with the equality which all men are in, in respect of jurisdiction or domination one over another, which was the equality I there spoke of as proper to the business in hand, being that equal right that every man hath to his natural freedom, without being

subjected to the will or authority of any other man (Locke 1969, p. 147).

The equality which Locke recognizes, in short, is not an equality of goods or attributes but rather the equal right of all individuals to be free of arbitrary domination. All people have this right equally. At the same time they have the right to enjoy greater status and precedence in decision making if their physiological capacities, endeavour or birth has provided them with some advantage that it any way makes it possible for them to lawfully gain these rewards.

Because human capacities are not distributed evenly through mankind, Locke argued, some individuals can labour more productively than others. While the world remained the common property of all, such individuals were prohibited from utilizing these capacities to increase their share of the world's wealth. However, given that mankind collectively owned the earth, it was not necessary for the people to retain equality of ownership. If they so desired, people could choose to adopt some other pattern of resource distribution. As noted above, to sustain this position it was necessary for Locke to explain how such a decision could have been reached. He did so by laying aside the claim that the uneven division of the world's economic resources was a consequence of a unanimous decision taken freely at a mass meeting attended by the whole of humanity. Rather, he suggested that agreement had been achieved by the people choosing to adopt the use of an instrument which enabled them to vote on this topic without ever having to meet. This wonderful device was money, and the system of economic distribution chosen was the allocation of resources on the basis of individual capacities and industriousness (Locke 1969, p. 144).

That the decision to abandon economic equality was freely taken was proven by the fact that durable metals had been chosen as the primary instrument of exchange. Gold and silver, Locke observed, had little intrinsic capacity to sustain human life. Even so, the people chose to elevate these particular elements to the status of money. Locke concluded that this was because there was no limit to the extent to which these resources could be accumulated and stored. Hence, this showed that the people had chosen to support the unlimited accumulation of wealth. Such a decision must have been taken freely, for individuals did not need gold and silver as such in order to live. These facts indicated that humanity had also chosen to support an uneven distribution of the world's resources. Locke claimed this would have been an obvious result of permitting people with differing levels of ability to engage in unlimited accumulation (Locke 1969, pp. 143–144).

Finally, there remains the question of why Locke believed people would have chosen to give up the security provided by the equal ownership of the world's wealth in exchange for the right to unlimited accumulation. The latter freedom, he noted, could only be had at the cost of forgoing economic equality. There was, in short, a cost in choosing to abandon equality of goods for equality of opportunity. Locke's explanation for why humanity chose the second of these options was founded on his belief that nature 'has put into man a desire of happiness and an aversion to misery' (Locke 1961, p. 27). Consequently, people faced with a choice between two goods will always take that which provides the greatest utility 'for no rational creature can be supposed to change his condition with an intention to be worse' (Locke 1969, p. 186; Brogan 1959). Humanity had chosen opportunity over security, then, because the people had decided that by so doing their nett utility would be enhanced.

RELATIONS BETWEEN PROPERTY OWNERS

By developing his theory of the origin of property, Locke countered Filmer's accusation that the consent theorists could not justify private property. Having achieved this objective, it was a relatively small step to then invent the property-defending state. All that was now required for a government to be created was for the property owners of a region to decide that they would pass certain of their powers to a collective body. Such an act did not contravene natural law as this action only concerned the property of the individuals involved. Having justified property rights and the state, Locke proceeded to discuss the nature of relations between property owners. Given his belief that all individuals own some property, even if this is no more than their life, liberty and capacity to labour, all relationships formed to promote a common endeavour are partnerships between property owners. However, it does not follow that partners will necessarily be equals. Locke appears to have accepted that the relative standing of partners will depend on the quantity of property each puts into the relationship and the respective degree of need each has for the other.

Locke sketched his general conception of the nature of partnerships in his comments on the employment relationship. As with any other partnership, he accepted that employer–employee relations should be founded on a freely negotiated agreement. The provisions that bargainers could choose to include in this contract were without limit, save only that they complied with the law. This latter need necessarily meant that the contract could not exist in perpetuity (for this would be slavery), and that its provisions not be subject to arbitrary modification during its lifetime:

> Master and servant are names as old as history, but given to those of far different condition; for a freeman makes himself a servant to another by selling him, for a certain time, the service he undertakes to do in exchange for wages he is to receive; and though this commonly puts him into the family of his master and under the

ordinary discipline thereof, yet it gives the master but a temporary power over him and no greater than what is contained in the contract between them (Locke 1969, p. 162).

Locke accepted that when human beings negotiate an employment contract, employer and employee should meet as agents free of arbitrary domination by any other. From this particular perspective they are equals irrespective of what level of inequality may exist in other areas. Hence, any contract forged between them to facilitate the exchange of their respective commodities is from this limited perspective a contract between equals (Vaughn 1980, pp. 83–84, 156-157). That one or the other of the bargainers may have a desperate need for the commodity being offered by the other, the intensity of which is not reciprocated by this other, does not for Locke negate the voluntary nature of any contract that may be negotiated. As Dunn (1967, p. 157) has put it, for Locke, 'Voluntary action does not, of course, imply the absence of motive, even of overwhelmingly powerful motive'.

Locke did not believe, however, that employers and employees normally meet as equals in all respects. He accepted that the latter have less access to economic resources. Certainly this was the case with handicraftsmen and labourers, whom he accepted tended to live a 'hand to mouth' existence (Locke 1963, pp. 23–24, 57). He acknowledged that where market forces induced an insufficiency of labour from the employers' perspective, the bargaining power of workers could be enhanced and their wages might consequently rise above a bare subsistence. However, he suggested that this was not the norm. Indeed he believed that, even if they acted collectively, workers seldom had sufficient bargaining power to match that of the employers. Of the struggle between classes over the distribution of society's wealth Locke noted:

> This pulling and contest is usually between the landed man and the merchant; for the labourer's share, being seldom more than a bare subsistence, never allows that body of men time or opportunity to raise their thoughts above that, or struggle with the richer for theirs (as one common interest) unless when some common and great distress, uniting them in one universal ferment, makes them forget respect, and emboldens them to carve to their wants with armed force; and then sometimes they break in upon the rich, and sweep all like a deluge. But this rarely happens but in the mal-administration of neglected or mismanaged government (Locke 1963, p. 71).

Where bargainers have differing levels of need for commodities being offered in exchange, there is a likelihood that this fact will become manifest in the final terms of the agreement. It is also likely that, where the exchange process requires the creation of a partnership, the bargainer with the lesser degree of need will tend to come out of the bargaining process with the more advantageous or senior position. Locke accepted that these consequences of unequal need amongst bargainers would generally characterize the employment relationship. Under normal circumstances, he noted, the employee conceded the employer authority over their partnership and agreed to accept the 'ordinary discipline' of the latter (Derringh 1980, pp. 140-212; Hundert 1977). In Locke's terminology the employer was invariably the 'master' and the employee the 'servant'. The latter accepted this lesser position because the utility lost by becoming the servant of another was more than offset by the wages received. As Locke put it: '[T]he authority of the rich proprietor and the subjection of the needy beggar began not from the possession of the lord, but the consent of the poor man who preferred being his subject to starving' (Locke 1969, p. 34). That the employer should enjoy an authority over the employee was not the way things had to be, for bargainers were free to negotiate alternative arrangements, but this was the outcome Locke accepted would normally occur (Locke 1969, p. 162).

Locke applied the principles utilized in his analysis of the employment contract to his discussion of other social covenants. Not the least of these was the marriage partnership. Here, once again, we are presented with two individuals equally possessing their natural freedoms. By a process of negotiation they forge a conjugal contract, the provisions of which are constrained only by natural law and, if in civil society, by those laws of the state which are consistent with natural law. That there should be an equality between prospective marriage partners was normally accepted as a given by consent theorists. However, their conception of what this equality involved was very limited in character. Grotius (1925, p. 234) and Pufendorf (1927, p. 95), for example, confined women's natural conjugal freedom merely to the right to choose whom to marry. The husband's absolute authority in marriage they saw as a necessary condition of the relationship. Locke, on the other hand, argued that 'the ends of matrimony requiring no such power in the husband, the condition of conjugal society put it not in him, it being not at all necessary to that state' (Locke 1969, p. 161).

To argue that men had no divine right to dominate the marriage relationship was a very radical hypothesis for seventeenth-century England. It was a clear criticism of those laws that constrained women's freedoms and held up a model of what should be that was not to become legal fact for another two centuries. Why Locke adopted this radical posture is a matter of conjecture. It should be noted, though, that to accept the alternative, that is the claim that husbands had a natural right to a dominant position within marriage, would have undermined his argument that Eve was not Adam's natural subordinate. This undermining would have destroyed his thesis that regents could not base their absolutist claims on the supposed powers given by God to Adam. To sustain his position as regards the King's claims, Locke needed to argue that wives and husbands were free to arrange their relationships as they wished, with neither being the natural subordinate.

Acknowledging that Locke was in a situation where the denial of women's natural equality was difficult to render compatible with his political needs, however, is not to suggest that he adopted this position merely because he had no choice. To do so would be to unjustly deny him the moral credit he deserves for challenging the perceived wisdom. His friend James Tyrrell (1681, pp. 14, 110), when faced with this same difficulty, could not bring himself to accept women's equality, as indeed very few of Locke's Whig contemporaries could do. It is therefore to his credit that when faced with this situation he maintained consistency and insisted that women's natural rights were no less than those belonging to men. It is true that Locke accepted that wives would normally be the lesser partner in marriage, but his reasons for doing so were not inherently sexist. By this is meant that he did not utilize criteria for explaining the nature, and assessing the justice, of relations between men and women that were different from those he applied to relations between men.

Locke's explanation and justification for why men were normally the senior partner in marriage was similar to his explanation for why the employer was normally the boss. In short, men's greater strength and consequent abilities enabled them to negotiate a superior position with their prospective brides. As did employees, women consented to this lesser position because they accepted that this was a cost they had to pay for economic security. Again, as with the employment relationship, Locke insisted that there was nothing inherent in marriage that demanded that one or other of the partners have the senior position. Conjugal partners were free to negotiate whatever marriage terms they wished. The only concessions to the uniqueness of the marriage covenant that Locke was willing to acknowledge was that it had to be compatible with the attainment of the primary purpose of marriage, that is 'the continuation of the species'. This meant, first, it had to be agreed that both partners would have access to the body of the other for purposes of procreation. Second, both had to agree to remain with the other for at least as long as was required to enable their common offspring to reach an age where they could fend for themselves. Third, both must agree to provide the degree of support required to ensure their children received adequate nurturing. Beyond these provisions there were no conditions which the partners had to include in their covenant:

> Conjugal society could subsist and attain its ends without it [that is the rule of husbands]; nay, community of goods and the power over them, mutual assistance, and other things belonging to conjugal society, might be varied and regulated by that contract which unites man and wife in that society as far as may consist with procreation and the bringing up of children till they could shift for themselves, nothing being necessary to any society that is not necessary to the ends for which it is made (Locke 1969, pp. 161–162; Shanley 1982, p. 93).

For Locke then, the same restrictions and freedoms applied to the marriage contract as applied to any other covenant. Most importantly, the property rights of both partners, both corporeal and spiritual, could not be arbitrarily infringed. Consequently, just as a people could not grant the state absolute power over their property, a wife could not grant her husband the right to absolute authority over her life, even if she so wished. To do so would alienate a property she does not have the power to give away. Nor may a man confiscate for his own use the goods a woman brings to the marriage merely because the couple have chosen to marry. This was her property and hence part of her being and as such could not be expropriated against her will.

For Locke, the marriage relationship created no theoretical difficulties with these forms of property. However, there was a problem with the property which a husband and wife, by common endeavour, accumulated during the period of the marriage. As this wealth was the product of their common labours, the husband could have no right to arbitrarily utilize it as he wished. 'For as to the wife's share, whether her own labour or compact gave her a title to it, it is plain her husband could not forfeit what was hers' (Locke 1969, p. 216). This left unresolved, however, how day to day decisions regarding the use of this common property were to be determined. It was here that Locke observed that, as the male was the 'abler and stronger' of the two sexes, family decision-making power, in the last instance, tended 'naturally' to fall to the husband. It needs to be stressed that Locke believed this development to be a tendency, not a universal phenomenon. He was quite explicit in insisting that husbands did not inevitably have final power of decision making. Indeed, he scoffed at those who suggested marriage conveyed this right on husbands. When doing so, he pointed out that, within England, no one accepted that a queen who married one of her subjects consequently became the subordinate of this individual (Locke 1969, p. 37). Moreover, Locke observed that even while it was true that the power of ultimate decision over common goods normally fell to the husband, this was not the way things had to be. 'Community of goods and the power over them' within marriage, he insisted, could be varied and regulated as the partners wished, so long as the interests of any offspring were protected (Locke 1969, p. 162).

Pateman (1987, p. 106) has denied that Locke accepted that both sexes had an equal right to be free of subjugation. He could not have done so, she insists, because in the *Two Treatises* he accepts that women are natural subordinates and a 'natural subordinate cannot at the same time be free and equal'. Pateman, however, misses Locke's point that there can be equality between individuals in certain areas of social life without there necessarily being equality in all others. It was not the case that Locke depicted women as men's 'natural subordinates'. Indeed, as has been shown, it was critical for his refutation of absolutism that any claim that husbands had a natural right to dominate their wives be denied. Even if he believed this was the case, therefore, Locke could not have conceded that women were the natural subordinates of men. Locke accepted that men would normally be the dominant partner in the marriage relationship. His explanation for this, though, was not founded on a belief that women were men's natural subordinates. Rather, it was founded on his theory of property and his understanding of the relationship that would normally exist between property owners who have differing levels of need for each other's services but who nonetheless choose to forge a partnership.

What Locke argued, in short, was that men commonly enjoyed a natural advantage when bargaining over the provisions of the marriage partnership as a consequence of the fact that women were physically the weaker sex. Men's greater strength was an advantage because it enabled them to undertake certain significant manual tasks much more effectively than could women. Consequently, because most men had this overall advantage, Locke accepted that, just as employers normally negotiated the senior position within the employment relationship because of their greater advantages, prospective husbands normally had the capacity to negotiate a superior position within marriage.

Why the strength advantage was important in the shaping of relations between the sexes, then, was because it gave men a greater ability to undertake those activities which required high levels of physical capacity. In seventeenth-century England, two fundamental activities which would have fallen within this category were soldiering and certain types of productive labour. Traditionally, the first had been of great importance amongst the ruling strata. Its significance had, however, declined greatly since the period of high feudalism when the rulers had, in effect, been a military class. Even so, despite its diminished significance, the respective military capacities of the sexes remained a significant factor influencing the ideological perspective of those who were members of the dominant sector. Much more significant for the overwhelming bulk of this agrarian population, however, would have been the extent to which the differing muscular capacities of the sexes influenced their respective ability to undertake heavy manual labour. That Locke might have believed this factor could enable the majority of husbands to gain a negotiated precedence in their relations with their wives has been denied by Clark (1979, p. 31) on the grounds that women are 'as able to labour as men'. The point is, however, that Locke did not believe that this was the case. He accepted that heavy physical work was an activity, a 'stress of labour', which women were less capable of undertaking than men (Locke 1954, p. 490).

Whether or not Locke was correct as regards the respective labouring abilities of the sexes is an issue for debate. But what we do know is that Locke was aware that their respective productivities were reflected in the relative wages paid to men and women. It should also be noted that there is evidence to suggest that this was a valid belief (Roberts 1979; Snell 1981; Middleton 1988). Irrespective of the validity of Locke's hypothesis, what is clear is that he believed it to be the case that women's lesser physical strength rendered them less capable than were men of undertaking heavy physical labour. That this was so is important for it enables us to comprehend how Locke could believe men would tend to emerge from marriage negotiations as the senior partner. Locke lived in a society where the economic security of the overwhelming majority of families was greatly dependent on the capacity of people to periodically undertake heavy physical labour. Indeed, even the livelihood of the gentry and the aristocracy, classes that did not actually engage in manual labour, was partially dependent on this ability. This was because the mass of surplus value these classes could extract from employees or tenants was influenced by the level of the latters' labour productivity.

Believing that men's greater muscular capacity gave them an enhanced ability to undertake manual labour would, in such a situation, amount to accepting that the majority of men entered the marriage negotiations with a decided economic advantage. Locke does not appear to have believed that women had any natural attribute which might be a bargaining tool as effective as that which he accepted was enjoyed by men. Consequently, he could rationally conclude that males entered these negotiations with a lesser need for that which women had to offer than the need women had for that which could be offered by men. Both prospective marriage partners could offer the other companionship, sex, children and productive labour. But the man could also offer a level of economic security and protection from the violence of others which very few women could match. Given this situation and his understanding of the likely outcome of bargaining between individuals with differing levels of need for each other's services, it is reasonable to assume that Locke would have considered it normal for the male to negotiate a senior position within marriage. In short, he would have considered that a wife promising to honour and obey her husband, while he only pledged to keep her in sickness and in health, was a normal outcome of such an uneven relationship.

CONCLUSION

In his reply to Filmer, Locke sought to undermine political absolutism by disabusing those who feared that to deny divine regency was to weaken political stability, property rights and husbands' authority. In seeking to attain his objectives, Locke advanced an explanation and justification for male seniority which rejected the claim that their superior position was divine in origin. By so doing Locke aided women in their struggle to free themselves from the binds of a theological determinism which decreed that they were forever fated to a condition of subservience to men. Given the extent to which religion and the story of Adam and Eve had traditionally shaped people's view as to the 'correct' relationship between men and women, this was no mean feat. As O'Donnell has observed, to undermine this perspective was a contribution of tremendous significance, greatly aiding the efforts of those who insisted that, in terms of spirituality, rationality, intelligence and natural rights, women were the equals of men.[1]

> The Christian patriarchal political and cultural system – whereby every avenue of power within society is in male hands – is ideologically rooted in the story of Adam and Eve. The birthright priority whereby males rule females, the innate distinctions presumed to fit males for domination and females for submission, is contained within the story. In the deepest sense, Adam's mastery of Eve precludes her claims to autonomous identity, while Adam's God-given power to name the creatures of the earth insures his right to define Eve with his own words. Locke's empiricism undercuts the story ... because it insists that the human mind become aware of itself and its own powers (O'Donnell 1979, pp. 161–162).

In place of the theological argument advanced by the absolutist theorists Locke substituted an economic argument which, while retaining links to theology, took debate far down the secular path which the economics discipline was eventually to follow. In the process, Locke helped to lay the foundations upon which subsequent debate on the social position of women was to be based. Contract, bargaining, relative productivity, utility and opportunity cost: these were the critical elements in Locke's explanation of men's superior social position. In the bargaining process, women, acting as free agents, conceded men a precedence in the marriage contract because they recognized that their overall utility would be thereby enhanced. The greater economic security attained had a cost, but the price was less than the utility forgone.

Advocates of the new household economics, with their overarching interest in the nature of intra-family economic relations and the concept of intra-family contracts, might well recognize a similarity between this argument and some of their own work. Indeed, if they were to claim Locke as an early advocate of their approach to the study of the family, they would be justified in doing so. Likewise, feminist economists, with their critical approach to the issue of discrimination, might well claim Locke as an early supporter of the right of women to be treated as equals with men. If they were to do so, they would be joining feminist philosophers such as Squadrito (1979, p. 10), who, although she fails to comprehend his economics, can perceive Locke's underlying commitment to sexual equality and can thus argue:

Relative to his contemporaries ... Locke took an extremely liberal position on sexual equality. These views, like most of his work, were considered radical and dangerous: indeed, some of his ideas about women did not become respectable until the twentieth century. We cannot rank Locke among the great fore-mothers of the feminist movement, but we should accord him his place among those whose insight and courage contributed to its development.

To modern readers such as Clark (1979) and Pateman (1987), Locke's thesis has appeared merely as a new justification for patriarchy. It has been perceived as little more than a construct advanced to enable an outmoded justification for women's enslavement to be jettisoned while ensuring women remained men's subordinates. Such a verdict, however, is unjustified. In the context in which he wrote, that is, a society which granted husbands total control of a wife's property and conceded him the right to beat her all but to death, Locke's work was without doubt both progressive and emancipatory. It depicted women as beings who were rational and who were entitled to the natural law rights that automatically accrued to all rational beings. This meant they had the right to freely possess their lives, liberty, goods and the products of their labour. Moreover, his argument placed an onus on men to justify their demand that they be given a superior ranking within marriage, rather than merely assuming they should enjoy this position simply because they were men. It denied husbands and fathers the right to use violence against females and accorded women the right to strive to find ways to overcome men's natural advantages. All in all, therefore, Locke's work was a valuable theoretical contribution to the process of women's emancipation. Certainly his contribution was a great advance on the traditional argument which simply stated that God had decreed that women were subservient to men and must therefore remain so in perpetuity.

REFERENCES

Anonymous (1970), *An Essay In Defence of the Female Sex*, New York: Source Book Press.

Ashcraft, R. (1986), *Revolutionary Politics and Locke's Two Treatises of Government*, Princeton: Princeton University Press.

Ballard, George (1985), *Memoirs of Several Ladies of Great Britain*, Detroit: Wayne State University Press.

Bourne, Henry (1969), *The Life of John Locke*, vol. 2. Darmstadt: Scientia Verlag Aalen.

Brogan, A.P. (1959), 'John Locke and Utilitarianism', *Ethics* **64** (2), 79–93.

Butler, M.A. (1978), 'Early Roots of Feminism: John Locke and the Attack on Patriarchy'. *The American Political Science Review* **72** (1), 135–150.

Celetano, E.J. and I. Noy (1981), *Development of Occupational Physical Selection Standards for Canadian Forces Trades: Performance Considerations*, DCIEM Report No. 82-R-29, Ontario: Department of National Defence.

Clark, L.M.G. (1979), 'Women and Locke: Who owns the apples in the Garden of Eden?' in L.M.G. Clark and L. Lange (eds), *The Sexism of Social and Political Theory - Women and Reproduction from Plato to Nietzsche*, Toronto: University of Toronto Press, pp. 16–40.

Cranston, Maurice (1957), *John Locke: A Biography*, New York: Macmillan.

Derringh, F.W. (1980), 'Personal Autonomy and Locke's Theory of Property. With Special Attention to Modern Commentators', Ph.D. Thesis. Columbia University, University Microfilms.

Dewhurst, K. (1984), *John Locke 1632–1704: Physician and Philosopher*, London: Garland Publishing Inc.

Dunn, J. (1967), 'Consent in the Political Theory of John Locke', *The Historical Journal* **10**, 153–182.

Dunn, J. (1984), *Locke*, Oxford: Oxford University Press.

Filmer, Robert (1969), 'Patriarcha or the Natural Power of Kings', published as an addendum to John Locke. *Two Treatises on Government*, New York: Hafner Publishing.

Fox-Genovese, E. (1977), 'Property and Patriarchy in Classical Bourgeois Political Theory', *Radical History Review*, **4** (1), 36–59.

Groenewegen, P.D. (1989), 'New Light on the Origins of Modern Economics', *The Economic Record*, **65** (189), 136–149.

Grotius, Hugo (1925), *The Law of War and Peace*, Indianapolis: Bobbs Merrill Inc.

Harrison, John and Peter Laslett (1971), *The Library of John Locke*, Oxford: Clarendon Press.

Hearnshaw, F.R.C. (1931), *The Social and Political Ideas of Some Great French Thinkers of the Age of Reason*, New York: Barnes and Noble.

Hundert, E.J. (1977), 'Market Society and Meaning in Locke's Political Philosophy', *Journal of the History of Philosophy*, **15** (1), 33–44.

Kinnaird, Joan (1979), 'Mary Astell and the Conservative Contribution to English Feminism', *The Journal of British Studies*, **19** (1), 53–75.

Laslett, Peter (1953), 'Masham of Otes: The Rise and Fall of an English Family', *History Today*, **3** (8), 535–543.

Laubach, Lloyd L. (1976), 'Comparative Muscular Strength of Men and Women: A Review of the Literature', *Aviation, Space and Environmental Medicine*, **47** (5), 534–542.

Locke, John (1954), 'Midwifery Notes' published in K. Dewhurst, 'Locke's Midwifery

Notes', *The Lancet*, **2** (5), 490–491.

Locke, John (1961), *An Essay Concerning Human Understanding*, London: Everyman's Library.

Locke, John (1963), 'Some Considerations of the Consequences of Lowering the Interest and Raising the Value of Money', *The Works of John Locke*, vol. 5, printed for Thomas Tegg and others, 1823, Darmstadt: Scientia Verlag Aalen.

Locke, John (1968), 'Locke to Mrs Clarke', in James Axtell (ed.), *The Educational Writings of John Locke*, Cambridge: Cambridge University Press: pp. 344–346.

Locke, John (1969), *Two Treatises of Government*, Cambridge: Cambridge University Press.

Locke, John (1979), *The Correspondence of John Locke*. vol. 4, S. De Beer (ed.), Oxford: Clarendon Press.

Masham, D. (1705), 'Occasional Thoughts in Reference to a Vertuous or Christian Life', London: A. and J. Churchill.

Michel, Robert H. (1978), 'English Attitudes Towards Women 1640–1700', *Canadian Journal of History*, **13** (1), 35–60.

Middleton, Chris (1988), 'Gender Divisions and Wage Labour in English History', in Sylvia Walby (ed.). *Gender Segregation at Work*, Philadelphia: Open University Press, pp. 5–73.

Mitchell, Neil J. (1986), 'John Locke and the Rise of Capitalism', *History of Political Economy* **18** (2), 291–305.

O'Donnell, S. (1979), 'Mr Locke and the Ladies: The Indelible Words on the Tabula Rasa', *Studies in Eighteenth Century Culture* **8** (2), 151–164.

O'Donnell, S. (1984), 'My Idea in Your Mind: John Locke and Damaris Masham', in Ruth Perry and Martine Brownly (eds), *Mothering the Mind*, New York: Holmes and Meier, pp. 28–46.

Pateman, Carole (1987), 'Feminist Critiques of the Public/Private Dichotomy', in Anne Phillips (ed.), *Feminism and Equality*, Oxford: Basil Blackwell, pp. 103–127.

Perry, Ruth (1986), *The Celebrated Mary Astell*, Chicago: University of Chicago Press.

Pufendorf, Samuel (1927), *De Officio Hominis et Civis Juxta Legem Naturalism Libri Duo* (translated by G.F. Moore), Oxford: Oxford University Press.

Richards, E. (1974), 'Women in the British Economy Since About 1700: An Interpretation', *History* **59** (3), 337–357.

Roberts, M. (1979), 'Sickles and Scythes: Women's Work and Men's Work at Harvest Time', *History Workshop* **7** (1), 3–28.

Schochet, G.J. (1975), *Patriarchalism in Political Thought*, Oxford: Basil Blackwell.

Shanley, Mary Lyndon (1982), 'Marriage Contract and Social Contract in Seventeenth-Century English Political Thought', in Jean Bethke Elshtain (ed.), *The Family in Political Thought*, Brighton: The Harvester Press.

Smith, F. (1916), *Mary Astell*, New York: Columbia University Press.

Snell, K.D.M. (1981), 'Agricultural Seasonal Unemployment, The Standard of Living and Women's Work in the South and East, 1690–1860', *The Economic History Review*, **34** (3), 407–437.

Snook, Stover H. and Vincent M. Ciriello (1974), 'Maximum Weights and Work Loads Acceptable to Female Workers', *Journal of Occupational Medicine* **16** (6), 527–553.

Squadrito, K. (1979), 'Locke on the Equality of Sexes', *Journal of Social Philosophy*, **10** (1), 6–11.

Stone, Lawrence (1977), *The Family, Sex and Marriage in England 1500–1800*, London: Weidenfeld and Nicolson.

Tyrrell, James (1681), *Patriarcha Non Monarcha*, London.

Vaughn, Karen (1980), *John Locke: Economist and Social Scientist*, Chicago: University of Chicago Press.

NOTES

1. Despite her recognition of the valuable contribution Locke's psychology made to the emancipation of women, O'Donnell failed to comprehend Locke's understanding of the part played by the differing attributes of the sexes in the bargaining process. This leads her to believe that Locke accepted that husbands had a right to dominate their wives. Consequently, she qualifies seriously her enthusiasm for his efforts in a manner which is unjustified.

4.   Biology and Environment: Montesquieu's Relativist Analysis of Gender Behaviour

Chris Nyland

Poulain de la Barre, Hobbs and Locke sought to account for gender status by discussing 'man' and 'woman' largely in the abstract.   By contrast, the contribution of Charles Secondat, Baron de Montesquieu (1689–1755), was that he pioneered the systematic analysis of the ways in which patterns of gender behaviour emerge from the interaction between the environment and human biology in specific real world situations.   Montesquieu believed that there are similarities and differences between the sexes which are common to all people.   The environment of specific societies shapes these human attributes, causing wide diversity in gender behaviour across communities.   In this examination of Montesquieu's gender relativism the study begins by outlining his understanding of the differences that exist between the sexes. His belief that these differences are given shape and significance by the environment is then examined.   Finally, Montesquieu's contribution is situated within the history of the economics of gender. The key point made in this last section is that Montesquieu's highlighting of the fact that both biology and the environment shape gender behaviour was of importance to the development of the economics of gender relations.   It was important because his work focused attention on the limits of attempts to analyse gender behaviour outside of the concrete conditions in which real men and women are situated.   It was also important because it provided a methodological foundation upon which Adam Smith, by combining Montesquieu's relativism with the notion of economic progress, was able to build his stages theory of gender behaviour.

THE NATURE OF THE SEXES

Montesquieu believed the sexes shared an equal right to life, liberty and the ownership of property.   In both *The Persian Letters* and *The Spirit of the*

Laws, he insisted that absolute power exercised by one sex over the other had no justification in natural law and was both despicable and a form of tyranny. He also believed that daughters and sons had an equal right to be nurtured adequately and that there was no natural reason why sons should have any greater claim over their parents' estate than had their sisters (Montesquieu 1949, vol. 2, p. 62). At the same time Montesquieu did not believe that the natural attributes of men and women are identical. He accepted that wives had a 'natural dependence' on their husbands (Montesquieu 1949, vol. 2, p. 65) and that consequently it 'is contrary to reason and nature that women should reign in families' (Montesquieu 1949, vol. 1, p. 108).

Montesquieu asserted that husbands invariably head families because the 'natural weakness' of wives 'does not permit them to have the pre-eminence' (Montesquieu 1949, vol. 1, p. 108). As has been shown in Chapter Three the fact that men and women can be equal in terms of their natural rights, yet unequal in terms of their natural attributes and hence of their eminence, was a thesis developed by Locke in his *Two Treatises on Government*. Montesquieu, however, had a less flattering view of women's natural attributes than did Locke. The latter merely accepted that women had less muscular strength than men. Montesquieu, on the other hand, while believing women had greater physical charms, was convinced that women's 'weakness' was both physical and mental in character.

> Nature, which has distinguished men by their reason and bodily strength, has set no other bounds to their power than those of this strength and reason. It has given charms to women, and ordained that their ascendant over man shall end with these charms (Montesquieu 1949, vol. 1, p. 252).

The source of women's relative lack of reason Montesquieu located in the menstrual cycle. This was a point he made clear in his *Essay on the Causes Which Effect the Spirit and Character*.

> The differences of the sexes must also diversify the mind. The periodical revolution that occurs in women has a very extensive effect. It attacks the very mind. The cause is known to be a fullness which increases continually throughout a month or thereabouts, after which the blood, which is found to be in excess, forces its own passage out. Now, as this quantity changes her every day, her mood, her character must also change (Montesquieu 1951, p. 45).

One other natural difference that Montesquieu believed to exist between the sexes relates to the sex drive. He asserted that nature had given to men a 'boldness', while to women it had given a 'shame'. Men's natural boldness drove them to strive to seduce women. Women's shame, on the other hand, induced them to act with a 'modesty' which helped to reduce the likelihood they would engage in extra-marital sexual activity. This restraint limited the chance that women would give birth to children who could not be nurtured adequately. Men's boldness and women's modesty, he argued, react upon each other and in a properly functioning society induce an equilibrium which contributes to species preservation.

Montesquieu held that men who refused to assert their natural boldness and women who declined to pay due heed to their natural modesty failed to act in accordance with the laws of nature. On the basis of these beliefs he insisted that homosexuality was a crime against natural law and that women who were not virtuous were behaving unnaturally. Thus of women he observed:

> It is then far from being true that to be incontinent is to follow the laws of nature; on the contrary, it is a violation of these laws, which can be observed only by behaving with modesty and discretion (Montesquieu 1949, vol. 1, p. 259; see also vol. 2, p. 2).

THE ENVIRONMENT AND SEX DIFFERENCES

Humans' reproductive organs apart, it appears then that Montesquieu believed there were four primary innate differences between the sexes. These relate to natural charms, inclination to engage in extra-marital sexual activity, physical strength and reason. Women, he suggested, have a natural relative advantage in the areas of charm and capacity to resist sexual licence. Men, on the other hand, have a relative advantage as regards physical strength and reason. Montesquieu did not believe, however, that sex differences alone could explain the respective status of the sexes. Cross-national studies convinced him that patterns of gender behaviour emerge from the interaction between human biology and the concrete natural and social environment within which individuals are situated. Seventeenth-century scholars who sought to explain gender behaviour, such as Grotius, Pufendorf and Locke, focused their attention primarily on the abstractions that are 'man' and 'woman'. These analysts tended to assume that the natural differences between the sexes were sufficient to explain their relative status. Consequently, they gave little consideration to the manner by which specific environmental conditions shape relations between the sexes across cultures. What distinguished Montesquieu's contribution to gender analysis, on the other hand, was the great emphasis he placed on the fact that context can induce great diversity in the relative social position of men and women.

The importance Montesquieu placed on the natural and social context when discussing gender relations replicated the stress he placed on the environment whenever he sought to explain social behaviour. His sensitivity to variation convinced him that populations differ because the needs, institutions and material conditions of nations are characterized by wide variation. He was adamant that humans are flexible beings shaped by the ideas and impressions around them. As Stark (1960, p. 76) has so correctly observed, it is Montesquieu's acceptance, indeed insistence, that human beings are part and parcel of the environment in which they exist, that transports his analysis beyond the whole rationalist era.

> Those before him had always seen the timeless individual apart from society, and ideas as his proper product; Montesquieu began to see the time-bound individual *in* society, and his ideas as special variations of a general theme. To grasp the meaning of any law, and indeed any idea, out of the concrete situation from which it had sprung was one of his overruling ambitions, perhaps the controlling ambition of his life (Stark 1960, p. 76).

Given his belief that humans are necessarily a product of their concrete situation, Montesquieu was highly critical of analysts who began with an abstract system and only subsequently looked for their proofs in the material world. He castigated those rationalists, for example, who attempted to assess the relative value of monarchy and the popular state in the abstract. By so doing, he insisted, they ignored the fact that in the world there exist many kinds of monarchy and popular state and that consequently the question raised is far too vague to be capable of a sensible answer.

Montesquieu's awareness that contextual factors can induce wide diversity in the behaviour of populations was accompanied by a belief that the manner by which context shapes people's behaviour is not merely a matter of chance. Physical bodies, he argued, tend to relate to each other in particular ways because their relations are governed by natural rules or laws.

> These rules are a fixed and invariable relation. In bodies moved, the motion is received, increased, diminished, or lost, according to the relations of the quantity of matter and velocity; each diversity is uniformity, each change is constancy (Montesquieu 1949, vol. 1, p. 2).

To the extent that humans are physical beings, they too are related to other physical objects in ways that are constant. Thus he observed that: 'Man, as a physical being, is like other bodies governed by invariable laws'. (Montesquieu 1949, vol. 1, p. 3). This constancy tends to be manifest in the nature of the communities which humans establish. All societies, for example, will develop behaviour patterns designed to ensure that they have a means of attaining food. Likewise societies will invariably adopt patterns of gender behaviour that reflect the relations that exist between the sexes as physical beings. However, the specific manner by which these physical relations become manifest can vary greatly as a consequence of differences in the natural and social environment of nations. Their manifestation will also tend to vary because, as intelligent beings, humans enjoy a significant degree of free will.

> [T]he intelligent world is far from being so well governed as the physical. For though the former has also its laws, which of their own nature are invariable, it does not conform to them so exactly as the physical world. This is because, on the one hand, particular intelligent beings are of a finite nature, and consequently liable to error; and on the other, their nature requires them to be free agents. Hence they do not steadily conform to their primitive laws; and even those of their own instituting they frequently infringe (Montesquieu 1949, vol. 1, p. 2).

In other words, though humans are a product of their biology and environment, they are not mere slaves of these forces. As self-conscious beings, they enjoy a degree of independence from both biological and contextual influences.

Montesquieu was convinced that the stress he believed analysts needed to place on context would not necessarily confront the scholar with a world which appeared to be the product of blind chance and arbitrary caprice. Order could be extracted from the vast diversity characterizing human societies by extending the range of Locke's 'science of man' into the whole realm of social phenomena. This would require the empirical and comparative study of law and government, political economy, social institutions and the history of civilizations. The object of such study must be the identification of the relations that necessarily exist among phenomena and are the cause of human activity. Explanations for social behaviour that merely emphasize fortune and free will should be rejected and it must always be remembered that:

> It is not chance that rules the world ... There are general causes, moral and physical ... All accidents are controlled by these causes. And if the chance of one battle – that is, a particular cause – has brought a state to ruin, some general cause made it necessary for that state to perish from a single battle. In a word, the main trend draws with it all particular accidents (Montesquieu 1965, p. 169).

The general causes that Montesquieu accepted as the primary determinants inducing variation in human behaviour across nations were natural and social in character. This applied both to behaviour in general and to gender behaviour. That he believed the natural environment can shape relations between the sexes is made explicit in his discussion of the effect of climate on the human body. Stark (1960, p. 119) has observed that this aspect of Montesquieu's thinking can be characterized philosophically as the development of Locke's sensationalism on the physiological side.

Montesquieu believed that humans are born with a physiology that is largely a blank sheet. How the body develops and matures subsequently depends on the sensations received, and the nature of these sensations is determined by the context in which people are nurtured.

Utilizing this sensationalist perspective, Montesquieu sought to explain why men tend to drink alcohol in northern Europe but not in North Africa, and why the people of Russia are supposedly less sensitive to physical pain than are the populations of warmer climates. As far as gender behaviour is concerned, he used the notion that climate shapes relations between the sexes to explain why polygamy tends to be common in the Middle East but is largely unknown in Europe. He suggested that this latter phenomenon was caused by the fact that 'in the Countries of the South there is a natural Inequality between the two Sexes' (Montesquieu 1949, vol. 1, p. 251). The essence of his argument was that in hot countries, women tend to mature physically at a much earlier age than they do in cooler nations. Hence they tend to be relatively young when they marry, lose their beauty and reach menopause. They do not, however, mature intellectually any faster in these regions. Consequently, when women are physically ready for marriage they seldom have the intellectual capacities of their much older husbands. This inequality in capacities, induced by the different ages at which the sexes marry, is continued even after women attain rationality with the passing of the years. For while the women of hot climates gain intellectually as they age, they all too soon lose the primary instrument they have for exerting influence over men, that is their physical charms. As a consequence, men are able to dominate women to such an extent that they can even take multiple wives.

In the cooler climates, on the other hand, women's physical maturation is less rapid. Consequently, they reach the time of menarche at an age when their reason has had greater opportunity to develop and hence are both rational and physically beautiful when they are ready to marry. Having both of these attributes at the same time enables them to negotiate a more equal marriage relationship than can be realized by their equivalents in warmer regions (Montesquieu 1949, vol. 1, pp. 251–252).

Montesquieu's claims regarding the effect of climate on gender behaviour are of course invalid, and were soon dismissed even by his admirers. His argument was seen to be flawed if for no other reason than that the gender behaviour of particular populations is known to have varied historically even though the climate has remained constant. It was also clear to many that the argument was built on a number of unexplained assertions. The claim that husbands are generally older when they marry, for example, is incorporated into the argument without explanation. Montesquieu's failure to explain this latter fact is unfortunate as it is critical to his thesis. This is especially so given his claim that men in hot climates tend to be 'bolder' than their counterparts in the cooler nations and therefore presumably more eager for the pleasures of marriage. However, while these criticisms are justified their significance should not be allowed to cloud the great importance of Montesquieu's emphasis on the extent to which context can shape gender relations. Moreover, it should be noted that Montesquieu believed climate was only one of the factors determining gender behaviour. Climate, he thought, helped explain why polygamy appears only in certain parts of the world. But he did not believe climate alone could explain this phenomenon. Rather, as with the many other examples of cross cultural diversity that he strove to explain, Montesquieu argued that the marriage form adopted by societies was invariably a manifestation of:

> [T]he changing moral habits, beliefs, general attitudes of a particular society, at a particular time, on a particular portion of the earth's surface, played upon by the physical and spiritual influences to which their place and period exposes human beings (Berlin 1955, p. 289).

As well as believing that the natural environment influences gender behaviour, Montesquieu was also convinced that the social structure of societies was a critical factor shaping male–female relations. He highlighted this fact by examining the gender behaviour that characterized what he believed to be the three basic forms of government. In each case he sought to show that gender relations are a product of both the innate attributes of human beings and the politico–economic environment.[1] Montesquieu's three 'species' of government were the republican, the monarchic and the despotic. Each of these ideal types was perceived as being motivated by its own unique principle which inspires the lives of the population and must animate the regime if it is to function effectively. Montesquieu drew his ideas regarding these differing forms of government from the historical record and from close study of the nations of contemporary Europe and Asia. Thus, his depiction of the republican way of life is based primarily on the history of Greece, Rome and Venice; his ideas on monarchy were founded on the experience of France and the feudal order in general, and his sketch of despotism on the accounts of contemporary travellers in Persia and Turkey (Stark 1960, p. 5).

GENDER BEHAVIOUR IN A REPUBLIC

Montesquieu began his analysis of how the politico-economic character of societies influences gender relations by examining the republican form of government. This type of regime he defined as 'that in which the body, or only a part of the people, is possessed of the supreme power' (Montesquieu 1949, vol. 1, p. 8). In these societies the principle that activates the population is civic virtue, meaning a devotion to the common good. The population of a republic must, to a significant degree, be willing to place the interests of the nation before individual interests. This commitment to civic virtue Montesquieu believed to be fundamental to the survival of all republics. If virtue does not characterize this form of society, the regime will invariably degenerate and become either monarchic or despotic. It will do so because in a republic the people have a significant degree of autonomy and personal freedom and the state cannot easily compel individuals to provide the resources it needs to function effectively. Consequently, the state must rely on people's acceptance that all citizens have a duty to contribute to the overall preservation of the community.

The danger that a republic will lose its virtue and consequently degenerate is especially grave in a nation which is capable of producing an economic surplus sufficient to enable a degree of luxury to be enjoyed by the population. This development is a threat to the republic because the experience of luxury tends to lead human beings to become enamoured with the personal pleasures that wealth can provide. Should they succumb to this temptation, people will tend to become resentful at having to forgo any significant portion of their wealth in the form of taxes levied to provide for the common good. In short, the experience of luxury leads to the denial of both frugality and the collective interest.

> In proportion as luxury gains ground in a republic, the minds of the people are turned towards their particular interests. Those who are allowed only what is necessary have nothing but their own reputation and their country's glory in view. But a soul depraved by luxury has many other desires, and soon becomes an enemy of the laws that confine it (Montesquieu 1949, vol. 1, p. 96).

Montesquieu held that the requirement that republics abjure luxury explains the character of the laws that republican legislatures tend to enact to regulate women's sexuality. He argued that 'in women, a violation of chastity supposes a renunciation of all virtue' (Montesquieu 1949, vol. 2, p. 65). As frugality is most decidedly a virtue, it follows that if women deny their natural modesty they will be led to renounce a commitment to frugality. Their consequent embracing of luxury will, in turn, lead to depravity and indeed threaten the very existence of the republic.

> So many are the imperfections that attend the loss of virtue in women, and so greatly are their minds depraved when this principal guard is removed, that in a popular state public incontinency may be considered as the last of miseries, and as a certain forerunner of a change in the constitution (Montesquieu 1949, vol. 1, p. 101).

Thus it is the danger which female incontinence poses to the nation's virtue and hence its political economy that explains why the classical republics, while allowing women a degree of freedom, demanded of them a particular gravity of manners. This was a form of gender behaviour, Montesquieu was convinced, that was quite proper in a republic and productive of highly beneficial results (Montesquieu 1949, vol. 1, p. 104; vol. 2, pp. 85–91).

> In republics women are free by the laws and restrained by manners; luxury is banished thence, and with it corruption and vice ... In the cities of Greece ... such were the virtue, simplicity, and chastity of women ... hardly any people were ever known to have had a better and wiser polity (Montesquieu 1949, vol. 1, pp. 102–103).

Before proceeding, it is important to be clear about what Montesquieu is arguing in his discussion of the status of women in republics. His point is that in these societies gender behaviour is not simply a matter of chance, of biology or of the population's beliefs as to what is right and wrong. Rather, relations between the sexes are shaped by the interaction of biology and the politico-economic character of these regimes. In short, his argument recognizes concomitantly both constancy and diversity. It asserts that republican women abjure promiscuity and are virtuous both because modesty is a natural attribute of women *and* because this natural attribute is reinforced by the politico-economic character of the environment.

GENDER BEHAVIOUR IN A MONARCHY

While female promiscuity especially endangers republics, Montesquieu believed it to be an offence which should be held in contempt and ignominy in all forms of society (Montesquieu 1949, vol. 1, pp. 258-259). This belief, together with his rejection of the right of men to enslave women, are the keys that resolve much of the ambiguity associated with his analysis of gender behaviour in monarchies. In the process of discussing the nature of monarchy, Montesquieu sought to explain the flagrant public incontinence he believed was practised by the women of the Ancien Regime. That the women of France did in fact intermix with men and enjoy a degree of political power and sexual freedom that was unusual in eighteenth-century Europe is accepted by modern historians (Fox-Genovese 1984, p. 1). Thus Niklaus observes of Regency France:

> Husband and wife commonly lived apart in 'societe distincté', and their relationship became meaningless. Love itself was belittled and turned into a mere pastime, a fact which outraged women's deepest feelings ... Their enforced idleness and craving for greater freedom led to the excesses of the Regency and the prevalence of a mode of life dominated by pleasure ... They became arbiters of

taste and elegance, but their vanity and the relaxed code of behaviour engendered a sense of decadence rather than a spirit of freedom (Niklaus 1979, pp. 70–71).

Montesquieu believed the decadence he perceived in France was a consequence of the lack of virtue that tends to characterize monarchic regimes. He defined monarchy as a form of government 'in which a single person governs by fixed and established laws' (Montesquieu 1949, vol. 1, p. 8). While the regent is the centre of all power, there exist permanent intermediate and subordinate powers that have the right to restrain the monarch's ability to exercise his or her will capriciously. Of the mediating powers that temper the monarch's will, the most significant is the nobility, a class the regent invariably draws to the court, the better to contain their potential power.

The principle that activates the nobility and hence the populace in monarchies is the pursuit of honour. All ranks enjoy a relative status and individuals are rewarded according to their standing, the ambitious being provided with the opportunity to climb within their station or even move to a more honourable rank. The fact that the power to dispense privilege is concentrated in the monarch's hands ensures that the closer one approaches the throne the greater are the opportunities to attain the rewards dispensed by the monarch. Hence, honour in a monarchy amounts to a self-serving ambition and a craving for preference and distinctions.

Because they must constantly plot, scheme and betray others if they are to be successful, courtiers have no time for virtue – a point Montesquieu emphasized in his description of these individuals.

> Ambition in idleness; meanness mixed with pride; a desire of riches without industry; aversion to truth; flattery, perfidy, violation of engagements, contempt of civil duties, fear of the prince's virtue, hope from his weakness, but, above all, a perpetual ridicule cast upon virtue, are, I think, the characteristics by which most courtiers in all ages and countries have been constantly distinguished (Montesquieu 1949, vol. 1, p. 24).

The corruption of character that results from the nobles' denial of virtue and their luxurious style of life is compounded by the fact that the preservation of honour makes it imperative that they not undertake any form of labour or be subject to sumptuary laws.[2] The consequent decadence within the ruling class tends, in turn, to cause the population as a whole to become debased. This is because 'it is exceedingly difficult for the leading men of the nation to be knaves, and the inferior sort to be honest; for the former to be cheats, and the latter to rest satisfied with being only dupes' (Montesquieu 1949, vol. 1, p. 24). Thus the court acts as both a centripetal force drawing in the nation's power and wealth and a centrifugal influence dispensing moral corruption.

Montesquieu argued that the experience of France showed that the nobility's denial of virtue tends to debase men and women equally. Not wishing to deny themselves any pleasure, the men encourage the women of the nobility to come to the court. In this corrupt centre of wealth, power and privilege, women are thus provided with an opportunity to exploit their charms to the full. This was a chance they were quick to seize upon. When so doing, they also sought to transform the accepted notion of what constitutes desirable attributes away from those in which men have a relative advantage to those where women tend to excel, that is to beauty and wit.

Montesquieu's disapproval of the extent to which these tendencies had become manifest in eighteenth-century France is best captured by an observation made by Rica in *The Persian Letters*.

> When I arrived in France, I found the late king entirely governed by women, although at his age I think no monarch on earth had less need of them ... But there is no one employed in any way at the court, in Paris, or in the provinces who does not have a woman through whose hands pass all the favours, and sometimes the injustices, that he can give. These women are all in contact with each other; they form a kind of republic, whose members are continually active in mutual aid and service. It is like a state within a state; and anyone at court, in Paris, or in the provinces who observes the action of the ministers, magistrates and prelates, unless he knows the women who govern them, is like a man watching a machine work without knowing about the springs that drive it ... Do you think, Ibben, that a woman decides to become a minister's mistress so she may sleep with him? What a thought! Her purpose is to be able to submit five or six petitions to him every morning; and the natural goodness of these women shows itself in their eagerness to do favours for a host of unfortunate people, who in turn procure for them an income of one hundred thousand livres (Montesquieu 1964, p. 180).

The free intermixing of the sexes, encouraged by the luxurious character of monarchic life, not only tends to induce an unacceptable forwardness in women, but also encourages an equally reprehensible effeminacy in men. That Montesquieu believed this development was also very much manifest in France was made clear in his *Pensées et fragments inédits*:

> I was asked why there is no vogue today for Corneille, Racine, etc. I replied that it is because all those things for which intelligence is demanded have become ridiculous, and that indeed the evil lies even deeper than this. Men can no longer tolerate anything that has a fixed object: military men cannot tolerate warfare, officials cannot tolerate the office, and so on. We are coming to know generalities alone, and in practice these reduce themselves to nothing. It is our social intercourse with women which has brought us to this state, for they are dilettantes by nature. Today there is only one sex left; we have all become women as far as intellectual life is concerned. If one night our features were to change, no one would notice the difference (cited by Vyverberg 1958, pp. 166–167).

GENDER BEHAVIOUR UNDER DESPOTISM

As has been shown, Montesquieu took pains to illuminate how the political and economic character of republics and monarchies shapes gender behaviour in these two different types of society. The diversity in gender behaviour induced by the environment is even more starkly revealed when Montesquieu turns to study despotism. In this type of society, he argued, women are invariably enslaved by their men. Despotism he defined as unrestrained power exercised by one individual. It is a form of government 'in which a single person directs everything by his own will and caprice' (Montesquieu 1949, vol. 1, p. 8). The rulers of those 'monstrous' regimes, such as existed in Turkey and Persia, demanded absolute obedience from the population, the individual being considered merely an instrument of the despot's pleasure. 'Man's portion here, like that of beasts, is instinct, compliance, and punishment' (Montesquieu 1949, vol. 1, p. 27).

With unlimited power concentrated in the hands of the despot, fear is the animating principle of the regime. Civil law is little more than the capricious will of the ruler, and people possess their lives and liberty at the despot's discretion. The same applies to their property, and this is especially so where the despot chooses to intervene directly in trade. Commerce, Montesquieu insisted, must necessarily be a profession of people who are equal in terms of their property rights. However, the only form of equality accepted by the despot is that which decrees that all subjects are equal in that they are all slaves who live merely for the master's pleasure.

Montesquieu was convinced that the slave–master relationship that dominates despotic regimes has especially horrendous consequences for women. Citing the harems of the Middle East in support of his claims, he argued that the despot considers his wife a slave who happens to fulfil a particular duty. She is his property to do with as he wishes. Her physical closeness to the ruler, however, demands that she be kept in the most rigorous servitude lest she become the instrument of the ambitious usurper. Thus the relationship between husband and wife is one in which the former both possesses his wife as a slave and lives in constant fear that if her behaviour is not controlled rigorously she will be his undoing. This is a situation which the endemic fear within the society causes to be replicated in every household.

> In despotic governments women do not introduce, but are themselves an object of, luxury. They must be in a state of the most rigorous servitude. Every one follows the spirit of government, and adopts in his own family the customs he sees elsewhere established. As the laws are very severe and executed on the spot, they are afraid lest the liberty of women should expose them to danger. Their quarrels, indiscretions, repugnancies, jealousies, piques, and that art, in fine, which little

souls have of interesting great ones, would be attended there with fatal consequences (Montesquieu 1949, vol. 1, p. 102).

Women are consequently enslaved by their men. Montesquieu believed that this was a reprehensible act. However, he also believed that the men of nations such as Persia and Turkey had little choice but to adopt this form of gender behaviour. It was forced upon them by the very nature of the environment of fear that pervaded these countries. Thus, as with republican and monarchic societies, Montesquieu was convinced that the evidence showed that gender behaviour in despotic regimes reflected both biology and the politico-economic environment. Men's biological advantages enabled them to enslave women if they so chose, and in the despotic nations fear ensured that they took up this option.

Montesquieu's study of the experience of women in republican, monarchic and despotic regimes highlighted the limited character of the abstracted arguments of the rationalists, and it was this illumination above all that constitutes his great contribution to the study of gender behaviour. By the utilization of comparative and empirical studies he demonstrated, to an unprecedented extent, that gender behaviour is a function of human biology, free will and the natural and social environment. This means it is not possible to explain gender behaviour adequately merely in terms of biological differences and natural rights. Rather, analysis of the relations that exist between the abstractions 'man' and 'woman' must be extended to the examination of real men and women in the material world in which they are situated.

MONTESQUIEU AND THE DEVELOPMENT OF THE ECONOMICS OF GENDER

Montesquieu's analysis of the interaction of the human body and the environment pioneered the systematic examination of how gender behaviour is shaped by these two fundamental influences. A number of his conclusions regarding sex differences and the manner in which the factors that shape gender behaviour interact were invalid. Nevertheless, as Stark has observed, even where Montesquieu's conclusions do not hold water, the method he utilized to reach these conclusions renders them greatly to his credit.

[W]hatever the value of the results to which he comes, his method is direct. It is the true method of the sociology of knowledge – to comprehend the meaning of individual phenomena by relating them to the total life situation out of which they arise and with which they function, to see the genesis of customs and ideas in their essential connexion with the social background and underground in which they are rooted (Stark 1960, p. 43).

That it is Montesquieu's methodological contribution that gives his political economy its great significance has long been recognized by historians of economic thought. Commenting on Montesquieu's contribution to economic thought, Hutchison (1988, p. 220) has suggested that *The Spirit of the Laws* was: 'Outstandingly the most important French work for the history of economic thought between Boisguilbert and Quesnay'. As with Stark, it is Montesquieu's methodology that particularly impresses Hutchison.

What was so broadly and powerfully important and consequential for political economy, and for the social sciences, or social studies, in Montesquieu's work, was his fundamental methodological emphasis on cause and effect, and on regularities in the politico-economic world, together with, more specifically, his insistence on historical-institutional relativity, and on the importance of varying, particular, historical, geographical and climatic factors, together with other differing particular circumstances, in explaining the politics and economics of different nations (Hutchison 1988, p. 220).

Hutchison's evaluation reveals a clear appreciation of the importance of Montesquieu's methodological contribution to the development of the social sciences. He is very much aware of the importance of the latter's scepticism regarding claims of universal validity which do not take account of the history, geography, climate and traditions of particular societies. While he believes Montesquieu to be less radical in his relativism than Vico, he concludes that 'Montesquieu was certainly the great pioneer in our period of the historical and comparative method and approach in political economy, and in social studies generally, and one of the precursors of modern sociology' (Hutchison 1988, p. 221). Groenewegen has gone even further and observed that *The Spirit of the Laws* constituted nothing less than the great landmark which denotes the beginning of secular social science. Montesquieu's masterpiece, he suggests, 'liberated the social sciences from their former theological encumbrances and ... induced enormous activity in history, sociology, political philosophy, jurisprudence and of course, political economy' (Groenewegen 1983, p. 48). These evaluations of Montesquieu's contribution to economics rightly stress the significance of his methodology. However, it should be noted that he also made a number of useful additions to economic theory. This point was highlighted by Devletoglou (1963), who noted that Montesquieu developed an intelligent conception of national wealth and made contributions to the economics of agriculture, interest, international trade and population.

The foregoing outline of the place of Montesquieu in the history of economics literature shows that his methodological contribution to social analysis has been well appreciated. A point central to this paper, however, is that this appreciation has not extended to Montesquieu's study of gender relations. Indeed, this aspect of his work has gone unexamined by all economists who have studied his writings. Meek (1976, pp. 31–35), for example, recognized that Montesquieu made a contribution to the development of the four stages theory, but failed to note that part of this contribution was an examination of the relationship between the mode of subsistence and the relative status of the sexes.[3] Montesquieu asserted that in communities based on the agricultural mode of subsistence, women tend to have a degree of certainty and status because they are settled and are permanent members of a specific family. In hunting and pastoral societies, on the other hand, women have little assurance in their lives, and are treated with scant respect.

> These people wander and disperse themselves in pasture grounds or in forests. Marriage cannot there have the security which it has amongst us, where it is fixed by the habitation, and where the wife continues in one house; they may then more easily change their wives, possess many, and sometimes mix indifferently like brutes (Montesquieu 1949, vol. 1, p. 277).

The lot of women in hunting communities, Montesquieu suggested, was especially uncertain. This was because the men do not require women to ensure their own freedom or safeguard their means of subsistence. Conversely, in pastoral societies women enjoy at least some security because they cannot be abandoned easily by the men, as they play a vital role in the preservation of the latter's livelihood.

> Nations of herdsmen and shepherds cannot leave their cattle, which are their subsistence; neither can they separate themselves from their wives, who look after them. All this ought, then, to go together, especially as, living generally in a flat open country, where there are few places of considerable strength, their wives, their children, their flocks, may become the prey of their enemies (Montesquieu 1949, vol. 1, p. 277).

SCOTTISH DEBATE

At the end of his discussion of Montesquieu's economic thought, Hutchison observes:

Let us, in conclusion, re-emphasize that the great significance of *L'Esprit des lois* for the development of political economy in the eighteenth century, and after, lay in its fundamental, methodological approach, which was especially important in Scotland ... (Hutchison 1988, p. 224).

It has been argued in this chapter that Hutchison's observation regarding the importance of Montesquieu's methodology is very much applicable to the latter's contribution to the economics of gender. To appreciate fully the significance of his contribution to this area of study, however, it is necessary to be aware that Hutchison's reference to Montesquieu's influence in Scotland is equally germane.

Through much of the second half of the eighteenth century, the question of why gender behaviour differs across nations and time periods was the focus of a sustained debate in Scotland. An early sign of the influence that Montesquieu was to have on this debate appears in Adam Smith's Glasgow lectures (to be discussed in the next chapter). These lectures were important in the development of the economic analysis of gender behaviour, for it was here that Smith expounded the notion that gender relations are very much a product of the mode of subsistence. Utilising his four stages theory Smith argued that the social position of women was largely shaped by the manner in which societies attain their means of subsistence.[4] As societies progress through the various stages of development the economic environment is transformed, and this change in economic context is reflected in the changing status of women.

That Smith's lectures were influenced by the publication of *The Spirit of the Laws* has long been recognized. What has not been appreciated is the fact that Smith appears to have been especially taken by Montesquieu's ideas regarding gender relations. It is possible to attain a rough measure of the extent to which Smith was particularly taken by Montesquieu's study of gender by examining the direct citations Smith makes to this aspect of Montesquieu's work. By this measure, it would appear that the gender aspect of Montesquieu's masterpiece influenced Smith more than any other. Of the twenty-five references to Montesquieu that appear in the lectures, fourteen refer specifically to some aspect of gender behaviour. In his lectures Smith relied heavily on *The Spirit of the Laws* when he was dealing with the rights which accrue to an individual as a member of a family and consequently to the relations that exist between husbands and wives. He cited Montesquieu when discussing such questions as in what matter the laws of nature should regulate marriage and where they should be regulated by the state: for example, succession laws in relation to girls and boys; the origins of succession laws in different societies; the manner in which these laws were utilized in the classical republics in order to contain the power of women; the justification for divorce; and the causes and justification of polygamy (Smith 1978, pp. 41, 65, 145, 147, 151, 155, 156, 164, 173, 443, 444, 447).

In the *Lectures on Jurisprudence*, Smith makes many other observations regarding the place of women in society that have great similarity to ideas expounded in *The Spirit of the Laws*. For example, Smith shared Montesquieu's belief that it is a greater crime for women to act without modesty than it is for men. Whether such ideas were taken from Montesquieu, however, it is not possible to say. Such observations were widely accepted and discussed by many other seventeenth and eighteenth-century observers. It is just as likely that Smith may have taken these notions from David Hume, who was a more immediate influence, or may simply have learnt these commonly accepted 'truths' while sitting on his mother's knee.

Given Hume's relativism, his emphasis on cause and effect and the fact that he was a more immediate influence on Smith, it needs to be mentioned in passing that Hume's writings on gender behaviour all but failed to be cited by Smith in the *Lectures on Jurisprudence*.[5] Of the forty-three references to Hume in the *Lectures*, only one citation is related to his contribution to the study of gender behaviour. This one exception, however, is indicative. It suggests why the gender aspect of Hume's contribution was largely ignored and what it was that attracted Smith to Montesquieu's analysis. Most of Hume's writings relating to gender were concerned with such issues as why men prefer modest women and why there existed a double moral standard for the two sexes. With one exception these writings were abstracted from any context. It is therefore notable that Smith's single citation was drawn from this one exception. In his 'Of Polygamy and Divorce', an article in which Montesquieu's *Persian Letters* is cited, Hume begins by observing:

> As marriage is an engagement entered into by mutual consent, and has for its end the propagation of the species, it is evident, that it must be susceptible of all the variety of conditions, which consent establishes, provided they be not contrary to this end ... A man, in conjoining himself to a woman, is bound to her according to the terms of his engagement: In begetting children, he is bound, by all the ties of nature and humanity, to provide for their subsistence and education ... And as the terms of his engagement, as well as the methods of subsisting his offspring, may be various, it is mere superstition to imagine, that marriage can be entirely uniform, and will admit only of one mode or form. Did not human laws restrain the natural liberty of men, every particular marriage would be as different as contracts or bargains of any other kind of species (Hume 1964, pp. 231–232).

Hume follows up this very promising opening by citing a number of situations where divergent marriage forms had been adopted as a consequence of a particular social environment. This discussion, however, is very brief and insubstantial, and Hume very soon returns to the universalistic stance he normally adopted when discussing gender relations. His subsequent analysis of the cause of polygamy is totally abstracted from any environment, with the analysis conducted at the level of 'man' and 'woman'. Nevertheless, it was that brief moment when Hume ventured from his universalism towards relativism which Smith chose to point out to his students when discussing gender behaviour (Smith 1978, p. 153).

What can be inferred from this single reference to Hume's ideas regarding gender relations and the many references to Montesquieu is that Hume was not the significant influence shaping Smith's ideas regarding male–female relations.   Rather, what Smith found interesting was the relativism that pervades Montesquieu's contribution to the study of gender behaviour; in short, it was Montesquieu's systematic development of the notion that while innate differences between the sexes do exist, these differences alone do not determine gender relations.   Smith did not necessarily embrace Montesquieu's ideas regarding the innate differences between the sexes. As with Locke, he does not appear to have accepted that women's intellectual capacities were less than those of men. What he did accept was that while there are innate differences between the sexes, the social significance of these differences is variable. The combining of this fundamental, but uniquely developed, relativist perspective with the concept of economic progress was to be the path down which Smith's stages theory took the development of the economic analysis of gender behaviour. However, it was Montesquieu's gender relativism that pointed Smith the way to this path.

REFERENCES

Althusser, Louis (1972), *Politics and History: Montesquieu, Rousseau, Hegel and Marx* (translated by Ben Brewster), London: NLB.

Aron, Raymond (1965), *Main Currents in Sociological Thought*, New York: Basic Books.

Baum, John Alan (1979), *Montesquieu and Social Theory*, Oxford: Pergamon Press.

Berlin, Isaiah (1955), 'Montesquieu', *Proceedings of the British Academy*, **41**, 267–296.

Berlin, Isaiah (1980), 'Note on Alleged Relativism in Eighteenth-Century European Thought', *The British Journal for Eighteenth-Century Studies*, **3** (2), 89–106.

Bonar, James (1893), *Philosophy and Political Economy*, London: Swan Sonnenschein and Company.

Brumfitt, J.H. (1972), *The French Enlightenment*, London: The Macmillan Press.

Chamley, Paul E. (1975), 'The Conflict between Montesquieu and Hume. A Study of the Origins of Adam Smith's Universalism' in Andrew S. Skinner and Thomas Wilson (eds), *Essays on Adam Smith*, Oxford: Clarendon Press.

Cox, Iris (1983), 'Montesquieu and the History of French Laws', *Studies on Voltaire and the Eighteenth Century*, **218**, 592–600.

Crane, R.S. (1941), 'Montesquieu and British Thought', *The Journal Of Political Economy*, **49**, 592–600.

Cranston, Maurice (1986), *Philosophers and Pamphleteers*, Oxford: Oxford University Press.

Devletoglou, Nicos E. (1963), *Montesquieu and the Wealth of Nations*, Athens.

Fletcher, F.T.H. (1939), *Montesquieu and English Politics*, Philadelphia: Porcupine Press.

Fox-Genovese, Elizabeth (1984), 'Introduction' in Samian I. Spencer (ed.), *French Women and the Age of Enlightenment*, Bloomington: Indiana University Press, pp. 1–29.

Groenewegen, Peter (1983), 'Turgot, Beccaria and Smith' in Peter Groenewegen and Joseph Halevi (eds), *Altro Polo. Italian Economics Past and Present*, Sydney: Frederick May Foundation.

Groenewegen, Peter (1985), 'Turgot's Place in the History of Economic Thought: a Bicentenary Estimate', *History of Political Economy*, **15** (4), 585–616.

Groenewegen, Peter (1987), 'The International Foundations of Classical Political Economy in the Eighteenth Century: An Alternative Perspective' in Todd Lowry (ed.), *Pre-Classical Economic Thought*, Boston: Kluwer Academic Publishers.

Groenewegen, Peter (1989), 'New Light on the Origins of Modern Economics', *The Economic Record*, **65** (189), 136–149.

Hampson, Norman (1983), *Will and Circumstance. Montesquieu, Rousseau and the French Revolution*, University of Oklahoma Press.

Hebert, Robert (1987), 'In Search of Economic Order: French Predecessors of Adam Smith' in Todd Lowry (ed.), *Pre-Classical Economic Thought*, Boston: Kluwer Academic Publishers.

Hirschman, Albert O. (1977), *The Passions and the Interests – Political Arguments for Capitalism Before its Triumph*, Princeton: Princeton University Press.

Hulliung, Mark (1976), *Montesquieu and the Old Regime*, Berkeley: University of

California Press.

Hume, David (1964), *Essays. Moral, Political, and Literary*, London: Scientia Verlag Aalen.

Hume, David (1966), *A Treatise of Human Nature*, London: Everyman's Library.

Hutchison, Terence (1978), *On Revolutions and Progress in Economic Knowledge*, Cambridge: Cambridge University Press.

Hutchison, Terence (1988), *Before Adam Smith – The Emergence of Political Economy, 1662–1776*, Oxford: Basil Blackwell.

Klosko, George (1980), 'Montesquieu's Science of Politics: Absolute Values and Ethical Relativism', *Studies on Voltaire and the Eighteenth Century*, **189**, 153–177.

Kra, Pauline (1963), 'The Invisible Chain of the *Lettres Persanes*', *Studies on Voltaire and the Eighteenth Century*, **23**, 9–60.

Kra, Pauline (1979), 'The Role of the Harem in Imitations of Montesquieu's *Lettres Persanes*', *Studies on Voltaire and the Eighteenth Century*, **182**, 273–283.

Kra, Pauline (1984), 'Montesquieu and Women' in Samian I. Spencer (ed.), *French Women and the Age of Enlightenment*, Bloomington: Indiana University Press.

Martin, Kingsley (1962), *French Liberal Thought in the Eighteenth Century*, London: Phoenix House.

Mason, Sheila (1979), 'The Riddle of Roxane', in Eva Jacobs, W.H. Barber, Jean H. Bloch, F.W. Leakey and Eileen Le Breton (eds), *Woman and Society in Eighteenth-Century France*, London: The Athlone Press, pp. 42–54.

Meek, Ronald L. (1976), *Social Science and the Ignoble Savage*, Cambridge: Cambridge University Press.

Meinecke, Friedrich (1972), *Historicism. The Rise of the New Historical Outlook*, London: Routledge and Kegan Paul.

Montesquieu, C.L. (1949), *The Spirit of the Laws* (translated by Thomas Nugent), New York: Hafner Publishing.

Montesquieu, C.L. (1949a), 'Mes Pensées' in Roger Caillois (ed.), *Oeuvres Complètes de Montesquieu*, vol 1, pp. 973–1574.

Montesquieu, C.L. (1951), 'Essai Sur Les Causes Qui Peuvent Affecter les Espirits et les Caractères' in Roger Caillois (ed.), *Oeuvres Complètes de Montesquieu*, vol. 2, pp. 39–68.

Montesquieu, C.L. (1964), *The Persian Letters* (translated by George R. Healy), Indianapolis: The Bobbs-Merrill Company.

Montesquieu, C.L. (1965), *Considerations on the Causes of the Greatness of the Romans and their Decline* (translated by David Lowenthal), New York: The Free Press.

Niklaus, Robert (1979), 'Diderot and Women' in Eva Jacobs, W.H. Barber, Jean H. Bloch, F.W. Leakey and Eileen Le Breton (eds), *Woman and Society in Eighteenth-Century France*, London: The Athlone Press, pp. 69–82.

Nyland, Chris (1993a), 'John Locke and the Social Position of Women', *History of Political Economy*, **25** (1), Spring, 39–64.

Nyland, Chris (1993b), 'Adam Smith, Stage Theory and the Status of Women', *History of Political Economy*, **25** (4), Winter, 617–640.

Nyland, Chris (1993c), 'Poulain de la Barre and the Rationalist Analysis of the Status of Women', *History of Economics Review*, **19**, Winter, 18–33.

O'Reilly, Robert (1973), 'Montesquieu: anti-feminist', *Studies on Voltaire and the Eighteenth Century*, **102**, 143-156.

Pangle, Thomas L. (1973), *Montesquieu's Philosophy of Liberalism*, Chicago: University of Chicago Press.

Pollard, Sidney (1971), *The Idea of Progress*, Harmondsworth: Pelican Books.

Pribram, Karl (1983), *A History of Economic Reasoning*, Baltimore: Johns Hopkins University Press.

Randall, John Herman (1962), *The Career of Philosophy*, New York: Columbia University Press.

Richter, Melvin (1977), *The Political Theory of Montesquieu*, Cambridge: Cambridge University Press.

Rosso, Jeannette G. (1977), *Montesquieu et la Féminité*, Pise: Libreria Goliardica Editrice.

Shackleton, Robert (1961), *Montesquieu. A Critical Biography*, Oxford: Oxford University Press.

Shackleton, Robert (1979), 'Madame de Montesquieu, with some Considerations on Thérèse de Secondat' in Eva Jacobs, W.H. Barber, Jean H. Bloch, F.W. Leakey and Eileen Le Breton (eds), *Woman and Society in Eighteenth-Century France*, London: The Athlone Press, pp. 229–242.

Shackleton, Robert (1988), *Essays on Montesquieu and on the Enlightenment*, David Gilson and Martin Smith (eds), Oxford: The Voltaire Foundation.

Shklar, Judith N. (1987), *Montesquieu*, Oxford: Oxford University Press.

Smith, Adam (1978), *Lectures on Jurisprudence* (edited by R.L. Meek, D.D. Raphael and P.G. Stein), Oxford: Clarendon Press.

Spengler, Joseph J. and William R. Allen (eds) (1962), *Essays in Economic Thought - Aristotle to Marshall*, Chicago: Rand McNally and Company.

Spruell, Shelby O. (1980), 'The Metaphorical Use of Sexual Repression to Represent Political Oppression in Montesquieu's Persian Letters', *Proceedings of the Annual Meeting of the Western Society for French History*, **8**, 147–164.

Stark, W. (1960), *Montesquieu. Pioneer of the Sociology of Knowledge*, London: Routledge and Kegan Paul.

Stewart, Dugald (1980), 'Account of the Life and Writings of Adam Smith, LL.D' in W.P.D. Wightman and J.C. Bryce (eds), *Adam Smith; Essays on Philosophical Subjects*, Oxford: Clarendon Press.

Strong, Susan (1985), 'Why a Secret Chain? Oriental Topoi and the Essential Mystery of the *Lettres Persanes'*, *Studies on Voltaire and the Eighteenth Century*, **230**, 167–179.

Trevor-Roper, Hugh (1963), 'The Historical Philosophy of the enlightenment', *Studies on Voltaire and the Eighteenth Century*, **27**, 1667–1687.

Vaughan, C.E. (1925), *Studies in the History of Political Philosophy Before and After Rousseau*, New York: Russell and Russell.

Vyverberg, Henry (1958), *Historical Pessimism in the French Enlightenment*, Cambridge, Massachusetts: Harvard University Press.

NOTES

1. The term 'politico-economic' is borrowed from Hutchison's *Before Adam Smith* (1988, p. 220), though Hutchison does not explain what he means by the term. In this paper it is accepted that it relates to Montesquieu's belief in the unity of the political and economic domains, and more specifically to the relationship that exists between the constitutional and the commercial character of societies. Montesquieu believed that a particular form of government will all but invariably be characterized by a corresponding form of commerce. That Montesquieu in fact saw the economic and the political as related in this unitary manner is supported by his comments regarding commercial and constitutional form: 'Trade has some relation to forms of government. In a monarchy, it is generally founded on luxury; and though it be also founded on real wants, yet the principal view with which it is carried on is to procure everything that can contribute to the pride, the pleasure, and the capricious whims of the nation. In republics, it is commonly found on economy. Their merchants, having an eye to all the nations of the earth, bring from one what is wanted by another ... This kind of traffic has a natural relation to a republican government: to monarchies it is only occasional. For as it is founded on the practice of gaining little, and even less than other nations, and of remedying this by gaining incessantly, it can hardly be carried on by a people swallowed up in luxury, who spend much, and see nothing but objects of grandeur' (Montesquieu 1949, vol. 1, p. 318).

2. Not engaging in the creation of wealth, the nobility is necessarily a parasitic class. It attains its income by depriving another part of the population of the product of its labour. But if those who are exploited are to live, it is necessary that the nobility be allowed to consume that which it has expropriated. To do otherwise would deny a livelihood to the poor, who must labour at the production of the luxury goods desired by the nobility in order to win back some of the wealth their exploiters have taken from them. Hutchison (1988, p. 223) has asserted that Montesquieu approved of luxury spending and believed that '[c]ommerce led to riches, riches to luxury, and luxury to "the perfection of the arts"'. He also asserts that Montesquieu believed commerce to have a beneficial effect on human behaviour. Hutchison's assertions are invalid as universal truths. It is true Montesquieu believed that commerce leads to riches, but he accepted that riches gained by commerce lead to frugality and virtue rather than to luxury: 'This is because the spirit of commerce is naturally attended with that of frugality, economy, moderation, labour, prudence, tranquillity, order, and rule' (Montesquieu 1949, vol. 1, p. 46). Likewise, while Hutchison is correct in claiming that Montesquieu supported luxury spending in monarchies, he is incorrect in his assertion that Montesquieu generally approved of this form of expenditure. Rather, his comments in this regard were part of his indictment of the Ancien Regime. He believed it was necessary that the nobility engage in luxury spending and indeed that they gorge themselves, but this was only because this sector of society so exploited the people: 'Were the rich not to be lavish, the poor would starve' (Montesquieu 1949, vol. 1, p. 97).
   As for the claim that commerce leads to the perfection of the arts, Montesquieu in fact argued that the pervasive concern for material goods and the accumulation of wealth which tends to be induced by the spirit of commerce stifles interest in the arts and 'the beautiful and useless things which ornament and can inspire human life' (Pangle 1973, p. 151). Finally, while it is true Montesquieu believed commerce improves manners, he also believed that it has a number of adverse effects on human behaviour. He suggested that the development of commerce invariably involves the loss of certain basic human decencies, with many of the factors that unite human beings, such as friendship and the requirement that one afford hospitality to a stranger, tending to be replaced by the cash nexus: 'But if the spirit of commerce unites nations, it does not in the same manner unite individuals. We see that in countries where the people move only by the spirit of commerce, they make a traffic of all the humane, all the moral virtues; the most trifling things, those which humanity would demand, are there done, or there given, only for money' (Montesquieu 1949, Vol. 1, pp. 316-317).
   Moreover, commerce tends to engender a constant fear in individuals. Thus the English, the most commercial of people, experience a perpetual unease, with every individual tending to see all others as competitors who would deprive them of their goods were they not constantly

on their guard.

It is important that Montesquieu's ideas regarding the effects of commerce and luxury on human behaviour be recognized. This is not least because these issues subsequently played an important part in the contribution to the economics of women's status advanced by disciples of Montesquieu such as John Brown and Antoine Thomas. What these latter correctly perceived in *The Spirit of the Laws* was not the unqualified affirmative perspective suggested by Hutchison. Rather, they saw a relativistic argument which accepted that in certain circumstances luxury tends to enhance the conduct of humanity and in others lead it to debasement. This point has been well captured by Vyverberg (1958, p. 162), who observed of Montesquieu in this respect: 'His general conclusion was that luxury tends to refine primitive peoples, and to ruin well-ordered states when carried to excess'.

3. The failure of economists to examine Montesquieu's contribution to gender analysis cannot be excused on the grounds that this aspect of his work has gone unnoticed by historians. Scholars in other areas of history have commented extensively on his writings on gender behaviour (O'Reilly 1973; Shackleton 1979; Kra 1984). This important work has produced divergent assessments of his views regarding the place of women in society, particularly as regards the question of whether he was a feminist, an anti-feminist or a misogynist. The issue of his relativism has attracted less attention. An important exception in this last regard is Kra's 1984 paper *'Montesquieu and Women'*. This valuable work highlights the importance of his empiricism, relativism and breadth of vision. Unfortunately, however, it is seriously undermined by the belief that Montesquieu discarded 'the notion of the natural inferiority of women' (Kra 1984, p. 272). As a consequence of this mistaken belief, Kra overemphasizes the importance Montesquieu placed on context and misses the complex interaction he perceived between the unique conditions that characterize individual societies, the innate attributes of human beings and free will. In short, Montesquieu rejected simplistic biological determinism when explaining gender behaviour but he also rejected the claim that biology could be ignored. Consequently, he dismissed out of hand analysts such as Poulain de la Barre, who argued that men's universal dominance could be explained purely in terms of the social environment (Nyland 1993c). He asserted that these individuals could not possibly be serious and hence, when advancing such propositions, were presumably merely being gallant (Montesquieu 1964, p. 64).

4. The four stages theory held that society normally progressed through four distinct and consecutive stages, each of which corresponded to a different mode of subsistence. These stages were hunting, pasturage, agriculture and commerce. To each mode of subsistence there corresponded appropriate sets of beliefs, institutions, mores and manners (Meek 1976, p. 2).

5. See in particular 'Of Polygamy and Divorce' and 'Of Love and Marriage' from the *Essays*; and from the *Treatise* see 'Of the Amorous Passion, or Love Betwixt the Sexes' and 'Of Chastity and Modesty'.

5.   Adam Smith, Stage Theory and the Status of Women

Chris Nyland

Economists who seek to analyse the social position of women often assert that while men's greater physical strength may be an important factor influencing the relative status of the sexes in less-developed societies, it is of no great significance in a modern, industrialized economy. This assertion is founded primarily on the assumption that the developed nations have progressed to a stage where physical strength is no longer a significant factor influencing the individual's productive capacity or ability to exert authority over others. The notion that technical progress tends to modify the status of women, by transforming the social significance of physiological differences between the sexes, has played an important role in the economic analysis of women's social position since the seventeenth century. This paper contends that Adam Smith made a major, though neglected, contribution to the development of this important idea.[1]

It is argued in the chapter that Smith developed an explanation of women's status that centred on the means by which societies attain the material requirements of life, that is, on their mode of subsistence. His argument drew upon his belief that societies tend naturally to progress through distinct economic stages as they develop. Each of these stages is characterized by a different mode of subsistence, with each stage having unique primary sources of authority and status. This process of progression was held to have fundamental significance for women. Smith believed that in the earliest stages of economic development, women were disadvantaged by their biology in the competitive struggle for authority and influence. However, as societies progress to the commercial stage of development, the innate differences between the sexes tend to become of decreasing social significance. By advancing this argument, Smith made a fundamental contribution to the development of the economic analysis of the social position of women. His contribution was fundamental for two reasons. First, it offered an alternative to the views of the time which was to prove highly constructive and influential. Second, it provided a theoretical challenge to the belief that women would always remain the subservient sex.

Smith was not the first theorist to suggest that the social standing of women was related to the mode of subsistence and to stages of economic development. Turgot (1973, pp. 80–82) and Rousseau (1952, p. 350) had argued, in 1751 and 1755 respectively, that the status of women was linked directly to the means by which societies produced the material requirements of life. Further, they argued that humanity's means of obtaining these needs tended to progress through distinct stages over time.[2] However, the contributions made by these theorists to the consideration of women's social condition were relatively brief and undeveloped. Moreover, they were rationalistic rather than empirical in character. Smith, on the other hand, undertook a relatively detailed examination of this notion and utilized it systematically as a device to analyse the historical record. By so doing he transformed the idea that women's social position is primarily a function of the mode of subsistence from an abstract hypothesis into an argument founded on historical fact.

SMITH AND MONTESQUIEU

John Millar has reported that, in his lectures on justice, Smith 'followed the plan that seems to be suggested by Montesquieu' (Smith 1853, p. xvii). It would also appear to have been the case that Smith derived a number of his key ideas relating to women from this theorist. When discussing women's social standing, Smith makes numerous references to Montesquieu. He sometimes disputes the latter's claims. For example, while he accepted Montesquieu's belief that men were by nature physically stronger than women, he does not appear to have accepted the latter's claim that females had less innate intellectual capacity. In Smith's discussion of women's place in society, there is no suggestion that he believed women to be intellectually or spiritually inferior to men. Even so, it is clear that he learned much from Montesquieu and accepted the latter's relativist view of women's place in society. Most importantly, he accepted the fact that, while there are certain biological differences between the sexes which are constants, the social significance of these differences is variable. Consequently, he abandoned the very high level of abstraction that had been adopted by his rationalist forebears in the Chair of Moral Philosophy at Glasgow when analysing relations between the sexes.

Traditionally, theorists who discussed the woman question had done so by considering the relations that exist between the abstractions that are man and woman or husband and wife.[3] By contrast, as was shown in the last chapter, Montesquieu analysed women's social position by way of a relativist methodology. This emphasized cause and effect and highlighted the importance of relating innate differences between men and women to their cultural, physical and economic environment. His so doing led Montesquieu to conclude that, though women might have less innate intellectual and muscular capacities than men, the social relevance of this constant could vary dramatically given appropriate changes in the social and physical environment. Therefore, the theorist who wishes to explain the social position of women can say little if analysis is confined to a very high level of abstraction. To explain women's place in society, the theorist must adopt a relativist perspective which places the sexes in a social context.[4]

Montesquieu expounded his relativist view of women's social position both in the *Persian Letters* and *The Spirit of the Laws*. The latter work, in particular, received an enthusiastic welcome in Scotland from theorists such as Hume and Smith.[5] Like Montesquieu, these men accepted the 'uniformity of the human constitution' and were concerned to explain the apparent contradiction between universalism and the existence of clear diversity in the behaviour of nations. However, while accepting the value of Montesquieu's relativist and comparative methodology they did not accept the degree of emphasis he placed on climate and geography as factors explaining social diversity. For Hume and Smith, the character of a people is formed by custom, with national customs arising and altering as a consequence of imitation. In this process the ruling classes and the state play an especially significant role in setting the standards of correct behaviour (Chamley 1975). Therefore Hume and Smith believed that to explain the character of a population the theorist needs to concentrate on the society's historical record and class structure rather than its climate. What needs to be identified are those historical factors which gave rise both to the adoption of particular customs and to the subsequent supplementation of these customs by others.

Smith primarily advanced his ideas regarding the place of women in society when discussing the rights which belong to the individual as a member of a family.[6] As part of this project he sought to identify the environmental factors which determine intra-family patterns of authority. Further, he sought to explain why authority patterns tend to change over time.[7] He believed that there were four basic sources of authority which existed irrespective of the nature of a society.

> The causes or circumstances which naturally introduce subordination, or which naturally, and antecedent to any civil institution, give some men some superiority over the greater part of their brethren, seem to be four in number (Smith 1966, p. 200). 1st, superiority of age and of wisdom which is generally its concomitant. 2dly, superior strength of body; and these two it is which give the old an authority and respect with the young. 3d, superior fortune also gives a certain authority, *caetereis paribus*; and 4thly, the effect is the same of superior antiquity when everything else is alike; an old family excites no such jealousy as an upstart does (Smith 1978, p. 321).

In his analysis of authority, Smith argued that there tends to be a close connection between a community's mode of subsistence and the relative significance of these four sources of authority. Moreover, he insisted that the development of the mode of subsistence invariably transforms the relative significance of these sources of status and power. This variability, in turn, influences the customary distribution of rights between the sexes in both the family and the wider society. Smith's argument can best be illustrated by looking in turn at each of his four idealized economic stages.

THE AGE OF HUNTERS

In Smith's 'hunting' stage of development, life is sustained by the gathering of the fruits of nature with the dominant activities presumed to be hunting and fishing. Property is almost non-existent, communities are very small in size and there is no established magistracy. Collective problems are resolved democratically by the whole community. The only individuals with a disproportionate degree of authority in these societies are those with 'superior wisdom, valour, or such like qualifications' (Smith 1978, p. 202). Moreover, even these privileged individuals are only able to gain the allegiance of others if they agree to share the benefits of their greater attributes. In other words, community members offer these favoured individuals a greater degree of influence in return for the utility the former can gain by obtaining a share of the greater material benefits that accrue to those with greater personal attributes.

Smith accepted that in these simple communities women experienced a significant degree of influence. However, he did not believe that they normally enjoyed the degree of authority that accrued to adult males. This was because, while women might be capable of matching men's longevity and intellectual capacities, they were not men's equals in terms of physical strength. This fact, together with their physically debilitating role in reproduction, meant that women were not the equals of men either as hunters or as warriors. These were two of the most fundamental activities required for survival in the hunting stage of development. They were also two of the primary sources of status, the authority of individuals being largely determined by their personal capacities in these areas. Hence, because distinctions in status and authority were solely a function of personal attributes, women were structurally disadvantaged in hunting societies.[8]

Smith accepted explicitly that women's natural attributes would affect their ability to engage in manual labour and warfare.[9] He specified his views on the relative productivity of male and female labour when discussing the evils of slavery:

As it is for the labour of the slaves that the masters desire to have them, so it is chiefly male slaves which they procure as they are most able to sustain a great degree of hard labour. The women are not of such strength, and are therefore not much coveted (Smith 1978, p. 193).

Smith suggested that the esteem of male hunters would have also been enhanced by their military capacities. He believed that for hunting societies a social priority as fundamental as the attaining of sustenance was the ability to defend the community. Hence in hunting societies 'every man is a warrior as well as a hunter' (1966, p. 182). Smith acknowledged that women were able to engage in warfare, but he did not believe they were capable of matching men at this activity:[10]

> Amongst the Calmucks and some other nations, the women fight as well as the men. They are, as being weaker, not so good soldiers, but they have their horse, their bows and arrows as well as the men (Smith 1978, p. 229).

The degree of status that Smith believed warriors in hunting communities derived from their capacities in battle is indicated by the type of individual he thought warrior communities would customarily select as their leader:

> At the head of every small society or association of men we find a person of superior abilities; in a warlike society he is a man of superior strength, and in a polished one of superior mental capacity (Smith 1978, p. 401).

Smith's understanding of the type of individual who would tend to be the leader in a warrior community also had implications for who would lead the family in this type of society. He believed the head of a family was invariably the person who contributed most to its economic and military security. 'The head of the family is the person on whom the others are all naturally in a great measure dependent for their support and defence' (Smith 1978, p. 176). In a hunting and warrior society this was the husband and father.

The individual's capacity to contribute to the family's material well-being was, therefore, the prime factor determining the relative authority and standing of family members. That Smith believed this was the case he made even more explicit in his discussion of the nature of the relationship that exists between male and female slaves who cohabit. Smith notes that because a male slave cannot provide a wife with economic or military security, he has no right to claim a position of seniority in their relationship. Indeed, he does not even have the right of fidelity:

> [T]hat which creates the obligation to fidelity in the wife was altogether wanting when a male and female slave cohabited together. When a man takes a wife she comes to be altogether under his protection; she owes her safety and maintenance (especially in the lower ranks) intirely to her husband, and from this dependence it is

that she is thought to be bound to be faithfull and constant to him. But a female slave who cohabits with the male one has no such obligation; she is not maintained by his labour, nor defended by him, nor any way supported; all this, as far as she enjoys it, she has from her master, who will take care of every thing which may enable her to perform her work the better (Smith 1978, p. 178).

In other words, being a man is not sufficient of itself to elicit seniority within marriage. What is required for the custom of male headship to be established and maintained is for the husband to be capable of providing a material contribution to the wife's well-being sufficient to induce her to accept a lesser position in the marriage relationship.

THE AGE OF PASTURE

Smith argued that, while societies remained in the hunting stage of development, women would continue to enjoy a significant degree of authority. However, this situation would change when societies adopted the nomadic, pastoral mode of subsistence. The primary factor inducing this transformation is the emergence of two new sources of power upon which individuals can found a claim to a disproportionate degree of authority in social institutions. These are wealth and lineage. As there is little property in hunting societies, Smith held, it is not possible for individuals to gain great influence over the community by buying the allegiance of others or by being born of noble parentage. But once societies adopt the practice of pasturage, it becomes possible for some families to become very rich by building up large herds or flocks. As this process develops, those individuals unsuccessful at amassing wealth become dependent on the rich for their well-being. Wealthy families thus gain great authority over other community members.

In Smith's pastoral societies wealth becomes the most important source of authority, and the rich become the primary influence determining the customs of a nation. The wealthy of these societies have little to spend their riches upon but the purchasing of the allegiance of the population. This is because there does not exist any significant manufacturing or trading sector which can provide them with alternative sources of utility. Moreover, the authority of the rich will be enhanced from generation to generation as a consequence of the respect families attain when their wealth is of long standing. It will also be enhanced by the propensity of the poor to admire those with wealth (Smith 1978, pp. 40, 401).

While wealth is the primary source of authority in pastoral societies, military prowess also remains an important source of status. Domestication of animals provides individuals with the opportunity to accumulate wealth by either breeding bigger herds or stealing the herds of others. However, while these opportunities for wealth enhancement are created by the development of the pastoral mode of subsistence, the danger is also created that one's own property might be attacked:

> If they conquer, whatever belongs to the hostile tribe is the recompense of the victory. But if they are vanquished, all is lost, and not only their herds and flocks, but their women and children, become the booty of the conqueror. Even the greater part of those who survive the action are obliged to submit to him for the sake of immediate subsistence. The rest are commonly dissipated and dispersed in the desert (Smith 1966, p. 183).

Because of these possibilities and dangers, pastoral communities necessarily remain warrior societies. Every man must be both a shepherd and a soldier. Accordingly, great esteem and hence authority accrues to those individuals who have the personal attributes required for success in battle.[11] Within each family, this will mean the adult males. Thus, while the development of the pastoral stage brings into existence new customs which base authority primarily on property, the character of this mode of subsistence ensures that certain personal attributes remain primary sources of authority. This situation is advantageous to men and perpetuates the existence of inequality between the sexes, ensuring that adult males enjoy greater authority within both the community and the family.

Smith argued that the possibilities and dangers which are inherent in the very nature of the pastoral mode of subsistence lead directly to the creation of the state. This development, in turn, leads to further inequality between the sexes. Pastoral communities are compelled to band together to establish a central authority that can provide for their collective security. For Smith the state exists to protect the rights of those with property from those who would infringe these rights. However, it is important to note that he believed that it was not only the rich who wished to see property rights defended in the age of pasture:

> Men of inferior wealth combine to defend those of superior wealth in the possession of their property, in order that men of superior wealth may combine to defend them in the possession of theirs. All the inferior shepherds and herdsmen feel that the security of their own herds and flocks depends upon the security of those of the great shepherd or herdsman; that the maintenance of their lesser authority depends upon that of his greater authority, and that upon their subordination to him depends his power of keeping their inferiors in subordination to them (Smith 1966, p. 203).

The state is at first a relatively weak institution. Therefore, Smith argued, it tends to be wary of 'intermeddling' in the affairs of individuals. Where disputes arise, the central authorities will seek to bring about reconciliation rather than judge and punish. But to be able to maintain any level of government, the state must be able to establish at least some degree of jurisdiction over the population to be ruled. Smith insisted that the only way this could be achieved, while the state remained weak, was by the devolution of power to the various regions:

> Government is far advanced before the legislative power can appoint judges at pleasure ... This could not be done in an early society. The people would not submit themselves in that manner. The government therefore would find it necessary to take advantage of the superiority and authority of certain persons who were respected in the country and put the judicial power into their hands (Smith 1978, p. 187).

Smith observed that this process of devolution would greatly influence the distribution of power within the family.[12] In order to ensure the state's ability to rule at this fundamental level, the authority of the family member who had greatest respect, that is, the adult male, would need to be strengthened. Thus those with greatest esteem in the community, that is, the rich men, 'endeavoured by all means to strengthen the power of the husband and make him as absolute as possible' (Smith 1978, p. 440; see also pp. 143, 176, 187).

Smith's theory of the origin of the state suggests yet another reason why rich men would have supported the rights of all husbands to a superiority within their own homes. His belief that those individuals with a small amount of property will ally themselves with those who possess large properties might well be analogous to the relationship between the sexes. In short, rich men establish a reciprocal understanding with men of lesser wealth in order to ensure that men of all classes are able to dominate the women of their own families.

Smith suggested that the customary rights attained by husbands in the pastoral stage of development, as a consequence of men's natural attributes and the aid they receive from the state, tends to be almost absolute. He observed that, once men gain control of state power, they 'generally are very severe on the women'. Having the ability to make laws relating to the family, 'they generally will be inclined to curb the women as much as possible and give themselves the more indulgence' (Smith 1978, pp. 146–147). Two areas of law that he suggested tend to be particularly significant in this regard are those relating to inheritance and divorce. Amongst shepherds, men are normally given legal control of any inheritance their wives may bring to a marriage, and only men are allowed to dissolve the marriage. Smith cited early Rome as an example of the distribution of power between the sexes that this process tends to produce in pastoral communities:

> [T]hat some sort of government might be preserved in them they strengthend the authority of the father of the family, and gave him the power of disposing of his whole family as he thought proper and determining with regard to them even in capital cases. By this means the father possessed a power over his whole family, wife, children, and slaves, which was not much less than supreme (Smith 1978, pp. 143–144).

THE AGE OF AGRICULTURE

Women's status does not tend to improve in Smith's agricultural stage of development. He suggested that populations that progress to this stage continue to live in perpetual danger of being attacked by other communities. Hence, the building of fortified towns and castles characterizes this stage of development and every husbandman 'is a warrior or easily becomes such' (Smith 1966, p. 184). Smith suggested that there were three fundamental economic reasons why high status continues to accrue to the warrior throughout this stage of development. First, the means by which these communities produce their livelihood gives men ample time to engage in warfare. Because of the nature of agricultural production, men can afford to be absent from their farms during the months between sowing and harvest. This is because their crops continue to grow while they are away, and what work needs to be done during this period 'can be well enough executed by the old men, the women, and the children' (Smith 1966, p. 185; see also Smith 1978, p. 229):

> [Husbandmen] can all go out to war as easily as the shepherds. In this state the campaigns were only summer ones. They continued but three or four months in the middle of the summer, after the spring and before the harvest work. They could easily be absent in the intermediate time, as the corn grows and the crop comes on, if the season favours, as well as if they were at home (Smith 1978, p. 229).

The second fundamental reason for the high status of the warrior in the agricultural stage of development is the fact that there is yet to emerge any significant manufacturing or trading sector. In consequence, the wealthy still have only a small range of commodities upon which they can spend the surplus they extract from their subordinates. For this class, the primary purchasable source of utility remains the allegiance, subservience and willingness to obey of others. Included in the duties that a lord's wealth can purchase in agricultural societies is the agreement of poorer men to follow him into battle:

> In a country which has neither foreign commerce, nor any of the finer manufactures, a great proprietor, having nothing for which he can exchange the greater part of the produce of his lands which is over and above the maintenance of the cultivators, consumes the whole in rustic hospitality at home. If this surplus produce is sufficient to maintain a hundred or a thousand men, he can make use of it in no other way than by maintaining a hundred or a thousand men. He is at all times, therefore, surrounded with a multitude of retainers and dependants, who, having no equivalent to give in return for their maintenance, but being fed entirely by his bounty, must obey him, for the same reason that soldiers must obey the prince who pays them (Smith 1964, p. 363).

The third economic pillar underpinning the high status of the warrior in agricultural societies is the fact that the agricultural mode of subsistence creates a decided use for soldiers. Slavery or serfdom, Smith suggested, invariably comes to characterize this stage of development with warrior lords actually owning the land. Consequently, the direct producers have little incentive to raise the productivity of their labour or make long-term investments which would enhance output. Were they to do so, the greater productivity would merely increase the surplus extracted by the lord. Given this situation, the only effective means landowners have of increasing their wealth and power is by taking that which belongs to others, that is, by 'extending his jurisdiction and authority over those of his neighbours' (Smith 1964, p. 343). Hence, the economic character of the agricultural mode of subsistence creates a supply of soldiers and an effective demand for their services.[13] While this remains the case, Smith argued, women were invariably considered inferior beings and the customs of nations ensured that they were not permitted any significant degree of equality with men.

Smith's observations regarding the status of women in agricultural societies related primarily to early Greece and Rome and to the situation in Western Europe following the collapse of the Roman Empire. While landholding remained on a small scale, as he suggested was the situation in early Rome, women had little upon which they could found a claim to any degree of equality:

> In the earlier periods of Rome, when there was but little wealth in the nation, the fortune a woman could bring to her husband or could possibly be in possession of was not so great as to entitle her to capitulate or enter upon treaty with her husband; she was content to submit herself to the power of the husband (Smith 1978, p. 144).

By these ancient marriages, which were performed either by *confarreatio* or *coemptio*, the wife became entirely the slave of the husband. He had absolute power over her, both of death and of divorce. Wives could not at that time give any great addition to a man's fortune. They brought either nothing with them or a very small matter, as seven acres of land were accounted a large estate. Wives were accordingly not much regarded in those times (Smith 1978, p. 66).

Moreover, the situation of women was not improved merely by the establishment of large landholdings. Smith argued that the barbarians who swept across Western Europe at the beginning of the fifth century, destroying in the process the Roman system of commerce, had developed economically and socially only to the early agricultural stage of development (Smith 1978, p. 107). Their marriage customs tended to reflect this fact:

> The savage nations which issuing out from Scandinavia and other northern countries overran all the west of Europe were in that state in which the wife is greatly under the subjection of the husband. By the small remains of the laws of those nations which have come down to our hands, this seems to have been very much the case. The

husband had then a very great authority over her and was allowed divorce in the same manner as formerly amongst the Romans, but the wife had no power of divorcing the husband (Smith 1978, p. 146).

The barbarians, however, did not establish small landholdings. Rather, the 'chiefs and principal leaders' enslaved the local population and divided the conquered territories amongst themselves, establishing vast estates over which they ruled. These estates were kept in existence from generation to generation. This permanence was required because of the need for both the rulers and the ruled of each estate to ensure that their collective strength was sufficient to defend themselves from the rapine and violence that characterized the agricultural mode of subsistence.

In such an environment, it was perceived to be critical that adequate manpower was available for defence. Hence women were not accorded high esteem and customs emerged that ensured the continuance of their social and domestic subservience. Smith claimed, for example, that in the initial period of chronic disorder, following the collapse of Rome, no woman was permitted to succeed to an estate. When in time this custom was subsequently modified, the tradition became that a woman could inherit property but she could not marry without the consent of the superior of the estate. This was justified on the grounds that it was the duty of the lord to ensure that her prospective bridegroom could fulfil the duties required of vassals. Above all else, this meant the ability to provide military service (Smith 1978, pp. 59–60, 249–250).

The continuance of the tendency for high status to accrue to warriors in the agricultural stage of development, Smith suggested, left women with no chance of gaining any significant level of equality with men. However, Smith was not a crude economic determinist. He allowed that non-economic factors could play a significant role in the shaping of social relations and customs. Thus he argued that women were seldom left totally at the mercy of their husbands, even in the most despotic of regimes. This was because fatherly and brotherly love would normally lead men to ensure that their female relatives were not mistreated beyond what was considered a socially acceptable degree. Further, he suggested that in feudal Europe women did not experience the level of social subservience that had been the lot of females in early Rome. This was because they found allies who were able to ameliorate some of the more excessive iniquities women were compelled to endure. These allies were the male functionaries of the Christian church.

Priests and monks became extremely influential during the period of regional absolutism which characterized society in the early middle ages. This was largely because people clung to the church as a means of ameliorating the powers of the local lord (Smith 1978, pp. 90, 188–190, 264–266). Smith claimed that this development proved a great boon to women. The men of the religious orders did not marry and this feature of their life tended to encourage them to adopt a more balanced perspective regarding relations between husband and wife than that adopted by the secular authorities. The most important single means by which the church aided women was by making divorce all but impossible for both men and women, whereas previously it had been only women who could not divorce. In this way women's authority was greatly enhanced:[14]

> This rendering divorces not easily obtainable gave the wife a more respectable character, rendering her in a great measure independent on the husband for her support. She was accordingly considered as a considerable member of the family, who had the same interest in the common stock as the master or the children; and from this it was that the wife after the demise of her husband came in for the same share as either of the other two parts of the family (Smith 1978, p. 47).

THE AGE OF COMMERCE

So long as the nations of Europe advanced no further than the agricultural stage of development, Smith accepted that, even with the aid of the church, women's ability to attain any significant degree of equality with males remained severely curtailed. In his analysis, what tended to change this situation was the gradual establishment of the commercial stage of subsistence. This development enabled women to increase their authority in both society and the home. It did so both by providing women with new sources of power which they could utilize in negotiating their relations with men and by undermining the social esteem that men gained as a consequence of their natural physical advantages.

As with his discussion of the agricultural mode of subsistence, Smith founded this part of his argument primarily on the history of ancient and modern Europe. He argued that if the opportunity exists to engage in trade, agricultural people will be led to strive to improve the quality of their manufactured goods. The growth of trade and manufacturing, he suggested, has two consequences of fundamental significance for women. First, it undermines the authority that accrues to men as a result of their greater innate capacity to act as warriors. Smith observed that, while nations remain in the pastoral and agricultural stages of development, all the free males of military age actively take part in warfare. However, with the emergence of commerce, the willingness of men to undertake military service is undermined because of the great opportunity cost necessarily involved in undertaking this form of activity in a commercial society:

> [A pastoral or agricultural state] could send out all those of the military age ... But in a state where arts, manufactures, and handicrafts are brought to perfection this is not

the case. They can not dispense with the labourers in this manner without the total loss of business and the destruction of the state. Every hour a smith or a weaver is absent from his loom or the anvill his work is at a stop, which is not the case with the flocks of a shepherd or the fields of a husbandman. Trade, commerce, can not go on, and they therefore will not go out to the wars. As one in 4 can go out in the former case, so not above 1 in 100 in those who are polished and cultivate the arts (Smith 1978, p. 230).

Smith argued that the development of trade and manufacturing acts as a corrosive influence on militarism, irrespective of the political character of a regime (Smith 1978, pp. 230–232). This is less so in slave societies, for there free men do not have to engage in productive labour. However, even in slave communities, the development of commerce tends to undermine the authority that customarily accrued to the warrior in earlier modes of subsistence. It does so first by increasing the quality of life that a man can enjoy by staying at home amongst his luxuries, as compared to the life he experiences while on campaign. Second and much more importantly, the development of manufacturing and trade provides the rich with alternative sources of utility upon which they can spend their wealth. This development reduces the capacity of the rich to purchase the allegiance of soldiers and hence undermines their ability to engage in constant warfare against both their neighbours and the central authorities.[15]

Commercialism, then, tends to undermine the willingness and the ability of both the wealthy and the tradesmen to act as soldiers (Smith 1978, pp. 232, 263–266). Consequently, the only men who can be induced to become warriors are those incapable of obtaining a living by any other means, that is 'the very lowest and worthlessest of the people' (Smith 1978, p. 232). In this environment, the authority that men can derive from those personal attributes which enable them to engage effectively in combat are greatly devalued amongst the wealthy and commercial classes. Hence the rise of commerce induces an enhancement in the relative status of women by demeaning what in earlier stages of development had been one of the fundamental sources of authority available to men.

The second means by which the commercial mode of subsistence enhances the relative degree of authority enjoyed by women is by making it easier for females to amass wealth. Smith argued that in the case of Rome, as the nation developed a substantive commercial sector, great riches were accumulated by individuals. Some of these rich men invariably left part or all of their wealth to their daughters. Consequently, some women became extremely wealthy and did so even though certain 'austere disciplinarians' did all they could to halt this development (Smith 1978, pp. 66-67). The authority that accrued to these heiresses as a consequence of their wealth made them less willing to accept the slave-like status that was customarily accorded to Roman wives. Given the opportunity to renegotiate the traditional marriage contract by the fact that their wealth gave them great bargaining power with prospective bridegrooms, these women demanded that their marriages involve a new set of arrangements:

> [W]hen the Romans became from a very poor a very wealthy people; and the women, who are in all polite and wealthy countries more regarded than they are by a poorer and more barbarous nation, came to have large fortunes which they could confer on their husbands; they could not submit, nor would the friends allow it, to the subjection that attended the old form of marriage. They therefore made certain concessions to one another; the husband, on consideration of the use of such large sums of money as they might sometimes receive, gave up some parts of his authority, and the woman on the other hand gave him the use of her portion during his lifetime (Smith 1978, p. 66).

Smith observed that the Romans' adoption of new marriage customs which enhanced the authority of wives was initiated by the rich. However, these new practices in time became the social norm. This was because of the desire of those who controlled the state to preserve family fortunes and because of the tendency of the lower classes to take their social lead from those with wealth (Smith 1978, pp. 144–145).

Smith did not believe that the greater authority that came to be enjoyed by Roman women concomitantly with the development of the commercial stage of economic development was merely an aberration or the result of a unique combination of political forces. This is indicated by the fact that he suggested that a similar enhancement of women's authority occurred with the rise of the commercial mode of subsistence in modern Europe. As with earlier commercial societies, he argued, the growth of manufacturing and trade in Europe undermined militarism by raising the opportunity cost of engaging actively in warfare. Once again, the importance for women of these developments lay in the fact that the status of the warrior declined and women were given a greater ability to accumulate property. With the development of commerce, the direct producers became less inclined to go to the wars and the landowners came to desire cash or payment in kind from their tenants rather than a willingness to follow them into battle. Smith suggested that the payment of this form of rent provided an historic opportunity for women:

> In the first period of the feudal government the succession of females was never allowed; for they could not perform any of the services required of those who were vassals either of the king or his nobles; they could neither serve him in the field nor in the council; and as they could not inherit so neither could their descendents by their right ... But in time the military fiefs came to be considered in most respects as property, and the services of the field were not always required, but were dispensed with for a certain gratuity. This gratuity, which they called [escuage], was often more esteemed than the performance of the actual services, and new fiefs were given out on that condition. The lords or feudal chiefs did not now exercise the jurisdiction themselves, but by their steward. In this state of things females could succeed in

every shape as well as males; they could pay the [escuage] and maintain a steward to exercise judgment on their tenants as well as men. From this time therefore females were admitted to the succession (Smith 1978, pp. 59-60).

It is clear from his observations regarding inheritance laws in pastoral and agricultural societies that Smith believed that an ability to inherit wealth is not of itself sufficient to ensure that women are able to attain any significant degree of authority. What is required for this development to take place is that women be able to inherit wealth and live in an environment where the people need not be constantly ready to defend their property and lives by military force. Smith appears to have believed that these two developments tend to exist concomitantly only in societies characterized by the commercial mode of subsistence.

CONCLUSIONS AND IMPLICATIONS

The key factor that distinguishes Smith's contribution to the economic analysis of women's social position is the role played by the mode of subsistence. By focusing his analysis on this element Smith was able to advance a systematic explanation for women's place in society through the ages. For Smith it is the means by which populations attain the material wherewithal required for survival that explains, above all else, both the authority and status enjoyed by women. These needs include food, clothing and shelter and, of equal importance, the requirements of defence. By concentrating on these material factors, Smith developed a systematic argument the use of which enabled the history of women to be explained with an unprecedented degree of rigor. It is this enhancement of economic theory's capacity to explain the history of women's place in society that gives Smith's contribution to the woman question its great significance.

Smith's emphasis on the economic dimension in his explanation of women's social position made his contribution inherently materialist in character. This is not to deny that he incorporated non-economic factors into his argument. He gave due heed to the political and legal dimension. Moreover, he noted the importance of fatherly and brotherly love and the role played by the church in the shaping of women's lives. Nevertheless, the weight he gave to the economic dimension suggests that those who seek to deny a materialist character in his historiography need to qualify their opinions at least in relation to gender status.

Skinner's general observation of 1975 best captures the role played by the economic dimension in Smith's contribution to the woman question:

Smith would appear to come close to Engels's general position in arguing that the economic finally asserts itself as the 'ultimate', rather than as the sole, determining factor. This carefully qualified view can be seen in many ways and is nowhere more obvious than in Smith's use of the economic stages which are offered as general categories in terms of which the experience of different peoples can be interpreted rather than as templates to which that experience must be made to conform (Skinner 1975, p. 175).

Smith's contribution to the analysis of women's place in society is materialist in another respect. He also founded his argument on natural differences between the sexes. The innate differences he chose to emphasize were only those related to strength and fecundity. Unlike Montesquieu, he does not appear to have accepted that women have any natural intellectual disadvantage relative to men. However, he followed the latter in accepting that there are natural differences between the sexes which, in appropriate circumstances, can be socially significant. The explanatory emphasis he placed on innate capacities made Smith no more a crude biological determinist than his stress on the economic made his work crude economic determinism. He believed men's greater natural strength and freedom from the encumbrances of fecundity were fundamental factors explaining women's lesser social position through history. However, because he followed the path pointed to by Montesquieu, he appreciated the fact that while biological differences are a constant, the social importance of these differences is a variable which is dependent on the human context. Indeed, by integrating biology, economics and history, Smith was able to develop a relativist argument which was a decided advance on Montesquieu's contribution to the woman question.

Smith's determination to found his argument on the process of economic development and on a limited number of natural differences between the sexes meant that his relativism was not dependent on dubious biological, geographic and climatic generalizations. His relativism was consequently more substantive than was Montesquieu's. For example, the latter's claim that women's social position was related closely to a nation's average temperature could be all too easily dismissed merely by pointing to the many nations which did not fit his argument. Smith was much more circumspect in his relativism and his use of biology and consequently was decidedly less vulnerable to this form of criticism.

Smith's contribution was also an advance on Montesquieu's discussion of the woman question in that, because of the weighting he gave to the economic dimension, he was not led to embrace the fatalism displayed by the latter. For example, Montesquieu accepted that women in hot climates would always remain subservient to men because of the adverse effect he believed high temperatures invariably exerted on their biological development. Smith, on the other hand, precisely because he believed that the process of economic development tended to carry societies to the higher stages of development, was led to conclude that women's lot was not and could not be so rigidly determined. Indeed, contained within his notion of progress was the suggestion that the process of economic development would tend to lead, if not to full equality between the sexes, at least to a decided improvement in the relative status of women.

Smith did not believe that progress through the various modes of subsistence would always improve women's social position. Clearly the transition from the hunting to the pastoral stage of development did little if anything to improve women's status. Nor did he believe that the path of economic development and hence the transformation of the authority accruing to women was necessarily a one-way street. This is indicated by his recognition that women's condition was set back by the reversion of Europe to the agricultural mode of subsistence following the collapse of Rome. Even so, Smith believed that the progress of societies tended towards commercialism and this stage of development offered women unprecedented opportunities to enhance their authority relative to men. This social change might not emerge as soon as there occurred a transformation in the economic base of society. Cultural lag is not at all incompatible with Smith's materialism. Nevertheless, it must be concluded, Smith believed that technical and economic progress in the long term tended to transform the social significance of the innate differences between the sexes. Further, he accepted that the process of economic development implied that human progress involved a movement towards greater equality between men and women.

REFERENCES

Battersby, Christine (1980), 'An Enquiry Concerning the Humean Woman', *Studies on Voltaire and the Eighteenth Century*, **193** (4), 1964–1967.

Bowles, Paul (1984), 'John Millar, The Four-Stages Theory, and Women's Position in Society', *History of Political Economy*, **16** (4), 619–637.

Chamley, Paul E. (1975), 'The Conflict Between Montesquieu and Hume: A Study of the Origins of Adam Smith's Universalism', in A.S. Skinner and T. Wilson (eds), *Essays on Adam Smith*, Oxford: Clarendon Press, pp. 274–305.

Dunbar, Robin (1991), 'Foraging for Nature's Balanced Diet', *New Scientist*, **131** (1784), 21–24.

Faust, Beatrice (1991), *Apprenticeship in Liberty*, Sydney: Angus and Robertson.

Haakonssen, Knud (1981), *The Science of a Legislator*, Cambridge: Cambridge University Press.

Hutcheson, Francis (1755), *A System of Moral Philosophy*, Glasgow: R. and A. Foulis.

Leavitt, R.R. (1971), 'Women in Other Cultures', in V. Gornick and B.K. Moran (eds), *Woman in Sexist Society*, New York: New American Library, pp. 407–420.

Marcil-Lacoste, Louise (1979), 'Hume's Method in Moral Reasoning', in Lorenne M.G. Clark and Lynda Lange (eds), *The Sexism of Social and Political Theory: Women and Reproduction from Plato to Nietzsche*, Toronto: University of Toronto Press, pp. 60–73.

Nyland, Chris (1991), 'The Women's Question and the Relativism of Poulain de la Barre and Montesquieu', Paper presented at the Sixth History of Economic Thought Conference, Monash University.

Nyland, Chris (1993), 'John Locke and the Social Position of Women', *History of Political Economy*, **25**, Spring.

Pocock, J.G.A. (1972), *Politics, Language and Time*, London: Methuan.

Pocock, J.G.A. (1975), *The Machiavellian Moment*, New Jersey: Princeton University Press.

Pufendorf, S. (1724), *De Officio hominis et civis juxta legem naturalem. Libro duo.* Supplementis & observationibus in Academiciae juventutis usum auxit & illustravit Gerschomus Carmichael. Editio secunda priore auctior & emendatior, Edinburgh.

Rendall, Jane (1985), *The Origins of Modern Feminism: Women in Britain, France and the United States 1780–1860*, Basingstoke: Macmillan.

Rendall, Jane (1987), 'Virtue and Commerce: Women in the Making of Adam Smith's Political Economy', in E. Kennedy, and S. Mendus (eds), *Women in Western Political Philosophy: Kant to Nietzsche*, Brighton: Wheatsheaf Books Ltd., pp. 44–77.

Rousseau, Jean Jacques (1952), 'A Dissertation on the Origin and Foundation of the Inequality of Mankind', in William Benton (ed.), *Great Books of the Western World*, London.

Skinner, Andrew S. (1965), 'Economics and History: the Scottish Enlightenment', *Scottish Journal of Political Economy*, **12** (1), 1–22.

Skinner, Andrew S. (1975), 'Adam Smith: An Economic Interpretation of History', in A.S. Skinner and T. Wilson (eds), *Essays on Adam Smith*, Oxford: Oxford University Press, pp. 154–178.

Skinner, Andrew S. (1979), 'Adam Smith: An Aspect of Modern Economics?', *Scottish Journal of Political Economy*, **26** (2), 109–123.

Skinner, Andrew S. (1982). 'A Scottish Contribution to Marxist Sociology?', in L. Bradley and M. Howard (eds), *Classical and Marxian Political Economy*, London:

Macmillan Press, pp. 79–114.

Smith, Adam (1853), *The Theory of Moral Sentiments*, London: H.G. Bohn.

Smith, Adam (1964), *The Wealth of Nations,* vol. 1, London: Everyman's Library.

Smith, Adam (1966), *The Wealth of Nations,* vol. 2, London: Everyman's Library.

Smith, Adam (1978), *Lectures on Jurisprudence* (edited by R.L. Meek, D.D. Raphael and P.G. Stein), Oxford: Clarendon Press.

Tomaselli, Sylvania (1985), 'The Enlightenment Debate on Women', *History Workshop Journal,* **20** (2), 101–124.

Turgot, A.R.J. (1973), *Turgot on Progress, Sociology and Economics,* (translated and edited by Ronald L. Meek), Cambridge: Cambridge University Press.

Winch, Donald (1978), *Adam Smith's Politics: An Essay in Historiographic Revisions*, Cambridge: Cambridge University Press.

NOTES

1. Smith's contribution to the economic analysis of the social position of women appears primarily in the lectures he gave at Glasgow. It is mainly for this reason that this paper concentrates on the argument advanced in the lectures. However, a second reason for this focus relates to the dating of Smith's contribution. Beginning in the 1770s, an extensive debate regarding the history of women through the ages emerged in both Scotland and France. It has been widely recognized by historians of economic and political thought that stage theory provided a central organizing theme in much of the literature produced by this debate (Bowles 1984; Tomaselli 1985; Rendall 1985, 1987). What has not been appreciated is the fact that Smith contributed to the development of this perspective. Moreover, as Smith's lectures date from 1762, it would appear his contribution was made at an earlier time than that made by any of the recognized discussants. Thus he deserves the credit that belongs to the pioneer.

2. The notion that women's social position could change in accordance with changes in the progress of humanity had also been argued by Poulain de la Barre in 1673. I have been unable to locate any evidence that Smith read any of Poulain's works, though Montesquieu had certainly done so (Nyland 1991).

3. Thus Locke, Grotius and Pufendorf's contribution to the discussion of women focused on the respective rights of wives and husbands in any form of society (Nyland 1993). Likewise, this level of abstraction was adopted by Carmichael (Pufendorf 1724) and Hutcheson (1755), Smith's predecessors in the Chair of Moral Philosophy at Glasgow.

4. The fact that Montesquieu was a major influence on Smith's ideas regarding women has been neglected in the literature. Rendall has published the only substantive study of Smith's notion of women's place in society. However, she chose to 'risk ... neglecting such fundamental contemporary influences as David Hume, and Montesquieu', confining her analysis only to the extent that Smith's ideas were influenced by 'civic humanism' (Rendall 1987, p. 45). Consequently, she fails to appreciate the significance of Smith's historicism and mistakenly concludes that his contribution 'was not profoundly original'.

5. Hume's approach to the consideration of women's place in society, however, appears to have been little affected by his reading of Montesquieu. Where he discusses the woman question he primarily utilizes the traditional methodology, making only passing acknowledgement to the importance of relativism. For details of Hume's ideas regarding women see Marcil-Lacoste (1979) and Battersby (1980).

6. When he discussed the individual's civil rights, Smith utilized the term 'man', but as he included wives within this category it is clear he was using this term synonymously with 'human being' (Smith 1978, pp. 141, 399).

7. In arguing that Smith sought to *explain* the distribution of rights within the family rather than to *prescribe* what these should be, this paper adds to the work of Paul Bowles (1984). Bowles' analysis of John Millar's use of stage theory in relation to the place of women in society has played a valuable role in negating the claims of individuals such as Haakonssen (1981) and Pocock (1972, 1975). These scholars argue that the Scottish Historical School used stage theory primarily to prescribe human conduct rather than to explain its character.

8. Modern anthropological studies generally validate Smith's ideas regarding the high status and favours that women in hunting and gathering societies customarily grant to the men who are the best hunters (Dunbar 1991; Faust 1991; Leavitt 1971). That Smith's argument suggested that there existed a structured inequality between the sexes in these communities has been missed by economists who have discussed the foundations of authority in his four stages of development. This omission is largely a consequence of the fact that analysts have invariably adopted a 'sex neutral' methodology when considering this topic, which does not consider the differing biological capacities of men and women.

9. Recognition that females have less capacity to engage in many manual activities than do men did not lead Smith to claim that women in hunting societies were incapable of providing their own sustenance. This was so even though he does not appear to have been

aware of the important gathering activities normally undertaken by women in these communities. Where he stated explicitly that they did require the assistance of men in the attaining of their subsistence was when they were pregnant or were breast-feeding. He accepted that in these circumstances the attaining of the child's material needs as well as her own would require 'a degree of labour to which the woman would be altogether unequal' (Smith 1978, pp. 142, 438).

10. The extent to which Smith believed physical strength was an important factor in battle is attested to by his discussion of the equalizing influence of the invention of firearms. Prior to the adoption of these weapons in warfare, 'Strength and agility of body were of the highest consequence, and commonly determined the state of battles' (Smith 1966, p. 189).

11. Smith notes that, because he lived in a pastoral society, Ulysses preferred to be considered a pirate rather than a merchant; 'A pirate is a military man who acquires his livelihood by warlike exploits, whereas a merchant is a peaceable one who has no occasion for military skill and would not be much esteemed in a nation consisting of warriors chiefly' (Smith 1978, p. 224).

12. Smith argued that, in the hunting stage of development, interfamily relations were not considered to be the business of the community so long as they did not infringe the rights of others. 'The affairs of private families, as long as they concern only the members of one family, are left to the determination of *the members of that* family' (Smith 1978, p. 201).

13. As part of his critique of Meek's claim that Smith was a materialist, Skinner (1975, 1979, 1981) has observed that it was primarily the *political* disorder and conflict characterizing Europe after the collapse of Rome that induced proprietors to alter the pattern of landholding and establish feudalism. The claim Skinner is attempting to advance is that Meek over-emphasizes the economic and hence materialist character of Smith's argument. More specifically, he wishes to weaken the link between Smithian and Marxist sociology identified by Meek. However, Skinner's argument is flawed because he gives inadequate emphasis to the fact that Smith argued that the underlying causes of the political instability were economic in character. They were economic in that they emanated, first, from the seasonal nature of agricultural production; second, from the slave-master relationship and the difficulties with raising labour productivity inherent in this relationship; and third, from the inadequate outlets available to the lords in which they could spend the surplus they extracted from their serfs or slaves. These are issues respectively of production, distribution and exchange. It was these economic factors which were the root cause of the political environment that Skinner chooses to over-emphasize.

14. Smith argued that permanency in marriage also enhanced the status of women by inducing men to take much greater care when selecting their wives. He claimed that this development, in turn, generated love in marriage for the first time. This was a phenomenon which he believed required a permanence in marital relations because it was difficult to sustain love in an environment where men could dispose of their wives with ease or, as in late Rome, where the institution of marriage was unstable because both partners had access to easy divorce (Smith 1978, pp. 146–150, 160).

15. In both Rome and feudal Europe, Smith argued, it was commercialism's weakening of the lords' political power that led to a strengthening in the power of the central government. This economic factor, Smith believed, was the fundamental element that undermined feudalism in Europe: 'A slave who can acquire nothing but his maintenance, consults his own ease by making the land produce as little as possible over and above that maintenance. It is probable that it was partly upon account of this advantage, and partly upon account of the encroachments which the sovereign, always jealous of the great lords, gradually encouraged their villeins to make upon their authority, and which seem at last to have been such as rendered this species of servitude altogether inconvenient, that tenure in villeinage gradually wore out through the greater part of Europe' (Smith 1964, p. 346) ... 'The power of the [English] nobles ... declined in the feudal governments from the same causes as everywhere else, viz., from the introduction of arts, commerce, and luxury. Their power consisted in the number of their retainers and tenants. The number of their retainers and

even of their dependants was owing to their plain and hospitable way of living ... But when elegance in dress, building, and gardening, cookery, etc. was introduced, it was no difficult matter to spend a fortune even as great as that of Warwicks, and by this means he would lose all his retainers except a few menial servants who could give him no influence' (Smith 1978, p. 261).

6. Women's Progress and 'the End of History'

Chris Nyland

The eighteenth century, which saw the first wave of optimism about the destiny of mankind, also saw it reach its highest point. It opened with a fair degree of agreement on progress in one field only: science and technology. Before its close, firm convictions had been expressed about the inevitability of progress in wealth, in civilization, in social organization, in art and literature, even in human nature and biological make-up. But the century ended in the explosion of the French Revolution, which shattered again the hopes particularly of those who had hoped the most (Pollard 1971, p. 31).

As the last chapter revealed, in his lectures on jurisprudence Adam Smith developed an explanation for women's social status that was underpinned by his four-stage theory of socio-economic evolution. Smith argued that the social condition of women is determined primarily by the interaction of the constant that is biology and the variable that is the mode of subsistence prevailing in a given location at a particular time. He also suggested that women's social standing tends to change as societies progress to what he perceived to be the higher socio-economic stages, with their status being greatest in commercial societies. Smith's contribution was an important milestone in the history of the economic analysis of women's status. This was due to the materialist nature of his argument and because he could explain the historical universality of male dominance in a way that denied that this universality implied women would always remain the subordinate sex. The latter aspect of Smith's contribution is grounded in the Enlightenment tradition in that it suggests that a pattern of change exists in human history and that the direction of this change is toward improvement from a less to a more beneficial state. In short, the argument offered women the hope that their status might be further advanced as the details of social governance were further refined. However, Smith's argument also had a decided conservative element stemming from the fact that, in arguing that commercial society is the highest stage of socio-economic evolution ever attained, Smith failed to consider whether further progress might yet carry humanity to socio-economic stages beyond capitalism. As Pollard (1971) has noted, scholars who have embraced the idea of progress can be considered in layers. Virtually all accept that humanity's knowledge of the physical world has progressed; a lesser number accept human governance has been enhanced; an even smaller proportion believe that with improved knowledge and practice humanity has become more moral and/or better natured; and at the peak of the apex are those 'hopeful enough to predict that the improvements in other spheres will ultimately lead also to an improvement in the physical, mental and spiritual capacities of man ... an enhanced power of creation ... and an intellect that would take the human future right out of the comprehension of the present' (Pollard 1971, p. 12).

Smith was an optimist, but his failure to carry his analysis of stage theory beyond capitalism makes it clear that he did not belong to the layer of progressives who were situated at the very peak of the apex. This is not to suggest that he believed that bourgeois Scotland was as good as it gets and that further social progress was not possible. Certainly his conservatism was muted compared to those scholars of the period who recognized that the notion of progress can encourage malcontents to hope that capitalism might one day be superseded as had the predecessors of this social system. The challenge to Enlightenment optimism sustained by these conservatives in the second half of the eighteenth century was held at bay by progressives prior to 1789. But when Revolution in France stimulated the poor to hope that the 'rights of man' might apply to them as well as to their 'betters', popular and intellectual enthusiasm for an end of history argument that could effectively dash such hopes became overwhelming.

This chapter argues that at the end of the eighteenth century the demands of the dispossessed for forms of equality that the middle and upper classes deemed unacceptable proved a major barrier to the further 'improvement' of women's status. Even before the Revolution there were individuals who sought to deny women the hope that society might one day evolve to a stage in which there would exist a full equality of the sexes. However, the notion of socio-economic evolution placed these gender conservatives in a bind. They wanted to promote the idea that capitalism had provided women with a level of equality never before known, for which they should be duly grateful. But at the same time they wanted to make it clear to women that there is an end point to social progress, that this point had been reached, and that to seek further progress was to risk all that had been thus far attained. One intellectual device utilized to convey this message involved the combining of stage theory with the tradition that held that the accumulation of wealth can cause the leaders of society to live lives so luxurious that they become decadent, degenerate and debased. However, this was an unfortunate argument for conservatives who resided in those societies in which the capitalist class was predominant. This was because the argument continued to acknowledge that social systems can become redundant and be superseded, and it suggested that capital accumulation, an activity at the very heart of capitalist economics and morality, can be a primary source of social decay. Nevertheless, by utilizing this argument, scholars such as John Millar and William Alexander were able to inject into the literature on the economics of women's status the notion that there are natural limits to how far women's social position can be advanced. Until the French Revolution, this tendency was countered successfully by progressives such as Condorcet, Wollstonecraft and Godwin, who dreamed of unending progress and insisted that human rights belonged equally to both sexes. However, the fear of democracy engendered amongst the elites of Europe by the Revolution created a great demand for an argument that would bring closure to the notion of social progress and ideally could do so while placing the blame for the 'end of history' onto the dispossessed. This chapter suggests that at the very end of the eighteenth century this was a need catered for by Thomas Malthus. The chapter begins by sketching the contribution to the economics of gender advanced by those writers concerned about the impact luxury can have on the long-term viability of communities. It then proceeds to explain why Millar's ideas were unacceptable to progressive feminists, and concludes by discussing why Malthus' contribution to gender analysis was a more appropriate device for a class satisfied with the status quo but determined to end the hopes of those women who dared to dream that the destiny of their sex had yet to be realized.

JOHN BROWN, ANTOINE THOMAS AND THE DANGERS OF ACCUMULATION

With the publication of Montesquieu's *The Spirit of the Laws,* the notion that there exist barriers to social transformation became an axiom informing a great deal of social analysis in France and Britain. However, the nature of the barriers emphasized by scholars and political activists tended to differ across these two nations. Liberals in France could not be satisfied with a descriptive social science that merely identified the nature of the existing obstacles. What they required was a polemical device that denied the *ancien régime's* claim that human beings are innately evil and thus in need of social repression. What was much more attractive to them was Locke's claim that at birth the minds of individuals are 'blank sheets' and that human mental and spiritual development are functions of the social environment. This allowed them to locate the primary obstruction to social transformation not in natural barriers but in the nature of the monarchy and the church. Having done so, they could then argue that with appropriate political reforms a context would be created that would enable human beings to realize their potential for goodness and thus render the absolutist state redundant. This emphasis on human malleability contrasts markedly with the position of liberals in countries where the capitalist class had seized effective control of the state and culture. By the late eighteenth century, scholars in these latter nations were becoming more concerned with explaining the material world than with determining the nature of the political and socio-economic limits to human progress. They consequently embraced with much greater enthusiasm those aspects of Montesquieu's contribution that sought to identify the *natural* limits to further social progress. As the intellectual representatives of a class and gender that had already attained their primary political objectives and now wished to prevent the extension of these gains to other classes, women and races, British and Dutch liberals found the 'natural limits' element in Montesquieu's work decidedly more attractive than did their French counterparts.

While there was a clear difference of views across the Channel, one aspect of Montesquieu's critique that found enthusiasts in both England and France was the claim that the accumulation of wealth can lead a significant proportion of the population to give themselves over to luxury, and in so doing pose a threat to the community (Sekora 1977; Ignatieff 1983; Berry 1994). John Brown's *Estimate of the Manners and Principles of the Times*, initially published in 1757–1758, for example, drew on the jeremiads of the 1740s that argued that the English elite had become martially supine as a consequence of the 'irregular and exorbitant sexual desires awakened among the elite by leisure and luxury' (cited in Ignatieff 1983, p. 334; Crimmins 1986). Focusing on the respective behaviours that he believed had become the norm for men and women in England, Brown sought to determine if 'the present ruling manners and principles of this nation may tend to its continuance or destruction'. Citing Montesquieu in support of his position, Brown argued that the history and development of nations is a product of 'general causes', and that the general cause of England's decadence was the fact that the primary guiding principle determining the behaviour of its men was 'a vain, luxurious and selfish effeminacy'. His estimate of women was no more flattering, though he held that with women decadence manifested itself in an unacceptable and unnatural boldness (Brown 1757–1758, vol. 2, p. 51). What makes Brown's contribution relevant to economics is his insistence that it was the 'exorbitant wealth' made possible by the rise of commerce that had induced this role reversal between the sexes. By wealth he meant 'every kind of useful possession; or money, which is its sign' and commerce he understood to be 'the exchange of wealth, for mutual benefit'. Brown argued that the effect of commerce on the ruling manners of a society tends to vary depending on the stage to which commerce has evolved.

> If we view commerce in its first stages, we shall see, that it supplies mutual necessities, prevents mutual wants, extends mutual knowledge, eradicates mutual prejudice, and spreads mutual humanity. If we view it in its middle and more advanced period, we shall see, it provides conveniences, increaseth numbers, coins money, gives birth to arts and science, creates equal laws, diffuses general plenty and general happiness. If we view it in its third and highest stage, we shall see it changes its nature and effects. It brings in superfluity and vast wealth; begets avarice, gross luxury, or effeminate refinement among the higher ranks, together with general loss of principle (Brown 1757–1758, vol. 1, p. 93).

This transformation comes about because the expansion of markets makes it possible for landowners to accumulate vast wealth without having to make any direct effort. Not having had to labour or save to accumulate their wealth, these individuals lack any spirit of industry; hence accumulation on their part leads them to adopt habits of luxury and indulgence. While this trend is initially manifest in pleasures that are coarse and rude, as commerce increases the range of pleasures it can make available, there is a tendency for the luxuries that are taken up to become more refined. Given this expanded opportunity, men come to despise the coarser modes of pleasure and with this latter development 'gross luxury is banished and effeminacy takes its place' (Brown 1757–1758, vol. 1, p. 96). Why the decadence induced by commerce is manifest as boldness on the part of women is because the manners of women are invariably a product of the behaviour of men. In other words, women are 'such, as the men chuse to make them'. Where the ruling manners of men are characterized by courage and generosity, an honourable regard for women will prevail. In these circumstances 'modesty, gentleness, and amiable demeanour, form the character of the women'. However, when men become effeminate all honourable regard for women is extinguished and a natural consequence 'riseth of itself'. The women, finding themselves neglected by the men, invariably conclude they have been left with no choice but to become assertive in order to ensure their self preservation.

Brown's argument was not an attack on wealth accumulation per se, but a criticism of England's failure to contain the prevailing decadence stemming from wealth. His solution to this problem involved both the enactment of laws designed to curtail the drift into degeneracy and the establishment of a state schooling system the curriculum of which was to be designed to ensure that boys grow to become masculine men and women remain the docile creatures of Brown's fantasies. His argument implied that the degeneracy associated with luxury is a natural outcome of economic development and wealth accumulation that can be managed, but only if this degenerative trend is countered by targeted and strictly enforced social policies.

In contrast to Brown's position, the supposed link between wealth accumulation, luxury and unacceptable gender behaviour in France took a form that was decidedly different. Across the Channel, the 'general cause' of social decay and inappropriate male–female relations was more commonly held to be the fact that the king had caused the monarchy to become a parasitic class. A scholar who drove home this message was Antoine Thomas who, in 1771, published a conjectural history of women's status. Unlike the positive depiction of women in Smith's history, the picture of women in Thomas' contribution was decidedly ungenerous. In an extended discussion of women's innate capacities, he asserted that they are physically and morally weaker than men, have less capacity for genius and less ability to undertake sustained mental effort, and have an imagination that reflects reality rather than being creative. Given women's many natural 'weaknesses', he held that it was 'idle' to imagine that women could ever match the achievements of men except perhaps in the domestic sphere, this being an arena especially suited to women's nature.

In his 1771 *Essay on the Character, The Manners, and the Understanding of Women, in Different Ages* Thomas made clear his views. This work was a long time being published because of difficulties Thomas experienced with the censors. The goal of the volume was to identify 'the various sorts of merit which have distinguished the most celebrated women in the different periods of history' (Thomas 1781, pp. vii–viii). As with Smith, he began his analysis by considering the status of women in 'savage' societies, conjecturing that in these communities the lot of women is extremely miserable. This is because the males are indolent when not engaged in hunting or warfare and hence make little effort to enhance the lives of others. Uncaring of others, 'savage' men perceive women as nothing more than slaves existing merely to provide them with sex and labour. Having offered this brief assessment, Thomas moves rapidly to classical Greece where he claimed the two primary qualities deemed meritorious in women were courage and chastity. The first attribute he equated with the bravery demanded of the warrior. While women's lesser physical strength prevented them from engaging successfully in warfare, they gained merit by inspiring their men to be courageous. Chastity, by contrast, required abstinence; but this was not an attribute that human beings could be expected to embrace spontaneously. Consequently, the Greeks sought to protect this source of status for women by creating and maintaining what they deemed was an appropriate environment which involved confining them to the home – an institution that was held to be particularly resistant to corruption.

Thomas accepted the wisdom of the Greeks' approach to gender relations, arguing that where women are active in public life they are less honoured and enjoy less status than when they remain at home. The emphasis he placed on the positive effect of the home environment and the negative consequences of public life for women was continued in his subsequent analysis of women's status in Rome. He divided Roman history into three epochs, declaring that in each what was deemed meritorious was determined by the general spirit of the age. As Rome was militarily secure during its initial period of expansion, it was decency rather than courage that was the primary source of merit, and this the more so as throughout the period of the Republic the Romans remained a hardworking and austere people. For women, this was a time of great esteem and was so because this was a time when they:

> ... were shut up in their houses, where their rude and simple virtue was directed entirely by nature, and uninfluenced by what we call amusements; so unpolished as only to know how to be wives and mothers; chaste, without supposing it possible for them to be otherwise; tender, without having learned how to define the word; occupied in their duties, and ignorant that there were other pleasures, they passed their lives in retirement, to nourish their children, to raise for the republic a race of labourers and soldiers, and even employed part of the night in working for their husbands, with the distaff or the needle (Thomas 1781, pp. 29–30).

Thomas argued that this idyllic situation was undermined when the women of Rome began to take an active part in public life and consequently became more concerned with displaying their public talents than with maintaining the domestic virtues. He held that this negative development was the product of a thousand different influences, but of greatest significance was the fact that as Rome grew wealthy, it became possible for some women to cease engaging in productive activity. As a consequence of this development, women of wealth became disdainful of the traditional sources of merit that their mothers had deemed important and, as this perspective took hold, wealthy women began to seek merit by engaging in 'elegant employments'. In taking up these new activities, women left the home and developed their relations with men and, as they did so, decency was steadily abandoned with both men and women becoming debased, their lives degenerating into wanton sexual depravity, homosexuality, abortion etc.

> Then vice had no restraint: the rage for public spectacles brought the greatest and most vile licentiousness into fashion ... The debauched dreaded fecundity: they learnt to counteract nature, and brought to perfection the horrible art of procuring abortions. The passions were every day renewed, to be every day satisfied: the women, abandoning themselves to everything, and disgusted with every thing, multiplied in Rome the monsters of Asia, and had their slaves mutilated, to satisfy the new caprices of an imagination fatigued with pleasures (Thomas 1781, pp. 37–38).

Thomas' third Roman epoch began near the beginning of the third century.

The general spirit that characterized this period was a mixture of continence, courage and sanctity, the major influence creating this new spirit being the rise of Christianity with its respect for marriage and proscription on debased pleasures. The message in this part of his history is that while wealth accumulation can induce decadence, this consequence can be contained if communities establish and sustain highly moral social institutions. Having made this point, Thomas proceeded to trace the manner in which changes in the ways European women attained status took place over the next fifteen hundred years. Throughout his tale, the dangers associated with luxury remain a constant theme, becoming especially important when he turned to discuss contemporary France. He argued that while the French aristocracy remained a military class that provided protection and governance to the community, neither its women nor its men became debased. They became so only when they ceased to be productive and committed themselves to luxurious idleness. The blame for this last development Thomas placed directly on the monarchy, holding that the primary cause of the prevailing decadence amongst the French ruling class was the King's decision to confine his nobles to the Court in order to better control their political activities. By so doing, the monarch rendered the aristocracy a parasitic class that no longer drew status by participating in the governance of the provinces or the management of estates. Rather, in the Court, both sexes became convinced that the most effective way to gain status was to 'participate in society' and to show that they had the resources needed to fully live lives of luxury. As this process unfolded, leisured women came to believe merit was best attained by consuming pleasure in all its forms rather than by undertaking the virtuous roles of wife and mother. Initially, the great social gulf that separated the aristocracy from that part of the population that remained productive acted as a sanitary corridor protecting the wider society. But once the capacity to live a life of luxury became the primary source of status, the aristocracy allowed the social barriers that separated them from the merely rich to dissolve, and thus the degeneracy of the aristocracy began to permeate and threaten the whole of France.

Thomas' history is a demeaning tale that asserts that even with the attainment of significant economic resources women cannot hope to attain the status of men. But in recognizing his conservatism, it should be appreciated that in the context of the *ancien régime* he was not simply defending the status quo. His argument that the social policies adopted by the king were the 'general cause' of the prevailing degeneracy was an attack on the regency that invited women to gain status by contributing to be overthrow of the political order. Moreover, in assessing his contribution it should be noted that the ideal of home and loving husband that he suggested was on offer was applauded by most French liberal women writers of the period (There 1999). Finally, as far as the women of the bourgeoisie were concerned, his history offered the hope that, if appropriate moral institutions could be established, they would gain the status that accrues to affectionate wives and lovers and could do so while continuing to enjoy their wealth (Thomas 1781, pp. 214–216).

MEANWHILE, IN SCOTLAND

As demeaning of women as was Thomas' history, his contribution at least has the merit that it was an appeal for resistance against a decadent tyranny. In Scotland, by contrast, the argument that wealth accumulation can be a source of social decay and that women should heed this danger and remain within the home amounted to nothing less than unadulterated conservatism. Two Scots of note who promoted this understanding were John Millar and William Alexander, both of whom borrowed from Smith's linking of gender relations and stage theory. Millar took up Smith's approach to gender analysis in his 1771 *Observations Concerning the Distinction of Ranks in Society*. He was intimately aware of Smith's ideas because he had attended his lectures as a student in 1752–1753 and subsequently joined Smith as a faculty member at Glasgow. The lectures were an experience that Millar's biographer reports 'touched off a spark that burned for many a year' (Lehmann 1960, p. 114). In the *Ranks*, he used stage theory as a tool to explore the 'amazing diversity to be found in the laws of different countries, and even the same country at different periods' (Millar 1960, p. 175). Like Smith, he embraced a materialism that held that as change occurs in the means by which communities attain their means of subsistence, corresponding modifications tend to occur in their laws and customs.

In the section of the *Ranks* that dealt with the status of the sexes, Millar sought to explain the social 'condition of women in different ages'. In so doing, he gave explanatory emphasis to the mode of subsistence, wealth accumulation and biological differences, though he embellished his mentor's work by offering important insights regarding the foundations of matrilineality, jealousy and the role that sexual desire can play in shaping gender relations (Bowles 1984; Olson 1998). He argued that as societies evolve through the various socio-economic stages, women's status is enhanced both by the increased resources they are able to control and by the level of difficulty men experience when seeking to gain access to their sexual favours. In the barbarous age, women were held to have little status because they were poor hunters and warriors and property ownership was unknown, and because there were no social barriers to sexual promiscuity. The latter factor was considered important because the individual was held to have little regard for pleasures that can be gained with little effort, and hence savage women gained no status from being able to provide men with sexual pleasure. By contrast, with the onset of the pastoral age women's status began to improve. This was because they became more productive as the labour process grew more complex, and with this development their families became disinclined to allow men free access to the resources their daughter's labour could produce. This denial of free access to women's bodies increased women's status because by being chaste they could control access to a pleasure; and with access made more difficult, both the prize and the individual who controlled this prize became more valued.

> Their condition is naturally improved by every circumstance which tends to create more attention to the pleasure of sex, and to increase the value of those occupations that are suited to the female character; by the cultivation of the arts of life; by the advancement of opulence; and by the gradual refinement of taste and manners (Millar 1960, p. 203).

Progress to the stage of agriculture further improved women's status. Families became more fixed in abode and amassed more property, and as a consequence the distance between the ranks was further increased, with families becoming even more inclined to limit who could wed their daughters. The greater productivity of agriculture also increased the need to protect one's wealth against invaders, and as a consequence unending warfare was the norm – a tendency that, when melded with men's frustrated sexual lust, generated the system of chivalry in which women were placed on pedestals. In this environment, men came to accept that women's attentions must be 'won', in combat if necessary, and hence were surely an 'item' of great status. Finally, in the commercial age, productivity and wealth accumulation reaches a stage that makes possible 'very important changes in the state of society and particularly in relation to women' (Millar, 1960, p. 218). In this world, both sexes engage in commercial activities and consequently interrelate on a daily basis, and women are able to gain status as a consequence of both their wealth and their intellect. Millar applauded this development but observed that the enormous increase in wealth accumulation that commerce makes possible was a problem, as it enabled the emergence of an elite class of leisured women. Being leisured, these women invariably sought ways to amuse themselves.

> Exempted from labour, and placed in great affluence, they endeavour to improve their enjoyments, and become addicted to all those amusements and diversions which give an exercise to their minds, and relieve them from languor and weariness, the effects of idleness and dissipation (Millar 1960, p. 224).

To this point, Millar's use of stage theory to explain the relative status of the sexes is not markedly different from that adopted by Smith, even if the latter did not have Millar's preoccupation with sex.   However, having rhapsodised on the wonderful world enjoyed by women in commercial societies, Millar took a fundamental deviation.   Along with most other Scottish intellectuals, Smith had little time for the claim that wealth accumulation can lead through luxury to depravity and decadence.   But in writing the *Ranks,* Millar broke with this position and appears to have done so because he was motivated by a desire not merely to explain the history of gender relations but also to fashion the nature of these relations.   This led him to lay aside the typical Scottish cynicism regarding the supposed negative consequences of luxury and embrace instead the arguments of the 1840s jeremiads.

In this part of his contribution Millar began by reminding the reader that women were particularly suited to the management of the home.

> Loaded by nature with the first and most immediate concern in rearing and maintaining the children, she is endowed with such dispositions as fit her for the discharge of this important duty, and is at the same time particularly qualified for all such employments as require skill and dexterity more than strength which are so necessary in the interior management of the family (Millar 1960, p. 219).

He then proceeded to argue that while the progress women had thus far attained was to be applauded, further 'improvement' in their status was not possible for this would endanger women's capacity to fulfil their duties within the home.   This was because there are natural limits to progress that, if breached, can cost women everything their sex had won through the ages. This section of the *Ranks* Millar titled: 'The effects of great opulence, and the culture of the elegant arts, upon the relative condition of the sexes'.   He insisted that the factor that makes it necessary to halt all attempts to further advance women's status is the same as that which brought them to their present enviable position, that is wealth accumulation.   Like Thomas, he held that the problem lay in the fact that with affluence women can become slaves to pleasure not only of the mind but also of the body, and if this dangerous possibility is not contained women can all too easily lose both their status and their families.

Seeking to exploit both men's fear of women's sexuality and the fear of bourgeois women that they might lose their property, Millar echoed Thomas by citing the history of classical Rome.   In commercial Rome, women's pursuit of pleasure and their determination to advance their position beyond the ideal that had prevailed in the earlier period of the commercial stage was not brought under control.   As a consequence: 'The bad agreements between married persons, together with the common infidelity of the wife, had a natural tendency to alienate the affections of a father from his children, and led him, in many cases, not only to neglect their education, but even to deprive them of their paternal inheritance' (Millar 1960, p. 227). From these musings, Millar concluded that the wealth and opulence women enjoy in commercial societies would be lost should they insist on attempting to further advance their status.

> Thus we may observe, there are certain limits beyond which it is impossible to push the real improvements arising from wealth and opulence. In a simple age, the free intercourse of the sexes is attended with no bad consequences; but in opulent and luxurious nations, it gives rise to licentious and dissolute manners, inconsistent with good order, and with the general interest of society. The love of pleasure, when carried to excess, is apt to weaken and destroy those passions which it endeavours to gratify, and to pervert those appetites which nature has bestowed upon mankind for the most beneficial purposes. The natural tendency, therefore, of great luxury and dissipation is to diminish the rank and dignity of the women, by preventing all refinement in the connection with the other sex, and rendering them only subservient to the purposes of animal enjoyment (Millar 1960, p. 225).

The notion that women had gained much from social evolution would put these gains at risk by demanding further progress, and that hence they should be content with being good wives and mothers, was also the theme of William Alexander's 1782 *The History of Women, From the Earliest Antiquity to the Present Time.* As did Millar, Alexander sought to trace women's 'progress from slavery to freedom, and to mark the various causes which have more or less accelerated or retarded that progress' (Alexander 1782, p. 153). He supported Millar's view that women's status rose as societies evolved through the basic socio-economic stages: 'Man in his rude and uncultivated state, forms his connection with women from a regard to the beauty of her person only, when he becomes civilised, he regards the qualities of her mind also' (Alexander 1782, p. 43). Thus Alexander argued that commercial women had become 'free' as a consequence of social evolution, but in making this point he was quick to add that their status does not, and cannot be expected to, equal that of men. This is because men are 'endowed by God' with superior attributes while women have qualities that at best can place 'men and women *nearly* on a level with each other' (Alexander 1782, p. 502).

The qualities Alexander ascribes to women are beauty, softness and persuasive force, attributes which few men 'have the power of resisting'. Echoing Millar, he claims the correct and natural role of women to be the care of their children, a role that is endangered:

> in proportion as women advance more towards that perfection, or rather

imperfection of politeness; where folly, fashion and the love of pleasure so much engross the affections as in most cases greatly to weaken, and in some totally to obliterate, a passion hardly less natural than that of self-preservation (Alexander 1782, p. 137).

Having warned of these dangers, Alexander decries the situation in Europe where nursemaids are employed, observing that 'there is scarcely to be found in Europe, a woman of family and fashion who will take the trouble of nursing her own child' (Alexander 1782, p. 145). He agrees that limited association between the sexes in properly functioning bourgeois societies is desirable because 'a man secluded from the company of women is not only rough and uncultivated, but a dangerous animal to society' (Alexander 1782, p. 492). However, he warns that too much female company is detrimental to men for 'it enervates the mind, and gives it such a turn for trifling, levity and dissipation, as renders it altogether unfit for the application which is necessary in order to become eminent in any of the sciences' (Alexander 1782, p. 497). Not surprisingly, the lessons Alexander drew from his history are similar to those reached by Millar. Women's progress through the four socio-economic ages is to be applauded, but it must be accepted the onward march of progress has reached an end point. In short, women can attain high status within the confines of bourgeois society but not beyond, and they need to accept that happiness and status are best attained by being good wives and mothers. Thus both Millar and Alexander agree that the end point to the rise of women had been reached and a refusal to accept this fact is bound to cause women to become debased and rendered 'subservient to the purposes of animal enjoyment' (Millar 1960, p. 225).

ACCUMULATION OR UNRESTRAINED FECUNDITY?

Millar's and Alexander's contributions were examples of eighteenth-century gender conservatism without the call to resist tyranny that at least partially redeems the work of Thomas. On gender, the two Scots read as men who are satisfied with their world and fear any trend that would carry social progress beyond the status quo. As Alexander's work seems largely derivative, the following discussion focuses on Millar, though is equally applicable to both men. Medick and Leppert-Fogen (1974) have observed that Millar's endorsement of free market relations alongside the invectives he launched against monopoly, corruption and inequality suggest the mind of a 'petty bourgeois' motivated by a vision that sought to 'stop time' at the moment of petty commodity production. That Millar wished to bring history to an end has been accepted by Ignatieff (1983). Ignatieff doubts, however, that Millar was a spokesman for the petty artisan, noting that at the time he published the

Ranks, Millar was arguing that the property qualification for the franchise had already 'descended too low to the dregs of the people'. More convincingly, he argues that Millar expressed the perspective of the broad middle class and gentry of the 1770s with its commitment to the prevailing distribution of power in Britain. What undermined Millar's opposition to further social evolution, Ignatieff suggests, was in fact his rejection of the notion that human wants are insatiable and his incapacity to accept that market relations are a bond sufficient to hold society together as a unity. He was a fatalist convinced that economic development would eventually induce satiation and lack of incentive and that commodification of social relations would eventually weaken social bonds and in so doing engender despair and decay.

Irrespective of the validity of the foregoing positions, it remains the point that there is a consensus that Millar was an 'end of history' theoretician. The relevance of this point has been lost on Olson (1998), who has queried why it is that feminists such as Wollstonecraft failed to embrace Millar's work. He suggests that the answer may lie in the fact that Millar embraced an historical method while Wollstonecraft built her arguments around the claim that humans are everywhere the same, differing only according to the environment. But in offering this explanation, Olson misses the point that Wollstonecraft was a deeply committed progressive who fully embraced the hopes of the Enlightenment (Trouille 1991; Todd 2000). As such she could not possibly welcome an 'end of history' argument that asserted that, if women were to seek to further their position beyond that already achieved, they were doomed to be rendered little more than animals. Olson likewise queries why it was that Millar's broader contribution to social analysis disappeared from political discourse from the late 1790s. He suggests the mixture of radical liberalism and conservatism that made up his thought meant that he had no natural audience during the period of reaction that followed the French Revolution – a situation compounded by the tendency to discount philosophical history that became the norm in this period. These arguments have merit, but they miss the point that the reaction generated by the enthusiasm with which the French lower classes embraced the Revolution and democracy rendered unacceptable the whole notion that societies can become redundant and be replaced by more highly evolved forms of community. From the 1790s this was a view of history that was largely left abandoned until given new life by Marx as the materialist conception of history. Millar's work was also unacceptable in an age of bourgeois reaction for he argued that the accumulation process could prove a cancer that would eventually bring capitalism to an end; and he denied that market relations were a cement capable of unifying societies. Together, these elements of Millar's argument rendered his 'end of history' argument totally unsatisfactory to post-1790 Europe. What the conservatives and reactionaries of the period needed was a story that applauded wealth accumulation while making it clear that, for reasons for which property owners could not possibly be blamed, progress beyond the status quo was impossible. In 1798 Malthus sought to cater for this need. He did so by offering an argument that challenged the broad hopes of the Enlightenment, in a manner that applauded wealth accumulation and showed 'scientifically' that it was naive of women to hope that one day they might cease to be social subordinates.

Malthus' well known depiction of humanity as a species perpetually overbreeding because of a barely resistible animal desire to copulate, however miserable the consequences, was a deadly thrust against the Enlightenment. As Binion (1999, p. 566) argues, his essay on population 'with its scientific law against any happy, harmonious republic of virtue, probably did more to dash the high hopes of social progress raised by the Enlightenment than did any other modern work of the pen'. His argument that 'more mouths than bread' is an inevitable consequence of the 'passion between the sexes', and this particularly so amongst the lower classes because of their low moral standards, carried the clear and explicit message that those people whose hopes were located at the apex of progressivism were excessively idealistic if not inane. To ensure that this aspect of his message was not missed, Malthus named as the targets of his work Condorcet and Godwin, the two eighteenth-century scholars whose hopes were indeed situated at the very pinnacle of the progressive dream.

Plasmeijer (1999) has suggested that the fact that Malthus targeted Godwin as well as Condorcet suggests that he had the skills required of a marketing manager charged with turning a scientific volume of dubious intellectual value into a best-seller. Godwin was a brilliant target for an opportunistic marketer because at the time the first edition of Malthus' *Essay* appeared, a major scandal involving Godwin was the 'talk of the town'. In January 1798, Godwin shocked the public when he published his *Memoirs of the Author of the Vindication of the Rights of Woman*. This highly emotional volume traced the life of Godwin's recently deceased wife Mary Wollstonecraft and detailed her attempt to live the life of an independent woman, her defence of the French Revolution, her extra-marital love affairs and love-child, and her attempted suicides. When first published in 1792, the *Vindication* had been very well reviewed, but once the poor became a force in the French Revolution and both aristocrat and bourgeois perceived that progress was creating a common enemy, both Wollstonecraft and Godwin became targets for both class and gender conservatives. The publication of the *Memoirs* made them particularly easy marks. A constant theme in these attacks was the denunciation of their joint assertion that marriage is a fraud and their claim that women should enjoy all the freedoms available to men. The advocating of these claims was held to be indicative of the subversive and licentious behaviour that typified the progressives who had encouraged the masses on to the streets of Paris. As Plasmeijer notes:

> The conservatives took advantage of the situation and started throwing dirt. The fuss was pretty nasty. The *Anti-Jacobin* made noise about almost every immorality Wollstonecraft was supposed to represent, from unorthodox sexual behaviour to the non-payment of creditors. The noise lasted years and obscenities were not eschewed. As late as 1801 a 'poet' thought that Godwin had not suffered enough.

> William hath penn'd a wagon-load of stuff
> and Mary's life at last he needs must write,
> Thinking her whoredoms were not known enough,
> Till fairly printed off in black and white.
> With wondrous glee and pride, this simple wight
> Her brothel feats of wantonness sets down;
> Being her spouse, he tells, with huge delight,
> How oft she cuckolded the silly clown,
> And lent. O lovely piece!, herself to half the town.

> The title of the poem, the 'Vision of liberty', indicates clearly what the fuss was about. By destroying Godwin's and Wollstonecraft's intellectual and moral reputation conservative England tried to discredit the ideals of the French revolution (Plasmeijer 1999, p. 3).

As Plasmeijer notes, this was an effort into which Malthus threw himself with enthusiasm. His contribution was distinguished by the way in which he advanced himself as the dispassionate scholar who, by the use of science, could 'prove'that the progressive's dreams of human equality were at odds with the 'natural laws of society'. But while Plasmeijer makes an imporant point in highlighting the fact that Malthus was playing the part of opportunist marketeer in attacking Godwin, if this point is to be fully appreciated, we should not miss the point that Nicholas Condorcet was the second target identified in the *Essay* of 1798. Why this point should not be missed is because of course 1798 was the year Sophie Condorcet published her attack on economic inequality. Hence, by attacking both Godwin and Nicholas, Malthus would have increased the impact of his message; for his story became that these progressives posed a threat not only to the family but to wealth as well. In unleashing his tract Malthus took care to play the part of the English gentleman who, of course, would not publicly attack a lady. Hence he did not name Mary or Sophie, but rather pointed to their husbands. But in 1798 the point that these men had married women who promoted ideas alien to conservatives would not have been missed. That the reader's attention would have been drawn to the wives of the two men he ensured by pointing out that Godwin had asserted that marriage is a fraud.

Having captured the public's attention, Malthus drove home his message. Re-reading stage theory as a constant fight against hunger, he argued that the only hope for humanity lay in finding ways to inculcate the lower classes with bourgeois virtues. This was to be achieved by the introduction of universal suffrage, state-run education for the poor, the establishment of a free nationwide labour market, and the generation of a taste for affluence and hence a desire to delay marriage in order to first accumulate wealth. What was not needed was any restraint on the right to accumulate wealth or a weakening of men's right to predominance within the institution of marriage. Both of these activities were moral instruments humanity had established to protect itself from the population explosion that would be inevitable should the licentious behaviour of the kind engaged in by Wollstonecraft, or the redistribution of income advocated by Sophie Condorcet, become social norms.

Malthus made explicit his belief that the preservation of a form of marriage in which women are the subordinate partner was an absolute necessity. Having shown to his satisfaction that the existing distribution of property was part of the natural order, he proceeded in the *Essay* to discuss 'commerce between the sexes'. He began by noting that one important moral means by which societies had traditionally contained their numbers was by making it a disgrace for a parent to bring more children into the world than can be provided for adequately. The need to ensure that this did not happen also explained why communities 'naturally' held it to be worse for a woman to have a child out of wedlock than it was for a man. This was because it 'could not be expected that women should have resources sufficient to support their own children' Malthus thought this double standard was unjust but inevitable.

> That a woman should at present be almost driven from society for an offence which men commit nearly with impunity, seems to be undoubtedly a breach of natural justice. But the origin of the custom, as the most obvious and effectual method of preventing the frequent recurrence of a serious inconvenience to a community, appears to be natural, though not perhaps perfectly justifiable (Malthus, 1798, p. 10).

Marriage being established as an indispensable institution, 'inequality of conditions must necessarily follow'. As women are less capable than men of producing their needs, they are 'naturally' more dependent on their husbands than are men on their wives, and hence the wife has little choice but to accept subordination. Again, all this was held to be in accordance with the laws of nature against which it is folly to struggle and vain to hope that things might be different.

Malthus had not wished to deny humanity the hope that their lives might improve, but rather wanted to dash what he saw as the wild fantasies of Condorcet, Godwin and Wollstonecraft. For conservatives, however, the argument was all too neat, for it was an instrument that could very effectively be shaped to deny the very notion of progressive social evolution while concomitantly justifying accumulation and the selfishness of the affluent. Given that this was the case, it was an argument that was soon put to uses that went far beyond those Malthus intended. In the process, political economy was transformed from a progressive to a dismal science whose proponents saw their field as the study of scarcity. With this development, few were inspired few to lift their eyes beyond the minimalist promises offered by those whose notion of the limits of progress remained situated at the base of the apex of progressivism. Not until the notion of socialism inspired new dreams of what the future might entail did women again begin to hope that the destiny of womankind might not yet have been realized.

REFERENCES

Alexander, William [1782] (1995), *The History of Women, from the Earliest Antiquity to the Present Time,* (with a new Introduction by Jane Rendall).

Berry, Christopher J. (1994), *The Idea of Luxury. A Conceptual and Historical Investigation,* Cambridge: Cambridge University Press.

Binion, Rudolph (1999), 'More Men than Corn: Malthus versus the Enlightenment, 1798', *Eighteenth-Century Studies,* **32**, (4), 564–569.

Blum, Carol (1999), 'Forum: Demographic Thought and Reproductive Realities: From Montesquieu to Malthus', *Eighteenth-Century Studies,* **32**,(4), 535–536.

Bowles, John (1984), 'John Millar, the Four Stages Theory and Women's Position in Society', *History of Political Economy,* **16**, (4), 619–639.

Brown, John (1758), *An Estimate of the Manners and Principles of the Time,* London.

Crimmins, James E. (1986), 'The Study of True Politics: John Brown on Manners and Liberty', *Studies on Voltaire and the Eighteenth Century,* **241**, 65–86.

Godwin, W. 1798 (1987), *Memoirs of the Author of the Rights of Woman,* Hants: Penguin Books.

Hecht, Jacqueline (1999), 'From Be Fruitful and Multiply to Family Planning: The Enlightenment Transition', *Eighteenth-Century Studies,* **32**, (4), 536–551.

Ignatieff, Michael (1983), 'John Millar and Individualism' in Istvan Hont and Michael Ignatieff (eds), *Wealth and Virtue: The Shaping of Political Economy in the Scottish Enlightenment,* Cambridge: Cambridge University Press, pp. 317–343.

Lehmann, William C. (1960), *John Millar of Glasgow 1735–1801,* Cambridge: Cambridge University Press.

Malthus, Thomas (1798), *An Essay on the Principle of Population,* <http://www.ac.wwu.edu/~stephan/malthus/malthus.0.html>

Medick and Leppert-Fogen (1974), 'Frühe Sozialwissenschaft als Ideologie des Kleinen Bürgertums: John Millar of Glasgow, 1735–1801' in H.U. Wehler (ed.), *Sozialgeschichte Heute: Festschrift für Hans Rosenberg,* Gottingen, pp. 22–48.

Millar, John [1791] (1960), 'The Origins of the Distinction of Ranks', in William C. Lehmann, *John Millar of Glasgow 1735–1801,* Cambridge: Cambridge University Press.

Olson, Richard (1998), 'Sex and Status in Scottish Enlightenment Social Science: John Millar and the Sociology of Gender Roles', *History of the Human Sciences,* **11**, (1), 73–100.

Plasmeijer, Henk W. (1999), 'The Talk of the Town 1798', *History of Economics List,* <ww.eh.net?HE/hes_list/Editorials/plasmeijer.php>

Pollard, Sidney (1971), *The Idea of Progress,* Middlesex, England: Penguin Books.

Sekora, John (1977), *Luxury: The Concept in Western Thought, Eden to Smollett,* Baltimore: Johns Hopkins University Press.

There, Christine (1999), 'Women and Birth Control in Eighteenth-Century France', *Eighteenth-Century Studies,* **32**, (4), 552–564.

Thomas, M. (1771, 1773), *Essay on the Character, Manners, and Genius of Women in Different Ages* (translated by M. Russell) London.

Todd, Janet (2000), *Mary Wollstonecraft. A Revolutionary Life,* London: Weidenfeld and Nicolson.

Trouille, Mary (1991), 'A Bold New Vision of Woman: Stael and Wollstonecraft Respond to Roussseau', *Studies on Voltaire and the Eighteenth Century,* **292**, 293–336.

7. Condorcet and Equality of the Sexes: One of Many Fronts for a Great Fighter for Liberty of the Eighteenth Century

Peter Groenewegen

Among the causes of the progress of the human mind that are of the utmost importance to the general happiness, we must number the complete annihilation of the prejudices that have brought about an inequality of rights between the sexes, an inequality fatal even to the party in whose favour it works. It is vain for us to look for a justification of this principle in any differences of physical organization, intellect or moral sensibility between men and women. This inequality has its origin solely in an abuse of strength, and all the later sophistical attempts that have been made to excuse it are vain (Condorcet [1795] 1955, p. 193).

Liberty was the most sacred aspect of Condorcet's many social objectives reflected in the various political campaigns he mounted during the greater part of his eighteenth-century lifetime. In this, he was a faithful son of the Enlightenment as well as a true friend of Voltaire, Turgot and D'Alembert, to name but three of the many famous men he encountered, and befriended, during his lifetime of half a century.

Although during much of his early life Condorcet had limited himself largely to his mathematical studies, he wrote Turgot in 1773 that already at the age of seventeen he had been turning his mind to matters of justice and virtue, more specifically to whether 'self interest prescribed for mankind to be just and virtuous' (Arago 1891, p. x; Condorcet to Turgot, 13 December 1773, in Condorcet 1841, vol. 1, p. 220). His first preserved writings on such matters were devoted to the defence of economic freedoms. In these, he strongly argued for free trade, with special reference to the grain trade (in his *Letter by a Husbandman of Picardy*, 1775, addressed to Necker who had defended a regulated grain trade against the trade liberalization measures which Turgot was introducing during his term as Finance Minister). In this *Letter*, Condorcet claimed that every husbandman loved liberty and peace, that the maintenance of liberty was invariably just *and* useful, and even that liberty of thought ought to be fully admitted in debates of this nature (Condorcet, [1775a] 1847, pp. 488, 492, 497). His attack on the corvée during the same year (Condorcet, 1775b, 1847) was written in part to uphold the principle of the freedom of labour, and had likewise been designed to assist the reform initiatives of his friend Turgot (cf. Condorcet, [1783], 1997, pp. 61–65). A dictionary article on 'Monopoly and Monopolists' described this practice as the very opposite of liberty and hence a great evil for the general public, particularly when it was exercised in the traffic of staples, such as grain and salt. The salt monopoly was in fact a state-owned one, farmed out to private interests for fiscal reasons (the gabelle), the harsh punishments for the infringements of which Condorcet likewise severely condemned around this time (Condorcet, n.d., 1847, pp. 459-470, 473-474) in a plea for criminal justice which drew on the liberal sentiments on such matters of Beccaria, Montesquieu and Voltaire (ibid. p. 487). Another striking manifestation of Condorcet's wide-ranging quest for the cause of liberty and justice is his 1781 plea for the abolition of negro slavery, depicted as a blot on freedom in the newly independent United States, and in the context of which Condorcet likewise pleaded for full freedom for another, long oppressed race, the Jews, with respect to both the ownership of property and the practice of their religion (Condorcet, 1781, pp. 503-543, esp. p. 530).

In the years following the French Revolution of 1789, Condorcet involved himself heavily in the new representative institutions it spawned, including both the National Assembly and the National Convention. Over those years and through his involvement, he laboured assiduously for a wide range of crucial freedoms in the economic, the political and the social sphere. Much of this fight was conducted through the writing of numerous pamphlets and articles and the drafting of edicts to secure the separate manifestations of liberty. These demanded freedom of religion and worship, freedom of trade and industry, freedom of emigration and of domestic population movement, freedom of speech and of the printed word; these freedoms were to be preserved through a free constitution with equality of all citizens, before the law, and to be maintained through a system of just taxation based on egalitarian principles and proclaimed as the necessary price to be paid for freedom. Among his many writings in support of freedom and equality in these four hectic years, Condorcet in July 1790 also published an item dealing with the 'Admission of Women to the Freedom of the City' and, in 1792, a plea for the right to public education for all. Condorcet's last work, a quotation from which is reproduced at the start of the chapter, reiterated the principle of equality for the sexes in all its generality as an essential component of human progress towards perfectibility. In a very concise and clear manner it also showed his understanding of the root cause of women's subordinate position and his thoughts on those who attempted to justify their subordination. In short women's subordinate status has its origin solely in an abuse of strength.

The remainder of this chapter concentrates on Condorcet's specific pronouncements on the need for equality of the sexes and hence on granting full freedom to the female half of the nation. It does so in three separate sections. The first presents further background to Condorcet's life and work. The second examines in detail his views on equality of the sexes as expressed in the three products from his pen during the 1790s already mentioned. A third section offers some conclusions, including some discussion of the impact this part of his work had on subsequent eighteenth-century and early nineteenth-century writers.

CONDORCET'S LIFE

Condorcet was born on 17 September 1843, at the village of Ribemont in Picardy. His father, M. Caritat, was a cavalry officer, and the younger brother of a noted archbishop of Vienna, M. d'Yse de Saléon.[1] His father died when he was four years old, so he was largely brought up by his mother, Mlle de Gaudry, who was a *dévôt*. Not surprisingly, she dedicated him to the virgin and to the 'blanc'; she also apparently dressed him in women's clothes for the first eight years of his life. Given the circumstances of his birth, he was brought up among the nobility and clerics (Condillac was one of his uncles), leading a sheltered life which prevented any participation in physical sports and entailed a private education for him until he was eleven years old (in 1753). He then attended a Jesuit school for three years, completing this part of his education as second in his class. In 1756 he entered the Collège de Navarre in Paris for mathematical studies, at which he worked assiduously, specializing in the still newish integral calculus. His brilliance at mathematics brought him to the attention of Clairaut (the mathematician and astronomer) and the friendship of d'Alembert, who by then had already stepped aside from his original joint editorship of the *Encyclopédie* with Diderot. As mentioned previously, by the age of seventeen (that is, during the early 1760s) he later claimed to have also been involved with issues of justice and virtue, but mathematics remained his main occupation at least until the late 1760s. His *Essai sur le calcul integral*, published in 1765, gained him election to the Academy of Sciences in 1769, a body whose permanent secretary he became as successor to Grandjean de Fouchy in 1773 (until 1788). The French Académie did not elect him to membership until 1781.

Condorcet probably met Turgot through d'Alembert, or at the salons of Mme de Geoffrin or Mlle de l'Espinasse, some time during the late 1760s when Turgot was already the intendant of Limoges. Their collaborative economic work in any case did not begin until the 1770s, after Turgot's elevation to Minister of Finance. Correspondence between the two commenced in April 1770. D'Alembert definitely introduced Condorcet to Voltaire by taking him to visit that philosopher in 1770 at his sojourn of exile in Ferney. Their preserved correspondence also dates from that year, more precisely, 10 October 1770. Condorcet's other distinguished correspondents whose letters have been published as part of his *Works* include Mlle de l'Espinasse, Frederick the Great, King Stanislaus of Poland, Benjamin Franklin and Joseph Priestley.

After Turgot had been made Finance Minister in August 1774, he appointed his friend Condorcet to the position of Inspector of Money (*hôtel des monnoies*). During Turgot's earlier period as Minister of the Navy, Condorcet had bombarded him with suggestions ranging from the useful (a proper edition of Euler's *Théorie complète de la construction et de manoeuvre des vaissaux* as well as the introduction of some naval instruments by Magellan) to the almost ridiculous (the imposition of a charge on farmers of church lands to replace the corvée). Other schemes for abolishing the corvée were contained, as mentioned already, in some of his economic writings of the 1770s, namely the encyclopaedia article on 'Monopoly and Monopolists', his *Letter to Necker on regulation from a husbandman of Picardy,* and his *Reflections on Criminal Justice*. Condorcet reviewed the whole of Turgot's administrative career, with special reference to his two years as minister until 1776, in the *Life of Turgot* he published in 1786, five years after Turgot's death.

Other writings of the 1780s have already been mentioned, such as his *Reflections on Slavery in the United States*. His *Essai sur l'Aplication de la Probabilité des decisions rendues à la pluralité des voix* (published in 1785) attempted to solve the jury problem, more than 150 years later influencing modern social choice theory as pioneered by Arrow, Guilbaud and Black (see Moulin and Young 1987, vol. 1, pp. 566–567). To its preparation he brought to bear his mathematical skills and his work on probability theory. At the end of the 1780s came his analysis of the influence of the American Revolution on Europe, written itself on the eve of the French Revolution, and dedicated to Lafayette, who had fought for freedom in the new world as a representative of the old world (*ancien régime*) of France. Wide-ranging as these reflections were, they did not give any discussion to the issue of women's freedom, largely because such freedom, and the vote for women, had not been conceded by the founding fathers of the American Constitution.

In 1786, Condorcet married Sophie de Grouchy, a woman twenty-three years younger than himself and reputed to have been at the time one of the most beautiful women of Paris. Given de Grouchy's feminism, this event may explain his greater interest in women's issues during the 1790s. She died in 1822, her literary claim to fame being the notes she appended to her translation of Smith's *Theory of Moral Sentiments* into French, which was published in 1798 as the third translation. Most importantly, she assisted her husband greatly in editing her father's collected works (see Brookes 1980; De Lagrave 1989, pp. 434–442).

From 1790 to 1794, Condorcet produced an enormous amount of material on administrative and contemporary political and economic issues in articles and speeches partly written while a member of the National Convention and the National Assembly. Among these are his recommendations for the establishment of a national system of education (Condorcet, 1791–1792) and his contributions to republican views including his vote for exile rather then for the execution of the king. During the terror of 1793–1794, he was tried and sentenced to death in absentia in October 1793 for crimes against the republic. Being forewarned of this fate, he evaded captivity and death for many months by hiding in the house of a widow, Mme Vernet, who ran a simple boarding house. It was then that he wrote his famous *Sketch for a Historical Project of the Progress of the Human Mind*, unaided by any research material. In April 1794, Condorcet left his hiding place out of his growing fears about the danger in which his presence at her house was placing Mme Vernet. He was captured on 7 April, his disguise a as carpenter becoming suspect when he ordered a twelve-egg omelette in an inn at Camart. He was taken to prison in Paris. He died not long after his arrival there, either from hunger and exhaustion or, more likely, from suicide by taking poison which he had kept hidden on his person for that purpose.

During the 1840s, Condorcet's collected works were published by his son-in-law, A. Condorcet O'Connor, and M.F. Arago, a successor to Condorcet in the position of 'permanent' secretary of the Academy of Science. Much of the actual editing work was apparently done by his daughter, Eliza. These have never been re-edited, interest in Cordorcet's work having waned considerably, perhaps partly because of his 'turgid and rhetorical style' and the highly abstract nature of his thought (Schapiro 1930, p. 177). The historical picture of human progress is an exception, as is his *Life of Turgot,* his voting scheme and, as shown in the next section, his early plea for political rights and equality for women, produced as part of his immense literary output during the French revolution.

CONDORCET'S VIEWS ON EQALITY OF THE SEXES

Condorcet's writings on women's rights and the role of women date from the French revolutionary period of the 1790s. The first is a relatively short article dealing with the admission of women to the rights of the city, dated 3 July 1790 and included in volume X of the *Works* (Condorcet O'Connor and Arago 1847, pp. 121-130). The second is his plea of 1792 for public instruction for all, and the third is his last and most famous work, the *Sketch of a Historical Picture of the Progress of the Human Mind*, written during 1794 and posthumously published in 1795. These form the basis for his reputation as an enthusiastic exponent of women's rights, a firm supporter of equality of husband and wife before the law, and a staunch believer in the 'equal intellectual capacity of the sexes except in the highest forms of science and philosophy' (Schapiro 1930, p. 177, cf. Morley 1886, pp. 249–250).

In 1790, Condorcet raised the issue that both philosophers and legislators (hence implicitly including himself) had treated violations of natural rights solely from the perspective of the rights of man. They had thereby excluded, or deprived of those rights, at least half of the human species, that is, in contemporary France, the rights of twelve million women. He then asked rhetorically that if this neglect 'was not to be described as an act of tyranny, it was necessary to demonstrate either that the rights of women were not absolutely identical to those of men, or that they were incapable of exercising them' (Condorcet 1790, pp. 121–122).

Condorcet himself by then had no doubts whatsoever as to what the answer to this question was. Women, in having the same qualities as men with respect to a capacity for acquiring moral notions and for acting on them, must necessarily have the same rights as men. He put this principle even more strongly; either there are no human rights, or they are the same for everyone, irrespective of religion, race or gender (Condorcet 1790, p. 122). This was the crux of the matter.

In a series of varied arguments, Condorcet then demonstrated the truth of this simple proposition. He noted the quality of famous empresses and queens (Elizabeth of England, Maria Theresa of Austria-Hungary, the Catherines of Russia) and found them to be in no way inferior to kings like Louis XIV or XV, or, for that matter, Henry IV. Likewise he argued that when comparing the potential of men and women for high office in government, men were not assured of a preference based on their experience, since they had little reason to be proud of their record in this regard.

The same applied to what was known about the qualities of women as against those of men. Women, he claimed, clearly had the upper hand in the homely virtues and those associated with kindness; they were at least men's equals in understanding, in wisdom and in the ability to reason; while their smaller appreciation as yet of matters of justice and the law came from their artificially induced inferior education in such matters at the behest of men. Nor, in Condorcet's view, could the then *current de jure* powers of married status for women relative to those for men be used as an argument to deprive women of their political rights.

Likewise, Condorcet argued, the arts of public office, such as the ability to conduct public debate and oratory, were less discernable in women at the present time because they had long been prevented from practising them. Their well known skills in private displays of such attributes showed that they would quickly learn to adapt them to public use if permitted to exercise them in this manner. Nor would they then be protected by the customary politeness of men in society which currently prevailed in public differences of opinion among members of the opposite sex. It also could not really be argued that if all women were given the right to actively participate in politics, all of them would immediately abandon their domestic responsibilities, their child rearing or even their needlework. Only a small minority would do so, exactly as was the current situation with respect to male politicians. Given the facts, Condorcet concluded, and because women had acted as royal regents in France and were now able to function as merchants of fashions in Paris (as a consequence of the 1776 abolition of the guilds by Turgot), surely they now also deserved the full political rights of citizens of a city unless it could be clearly and unambiguously demonstrated that women were inferior to men in general. The last was an impossibility according to Condorcet. Women deserved full political rights as free citizens of the republic.

In 1792, Condorcet drafted an Edict on National Education *(Sur l'instruction publique)* for deliberation by the National Convention. It provided for universal, compulsory education, with full liberty for teachers, whose technical competence was to be guaranteed by the State. It was to be combined with a system of free scholarships as a form of educational stepping stone to secure greater equality for the population. The last embodied the most generous proposal for making public education more accessible ever to have been put forward: it was a characteristic project for a staunch believer in equality such as Condorcet.

Of particular relevance to this chapter, Condorcet's proposal for public education was to apply to women as well as to men. His decree specifically argued for the admission of women to the study of the natural sciences, particularly innovative when it was still the prevailing belief that women would lose their modesty if they were permitted to study subjects like biology. The arguments given by Condorcet for the extension of compulsory education to women were many. Women had to be able to teach their children satisfactorily in the crucial early years of their existence. If women stayed uneducated, the curse of ignorance, and hence of inequality, would be introduced into the family, and sons would regard their mothers with contempt. Moreover, men would more generally retain, and enhance, their intellectual pursuits if they were able to share them with women. Most importantly, women had a natural right to education, and the joint education of the sexes would greatly enhance public morality and foster a greater democratic spirit of equality by squashing this important manifestation of inequality in society. It would also generate useful competition between the sexes (Condorcet 1791–1792, pp. 222–228). Surprisingly, Condorcet did not introduce economic arguments in favour of universal eduction; perhaps his strong belief in the social value of the family prevented him from giving serious consideration to the possibility of women's valuable contribution to the national labour force (Condorcet 1791, pp. 215–222). This omission persisted in much of the ensuing literature for virtually the next 75 years, as Evelyn Forget has reminded me.

Condorcet finally examined the position of women more broadly in a historical setting, when he sketched the progress of the human mind in its various stages. The situation of women, however, was only raised in three of these,[2] that is, in the primitive, first stage of society, in its third stages of agriculture, and the, briefly, in the tenth or final stage which looked forward to the future.

In the first stage, when men were still united in tribes, women were immediately depicted as naturally placed in a subsidiary position, a phenomenon which Condorcet explained as deriving from their inability to participate in war or in long hunting expeditions. More positively, he illustrated that their role was to gather and collect edible fruits, nuts and plants and occasionally to grow edible plants around the huts of the camp, all qualities which collectively condemned them 'to a sort of slavery'. Smith's contribution is pure conjectural history, without any evidence, an omission partly excusable because Condorcet wrote the piece while in hiding and without any access to research materials. There were also important silences in this discussion of the first stage. Why women were immediately subordinated to menial tasks in hunting society, and why their roles in childbearing and child rearing were not mentioned in this context, or explained, is not indicated by him. The origin of the divisions of society, on which Condorcet's discussion of the first stage ends, is a division of male society only. It only discussed hunter–warriors and rulers–educators–priests in this context. Women's roles were not mentioned in Condorcet's final segment on the first stage of human progress.

The second, pastoral stage, perhaps a bow to biblical, patriarchal historical tradition, largely ignored women altogether, even when the family was briefly, but generically, mentioned. There is, however, a brief reference to the fact that women's slavery 'lost some of its rigour and [that] the wives of the rich were exempted from arduous work' (Condorcet [1795], 1955, p. 20).

The third or agricultural stage further enhanced the situation of women. A more sedentary form of life:

established a greater equality between the sexes. Women were no longer considered merely as useful objects, slaves in all but their proximity to their master. Men came to see them more as companions, and finally learnt how much they could contribute towards masculine happiness. However, even in the countries where they were most respected and where polygamy was forbidden, reason and justice were not pursued to the extent of a complete reciprocity of duties, nor was equality admitted either in the right of separation or in the punishments for infidelity.

The history of this form of prejudice and its influence on the fate of the human race must figure in the picture that I have undertaken; and nothing will serve better to show the extent to such happiness depends upon the progress of reason (Condorcet 1795, pp. 27–28).

Condorcet indicated at this stage that the history of this form of prejudice, presumably that exercised against women, would play a major role in his picture and overview. For reasons which are unexplained, he never in fact did so. Thus the fourth stage, devoted to early Greek development, fails to mention women. The same applies to the fifth stage, which deals with the progress of the sciences from what Condorcet described as their division to their decline, hence falling within his history in the stages from Greece and Rome up to the early Middle Ages. The sixth stage, examining the decadence of knowledge in East and West up to the Crusades, likewise excludes women as an explicitly mentioned group from the discussion, as does the seventh stage (covering the early progress of science up to the invention of printing), the eighth stage (from printing to the time when philosophy and the sciences shook off the yoke of religious authority), and even the ninth stage (which took Condorcet's account of human progress from the time of Descartes to the foundation of the French Republic in 1792). The last mentioned stage dwelled freely on the rights of man, without in any way broaching their relevance for the other half of the species, to the existence of which with respect to such rights Condorcet had explicitly drawn attention four years earlier in the context of political rights. Only when discussing demographic statistics is the division of society as to sex, as well as age and occupation, briefly admitted (Condorcet [1795], 1955, p. 161).

Women briefly re-entered the discussion in the remarks on the tenth and final stage, devoted by Condorcet to the future progress of the human mind. This was designed by him to illuminate three important facets of progress: 'the abolition of inequality between nations, the progress of equality within each nation, and the true protection of mankind' (Condorcet [1795], 1955, p. 175). In discussing the third of these issues, Condorcet raised the need to eliminate that fatal inequality between the sexes solely attributable to the abuse by men of their superior, brute strength. If this inequality were abolished, Condorcet argued, the happiness of family life would be greatly increased, thereby favouring the progress of education and the practice of the domestic virtues, as he had argued two years before in his plea for universal education. The destruction of sexual inequality, or of the 'strongest and most irrepressible of all natural inclinations' would open the door to the universal diffusion of mildness and purity in manners by free choice rather than by hypocricy, shame, or 'religious terror' (Condorcet [1795], 1955, pp. 193–194). Perhaps Condorcet considered the precise nature of these blessings from abolishing the oppression of women so self-evident and obvious that he did not discuss them any further. Sexual equality is, however, clearly a necessary attribute if society is to progress to the perfectibility of its individual members.

It seems doubtful to read these final remarks, as Morley (1886, p. 250 n.1) appears to have done, as a requirement of 'free love' for the perfectibility of mankind. They were little more than a striking affirmation by a leading second generation enlightenment philosopher that any attempt to create a new, more perfect form of society required equality as a leading principle. As an essential part of such equality and perfectibility, Condorcet specifically listed the voluntary abolition of sexual inequality or, as he also had put it, the complete elimination of the traditional suppression of women by men, including that of wives by their husbands.

CONCLUSIONS

Condorcet's views on progress gained a considerable notoriety in the decades following his death. His emphasis on liberty also gained him followers, though not always ones who acknowledged the importance or influence of his work on these subjects.[3] However, his special pleas for political rights for women, and for their admission to universal education, as well as the emphasis he gave to sexual equality as an essential feature of human perfectibility, were less frequently recognized and commented on. Brailsford (1913, p. 198) argued, somewhat exaggeratedly, that Condorcet 'deserves in the gratitude of women a place at least as great as John Stuart Mill' as an advocate of women's rights, especially in the context of women's education. This totally ignores the seeming impact factor of their respective works.

Much of Condorcet's notoriety in the English-speaking world undoubtedly derived from his treatment by Malthus in his *Essay on Population* from the first edition onwards. Condorcet's work on progress is there held up to ridicule for ignoring the inevitable population consequences of his perfectibility model, partly by eliminating such consequences from what

Malthus described as unduly optimistic expectations about future productivity, growth in general and in food production in particular. Malthus devoted no less than two chapters of the first *Essay* to this subject, material which was reproduced without much change in the subsequent editions (Malthus [1798], 1986, Chapters 8, 9). James Mill ([1808], 1966, p. 123) likewise condemned Condorcet's views on progress as a 'golden dream' and hence of no practical consequence. As such, it passed into the literature of future commentries irrespective of any other features of its contents. Its hopes on equality of the sexes as an essential part of future progress likewise passed into oblivion, unremembered, until they independently gained acceptability in the reform agenda of a later century.

In France, Condorcet fared little better. The doyen of French political economy in the first decades of the nineteenth century, J.B. Say, is a good example. In his *Treatise of Political Economy*, he only mentioned Condorcet's name in passing in the introduction, as a contributor to economics in the 1760s together with Raynall and Condillac. Say clearly implied in his introductory remarks that these economic writers were far lesser lights in economics than the Physiocrats and Turgot during the development of the subject in the eighteenth century (Say, 1821, p. xxxv). Needless to say, Condorcet's advanced treatment of the need for equality for women in a just and progressive society gets no mention at all in Say's work.

The only major French thinker of the first half of the nineteenth century who recognized Condorcet's importance on these matters appears to have been Auguste Comte, the sociologist. Comte greatly admired Condorcet's work on progress as that of the true discoverer of historical method. Condorcet's application of that method, however, needed to be criticized, because it was deficient in several ways. First of all, his historical stages were badly sub-divided. For Comte, Condorcet was too much a product of the eighteenth century to have regarded his own era critically, and he tended to view it in fact as superior, if not sublime. Most importantly to Comte, Condorcet's futuristic view of progress was unscientific; the future cannot be predicted. However, in this context, Comte said nothing on Condorcet's system of particular relevance to this chapter – that is, on Condorcet's perception of the role of women (see Allengry 1899, pp. 35–38).

However, more recently it has been argued that Comte was not only himself very sympathetic to the rights of women issue, but that he admired Condorcet's strong support for women's political rights during the French revolution, which he described as an almost unique position on this subject among the *philosophes* (Pickering 1993, p. 145).[4] In this context it is surprising that Comte did not impart his respect for Condorcet to his friend J.S. Mill, who was like minded on women's rights, at least to the extent that he published a strong plea for their liberation, in his essay 'On the Subjection of Women', and in his earlier article, 'On the Enfranchisement of Women', neither of which recognized the pioneering effort of Condorcet in this cause. As shown at the start of the chapter, Mill's follower and friend John Morley in his writing did recognize both Condorcet's intellectual status and his strong support for women's rights.   Morley also attempted to explain why Condorcet's writings had more or less fallen into oblivion by the second half of the nineteenth century, a situation which up to now seems not to have altered greatly.   That Condorcet's work is of interest, and that his views on the rights of women were important contributions for the time when they were written, has hopefully been demonstrated in this chapter.   The opinions of such a lover of liberty and fighter for freedom are an important part of the legacy of true liberal thought of the eighteenth century.

REFERENCES

Allengry, Franck ([1899], 1984), *Essai Historique et Critique sur la Sociologie chez Auguste Comte*, Paris: Slatkine Reprints.

Arago, M.F. (1891), 'Vie de Condorcet', in A. Condorcet O'Connor and M.F. Arago (eds), *Oeuvres de Condorcet*, Paris: Firmin Didot Frères, vol. I, pp. ii–clxii.

Badinter, Elizabeth and Badinter, Robert (1988), *Condorcet, un intellectuel en politique*, Paris: Fayard.

Brailsford, H.N. (1913), *Shelley, Godwin and Their Circle*, London: Williams and Norgate.

Brookes, Barbara (1980), 'The Feminism of Condorcet and Sophie de Grouchy', *Studies on Voltaire and the Eighteenth Century*, **189**, 297–361.

Condorcet, Jean-Antoine Nicolas Caritat, Marquis de (n.d. 1847), 'Monopole et Monopoleur', in E. Daire (ed.), *Mélanges d'écomomie politique*, Paris: Guillaumin, vol. 1, pp. 459–470.

Condorcet, Jean-Antoine Nicolar Caritat, Marquis de ([1775]a, 1847), 'Lettre d'un Laboureur de Picardie à M. Necker, Auteur Prohibitif à Paris', in E. Daire (ed.), *Mélanges d'économie politique*, Paris: Guillaumin, vol. 1, pp. 483–500.

Condorcet, Jean-Antoine Nicolas Caritat, Marquis de ([1775b], 1846), 'Réflexions sur la Jurisprudence criminelle', in E. Daire (ed.), *Mélanges d'économie politique*, Paris: Guillaumin, vol. 1, pp. 471–482.

Condorcet, Jean-Antoine Nicolas Caritat, Marquis de ([1781], 1847), 'Réflexions sur l'esclavage des nègres', in E. Daire (ed.), *Mélanges d'économie politique*, Paris: Guillaumin, vol. 1, pp. 503–543.

Condorcet, Jean-Antoine Nicolas Caritat, Marquis de ([1783], 1997) *Vie de Monsiur Turgot*, Paris: Association pour la diffusion de l'économie politique.

Condorcet, Jean-Antoine Nicolas Caritat, Marquis de ([1787–1789], 1847) 'De l'influence de la Révolution de l'Amérique sur Europe', in E. Daire (ed.), *Mélanges d'économie politique*, Paris: Guillaumin, vol. 1, pp. 544–565.

Condorcet, Jean-Antoine Nicolas Caritat, Marquis de ([1790], 1847), 'Sur l'Admission des Femmes au Droit de Cité', in A. Condorcet O'Connor and K.F. Arago (eds), *Oeuvres de Condorcet*, Paris: Firmin Didot Frères, vol. 10, pp. 121–130.

Condorcet, Jean-Antoine Nicolas Caritat, Marquis de (1791–1792), 'Sur l'instruction publique', in Condorcet O'Connor and M.F. Arago, *Oeuvres de Condorcet*, Paris: Firmin Didot Frères, vol. 7, pp. 167–573.

Condorcet, Jean-Antoine Nicolas Caritat, Marquis de ([1795], 1955), in June Barraclough (ed.), *Sketch for the Historical Picture of the Progress of the Human Mind*, Wesport, Conn: Greenwood Press

De Lagrave, Jean-Paul (1989), *Condorcet, Mathématicien, Économiste, Philosophe, Homme Politique*, Paris: Minerve.

Destutt de Tracey, A.L.C. (1926), *De L'Amour*, with an introduction by Gilbert Chinard, Paris: Société d'édition les Belles-Lettres

Malthus, T.R. (1798, 1986), 'An Essay on the Principle of Population', in E.A. Wrigley and David Souden (eds), *The Works of Thomas Robert Malthus*, vol. 1 London: William Pickering.

Mill, James (1808, 1966) 'Commerce Defended', in Donald Winch (ed.), *The Selected Economic Writings of James Mill*, Edinburgh: Oliver and Boyd, pp. 85–159.

Morley, John (1886), 'Condorcet', in *Critical Miscellanies*, London: Macmillan, vol. 2, pp. 163–255.

Moulin, H. and H.P. Young (1987), 'Condorcet, Marie Jean Antoine Nicolas Caritat, Marquis de (1743–1794)', in John Eatwell, Peter Newman and Murray Milgate (eds), *The New Palgrave, A Dictionary of Economics,* vol. 1, London: Macmillan, pp. 566–567.

Pickering, Mary (1993), *Auguste Comte – An Intellectual Biography,* vol. 1, New York: Cambridge University Press.

Robinet, J.F.E. (1968), *Condercet, Sa Vie, Son Oeuvre,* New York: Slatkine reprints.

Say, J.B. (1821), *A Treatise on Political Economy,* New York: Augustus M. Kelley, 1971.

Schapiro, J. Salwyn (1930), 'Condorcet, Marie Jean Antoine Nicholas Caritat, Marquis de', *Encyclopaedia of the Social Sciences,* New York: Macmillan, vol. IV, pp. 176–177.

NOTES

1. There are now several detailed studies of Condorcet's life. The biographical detail in this section is drawn largely from material contained in Arago (1841) and Morley (1886). In addition, see Robinet (1968), Baninter and Badinter (1988) and De Lagrave (1988), to which Evelyn Forget kindly drew my attention.
2. Occasionally, individual women are mentioned in passing. Examples are Mary the mother of the Messiah, and the woman who allegedly claimed a small sum of money from the prophet Mohammed (Condorcet, [1795], 1955, pp. 71, 86).
3. Thus Brailsford (1913, p. 92) suggests that Condorcet's views were a major source in the preparation of the second edition of Godwin's *Political Justice*, though his name is never mentioned in that work.
4. The almost unique position of Condorcet on this matter among the eighteenth-century *philosophes* in some respects makes his work on the subject even more important, and its comparative neglect since the mid-nineteenth century even more difficult to understand. Evelyn Forget, in this context, mentions *De l'amour* by Destutt de Travey (1754–1836), not actually published until 1926 because of its 'advanced' nature.

8. Cultivating Sympathy: Sophie Condorcet's Letters on Sympathy

Evelyn L. Forget

In 1798, Sophie de Grouchy, the marquise de Condorcet[1] published a translation of the seventh edition of Adam Smith's *Theory of Moral Sentiments* (1792) along with a series of eight 'letters' on the subject of sympathy. These letters are, in fact, substantial essays that allow us to discern how she read Smith. Intellectual historians have a tendency to privilege an author's intent, and to read the *Theory of Moral Sentiments* in order to determine what Smith actually meant, and how meaning was constructed in the context of a particular intellectual environment. As long ago as 1978, literary theorists such as Wolfgang Iser suggested that a reader's response is at least as interesting a question as an author's intent (Iser 1978). And Sophie de Grouchy is no ordinary reader. Her translation of, and commentary on, Smith's work allow us to see how a theory constructed in the intellectual context of the Scottish Enlightenment would be received by a different intellectual community. While de Grouchy shared much of the background that informed Smith's work, she could not write a commentary on sympathy during the Terror without taking into account recent French political experience and debate. And, I argue, her reading was not merely idiosyncratic, but rather representative of a particular group of intellectuals seized with the problem of adapting Enlightenment theory to the political reality of the Republic.

This essay reconstructs Sophie de Grouchy's reading of Smith's *Theory of Moral Sentiments*. Her letters offer a reading of Smith at variance with that emerging today from a vantage point two centuries after their publication. She read Smith through the lens of Rousseau and Scottish moral philosophy through the prism of French political experience. But it is precisely because she brings together two traditions that her essays provide insight into a particular time and place.

First, we examine the significance and reception of de Grouchy's translation and essays, and consider the value of these letters as historical documents that codify a particular response to Smith's *Theory of Moral Sentiments*. Section Three defines sympathy and establishes the foundation of de Grouchy's essays in a pleasure–pain calculus. Section Four follows her analysis into areas of morality, justice, and human rights, where she links the Rights of Man rhetoric, which cost her husband his life, to the concept of sympathy. Section Five establishes the links she draws between Rousseauvian educational theories and sympathy, and Section Six considers the role that institutional reform ought to play in nurturing sympathy.

De Grouchy's letters helped to shape a particular theoretical response to a society challenged by political upheaval. She argues that educators and social reformers, who take responsibility for nurturing social behaviour through the active cultivation of sympathy, are essential to a functioning civil society.

THE RECEPTION OF THE TRANSLATION AND LETTERS

De Grouchy had begun work on the translation in 1793, during the Terror which took the lives of her husband and many of her friends and family. Smith's work was already well-known in France. Within a year of its publication, the first English-language edition of *Theory of Moral Sentiments* (1759) was favourably reviewed in the *Journal Encyclopédique* (Raphael and Macfie 1976, p. 29). Moreover, de Grouchy's was not the first French translation. Marc-Antoine Eidous translated the first edition under the title *Métaphysique de l'âme* (1764). D.D. Raphael and A.L. Macfie note its limited success, citing contemporary evidence attributing its limitations to the translation rather than the original work (Raphael and Macfie 1976, p. 30). A second translation, this time of the third edition, by the abbé Blavet, appeared in 1774–1775. But the sixth edition, published shortly before Smith's death, was substantially revised (Raphael and Macfie 1976, p. 15f), and de Grouchy's translation of the seventh edition[2] is the first to contain these changes.

The importance of de Grouchy's translation, however, rests in a series of her own essays on the subject of sympathy that she appended to the translation in the form of 'letters' addressed to her brother-in-law, Pierre-Jean-Georges Cabanis, the eminent physiologist and ideologue.[3] The significance of these essays has occasioned some dispute. De Grouchy claimed that she was merely making explicit what was implicit or incomplete in Smith:

> Smith limited himself to noting the existence [of sympathy] and articulating its principal effects: I have regretted that he did not dare to push further; to penetrate to its first cause; to show finally how [sympathy] must belong to all beings who are capable of feeling sensation and of reflecting. You will see how I have had the temerity to supply these omissions (de Grouchy 1798, p. 357).[4]

Cabanis accepted de Grouchy's argument, and noted that 'Smith had made a very learned study which was nevertheless incomplete for want of his having linked it to physical laws, and which Mme Condorcet, by means of simple rational considerations, knew how to remove from the vagueness in which it was left by the *Theory of Moral Sentiments'* (Cabanis [1802], 1867, pp. 283–284). He went on to extend many of the ideas raised by de Grouchy.   Henri Baudrillart, however, who brought out the third edition of the de Grouchy translation in 1860, claims: 'The philosophical theory upon which these *Letters* on sympathy rest does not differ significantly from that of Adam Smith ... The points which the author of these letters disputes with Smith concern secondary matters.   She is, above all, an ingenious commentator' (Smith 1860, p. 434). While the letters and the translation went through many French editions, they apparently received no attention in Britain in the nineteenth century.

More recently, some historians have offered evaluations of the letters as commentary on Adam Smith, without a detailed consideration of their content. Lynn McDonald, for example, has claimed that de Grouchy disapproved of inequality of wealth more vehemently than had Smith (McDonald 1994, pp. 131–132; 1998b, pp. 125–127).   Deidre Dawson has argued that while Smith articulated a theory of 'sentiment' showing that it forms the basis of all human interactions, de Grouchy saw sympathy as the basis of practical action to reform society (Dawson 1991).   Others have seen the letters as an articulation of the social theory of the *encyclopédistes*.   Takaho Ando, for example, writes that de Grouchy's letters 'reinforced and gave a revolutionary character to the social thought of the lumières' (1994, p. 7).

Sophie de Grouchy, marquise de Condorcet, wife of the mathematician and revolutionary philosopher Nicolas Condorcet, advocate for the extension of political rights to all races and to women, intellectual intimate and translator of Tom Paine, was an active and involved observer of the political process.   She grappled with the issues raised in the *Theory of Moral Sentiments* at a particularly brutal point in French history.   She struggled with the question of what it is that holds societies together, that allows the continuation of civil society, at a time when a reasonable person might wonder whether such a thing were possible.   A supporter of revolutionary ideals, she saw a movement of unlimited potential spin out of control and claim the lives of many of its most promising advocates.   In the midst of this chaos, she articulated a coherent view of the role of sympathy in contemporary society – a view compiled of insights from many sources, including a particular reading of Adam Smith.

De Grouchy's attraction to the concept of sympathy is easily understood. Even today, writers are drawn to the idea that there is some kind of social glue that allows societies to cohere, especially in moments of social chaos.[5]   But is her commentary intellectually valuable?   Her letters take issue with Smith on two major points.   First, she argues that Smith does not clearly articulate the link between sensation, reflection and sympathy, and attempts to clarify the issue in a manner consistent with Smith's theory. In this, she has limited success. She never, for example, articulates a physiological mechanism by means of which physical sensation is linked to abstract ideas, a task Cabanis undertakes himself (Cabanis [1802], 1867, vol. 2, pp. 285–287). But she does locate the genesis of sympathy in a pleasure and pain calculus. Second, she attempts to extend Smith's investigation by asking how education and social institutions can be reconstructed so that sympathy is nurtured in society.

But her criticisms of Smith are somewhat ironic. In the two centuries since she wrote, we have considerable material on the evolution and implications of Smith's thought to which she did not have access. That material has allowed commentators such as Christopher Lawrence (1979) to sketch out Smith's debt to contemporary Scottish physiology, and others, such as Andrew Skinner (1995), to detail the educational implications of Smith's *Theory of Moral Sentiments*. As an interpretation of Smith's intention and achievement, de Grouchy's letters are of limited value. The letters, however, should be read as the attempt of an involved participant to address a particular set of social problems in a society stripped of all of the institutions, including the Church and the monarchy, that had previously given it order. And sympathy, whether or not de Grouchy understood the concept in the same way as did Smith, and whether or not she recognized the differences between her work and his, is, in her mind, the indispensable cement that holds a society together. What form did it take in Paris during the Terror? The philosophy of sympathy allows de Grouchy to construct a coherent set of social policies that afford key roles to educators and administrators. The first are responsible for nurturing social behaviour in individuals, and the second are responsible for creating and reforming institutions in accord with the principles of justice and human rights that she derives from a consideration of sympathy. Sections IV through VI reconstruct this analysis.

If that is all we could learn from these essays, that would be reason enough to read them, because their author was an interesting person in a dramatic time and place. But her essays and her translation do something more. They codify a particular response to a world challenged by political tumult, and serve as an often-unacknowledged source for subsequent writers. This is a difficult case to make because, except for Cabanis's acknowledgement of her work, there is little direct citation of her essays. Nevertheless, we know they went through three editions by 1860. More to the point, we can find indirect citations that demonstrate some of the difficulty involved in tracing their impact. For example, the physiologist and ideologue Pierre Roussel, according to an *Éloge* published by J.L. Alibert, was induced to insert 'in the *Actes de la Société médicale*, a curious note on sympathies' (Alibert [1806] 1820, p. xiv):

He had been especially determined to address this matter, by the publication of eight letters on the same subject, at the end of an excellent translation of Smith, by a woman of his intimate society, who, at that time, seemed to hold aloft at once the scepter of beauty and the torch of philosophy (Alibert [1806] 1820, p. xiv).

Alibert adds a footnote in which he claims that 'Smith himself,' were he still alive, would translate these letters because they were 'full of novel insights' (Alibert [1806] 1820, p. xiv). Alibert does not name her, and Roussel does not cite her.

We also have the witness of contemporaries. For example, François André Isambert, the author of a short biography of de Grouchy, acknowledges her influence on the social theory of the ideologues (Isambert 1855, p. 475). Tracing the impact of de Grouchy's essays is far beyond the scope of this paper. But we revisit the influence of these essays in the final section of this paper, and suggest two avenues where their traces might be found.

SENSATION, REFLECTION, AND SYMPATHY

De Grouchy attempts to articulate clearly the relation between physical sensation, intellectual reflection, and sympathy. She begins 'Letter 1' by defining sympathy as 'our disposition to feel in manner similar to that of another' (de Grouchy 1798, p. 357), and grounds her analysis in physical pleasure and pain. She claims that before we can understand the sympathy we feel for the moral suffering of another, we must first understand our sympathy for the physical pain of another.

We begin by examining our response to physical harm to ourselves. Every physical injury, she claims, creates a sensation composed of two parts. First, it causes local pain in the wounded area of the body (p. 357). And it produces, as well, a separate painful impression in all our organs. This second sensation always accompanies the same physical wound, but may also exist independently of it (p. 357). We know these are two distinct sensations because, at the moment the physical cause ceases, we feel both pleasure that the local pain has stopped, and a general sensation of malaise that may continue long after the local sensation has ended. This general sensation may be much more difficult to bear because it affects the brain, which is central to life, and which renders human beings both intelligent and capable of processing sensation (p. 358). This general sensation is renewed each time we remember the physical harm we have suffered (p. 358). Moreover, it can be reawakened by seeing the physical signs of pain exhibited by others who have suffered similar physical wounds (p. 359).

The general sensation, dependent upon the development of our mental capacity and our past experience of pain, in effect allows us to develop an abstract idea of pain that we feel not only when we remember our own experiences, but also when we see the evidence that others feel pain (p. 360). De Grouchy sees the evidence for this in the reaction of a baby who must develop the intelligence necessary to recognize the signs of pain before he sympathizes with another. Once that development has taken place, the infant will react to another's distress by crying. The reaction depends upon how aware the infant is of the signs of pain, how sensitive he is, how imaginative, and the extent to which his memory is developed through experience (p. 360). Similarly, seeing an old man in tears might suggest that he is very sensitive to the pain felt by others. In fact, she claims, his reaction is not the result of greater physical sensitivity (which is often reduced with age), but rather the result of the deterioration of his mental faculties. This extreme reaction of the aged is why they must be protected from particularly distressing sights (p. 363). Both the very young and the very old allow us to recognize the existence of a general or abstract sensation independent of the local physical sensitivity.

In a very imaginative individual, not only might the general sensation, or abstract idea, of pain be reproduced in one who witnesses another suffer, but the local pain itself might be felt, as in the case of the woman who, upon reading a medical treatise, develops all the symptoms of a pulmonary disorder (pp. 361–362). Similarly, a particularly painful wound may make such an impression on an individual that seeing another suffer a similar fate renews in that individual the local sensation he once suffered (p. 361).

Sympathy, in other words, is not an automatic response independent of reflection. Physicians, for example, who are sometimes the very cause of some intense local pain for others often seem, de Grouchy claims, not to react to the pain they have caused. This is not the result of insensitivity or lack of imagination, but of the knowledge that causing pain might ward off a yet more unpleasant outcome for a patient (pp. 363–364). The faculty of reflection, that is, can offset the more or less automatic physical reaction that occurs when we witness the suffering of another.

When we experience a physical pleasure, our reaction is very like that occasioned by physical pain. We feel a pleasant sensation locally, and a more general sensation of well-being that allows us to develop the abstract idea of physical pleasure (p. 368). In principle, this leads to a similar ability to sympathize with the physical pleasure felt by others. But physical pleasures are often more private than physical pain, giving less evidence through physical signs. For example, a grimace may signal pain, but a smile is less striking in the case of physical pleasure. Moreover, in the case of pleasure felt by another, our capacity to share their joy is often offset by a certain envy on our part (p. 368).

The composite nature of the feelings associated with pleasure and pain, the physical sensation and the general idea of happiness or pain that allows us to sympathize with others, is apparent in de Grouchy's analysis of how we sympathize with different people. In a state of society, she claims that we are all dependent upon one another and this dependence begins in infancy with the physical dependence of a child on its mother (p. 376). We all see those upon whom we are dependent as the source of our own pleasure and pain (p. 376). This very close tie means that we react to the pains and pleasures felt by those upon whom we depend almost as if they were happening to us. The reaction requires very little reflection, and is almost as strong as our own physical sensations (p. 377). Civilization extends this natural sympathy to two classes of people: those whom we believe can protect us, and those whose similar tastes and habits create a pleasant society. That is, we are tied to others by considerations of utility and pleasure (p. 378). This second is the source of all friendship and love, particularly when it is joined by a sort of 'enthusiasm'[6] that can create passion ('letter 3', pp. 386–407). As we extend the circle of our intimates and move further and further away from ourselves and engage in a greater number of anonymous interactions, the physical sensations upon which sympathy is based grow weaker, and the role of intellect and reflection grows stronger.

De Grouchy's argument has its counterpart in the taxonomy that Philippe Fontaine has drawn between 'empathetic identification',[7] which may be 'partial' or 'full', and 'sympathetic identification' (1997). He defines partial empathetic identification as an imaginative exchange of circumstances with another. Full empathetic identification refers to an exchange of circumstances and persons with another. That is, not only putting yourself in another's shoes, but putting yourself into another's shoes and imagining how you would feel if your character and experiences were identical to the other's. And sympathetic identification refers to what economists often call 'interdependent utility functions' – the idea that one person's well-being is affected by that of another. De Grouchy uses 'sympathy' ambiguously by this taxonomy, usually referring to what Fontaine labels 'empathy'. Her discussion of the physiological aspect of sympathy among intimates parallels 'full empathetic identification' and implies that one's well-being is dependent on that of another.

De Grouchy's contention that sympathy is rooted in both physiology and rationality implies that while human beings are naturally endowed with the capacity for sympathy, nature alone is insufficient to ensure its existence in society: 'The sentiment of humanity is a sort of seed deposited deep in the hearts of human beings by nature; the faculty of reflection nurtures it and helps it blossom' (p. 371).

And if individual sympathy were 'more cultivated' it may 'make sensitive to the wounds and needs of all humanity, that crowd of people who have become almost unaware of all that is not immediately tied to their existence and happiness' (p. 386). This cultivation of sympathy forms the subject of Section Five below.

De Grouchy extends the analysis of physical pleasure and pain to intellectual or moral pleasures and pains:

> We sympathize with physical pains and pleasures in proportion to the knowledge that we have, to our own experience, to their severity and affects; similarly we sympathize in general with moral pains and pleasures to the extent that we are susceptible to similar effects: I say in general, because there are undoubtedly hearts sensitive enough to be touched by wounds felt by others that they would never feel in the same circumstances, that is to say, wounds which imagination alone might appreciate and, as in the case of physical wounds one has never experienced, sympathy is excited by the vague idea of pain (de Grouchy 1798, p. 407).

In general de Grouchy argues (contrary to Smith) that we are more easily moved by physical harm that befalls another than by moral or intellectual harm (p. 409). Smith cites as evidence for his position the fact that plays about corporal pain rarely move us, while tragedies about moral events are more striking. De Grouchy argues that it is simply more difficult to stage physical events well, and so individuals who have never had a similar experience cannot imagine it and ridicule the result, while others who have had similar experiences avoid these events because the memories invoked are so distressing (pp. 409–410).[8]

One particular event, however, deserves special notice because of its political echoes. Smith finds events such as the dethroning of a king particularly moving, an outcome for which de Grouchy finds little evidence. Smith claimed that ordinary people sympathize with kings who are dethroned because the idea of their grandeur somehow elevates our ordinary sentiments and causes us to conspire in their happiness. De Grouchy, a committed republican, demurs:

> It seems to me that this affection is little known in the British Empire, that it is absent in the rest of Europe, and that it is at least very clear that it is absolutely opposed to the sentiment of natural equality that causes us to regard with jealousy, or at least severity, everything that is above us (p. 408).

This 'sentiment of natural equality' reappears throughout de Grouchy's letters, and leads to a discussion of morality, justice, and human rights.

MORALITY, JUSTICE, AND HUMAN RIGHTS

'It seems to me,' de Grouchy claims, 'that the preachers of virtue (except Rousseau) have not often enough traced the origins of moral ideas' (p. 432). The need to do good is an irresistible motivation for human beings 'governed by wise laws and raised without prejudice' (p. 433). This, she claims, is a simple extension of the analysis of sympathy we have undertaken. We feel pleasure when we aid another, especially if this act is preceded by reflection so that it is intentional (p. 433). This pleasure in doing good creates in us a satisfaction, and memory recalls and prolongs the physical sensation caused by our deed (p. 434). This sentiment becomes general and abstract, and is felt anew when we remember the good action without necessarily recalling the details of the particular circumstances afflicting another (p. 435). These acts become habitual, and tied to our idea of ourselves (p. 435). Just as in the case of all sympathy, the pleasure we feel in doing good is independent of the pleasure that the recipient of our goodwill feels. It persists in us even without a detailed memory of, or actual attention to, the details of another's experience (p. 435). Our satisfaction in doing good is heightened, as in the case of all sympathy, by our experience and our imagination (p. 438).

Similarly, we feel an abstract sentiment of pain when another suffers, and that feeling is particularly unpleasant when we are the cause of another's suffering (p. 436). The fear of remorse is sufficient to prevent most people from intentionally causing harm to others (p. 438). Indeed, the satisfaction created by recalling good actions and the remorse of remembering evil are two effective motives that influence all human action. These sentiments are universal and are the foundation of all human morality (p. 438).

The sentiment of satisfaction or remorse attached to our action is necessarily modified by reflection, and this leads us to the idea of moral good and evil which is 'the eternal and first rule that judges human beings before the laws, and which so few laws have consecrated and developed, and so many others have violated' (p. 440). We choose not necessarily the action that does the most good but the one that which causes us the most satisfaction (p. 441). Virtue, then, is defined as 'actions which give pleasure to others and are approved by our reason' (p. 441), while moral evil is 'action harmful to others and of which our reason disapproves' (p. 442). Reflection allows, for example, the creation of a small amount of harm to others in order to prevent a larger calamity, because the remorse we feel is overpowered by our feeling of satisfaction (p. 442). Evaluating our actions upon this abstract idea of moral good and evil becomes habitual (p. 443).

De Grouchy argues that ideas of justice and injustice are born of the abstract ideas of moral good and evil (p. 453). Justice must be based on the concept of 'rights', that is to say, 'of a preference commanded by reason itself in favor of an individual, such that even when his interest appears to us weaker than that of another in whatever particular circumstance, he must nevertheless be preferred' (p. 453). For example, an individual who, in a state of nature, troubles himself to cultivate a field has the right to the fruits of his harvest even though his harvest may exceed the need he has for it and even when the physical needs of another may be greater. De Grouchy claims this preference is based on his labour and not on his need (pp. 453–454). His right is based on the social requirement for a general law, based on reason and applicable to all, which relieves us of the need to examine motives and consequences in each particular case (p. 454). It is also based on sentiment, in the sense that the violation of a general law creates an injustice more harmful than the effects of a simple act of greed, and therefore must inspire in us greater repugnance (p. 454).

De Grouchy claims that the stingy farmer who chooses not to share his bounty commits a smaller wrong than a powerful neighbor who would mandate benevolence; the first lacks humanity, but the second violates a general law that reason dictates and that, in the general case, serves their common interests (p. 455). The good that might occasionally result from the violation of general laws is less than the advantages of their certainty (p. 455). If, in the case of absolute and extreme need, the needy engage in theft, morality must be tolerant. But excusing such a theft never means that the individual whose property was stolen has any less right to his property (p. 455).

A right like that of property is a positive right in the sense that it is a preference based on reason – the right to enjoy something. A right like liberty is a negative right in the sense that it only exists in the supposition that another has an interest in attacking one's liberty. Equality is like liberty (p. 456). In the case of moral good and evil, sentiment must submit to reason, which directs it to the most pressing end. In the case of justice and injustice, reason directs us to general laws, and to preferences based on general and reasoned motives. De Grouchy defines these reasoned preferences for one individual over another as 'rights' and argues that such a definition undermines the notion of the 'right of kings' (p. 457). The ideas of rights and justice raise the idea of the obligations we have towards one another. In general, 'one is obliged to do voluntarily all that another may, without infringing upon our rights, demand of us independently of our will' (p. 460).

De Grouchy argues that human beings are motivated to behave in accordance with general laws founded upon rights because reason tells us that the violation of such laws causes greater harm than their universal application (p. 457). Behaving in accord with reason creates an immediate pleasure of fulfilling an obligation, which is independent of the opinions of others. It raises us in our own eyes (pp. 462–463). But we also have a less lofty personal interest that reinforces this behaviour; everyone has rights, and the violation of anyone's rights threatens our own (p. 459).

In summary, physical sensation creates a composite idea composed of a local sensation of pain and a general feeling of unhappiness that invades all our organs. This general feeling is the source of our natural sympathy for the physical pain of others. Natural sympathy can be generalized to moral afflictions. Reflection is the source of our moral ideas, and our moral ideas are the foundation for the concepts of justice and injustice that necessarily lead to a consideration of rights. Moreover, and most importantly, de Grouchy argues that all other people who are subject to the same physical sensations and have the capacity to reason must necessarily have the same moral ideas. Moral ideas are not arbitrary but can rather be the subject of a certain science. Agreement with moral truths differs from agreement with mathematical or physical truths not because one is less arbitrary than the other, but because moral ideas depend on both reason and sentiment (p. 463). Morality, justice and human rights, de Grouchy claims, follow naturally from sympathy.

THE NEED TO NURTURE SYMPATHY THROUGH EDUCATION

De Grouchy argues that the educational system is at the heart of civil society. The purpose of education is less to create sympathy than to combat those aspects of society that stifle natural sentiments and replace them with vanity and egoism:

> What immense work must be put into education, not to develop or direct nature, but only to conserve the benevolent inclinations, to preserve natural sentiments from being snuffed out by prejudices, so accredited and so common, which corrupt at their source the sentiments of humanity and equality, sentiments as necessary to the moral happiness of each individual, as to the maintenance of equality and security in all the bonds of the social order! (de Grouchy 1798, p. 416).

Sympathy, being the fruit of both sentiment and reason, requires that individuals attain that elevation of mind that makes it possible to understand the nuances of abstract ideas: It is … to be desired that one of the principal objects of education ought to be to create the facility to acquire general ideas, to feel the general and abstract sentiments of which I have spoken, and common education is ordinarily very distant from this goal' (p. 450).

The ability to have abstract ideas:

> is a type of scale against which minds can be arranged to determine their elevation and their understanding. Those who have attained by reflection or a sort of instinct the habit of generalizing and extending their ideas never stop climbing. Those in whom the need to increase the number and extent [of their ideas] was prevented or snuffed out by other passions (and this is the multitude) rest at a certain level and never move (p. 449).

This is why it is so difficult to educate human beings 'even in their own interests'; (p. 449). First, 'one must find in their passions the strength to renovate an intelligence weakened by inaction or degraded by error', she argues, 'and then make them adopt truth either by seducing them through ingenious and striking presentations, or by captivating their reason by a logic so persistent they arrive effortlessly at the final goal' (p. 449).

Despite the important role that education ought to play in socializing individuals to live in accord with one another, de Grouchy recognizes that contemporary education seldom achieves this goal. She notes that the study of grammar, which precedes the others, begins by giving children some metaphysical ideas, but generally these are 'false ideas or, at least, very incoherent' (p. 450). Then children are required to learn language mechanically by translating authors whose thoughts they do not understand (p. 450). Then they are taught history 'isolated from the great results which alone make it useful, because otherwise it would be too easy for them to appreciate the abuses they must be taught to respect' (p. 450):

> They are raised amidst all the prejudices of pride and vanity which strip from them all feeling for the inalienable [*imprescriptibles*] rights common to all men, of true happiness, true merit, to give them the ideas of superficial pleasures and artificial pre-eminence, of which the respect and desire shrinks the mind, corrupts reason and extinguishes conscience (de Grouchy 1798, pp. 450–451).

The morality taught consists 'almost always of isolated precepts presented without order, minor duties mixed with the most sacred, announced in the same way and given the same importance' (p. 451). They are seldom led 'to seek in their own hearts eternal and general laws of good and evil, to listen for the sentiments that favor one and punish the other' (p. 451).

The study of science is introduced to children too late, and 'almost always rejected the moment the mind, already accustomed to be content with vague ideas, to occupy itself with words rather than things, finds difficult the reasoned and methodical presentation' (p. 451):

> Let us stop blaming nature for being stingy with great men; let us cease to be astonished that the general laws of nature are so little understood. How many times in this century has education given a mind the strength and rectitude to arrive at abstract ideas? How many times has it perfected the instinct for truth? (de Grouchy 1798, pp. 451–452).

Ordinary education as it is commonly practised is clearly not an effective means of nurturing sympathy.

The appropriate use of education is, however, an essential feature of a society intent upon encouraging moral behaviour and justice. De Grouchy argues that children are more educable than adults, and must be given the opportunity to exercise their sensibility so that it is developed to the extent to which it is susceptible (p. 365). This makes parents and teachers vital:

> How guilty you are, if you are more preoccupied with the success of your children than with their virtues; if you are more impatient to see them please in some circle, than to see their hearts boiling with indignation at the sight of injustice, their faces paling before unhappiness, their hearts treating all men as brothers! Care less for their graces, their talents, their careers; nurture in their souls all the sentiments that nature has placed there; make them susceptible to remorse and sensitive to the voice of honor and probity, that they may not see suffering without being tormented by the need to help (p. 366).

De Grouchy finds it apparent that 'the more sensibility is exercised, the more alive it becomes' (p. 364) and that 'emotion strengthens the soul, as exercise strengthens the body' (p. 384). Similarly, she argues that intellectual activity strengthens the ability to reflect (p. 421) and moral reflection is strengthened by habit and practice (p. 487).

De Grouchy acknowledges that even adults can be educated, although their bad habits make it difficult for educators to have an effect. Theatre and novels, for example, can allow adults to exercise their imagination and sensibility and, more rarely, their intellect (pp. 384–385). But de Grouchy is much more concerned about the negative effects of sympathy in adults, which she claims are much more frequently observed.

Her examples resonate with recent events. Among the effects of sympathy, for example, she cites the ability of a crowd to excite emotions and reinforce vague ideas by voicing what had not been articulated and stating what no individual dared say (p. 424). Similarly, the ability of some individuals to persuade others to their way of thinking depends upon the manipulation of sympathy: The impact that certain men exercise over those who hear them or read them profits from the dispositions of their souls, including sympathy: it is the result of an art less difficult than dangerous, but it ceases to be so when unveiled (de Grouchy 1798, pp. 426–27).

Individuals who can erase doubt by expressing ideas forcefully (p. 427) will be popular. Similarly, people who revive old ideas appeal to the vanity of mediocre individuals who associate new ideas with temerity and never forgive those who express them 'because such a project suggests a superiority which humiliates them' (p. 428). But the best way, she claims, for an orator to win minds is to attach opinions to general principles that are widely held, especially those received with 'enthusiasm' (p. 428).

The same principles that explain the effects of charismatic individuals are used by talented writers or artists. Writers who express themselves passionately move us. We can envision the writer feeling strong emotion, and that mechanically corresponds to our own (p. 429). They influence our opinions because we are more likely to believe that which makes a strong impression upon us. 'Such is the art of Rousseau, the model' (p. 430). 'Rousseau establishes opinion by the force of his sensitivity and logic; Voltaire by the piquant charm of his mind. One instructs men by touching them: the other, by enlightening and amusing them' (p. 431).

Because he excites the passions, de Grouchy argues, Rousseau's 'empire over souls' will survive long after Voltaire's appeal to rationality (p. 432).

NURTURING SYMPATHY THROUGH INSTITUTIONAL REFORM

Just as de Grouchy argues that the educational system is vital to a well functioning civil society but that its potential is wasted or perverted in contemporary society, so she argues that civil society requires that all of the informal and formal institutions of society must be such as to nurture the sympathy on which society must rest. She recognizes that one cannot observe human nature because it is impossible to separate human beings from the society in which they were formed in order to see what it is they might become (p. 466). But she claims, nonetheless, that human beings are by nature neither moral, evil, nor indifferent, but possess within themselves a motive to do good and none to do evil (p. 466).

De Grouchy claims that nature is less powerful than human institutions in shaping human action, and therefore one can transform human behaviour simply by reforming human institutions. If one can demonstrate that unjust behaviour may be attributed to vicious institutions and that without these institutions justice would prevail, then evil people are the consequence of policy errors. Similarly, if one can show that the existing educational system almost always weakens morality, then it follows that human beings who are 'formed and governed by reason' will behave more justly toward one another (pp. 467–468). De Grouchy, therefore, turns to institutional transformation in order to nurture sympathy and to encourage human beings to act in accordance with justice and reason.

Why do we see human beings tormenting one another? De Grouchy is clear; we create 'needs' out of social fantasies, but it is obvious that not all such needs can be met. Therefore we regard another's good fortune as leaving less for us: 'Civilized man, if he is governed by prejudices and bad laws, is naturally envious and jealous, and more so the more the vices of social institutions separate him from nature, corrupt his reason and make his happiness depend on the satisfaction of a great many needs' (p. 414).

We know this to be so because people only harm others to the extent that they believe the other's needs are exaggerated, she claims. It is not a natural misanthropy; it does not derive from personal viciousness, because most people can still sympathize with real misfortune, such as physical pain (p. 415). The rare exceptions 'are true monsters, whose evil can be explained by their education and circumstances' (p. 415).

De Grouchy claims that all motives that lead individuals to behave unjustly reduce to four: the passion of love, the pursuit of money, ambition, and *amour-propre* or vanity – often the motive and goal of the previous three (p. 473). Money is not a source of injustice in a society governed by reasonable laws, de Grouchy claims (pp. 474–475). Suppose the law stopped favouring the inequality of fortunes. 'Will injustice ensue from the natural inequality that will still come through differential conduct and differential birth rates, which are responsible for three quarters of the differences in land revenues [in agriculture]?' de Grouchy asks (p. 474). Not if the rest is equally shared, she concludes. Even a small amount of redistribution will eliminate the most dire poverty, which is the source of much desperate theft and other crime (p. 475).

In the case of industry, poverty is worse than in agriculture because land is kinder to the individuals it employs in the sense that they can, at least, provide their own subsistence, and because (she claims) land itself is the source of all wealth (p. 476).[9] Low salaries in industry are the source of poverty, and they result, de Grouchy contends, from laws that restrict business and allow wealth to accumulate in a few hands (p. 476). The unequal sharing of taxes similarly burdens the poorest class, which 'without property and without liberty, is reduced to count fraud among its resources, and cheats without remorse because conscience is soon enough extinguished by chains'[10] (pp. 476–477). Injustice based on need is rare without bad laws, she claims, although theft would remain a source of injustice even if the laws were revised (p. 478). Therefore, the first of the four motives – money – causes individuals to behave immorally largely because social institutions, as they are, create poverty. Transforming those institutions would eliminate poverty, and therefore allow the natural sympathy that is the foundation for morality to emerge.

Similarly, vanity and ambition, which are the sources of much injustice, are the work of social institutions (p. 478):

> It is social institutions alone that leave for all classes, all routes to fortune open to trickery, to intrigue, to cabals, to corruption, which separate from ambition the love of glory that ennobles it ... It is social institutions which, by consecrating hereditary rights (almost always abused from the first generation) furnish to the presumptuous mediocrity an infallible means of elevation (p. 479).

Vanity owes its existence to social institutions that favour personal interests over general interests (p. 480).

Social institutions are similarly responsible for immorality when love is the motive (p. 482). Most contemporary marriages, de Grouchy maintains, founded on property rather than love, encourage the spouses to behave badly toward one another (p. 484). Added to loveless marriages, she argues, is a society that allows the existence of an idle class for whom seduction is an occupation. Both are sources of immorality and responsible for much unhappiness (p. 484). A law that encouraged greater social equality between classes would lessen these factors, because it would virtually eliminate a leisured class (p. 484). Elevating the status of women would make them less vulnerable to seduction. Moreover, much immorality is the result of social institutions that make marital ties indissoluble (p. 485). A system that allowed divorce or even contemplated the possibility of temporary marriages would lessen such abuses (p. 485). It is society, she claims, that 'creates shackles out of marital laws and creates barriers between the two sexes that prevent the true knowledge of tastes and minds that are necessary to a true and happy marriage' (p. 485). Similarly, 'it is society that excites the vanity of men in the corruption of women, and that extends shame where it does not belong, such as to the status of illegitimate children or the breaking of a formal promise to marry' (p. 486).

In sum, de Grouchy argues that all four causes of injustice – money, ambition, love and vanity – are the consequences of formal and informal social institutions. Society encourages egoism and weakens conscience by creating the spectacle of others behaving badly (p. 487), and by furnishing excuses for bad behavior (p. 488). As vice becomes more common, it becomes more attractive as individuals dream of profiting by even more audacious projects (p. 488). She argues, however, that an ordinary conscience and reasonable laws are sufficient to make human beings just and good, unless social institutions have degraded them (p. 489).

Moving from the causes of injustice to its control, de Grouchy notes that injustice takes two forms: crimes subject to laws, and minor injustices which are not so subject, either because they are too unimportant or because the burden of proof would make them impossible to enforce (p. 491). She argues that the legal system, as it exists, exacerbates injustice. It is commonly understood, she claims, that it is not the severity of punishment that discourages crime, but rather its certainty (p. 491). Several criminal laws which create an incentive for differential enforcement, coupled with civil laws that favour inequality, cause many crimes to go unpunished. This impunity inspires more ambition in the criminals (p. 492). Similarly, judges ought not to have too much discretion, nor should favour and privilege exempt some criminals from legal provisions; otherwise, people will see the law as part of an oppressive system and 'laws which assault reason will not shape conscience' (p. 493).

Laws favouring inequality simply increase the number of people with nothing to lose. An individual with property not only believes that property is just and respects another's right to property; he recognizes that his own will be jeopardized by the need to pay restitution for criminal activity, or even to mount a costly defence (p. 494):

> The social order, by conserving to men their natural rights, puts them in a position of respecting one another, and these rights are guaranteed by the interest of each individual in his own happiness and tranquility rather than by law (p. 494).

Even artisans and farm labourers who must sell their labour to survive have a motive to respect the property of others, either because they do not have the funds to subsist during a period of unemployment or because they possess some small property in the form of clothes, furniture, and so on (pp. 497–498). The poorer an individual is, the more he fears the loss of his small resources. As soon as one hopes to possess anything, and in a well-governed country almost everyone has some property, one respects the property of others (p. 498). But extreme inequality separates the poor from the rich to such an extent, claims de Grouchy, that there is no mutual understanding between them. The rich cannot empathize with the needs of the poor, and the poor cannot imagine ever owning property, and so have no conception of the right of property (p. 500).

Lesser indiscretions, which are not subject to laws, are no less the result of existing institutions. Such actions are judged by each individual's desire to be respected for his reputation for probity and virtue (p. 500). But in contemporary society, de Grouchy claims, this motive is weakened because many rewards depend more on social position than on behaviour that earns general respect (pp. 500–501). Fraud and oppression are encouraged by too many obscure laws, by religious hypocrisy, by favour, or by inequality of fortunes that makes human beings strangers to one another. The poverty of a large class leads to fraud and mischief (p. 501) and trickery in buying and selling (p. 502). Abuse of power on the one side, and deprivation of natural rights on the other, isolates human beings from one another, and renders probity useless (p. 502).

Social institutions that ought to help human beings achieve happiness instead corrupt and degrade them. This is undoubtedly because, de Grouchy claims, 'no one has tried until now to use them to perfect nature' (p. 502). It is not only that vicious institutions make men indifferent to their duties and their interests in fulfilling them, but these institutions have created artificial needs (p. 502). Egoism, therefore, becomes a dominant passion. The man formed by these institutions:

> is not happy or unhappy in himself by insufficiency, by the good or bad use of his faculties, by deprivation or possession of objects. It is not his own thoughts and sentiments by means of which he judges and acts and enjoys; enchained on all sides by unjust laws, favored by fortune ... blinded and weakened by his interests, almost always in opposition to the voices of reason and humanity, satisfying outrageous

pretensions without being forced to justify them by true merit, and corrupt passions without universal condemnation and the call for remorse ... the opinion of others becomes the measure of his conscience, the necessary sanction for his pleasures, and the first condition of his happiness (de Grouchy 1798, pp. 503–504).

Although social institutions as they exist are a cause of injustice in society, de Grouchy argues that in a well-governed society these same institutions can be transformed in such a way that sympathy is nurtured:

> It is not difficult to show how reasonable laws may both add to the personal interest in being just, and cement the power of the conscience, even in regard to those objects of which it alone must govern and punish (p. 490).

Similarly, 'it is in considering what the laws may be, that philosophers permit themselves to attack those which lead to more abuses than advantages: this examination [is] demanded by all unbiased people and necessitated by too many abuses' (p. 495). And even those institutions governing intimate relations ought to be reconsidered:

> Suppose divorce were to be permitted to all the people; ... one would see at the same time, both that most of the unjust actions that love (or better the degradation of love) may cause to be committed, would no longer have a motive, and that the passion itself would lose, by the ease of its satisfaction, the dangerous power that it derives from the obstacles themselves (p. 485).

As in the case of education, not only is society as it exists the cause of social injustice, but society can be transformed so that social institutions play a stronger role in the elimination of injustice.

FURTHER CONSIDERATIONS

Sophie de Grouchy intended simply to extend Smith's analysis, as she read it, in two directions. She attempted to clarify the link between physical sensation and sympathy, but left the actual specification of the physical mechanism to Cabanis. In so doing, she created a theory of morality and justice that pays a great deal of attention to the concept of natural rights. She also attempted to extend the analysis by asking how sympathy, a concept so vital to society, might be encouraged. She had two answers: appropriate education can nurture sympathy by creating experiences that allow individuals to develop their ability to identify with one another, and by developing the capacity to reason. Social reform can remove those vicious institutions that are responsible for nurturing the sentiments of egoism and vanity and for snuffing out sympathetic tendencies.

De Grouchy's essays represent a blend of two different traditions. She pays homage to Smith, but it is not difficult to see de Grouchy's source in the ideas of the Revolution. Her educational analysis is distinctly and explicitly Rousseauvian, as we can see by the repeated laudatory references. Her references to natural human rights come directly from Revolutionary debates – debates that cost her husband his life only five years before she published this translation.[11] But is her analysis no more than an interesting portrait of a mind struggling with time-bound issues?

De Grouchy's letters were not ignored in France, but their impact cannot be determined simply by counting citations. As we have seen, citations were often sketchy. But we know that her letters were appended to three editions of her translation between 1798 and 1860. And as long ago as 1855, Isambert claimed that she influenced the ideologues, a group of social philosophers who looked to Destutt de Tracy and P.J.G. Cabanis for intellectual leadership, and who played a significant political role in the 1790s (Isambert 1855, p. 475).[12] The impact of the ideologues was even greater through their influence on early nineteenth-century social theory (Staum 1980). This paper can do no more than to suggest fruitful areas in which to look for evidence that these essays had an impact on social theory.

Much of the writing of the ideologues concerns, in one way or another, the way that individuals and the larger society are related to one another. These concerns are echoed by subsequent writers. For example, Richard Arena claims that the French liberal economists 'go beyond ... self-interest and take into account their social role within the normal working of the economic system' (Arena 2000). Jean-Baptiste Say, in particular, recognized that human beings are very much the products of their environment (Forget 1999, 2001b). The utopian socialists also considered human beings as individuals embedded in social networks. Individuals were again conceived as the product of the societies in which they found themselves (Forget 2001a; Manuel and Manuel 1979, p. 576; Folbre 1993). Both liberal economics and utopian socialism built upon a vision of society in which individuals are socialized creatures, and in which educators and administrators are given the responsibility for managing the socialization process. The particular shape that the analysis took in early nineteenth-century France owes something to de Grouchy's conceptualization of sympathy, even though Cabanis is much more likely to get the reference than did the latter.

De Grouchy's analysis of sympathy formed the basis of a social theory that encouraged social activism and that viewed education as a method to nurture the sympathy that she saw as vital to human society. If Smith recognized the power of society by, for example, claiming that there exists little innate difference between the philosopher and the street porter, de Grouchy was keen to use the power of education and social transformation, informed by philosophy, to make both philosophers and street porters all that human nature would allow.

REFERENCES

Alibert, J.L. (1806), 'Éloge historique de Pierre Roussel', in Pierre Roussel, *Système physique et moral de la femme, suivi d'un fragment du système physique et moral de l'homme, et d'un essai sur la sensibilité, et ... d'une note sur les sympathies ...,* seventh edition, Paris: Caille et Ravier, 1820.

Ando, Takaho (1983), 'Mme de Condorcet et la philosophie de la 'sympathie'', *Studies on Voltaire and the Eighteenth Century,* **216**, 335–336.

Arena, R. (2000), 'The French Liberal School in the Nineteenth-Century', in E.L. Forget and S. Peart (eds), *Reflecting on the Classical Canon in Economics: Essays in Honour of Samuel Hollander,* London: Routledge.

Boissel, Thierry (1988), *Sophie de Condorcet, Femme des Lumières,* Paris: Presses de la Renaissance.

Cabanis, P.J.G. (1802), *Rapports du physique et du moral de l'homme,* Paris: Victor Masson et fils, 1867.

Cabanis, P.J.G. (1956), *Oeuvres philosophiques,* edited by Claude Lehec and Jean Cazeneuve, Paris: Presses universitaires de France.

Chaussinand-Nogaret, G. (1984), 'La Marquise de Condorcet, la Révolution et la Rèpublique', *Histoire,* **75** 30–38.

Condorcet O'Connor, Èliza (1841), 'Notes biographiques sur Mme de Condorcet et sur Mme Vernet', in Robinet, 1893, *Condorcet. Sa Vie, Son Oeuvre,* Geneva: Slatkine Reprints, 1968.

Dawson, D. (1991), 'Is Sympathy So Surprising? Adam Smith and French Fictions of Sympathy', *Eighteenth-Century Life,* **15** (102), 147–162.

Folbre, N. (1993), 'Socialism, Feminist and Scientific', in M.A. Ferber and J.A. Nelson (eds), *Beyond Economic Man,* Chicago: University of Chicago Press, pp. 94–110.

Fontaine, P. (1997), 'Identification and Economic Behavior: Sympathy and Empathy in Historical Perspective', *Economics and Philosophy,* **13**, 261–280.

Forget, E.L. (1999), *The Social Economics of Jean-Baptiste Say: Markets and Virtue,* London: Routledge.

Forget, E.L. (2001a), 'Saint-Simonian Feminism', *Feminist Economics,* **7** (1), 79–96.

Forget, E.L. (2001b), 'Jean-Baptiste Say on Spontaneous Order', *History of Political Economy,* **33** (2), 193–218.

Grouchy, S. de (1798), 'Lettres à C[abanis], sur la Théorie des sentimens moraux', in Adam Smith, *Théorie des sentimens moraux,* translated from the 7th edition [1792] by Sophie de Grouchy, Marquise de Condorcet, Paris: F. Buisson.

Guillois, Antoine (1897), *La marquise de Condorcet. Sa Famille, Son Salon, Ses Amis,* Paris: Ollendorff.

Isambert, François André (1855), 'Condorcet (Marie-Louise-Sophie de Grouchy de)', in M. Hoefer (ed.), *Nouvelle Biographie Générale depuis les temps les plus reculé jusqu'à nos jours,* Paris: Fimin Didot Frères, 1853–1866.

Iser, Wolfgang (1978), *The Art of Reading,* Baltimore, MD: Johns Hopkins University Press.

Lagrave, Jean-Paul de. (1994), *Lettres sur la sympathie, suivies des lettres d'amour,* Montreal and Paris: L'Étincelle.

Lawrence, Christopher (1979), 'The Nervous System and Society in the Scottish Enlightenment', in Barry Barnes and Steven Shapin (eds), *Natural Order: Historical Studies of Scientific Culture,* Beverly Hills, CA: Sage.

Manuel, F.E. and F.P. Manual (1979), *Utopian Thought in the Western World,* Cambridge: Harvard University Press.

Marshall, D. (1988), *The Surprising Effects of Sympathy: Marivaux, Diderot, Rousseau and Mary Shelley,* Chicago: University of Chicago Press.

McDonald, L. (1994), *The Women Founders of the Social Sciences,* Ottawa: Carleton University Press.

McDonald, L. (1998a), 'Classical Social Theory with the Women Founders Included', in Charles Camic (ed.), *Reclaiming the Sociological Classics,* Oxford: Blackwell.

McDonald, L. (1998b), *Women Theorists on Society and Politics,* Waterloo, Ontario: Wilfrid Laurier University Press.

Raphael, D.D. and A.L. Macfie (1976), 'Introduction', in Adam Smith, *The Theory of Moral Sentiments,* Oxford: Oxford University Press.

Roussel, P. (1806), *Système physique et moral de la femme, suivi d'un fragment du système physique et moral de l'homme, et d'un essai sur la sensibilité, et ... d'une note sur les sympathies ...,* seventh edition, Paris: Caille et Ravier, 1820.

Skinner, Andrew S. (1995), 'Adam Smith and the Role of the Stare: Education as a Public Service', in Stephen Copley and Kathryn Sutherland (eds), *Adam Smith's Wealth of Nations: New Interdisciplinary Essays,* Manchester: Manchester University Press.

Smith, A. (1976), *The Theory of Moral Sentiments,* D.D. Raphael and A.L. Macfie (eds), Oxford: Oxford University Press.

Smith, A. (1860), *Théorie des sentiments moraux* (7th edition, translated by S. Grouchy), 3rd edition, Paris.

Staum, M. (1980), *Cabanis: Englightenment and Medical Philosophy in the French Revolution,* Princeton: Princeton University Press.

Stephens, W. (1922), *Women of the French Revolution,* New York: E.P. Dutton.

Taylor, Jane (1999), 'The Impossibility of Ethical Action: *Disgrace* by J.M. Coetzee (review)', *South African Mail and Guardian,* 27 July 1999, <http://www.mg.co.za/mg/books/9907/990727-disgrace.html>.

Valentino, Henri (1950), *Madame de Condorcet, ses amis et ses amours,* Paris: Perrin.

NOTES

1. For biographical data on Sophie de Grouchy, see Jean-Paul de Lagrave (1994), Thierry Boissel (1988), Guy Chaussinand-Nogaret (1984), Henri Valentino (1950), Winnifred Stephens (1922), Antoine Guillois (1897) and François André Isambert (1855).   Her daughter, Éliza Condorcet O'Connor, wrote biographical notes on Sophie's life. Grouchy was an ardent advocate of the principles that guided the French Revolution, a Girondist and an intimate of the ideologues, including Cabanis, Tracy, Garat, and others. She is best known for hosting a philosophical salon that brought together individuals of similar intellectual and social tastes. Note that she referred to herself as Grouchy; later biographers called her Sophie Condorcet. I have used the latter in the title because she is more commonly referred to in the secondary literature as Condorcet.
2. The seventh edition is essentially a reprint of the sixth.
3. In the first edition, her letters were addressed to 'C ...'. Cabanis was explicitly listed as the addressee for the first time in a posthumous edition (1830). Lagrave claims that Condorcet is the more likely addressee (Lagrave 1994, pp. 67–68n), but provides little convincing evidence. As an acknowledged expert in the physiology of sympathy, and an intellectual and personal intimate of the author, Cabanis seems a more convincing choice. The fact that the letters were published, and largely written, after Condorcet's death adds further, but not definitive, support. She was a *salonnière* and letters were her medium; she may well have written letters to a dead man.
4. All translations are my own.
5. The resonance of 'sympathy' in a period of political and social instability, even today, is reflected in a recent review of Coetzee's *Disgrace* in which the reviewer explicitly invokes the eighteenth-century idea of sympathy as relevant to South African society today (Taylor 1999).
6. 'Enthusiasm' recalls a religious sentiment. It is a passionate attachment independent of reason.
7. Fontaine is aware that 'empathy' is a word not available to eighteenth-century commentators. He notes that it was introduced into English by Titchener in 1909 as a translation of the German *Einfühlung*.
8. Consistent with his position on moral events, Smith claims that we rarely sympathize with another's feelings of love. De Grouchy, however, finds it 'astonishing that the passion of love appears always somewhat ridiculous' to Smith, who apparently believes that such a sentiment could only be shared by a 'frivolous youth who would judge love without having loved' (p. 412). Perhaps nowhere else is the intellectual distance between the moral philosopher and the *salonnière* so apparent.
9. Physiocratic doctrine is clearly an influence here.
10. The allusion to Rousseau's *Social Contract* is apparent in her choice of words.
11. In 1793, Condorcet, friend of Voltaire, Turgot, and Cabanis, was hiding from Robespierre's police when he was warned of an imminent raid. He escaped through the gates of Paris in disguise, only to be captured by the *sans culottes* in an obscure tavern. He died in their custody; either from a stroke, an embolism, or self-administered poison provided to him by his friend Cabanis.
12. Her intimacy with the ideologues, alluded to by Alibert (above, p. 323) is echoed by her various biographers who note both her personal and her intellectual ties.

9.   'Let There be no Distinction Between the Sexes': Jeremy Bentham on the Status of Women

Annie L. Cot

'One day arithmetick and accountantship will adorn a young woman better than a suit of ribonds and keep her warmer than a damnable dear manteau.'
William Petty

'On the ground of the greatest happiness principle, the claim of [the female] sex is, if not still better, at least, altogether, as good as that of the other; the happiness and interest of a person of the female sex, constitutes as large a portion of the universal happiness and interest as does that of a person of the male sex' (Bentham 1826, p. 108). More than a decade before Mary Wollstonecraft's *Vindication of the Rights of Woman*, Bentham begins to develop a radical view on the status of women in the society of his time, devoting many writings to demonstrating that, aside from some physical differences, the situation of inferiority of women is socially constructed and determined.

The topic appears as a strict application of his general utilitarian philosophy and economics. Pains and pleasures, supposedly measurable, form the basis of a moral arithmetic on which is laid the principle of utility. Rooted in a Newtonian epistemology, this new moral science should 'liberate' morals and legislation from tradition, prejudice and religion. When adding individual arithmetics, the principle of utility takes the form of the 'greatest happiness of the greatest number' principle, in which social happiness is defined as the sum of individual well-beings. A sum where: '[e]very individual in the country tells for one, no individual for more than one' (Bentham 1827, p. 334): every individual – free men and slaves, blacks and whites, aristocrats and indigents, men and women. Hence if, according to the newtonianism of the time, the validity of a principle depends on its generality, the happiness of mankind should include the happiness of 'the best half of the human species'.[1]

England is not the only country where the position of women was far from reaching this goal. 'In certain nations', writes Bentham in 1780, women, whether married or not, have been placed in a situation of perpetual wardship: this has been evidently founded on the notion of a decided inferiority in points of intellects on the part of the female sex, analogous to that which is the result of infancy or insanity on the part of the male. This is not the only instance in which tyranny has taken advantage of its own wrong, alleging as a reason for the domination it exercises, an imbecility, which, as far as it has been real, has been produced by the abuse of that very power which it is brought to justify (Bentham [1780] 1948, p. 268n).

Tyranny, imbecility, abuse of power: from these early remarks, Bentham will draw four fields of theoretical and political intervention on the specific status of women in modern societies. A first domain concerns sexual inequality – and more precisely the impossibility for women to have sex without conceiving chidren. This fight of Bentham's was part of a lifelong advocacy for contraception, decriminalization of both infanticide and abortion, and depenalization of prostitution (1. *If pleasure be not a good, neither is anything a good*). A second field is related to economic inequalities between men and women (2. *A peculiar disadvantage in finding occupation*). A third field concerns legal protection and laws on marriage and divorce (3. *The grimgribber, nonsensical reasons for absence of legal autonomy*). And a fourth field is devoted to education and enfranchisement (4. *Castrated minds?*).

IF PLEASURE BE NOT A GOOD, NEITHER IS ANYTHING A GOOD[2]

'You know', writes Bentham to his friend George Wilson in December 1786, 'it is an old maxim of mine, that interest, as love and religion, and so many other pretty things, should be free'.[3] This principle of individual freedom applied to private matters gives way to Bentham's position on women's sexuality. On a private ground, individual freedom involves the possibility of having sexual relations without becoming pregnant (through practices which fall under the general heading of contraception and of what Bentham calls 'sexual eccentricities'). On a social ground, the subject is linked to the much discussed population question.

Bentham always considered that women have less freedom than men as far as love relations are concerned. 'In all European countries', he writes in what he intended to publish as *An Essay on Paederasty*,

this propensity [to 'venereal enjoyment'] which in the male sex is under a considerable degree of restraint, is under an incomparably greater restraint in the female. While each are alike prohibited from partaking of these enjoyments but on the terms of marriage by the fluctuations and inefficacious influence of religion, the censure of the world denies it [to] the female part of the species under the severest penalties, while the male sex is left free (Bentham 1785, cited in Campos Boralevi 1984, p. 22).

Thus social discrimination suffered by women begins with the condemnation of their sexual lives:

> We come now to that class of desires for which no neutral name is found, – no name which does not present some accessory idea of praise or of blame, but especially of blame: the reason of which is easily discovered. Ascetism has sought to brand and criminalize the desires to which nature has confided the perpetuity of the species. Poetry has protested against these usurpations, and has embellished the images of voluptousness and love (Bentham 1782, p. 544).

Love is hence a privileged topic for applying the utilitarian *felicific calculus* to private action – and should therefore be a *non-agenda* for public intervention.

As often, Bentham offers here a classification. Sexual activities can be divided into two categories: those exercised 'in a manner conformable to rule, viz. the rule prescribed by public opinion', and those exercised 'in a manner unconformable to the same rule'.[4] The first category is again divided into two classes: those made 'potentially prolific' and those 'not potentially prolific', different by their 'effect' as well as by their 'object'. 'The operation has for its *effect* the preservation of the species, but has it for its *object* the production of that effect? No. ... The titled aristocrats of Europe, yes – but the savage of Asia, of Africa, of America, what cares he about the continuance of his race?'[5]

The second category – those 'not potentially prolific' – is divided into four classes: four deviations from the 'standard appetite'; *Error temporis; error loci; error sexus;* and *error species.*[6] Morals and religions condemn all sexual activities but the first class of the first category. But Bentham, who devoted many writings to what he named 'sexual non-conformity' or 'sexual eccentricities',[7] saw no possible condemnation of the other types of sexuality from the standard of the principle of utility:

> To what class of offences shall we refere these irregularities of the venereal appetite which are styled unnatural? I have been tormenting myself for years to find if possible a sufficient ground for treating them with the severity with which they are treated at this time of the day by all European nations: but upon the principle of utility I can find none (Bentham 1785, cited in Campos Boralevi, p. 41).

'Summa Felicitatis Ut Summa Veneris'

Hence a vigourous plea in favour of free physical love for both sexes, whether it be productive or not – a plea which Bentham cautiously writes in Latin. '*Si venus sit inter voluptates et felicitas constet ex voluptatibus (adeo ut*

summa felicitatis data summa infelicitatis est ut valor summae voluptatum)
summa felicitatis erit caeteris paribus ut summa veneris: quo casu, venus
productiva sit nec ne, quid refert?[8] Hence also Bentham's positions on birth
control measures, developed in a tract sent in 1797 – one year before the
publication of Malthus's *Essay* – to Arthur Young's *Annals of Agriculture*,
'Situation and Relief of the Poor':[9]

> Limit them [the poor]? – Agreed. – But how? – Not by prohibitory act – a remedy
> which would neither be applied, nor, if applied, be effectual ... When I speak of
> limitation, do not suppose that limitation would content me. My reverend friend,
> hurried away by the torrent of his own eloquence, drove beyond you, and let drop
> something like a spunge.[10]

The idea is twofold: First, it would be useless to prohibit sexual relations by
law – by 'prohibitory act'. Bentham later repeated this view in the manuscript
entitled 'Sex':

> In no other instance other than the act of sexuality has exercise of any act of sensuality
> been considered as being naturally subjected to any restrictive rule other than that rule
> of probity, by which injury to third persons is interdicted, and that rule of individual
> prudence by which *excess* is interdicted, *i.e.* that degree in which the act has for its
> consequence a quantity of pain ... more than equivalent to the pleasure'.[11]

Second, the contraceptive methods to be used are 'slow' remedies regarding
public relief on the poor question, but not as 'rough' as Malthus's recommended
abstinence.[12] Bentham often repeated this idea, playing on the question of
contraception what Himes calls a role of 'fountain-head' for James Mill, Francis
Place and John Stuart Mill.[13]

The social aspects of this plea in favour of sexual liberty are discussed at
length as part of the general question of the relation between population and
subsistence.[14] The different theoretical positions adopted by Bentham on the
subject are well known. A first standpoint was developed in 1780, in the
Introduction to the Principles of Morals and Legislation. There, a list of 'Public
Offences' includes 'offences against population', described as: '1. Emigration.
2. Suicide. 3. Procurement of impotence or barrenness. 4. Abortion.
5. Unprolific coition. 6. Celibacy' (Bentham [1789].1948, p. 288n). And
Bentham specifies: 'By *offences against population*, [I mean] such offences
whereof the tendency is to diminish the numbers or impair the political value of
the sum total of the members of the community' (Bentham [1789].1948,
p. 219n) – an idea coherent with the traditional thesis of a causal relationship
between population and wealth 'so that the greater the population, the greater
may *coeteris paribus* be this branch of the public wealth; and the less, the less'
(Bentham [1789].1948, p. 217n).

A few years later, in 1785, in a manuscript entitled 'Paederasty', Bentham's position has changed: 'If we consult Mr. Hume and Dr. Smith, we shall find that it is not the strength of the inclination of the one sex for the other that is the measure of the number of mankind, but the quantity of subsistence they can find or raise upon a given spot' (Bentham [1785], p. 396). The causal relationship is now reversed: it is the volume of population that depends on subsistence and wealth, and not the quantity of wealth that would depend on the quantity of population. A statement which leads Bentham to reject once again, in his notes on 'Population', all types of legal or political interventions destined to control the volume of population:

> Nothing ought to be done for the particular purpose of promoting population. Most of the measures that have been or would be pursued in this view are necessarily inefficacious, or otherwise needless. All of them are inexpedient as being coercive. The quantity of population is not limited by the desire of sexual intercourse, it is limited by the means of subsistence'.[15]

And these means of subsistence depend in turn on the demand for labour, which, according to Bentham's general theoretical construction, is itself subordinated to the quantity of capital invested in the industry. 'The facility of finding subsistence for children is in proportion to the demand for labour: and the demand for labour is in proportion to the relative quantity of capital already in store'.[16] Thus the same reverse correlation between population and wealth: 'The quantity of capital dispositive to industry remaining given, population can not be had but at the expense of wealth, nor wealth but at the expense of population: the more people there are, the poorer they will be: the fewer, the richer'.[17] – This is in effect central economic and demographic argument in favour of contraceptive methods.

Infanticide and Abortion

Coming back to the direct influence of these questions on the social position of women, Bentham extends his plea for a liberalization of contraception to an advocacy in favour of the depenalization both of infanticide and of abortion

Infanticide is described by Bentham as an 'act of which the principle of self-preservation is the present motive'.[18] And, once again, he seems preoccupied by the sole condition of women. 'To preserve her own reputation, the mother of a newborn illegitimate child destroys it. ... In the mind of the woman in question, the consideration of her own interest prevails over that of another being: her own a most momentous interest, the other an eventual rather than a real one. Supposing the discovery made, the whole life of the woman will probably be a life of bitterness: by the being whose life is finished as soon as begun, pain will not be felt in any shape. A more natural [practice] can scarce be found'.[19] Thus, no pain should be imposed upon infanticide mothers 'in the case of bastardy'. Bentham could not be more precise:

> By an absurd and undiscriminate penal law the mother is consigned to an ignominious death. This law, by what considerations has it been produced? Partly by antipathy towards the mother; partly, because of the resemblance which the case would be shown to have, taking but the mere physical appearances, to those really mischievous acts which under the name of murder are punished with that same punishment.[20]

And Bentham goes on:

> If, in the whole field of sensitive existence, there is a proper object of sympathy, it is the mother – a being who, to the physical agonies of parturition adds the mental agony produced by the immediate prospect of an everlasting infamy. Such is the being to whose cost for no rational cause that can be mentioned sympathy is in every breast changed to antipathy.[21]

The same tonality holds for Bentham's arguments in favour of abortion – even though Bentham's attitude on the subject also changed over the years.[22] After having adopted the common view that abortion was an offence against population, Bentham argues in terms of utility of the mother in his 1776 writings on the subject. 'There are cases where Abortion might be allowed; as in those where the child bearing threatens to be fatal'.[23] The calculus of utility should here help estimate:

> in which way the loss of happiness to be the greater: whether by the number of births prevented more than would be otherwise, in consequence of such a diminution in the abhorrence of the practice [of abortion] as such liberty might effect, if given; or by the loss of matrimonial and consequent comfort, which must be sustained by such of the females, so conformed who might otherwise be able to match themselves, if liberty be withholden. ... To a female of this unfortunate conformation one sees there is but this alternative – Abortion or a perpetual/privation of the sweets of marriage/sentence to the mortification of celibacy.[24]

The analysis could be carried further: abortion is both a private and a social act. In another manuscript, written in the 1780s, Bentham thus considers abortion 'in a two-fold point of view ... 1. as an operation dangerous to the health and even the life of the patient'[25] – an operation, hence, which 'does not seem to come within the competency of the legislators any more than any other medical operation: it is for the patient herself to choose between the risk and the advantage[26] ... [and] 2. as an act tending to diminish the force of the community'[27] – an act which should, as such, be 'considered as an offence ... under the head of offences against the public force'[28] and so legally condemned in the name of the greatest happiness for the greatest number.

A third step came in the 1800s, when Bentham wrote the manuscript of the *Institute of Political Economy*. The book is divided into two sections: *Science* and *Art*, the relation between the two being of an instrumental nature.[29] As far as science is concerned, 'Opulence is relative wealth, relation being had to population: it is the ratio of wealth to population. Quantity of wealth being given, the degree of opulence is therefore not directly, but inversely, as the population ... the fewer the sharers, the larger is each one's share' (Bentham [1801-1804], p. 319). Bentham then develops this thesis in a chapter on the art of population, divided under the classic two headings: *sponte acta*, and *agenda* and *non-agenda*. His views on population have not changed since 1785. First, if an increase of population is described as 'desirable', it 'results of course from the encrease of the means of subsistence; *and cannot be carried beyond them*' (Bentham [1801-1804], p. 361). Second, 'Populousness, like opulence, will thrive best, if all is left to the *sponte acta* of the individuals' (Bentham [1801-1804], p. 361). Third, among the '*agenda* and *non-agenda*'

> may be referred penal laws punishing for what is commonly meant by infanticide, for abortion, for irregularities of all sorts in the venereal appetite. ... For the penal laws of this class, an anxiety about population has never been anything but a pretence. In the principle of utility, they have no ground whatever. Of the establishment of these laws the historical causes are to be looked for exclusively in the cunjunct influence of the principles of asceticism and antipathy (Bentham [1801-1804], p. 362).

These are the two principles that Bentham had been fighting since the first versions of the *Introduction to the Principles of Morals and Legislation*.

The conclusion is clear: there are no valid reasons for punishing infanticide, abortion, or 'irregularities of all sorts in the venereal appetite' (Bentham [1801-1804], p. 362).

A PECULIAR DISADVANTAGE IN FINDING OCCUPATION

On a broader level, the general inequality between men and women concerns 'neglect and misery' (Bentham [1782], p. 545). This is for two reasons. The first reason is that women have less financial autonomy: '[i]n point of pecuniary circumstances, according to the customs of perhaps all countries, she is in general less independent', writes Bentham in the *Introduction to the Principles of Morals and Legislation* (Bentham [1780], pp. 58-59). The second reason is that, according to Bentham, the main source of poverty – and, hence, of prostitution – is unemployment (See Bahmueller 1981, p. 16).

Towards a Positive Discrimination

When Bentham turns back again to the question of indigence, in his *Principles of Penal Law*, he underlines the same points – and adds an important argument on the necessity for positive discrimination. Women are more subject than men to unemployment. One of the reasons for this is that men occupy their traditional positions. This situation is one of the causes and factors for prostitution. The text is very clear:

> Females, especially those a little above ordinary labour, have a peculiar disadvantage in finding occupation. Men ... even take possession of those labours which belong more properly to the other sex, and which are almost indecent in the hands of men. Men are found selling toys for children, keeping shops for fashion, &c.; making shoes, stays and dresses for women. Men are found filling the function of midwives. I have often doubted whether the injustice of the custom might be not redressed by the law, and whether women ought not to be put in possession of these means of subsistence, to the exclusion of men. It would be an indirect method of obviating prostitution, by providing females with suitable employments (Bentham [1782], p. 543).

Thus women could be kept away, by way of positive discrimination, from the four classes of poor.[30]

In other words, as Bentham had already written in a 1782 manuscript when composing the *Essay on Indirect Legislation*, compared with men, women suffered from marked disadvantages due to the 'superior activity, liberty, and perhaps dexterity of the men'.[31] Hence a proposition of using indirect legislation could be used to reserve some occupations for women: specially, writes Bentham, the occupations 'which seem particularly suited to the female sex and which can scarcely be practised without indecorum by the male are either shared in by the latter or engrossed'.[32]

Prostitutes: the Victims of Economic Inequality

The claim for sexual liberty was not the only reason why Bentham argued in favour of contraception. The shame cast upon 'fallen women' was another one: a shame which often led them to economic misery and prostitution. Listing 'the danger which accompany fornication', he mentions 'loss of reputation, to prevent that loss, abortion and infanticide, and, if discovery is made, prostitution, the inevitable consequence in many cases'.[33] Bentham's logical argument on prostitution is thus the same as the one he had used when discussing the case of abortion. Morally and socially, prostitution can be considered as full of 'evils' – as abortion was described as an 'abhorred' practice. In the manuscripts used by C.K. Ogden for the *Appendix* named 'Bentham on Sex' in his edition of *The Theory of Legislation*, Bentham assumes that 'female prostitution contains a net balance of evil ...: despondency, the result of perpetually experienced contempt, disease from excess, from contagion, from that habit of intoxication which is generally resorted to as a palliative'.[34] So many evils attached to the condition of the prostitutes enough disgrace to forbid any additional ignominy linked to legal punishment. 'There are some countries where the laws tolerate [prostitution]: there are others, as in England, where it is strictly forbidden ... Prostitution, prohibited as it is, is not less extended than if there were no law; but it is much more mischievous' (Bentham [1782], p. 545).

For Bentham, prostitutes are both factors and victims of prostitution; they should therefore be protected by the law instead of being submitted to penal actions brought against them. 'The condition of courtezans is a condition of dependence and servitude, he writes in his *Principles of Penal Law*: their resources are always precarious; they are always on the borders of indigence and hunger. Their names connect them with those evils which afflict the imagination. They are justly considered as the causes of those disorders of which they are, at the same time, the victims' (Bentham [1782], p. 545). A description which leads to a proposition of depenalization:

> The more this condition is naturally the object of contempt, the less necessary is it to add any legal disgrace. [Prostitution] carries with it its natural punishment – punishment which is already too heavy when every thing which should lead to commiseration in favour of this unfortunate class has been considered – the victims of social inequality, and always so near to despair (Bentham [1782], p. 545).

If the major causes of prostitution are economic causes, remedies should also be of an economic nature. Apart from depenalizing their activity, Bentham proposed 'to institute annuities' and to provide for some kind of retirement fund for prostitutes:

> It would be desirable to institute annuities, commencing at a certain age: these annuities should be adapted to this sad condition, in which the period of harvest is necessarily short, but in which there are sometimes considerable profits. The spirit of economy springs up with little encouragement ... as actual capital may yield a considerable annuity at a distant period (Bentham [1782], p. 546).

In the short term, as long as public opinion and civil law are not ready for depenalization, the 'National Charity Company'[35] could provide an asylum to prostitutes. Remedies for the condition of prostitutes or unmarried mothers include two special institutions: *Sotimion*[36] and *Nothotrophium*. These institutions would include an 'unchaste ward': a separate building were 'unchaste women' (prostitutes, unwed mothers, 'loose women', brothel-keepers, and 'procuresses') would be both separated from the other women housed by the

Company and aggregated with classes 'unsusceptible of that inconvenience'.[37] Plans for the *Sotimion* were designed 'for the preservation of female delicacy and reputation',[38] and those of the *Nothotrophium* as 'an asylum for the innocent offspring of clandestine love', in charge of welcoming illegitimate children on the basis of the principle *bene vivat qua bene latuit.*[39] And as in all of Bentham's plans which belong to the *u-topos* literary genre, long descriptions are devoted to details: the design of the chairs, the flower pots, the balconies, the list of the exercises and amusements that the resident would be allowed to take.[40] Lastly, legal protection would be provided to the mothers and the children, while 'left-handed' marriages were to be assumed by soldiers and sailors in order to protect the mothers and offer the children some sort of legitimacy.[41]

THE 'GRIMGRIBBER, NONSENSICAL REASONS' FOR ABSENCE OF LEGAL AUTONOMY

The third field of Bentham's preoccupation with the status of women concerns his favourite means for social reform: law and scientific legislation. Combining analysis and propositions of social reform, Bentham addresses the subjects on three major registers: the criticism of the status of women under English law; an advocacy in favour of a special protection for women; and marriage and divorce.

The Legal Subjection of the One Sex, the Legal Empire of the Other

English law was considered as particularly harsh to women by Bentham who, in his *Principles of the Civil Code*, brilliantly criticizes 'the difference of the condition of the two sexes, the legal subjection of the one, the legal empire of the other' (Bentham [1802], p. 351). Two examples will demonstrate. First is *Manent vestigia ruris.* 'There still exists an English law', states Bentham,

> which is a remnant of barbarous times: *manent vestigia ruris.* A daughter is considered as the servant of her father. Is she seduced, the father can obtain no satisfaction than a sum of money, the price of the domestic services of which it is considered that he may be deprived by the pregnancy of his daughter (Bentham [1782], p. 373).

Today's microeconomics would call this the opportunity cost of her ancillary services.

The second other example given by Bentham concerns the exclusion of the testimony of a wife against her husband before an English court – and hence the denying of any form of legal autonomy of a wife towards her husband. Compared with the Statute Book of the Swiss *Pays de Vaud*, according to which 'the testimony of two women, or girls shall be equal and neither more nor less than equal to that of a man',[42] the English law is not more advanced when it forbids the testimony of a wife against her husband. Behind the legal reasons, exclaims Bentham, '[t]he reason that presents itself as more likely to have been the original one, is the grimgribber, nonsensical reason, – that of the identity of the two persons thus connected' (Bentham [1827], p. 210, cited in Campos Boralevi 1984, p. 12).

The argument will often be repeated on different points of civil law. Like the legal settlement of successions, about which Bentham defends the idea of a necessary equality between men and women: 'Let there be no distinction between the sexes. Let what is said with regard to the one, be understood with regard to the one. The portion of the one shall always be equal to the portion of the other' (Bentham [1802], p. 335).

If There be any Difference, It Ought to be in Favour of the Weakest

In some cases, equality simply means equal division of wealth. In other cases, equality should imply special protection for women: measures to protect their 'delicacy' and 'sensibility' in courts;[43] or measures to protect them from sexual aggression and hence from social shame. Rape, for instance, should rather be punished by castration than by death – if it be to frighten potential criminals.

> Castration seems the most appropriate punishment in the case of rape, that is to say the best apt to produce a strong impression on the mind at the moment of temptation. It is expedient, then, on account of such scruples of modesty, that another punishment, as, for example, death should be employed, which is less exemplary, and consequently less efficacious (Bentham [1782], p. 411).

More generally, the arguments are many to justify these measures, in terms of comparative advantages. 'Why is a particular protection extended to females?' asks Bentham.

> *Answer.* A moral object is again in view: it is proper to inspire them with a most delicate sense of honour; and this object is attained by increasing the guilt of every injury done towards them. Besides, the law ought to inspire men with a disposition of peculiar regard for females, because they are not all beautiful, and beauty does not last for ever; whilst the men have a constant superiority over the women, on account of their superior strength.[44]

At last, as on the labour market, equality could also, from a utilitarian perspective, mean compensatory discriminations. 'If there be any difference', writes Bentham in the *Principles of the Civil Code*,

> it ought to be in favour of the weakest – in favour of the females, who have more wants, fewer means of acquisition, and are less able to make use of the means they have. But the strongest have had all the preference. Why? Because the strongest have made the laws (Bentham [1802], p. 335).

A Misery Too Great to be Tolerated Even in Slavery Itself

In the same line, Bentham was also an outspoken critic of the English marriage laws of his time, which he considered to be based upon physical strength and economic oppression by one sex of the other, going so far as to plead that a definitive union could be considered a sort of slavery.

According to him, the very institution of the family was built upon physical force. Under such circumstances, in case of conflict inside the family,

> [l]aying aside generosity and good-breeding, which are the tardy and uncertain fruits of long-established laws, it is evident that there can be no certain means of deciding it but physical power: which indeed is the very means by which family, as well as other competitions must have been decided, long before any such office as that of legislator had existence (Bentham [1780] 1948, p. 259n).

Hence a historical tradition which leads to what may appear as an 'order of things' to the legislator (Bentham [1780] 1948, p. 259n).

> For there were men and wives (or, what comes to the same thing, male and female living as man and wife) before there were legislators. Looking round him then he finds almost everywhere the male the strongest of the two; and therefore possessing already, by purely physical means, that power which he is thinking of bestowing on one of them by means of law. How then can he do so well as by placing the legal power in the same hands which are beyond comparison the more likely to be in possession of the physical? In this way, few transgressions, and few calls for punishments: in the other way, perpetual transgressions, and perpetual calls for punishments. Solon is said to have transferred the same idea to the distribution of state powers. Here then was *generalization*: here was the work of genius. But in the disposal of domestic power, every legislator, without any effort of genius, has been a Solon (Bentham [1780] 1948, p. 259n).

'So much for reasons', he says, before adding another 'motive' to that situation: 'that legislators seem all to have been of the male sex, down to the days of Catherine' (Bentham [1780] 1948, pp. 259-260n).

This inequality explains the double character of the institution of marriage: as a historical protection for women on the one hand, and as a potential submission to tyranny on the other.

Therefore marriage has historically represented progress in the condition of humankind in general and of women in particular:[45] 'it has trained up citizens', 'it has multiplied the social sympathies' and hence '[m]arriage, considered as a contract, has drawn women from the hardest and most humiliating servitude' (Bentham [1802], p. 349). But this does not acknowledge marriage in its present legal form, where '[t]he interests of the females have too often been neglected', as a result of history: At Rome, the laws of marriage were only the code of the strongest, and the shares were divided by the lion'(Bentham [1802], p. 355).

English law stipulates that the man should 'master' his wife, hence 'saving recourse to justice'. Bentham makes the point clear: 'I have said "saving recourse to justice" for it is not proper to make the man a tyrant, and to reduce to a state of passive slavery the sex which, by its weakness and its gentleness, has the greatest need for protection'(Bentham [1802], p. 355).

This theme will be repeated. From a utilitarian point of view, what John Stuart Mill will call the subjection of women implies a greater legal protection. Women have less financial autonomy, hence less social autonomy: what they need is legal protection more than a proclamation of equality. As part of this legal protection, they need the right to divorce.

The question is a delicate one in eighteenth-century English society and Bentham makes a cautious twofold statement about the advantages and disadvantages of divorce for women. On the one hand, he underlines with force the asymmetry of man and woman towards the duration of marriage; on the other hand, he claims the right for women to ask for a divorce when the 'tyranny' is too strong. The first statement pleads in favour of the protection insured by a long term marriage, the second one in favour of the right for women to ask for a divorce 'when tyranny is too strong'.

'If the law had not determined any thing respecting the duration of the marriage contract ... The object of the man in this contract might be only to satisfy a transient passion', writes Bentham in his *Principles of the Civil Code,*

and this passion satisfied, he would have had all the advantages of the union without any of its inconveniences. It cannot be the same for women: this engagement [marriage] has for her durable and burthensome consequences. After the inconveniencies of pregnancy, after the perils of child-birth, she is charged with the cares of maternity. Hence the union, which confers upon the man the pleasures only, is for the woman the commencement of long circle of pains, whose inevitable termination would be death, if she were not beforehand assured of the care and protection of a husband, both for herself and the germ which she ought to nourish in her bosom (Bentham [1802], p. 352).

The more so that a man could remarry more easily in the society of that time:

The woman has also a particular interest in the indefinite duration of the connexion:

time, pregnancy, suckling, cohabitation itself, – all conspire to diminish the effect of her charms. She must expect to see her beauty decline at a time when the strength of the man still goes on increasing: she knows, that after having spent her youth with one husband, she would with difficulty find a second; whilst the man would not experience a similar difficulty in finding a second wife (Bentham [1802], p. 352).

Therefore it is a necessity to preserve the rights of the woman when the man wants to get a divorce. Discussing the 'objections to the principle of the divorce', Bentham notes:

Objection. – The dissolubility of marriage will give the stronger of the two parties an inclination to maltreat the feebler, for the purpose of constraining its consent for the divorce. *Answer.* – This objection is well founded; it deserves the greatest attention on the part of the legislator. A single precaution, however, is happily sufficient to diminish the danger: in case of maltreatment, liberty to the party maltreated and not to the other. In this case, the more a husband desired a divorce for the purpose of marrying again, the more he would avoid behaving ill towards his wife, for fear lest certain acts should be construed as acts of violence intended to constrain her consent (Bentham [1802], p. 355).

But there is a second case considered by Bentham: 'when tyranny is too strong'. 'To live under the constant authority of a man that one detests is already a species of slavery', he writes in his *Principles of the Civil Code:* 'to be constrained to receive his embraces, is a misery too great to be tolerated even in slavery itself' (Bentham [1802], p. 353).

English law prohibited divorce unless there was adultery – and even so, writes Bentham, its price (five hundred pounds) makes divorce 'therefore accessible only to a very limited class' (Bentham [1802], p. 355). For the other women, the Panopticon could, here again, provide an 'asylum' for the wife of a 'tyrannical husband'. A perspective that could be desirable, although the conflict should be serious to exhange 'matrimonial comfort', home, and family, for 'celibacy under inspection – in company of her own sex only, and not of her own choice' (Bentham [1826], p. 108).

In the long term, the solution should therefore be a change in the law, and Bentham expounds two strong arguments in favour of divorce. First, 'The government which interdicts [divorces], takes upon itself to decide, that it understands the interests of individuals better than they do themselves' (Bentham [1802], p. 355): the result being that the 'effect of the law is evil or nul' (Bentham [1802], p. 355). Second, if, 'in all the civilized countries' women can get a separation for ill-treatment – but not a divorce, which means without permission to remarry – in that situation, '[t]he ascetic principle, the enemy of pleasure [results in the fact that] the injured wife and her tyrant are subjected to the same condition. This apparent equality covers great real inequality' (Bentham [1802], p. 355).

The conclusion leads to Bentham's usual statement: on the matter of divorce, as on others, '[o]pinion allows great liberty to the stronger sex, but imposes great restraint upon the weaker one' (Bentham [1802], p. 355).

CASTRATED MINDS?

Like all eighteenth-century reformers, Bentham believed in education as a way to improve the social status of women. 'For the benefit of the ruling few, as the bodies of some men, so the minds of all women are castrated. Pretended ignorance and insincerity forced on them, by knowledge alone they are disgraced'.[46] Lack of education, together with lack of power as a citizen, are thus pointed at as the major causes of women's social inferiority. And when Bentham remarks once more that 'men have a constant superiority over the women, on account of their superior strength', he adds that 'there may also, perhaps, be a superiority of mental strength, either derived from nature or acquired by exercise'.[47]

Chrestomathia

A 'mental strength', 'acquired by exercise': education will be the means for reshaping the social determination of sexual identities, the actual shaping being directed towards modesty and reserve.[48] Bentham inherits here both from a Hartleian conception of human nature as a product of education, experience and social prejudice, and from Helvétius's view of beings which can be sculpted by education and environment.[49] He therefore refuses to associate women's physical differences with their commitment to household work and to 'the exercise of their domestic duties': 'The men have their domestic duties as well as the women', he claims; 'it is not more necessary that women should cook the victuals, clean the house and nurse the children than it is that the greater part of the male sex should employ an equal share of their time in the labours of the workshop of the fields'.[50] Hence girls' education holds a central part in his *chresthomatic* project of education.

The instruction one can get in the *Chrestomathia* is designated for both sexes, but it is described as more useful for girls.

> In the whole of the proposed field of instruction ..., scarcely will there be found a spot, which in itself, custom apart, will not be, in respect of the information presented by it, alike useful to both sexes: some parts ... will even be found *more* useful to females than to males.[51]

Moreover Bentham proposes to adopt as a basic principle the 'well known fact, that girls are more docile and attentive than boys'. Hence,

> accordingly, in that part of their school time, which remains after subtraction of that which is applied to occupations appropriate to their sex, the degree of proficiency which, at the end of the year, they have attained, is not inferior to that which, in the whole of that same school time, has, within the same period, been attained by the boys (Bentham [1816] 1948, p. 56).

Bentham adds some specific knowledge according to the social ranking of girls. For these classes that he names *middling*, 'to whatsoever other branches of instruction the labour of female children be applied, needle-work will certainly not be regarded as one that can be omitted ...' (Bentham [1816] 1948, p. 56). For the *higher* classes, dancing and music represent 'two accomplishments the possession of which will ... be regarded as indispensable' (Bentham [1816] 1948, p. 56). But these classes, and the point is essential, should definitely be held outside school hours: 'For neither of these, it is evident, can any place be found in the proposed school. For uniting its benefits with those accomplishments, there remains therefore but two expedients; viz. the deferring of the accomplishments, either to a later *hour*, or a later *day*' (Bentham [1816] 1948, p. 56).

Hereafter prejudice will still be strong, but easier to fight. 'As to intellectual aptitude considered as applied to the field of thought and action at large', he writes in the essay 'Economy as applied to Office',

> two points require to be considered: in the first place, among writers for example, in how small a degree the superiority is on the side of the male sex; in the next place, how small is the number of those of the female sex whom laws and institutions have left unexcluded from the competition in comparison of those whom they have excluded (Bentham [1822], p. 98).

Reasons for the Exclusion None

The other instrument for women's emancipation is the right to vote. Here again, Bentham's position has been a radical one since his first writings. In 1789, he was working on a manuscript drawn up for the French Revolutionaries and centered on the question: 'Why admit women to the right of suffrage?' Bentham's discussion of the subject is coherent with his position on equality of rights. 'Why exclude them? Of the two sexes of which the species is composed how comes all natural right to political benefits to be confined to one? As to the custom which has prevailed so generally in prejudice to the disadvantage of the softer sex, it has tyranny for its efficient cause, and prejudice for its sole justification'.[52]

The two arguments of 'tyranny' and 'prejudice' shape Bentham's plea.

In his discussion of tyranny the situation of women is compared with that of 'negro' slaves, also excluded from the right either to vote or to stand for elections.

> As to the Negroes and the Women, were they by some strange accident to overcome the body of prejudice which opposes their admission with so much force, there could not be a stronger proof of a degree of mérit superior to any that was to be found among whites and among men.[53]

Moreover, tyranny also exists on a symbolic level. In a letter addressed to the Spanish *Cortes*, Bentham discusses the mode of election of *Ultramarian* deputies.[54]

> In their conception, have the female individuals of humankind each of them a soul belonging to it? ... If so it be that in their conception, and in the acceptation which, in that case, it is your duty to give to the Article, in female bodies there are no souls, then so it is that, by these 70,000 souls, we are to understand 70,000 male animals of the human species. ... But if the objects indicated by this number 70,000 are no other animals of the human species than those which are of the male sex, then so it is that we are compelled to understand that, in the conception of the proposer and adopters of this Article, such animals of the human species as are of the female sex have no souls.[55]

Concerning prejudice, the common argument to justify women's exclusion from the right to vote holds on to their supposed intellectual inferiority. Again, Bentham's answer in his 1789 pamphlet is a radical one.

> The English law does not recognize women's effective physical inferiority compared to men's, but refuses them political rights in the name of their supposed intellectual inferiority. ... Suppose the inferiority of faculties: the greater it is, the less their capacity of abusing the power in question. If they belong to the class of idiots, at least they do not to the class of mischievous idiots. If there are any points in respect of which their inferiority stands questionable, one should think it were the articles of bodily strength and personal courage. The English Common Law in its wisdom has determined otherwise. It calls them equally with the men to take upon them those offices the duties of which consist in apprehending vagrants and quelling riots. From those political rights which may be exercised without labour or hasard it excludes them with unrelenting care.[56]

Another argument is given by the many countries which have been ruled by female monarchs. 'But if no sensible inconvenience can be found to arise from entrusting them with the exclusive power of royalty, what danger can there be in their occupying so small a fragment of political power, and that in common with the other sex?'[57]

A few years later, when James Mill published his *Essay on Government*, Bentham wrote an extremely critical note on the famous passage where Mill asserted that women were deprived of their own interests and should therefore be excluded from the franchise, comparing them on this matter with children.

Mill's statement was the following:

> One thing is pretty clear, that all those individuals whose interests are indisputably included in those of other individuals, may be struck off without inconvenience. In this light may be viewed all children, up to a certain age, whose interests are involved in those of their parents. In this light also, women may be regarded, the interest of almost all of whom is involved, either in that of their fathers or in that of their husbands (James Mill [1828], p. 21).

A 'heresy'! This is how Bentham considered this position,[58] criticizing Mill for 'its [exclusionist] position, the object of which is to place all females under the absolute dominion of all males', and concluding: 'Reasons for the exclusion none'.[59]

Nearly thirty years after his 1789 tract, Bentham seems to have changed his position. On a 'practical' ground, the political fight for women's suffrage is described as 'altogether premature' for British society[60] – though this was not on the ground of principles, as Bentham still pled for the enfranchisement of women. Thus, discussing a recent speech of Fox's, who opposed women's rights in Parliament on the grounds of 'the law of nations and *perhaps* also the law of nature', Bentham discussed the word 'perhaps' with vehemence. 'Perhaps: A peremptory exclusion, by which one half of the species is excluded from that security for a regard to their interests, which in the case of the other half is pronounced indisputable' (Bentham [1809], p. 463).

Bentham called again in favour of women's enfranchisement in the *Catechism of a Parliamentary Reform*. But he later abandoned the argument and concentrated on the more realistic objective of male universal suffrage. The theme still reappears in some texts, such as 1819 *Radical Reform Bill*, where Bentham discusses the qualification of women as electors:

> Inconvenience there might be upon the whole, absurdity there would be none. Nor even would there be any novelty in it. In the India House, among the self-elected representatives of sixty millions of Hindoos, are females in any number ... Everywhere have females possessed the whole power of a despot ... Talk of giving them as here the smallest fraction of a fraction of such a power, scorn without reason is all the answer you receive. From custom comes prejudice (Bentham [1819], p. 567n).

From custom comes prejudice: the same arguments are used in the *Constitutional Code*:

> This custom of exclusion has been departed from in the case where the power is of the

highest grade. In countries in which the sex is not admitted to the smallest share in the constitutive power, it is admitted to the whole of the executive, coupled with the largest share of the legislative, and that without any constitutive power above it. And of experience, in England, as far as it goes, in this the highest rank of operative power, the decision is more of the female sex than of the male. In intellectual aptitude, Elizabeth of England showed herself in an incontestable degree superior to her immediate successor, and even to the nearest of her male and adult predecessors (Bentham [1826], p. 108).

Among the many groups excluded from universal suffrage, women are often compared with children, notes Bentham. But children are only refused temporarily, on the assumption that they are 'not yet competent to the management of [their] own affairs' (Bentham [1826], p. 108). Hence 'the exclusion thus put on the ground of age is not like the exclusion put on the ground of sex': gender, unlike age, is perpetual. In the case of women, there are no reasons of principle.[61] 'Why exclude the whole female sex from all participation in the constitutive power?' asks Bentham again. On the ground of 'practical' – or political – reasons, common prejudices give an answer: 'Because the prepossession against their admission is at present too general, and too intense, to afford any chance in favour of a proposal for their admission' (Bentham [1826], p. 108). But on the ground of principle, no reasons can be found. Hence

> [n]o reason can be assigned, why a person of the one sex, should as such, have less happiness than a person of the other sex. Nor, therefore, whatsoever be the external means of happiness, why a female should have less portion of those same means' ... If the possession of a share in the constitutive power, be a means of securing such equal share of the external means of happiness, the reason in favour of it, is therefore at least as strong in the case of the female sex, as in the case of the male (Bentham [1826], p. 108).

The argument goes even further: since women are subject to more physiological pain than men, and since they are to be excluded from 'the composition of a legislative or executive body', then, 'the principle of equality affords another reason, not merely for admitting the female sex to an equal share in the constitutive, but even to a greater share than in the case of the male' (Bentham [1826], p. 108).

As for the 'practical' consequences of this enfranchisement, they should concern a greater sexual freedom for women. 'Can practical good in any form be mentioned as likely to be produced from the admitting the female sex into a participation of the supreme constitutive power?', asks Bentham. 'Yes. The affording encreased probability of adoption to legislative arrangements placing sexual intercourse upon a footing less disadvantageous than the present to the weaker sex'.[62]

In an 1822 essay, Bentham again devotes a long discussion to franchise.

Question. Does the greatest happiness principle require that the female sex should be excluded from the participation in this function? *Answer.* Not any more than the males. ... As to intellectual aptitude, no reason has ever been assigned why, in respect of that branch of appropriate aptitude, this half of the species ought to be deemed inferior to the other. Of experience – of experience as far as it goes – as applied to the highest situation in the scale of operative power, the decision is more in favour rather of the female sex than of the male. In no two male reigns was England as prosperous as in the two female reigns of Elizabeth and Anne.[63]

Hence women's enfranchisement is legitimated both on the ground of principle and on the ground of practicality. But this does not mean that actual 'political states' are ready to take such legal and political measures. 'At the same time', writes Bentham with regret, 'there is no political state that I know of in which, on the occasion of any new constitution being framed, I should think it at present expedient to propose a set of legislative arrangements directed to this end' (Bentham [1826], p. 108). In other words, prejudice is still too strong. Prejudice was Bentham's lifelong enemy, but it might still explain some of his less advanced positions regarding enfranchisement. One famous example is his opposition to the election of women as members of the legislative assembly. The passage belongs to the 1791 *Essay on Political Tactics*. Discussing the general conditions of admission to the legislative assembly, Bentham asks the question: 'Ought females to be admitted?' His answer is: 'No!', and the explanation is the following: 'I have hesitated, I have weighed the reasons for and against. I would repudiate a separation, which appears an act of injustice and of contempt. But to fear is not to despise them ... and it ought not to wound their pride'.[64] Here Bentham adopts a mocking tone, denouncing the prejudices of the English political class – as well as of English society as a whole – against women, considered as too much of a matter of passion for such a serious assembly.

Removing them from an assembly where tranquil and cool reason ought alone to reign, is avowing their influence ... The seduction of eloquence and ridicule are most dangerous instruments in a political assembly. Admit females – you add new force to these seductions; and before this dramatic and impassioned tribunal, a discussion which only possessed the merits of depth and justice, would yield to its learned author only the reputation of a wearisome lecturer. All the passions touch and enkindle each other reciprocally. The right of speaking would often be employed only as a means of pleasing; but the direct method of pleasing female sensibility consists in showing a mind susceptible of emotion and enthusiasm. Everything would take an exalted tone, brilliant or tragical – excitement and tropes would be scattered everywhere; it would be necessary to speak of liberty in lyric strains and to be poetic with regard to those great events which require the greatest calmness. No value would be put but upon those things which are bold and strong; that is, but upon imprudent resolutions and extreme measures.[65]

England gives him an example, not without some irony:

> Among the English, where females have so little influence in political affairs – where they seek so little to meddle with them – where the two sexes are accustomed to separate for a time, even after family repasts, – females are not permitted to be present at the parliamentary debates. They have been excluded from the House of Commons, after the experiment has been tried, and for weighty reasons. It has been found that their presence gave a particular turn to the deliberations – that self-love played too conspicuous a part - that personalities were more lively – and that too much was sacrificed to vanity and wit.[66]

A FIGHT AGAINST PREJUDICE AND ASCETISM

Bentham's position regarding the status of women is therefore consistent with his twofold definition of the principle of utility.

> Nature has placed mankind under the governance of two sovereign masters, *pain* and *pleasure*. It is for them alone to point out what we ought to do, as well as to determine what we shall do. On the one hand the standard of right and wrong, on the other the chain of causes and effects, are fastened to their throne... The *principle of utility* recognises this subjection and assumes it for the foundation of that system, the object of which is to rear the fabric of felicity by the hands of reason and of law'.

What we shall do, what we ought to do: on the one hand a descriptive analysis, on the other a normative plan. On the one hand, the *felicific calculus*, which places happiness at the centre of the condition of humankind: on the other, the only proper measure of right and wrong: the principle of greatest happiness of the greatest number, with its four 'subsidiary ends', security, subsistence, abundance and equality.[67]

This simple sketch has two major consequences for what nineteenth-century social theorists would later call 'the woman question'. First, any oppression is contradictory to the principle of the greatest happiness of the greatest number (oppression of women as well as slaves, children, homosexuals, or religious minorities). There is no justification for oppression other than mere prejudice – even in the most elaborated philosophies.[68] Second, there is no pleasure which ought to be condemned if it does not affect the happiness of others. Therefore, utilitarianism has but one major enemy: the principle of ascetism, which,

> like the principle of utility, approves or disapproves of any action, according to the tendency which it appears to have to augment or diminish the happiness of the party whose interest is in question; but in an inverse manner: approving of actions in so far as they tend to diminish his happiness; disapproving of them in so far as they tend to

augment it.[69]

Hence the status given to the plea against the legal and social subjection of women: a fight of the 'greatest number' principle against all forms of oligarchical power of the 'ruling few'; a fight of enlightened reason against tradition; a fight of radicalism against the domination of ethics by any religion; a fight of the weak against the tyranny of the strong; a fight for responsibility of all citizens against prejudice; a fight for liberty against social constraints; and a fight whose echoes are still to resonate in our ears after more than two centuries.

REFERENCES

Bahmueller, Charles F. (1981), *The National Charity Company. Jeremy Bentham's Silent Revolution*, Berkeley, Los Angeles: University of California Press.

Ball, Terence (1980a), 'Utilitarianism, Feminism, and the Franchise: James Mill and his Critics', *History of Political Thought*, **1**, 91–115.

Ball, Terence (1980b), 'Was Bentham a Feminist?', *The Bentham Newsletter*, May, pp. 25–32, reprinted in Bhikhu Parekh (ed.) (1993), *Jeremy Bentham: Critical Assessments*, vol. 4, *Economics and Miscellaneous Topics*, London: Routledge, pp. 230–238.

Ball, Terence (1980c), 'Bentham No Feminist: A Reply to Boralevi', *The Bentham Newsletter*, May, pp. 47–48, reprinted in Bhikhu Parekh (ed.) (1993), *Jeremy Bentham: Critical Assessments*, vol. 4, *Economics and Miscellaneous Topics*, London: Routledge, pp. 255–257.

Baumgardt, David (1952), *Bentham and the Ethics of Today. With Bentham manuscripts hitherto unpublished*, Princeton: Princeton University Press.

Bentham, Jeremy (1785), 'Essay on "Paederasty"', edited by Louis Crompton, *Journal of Homosexuality,* vol. 3, (1978), 363–405 and vol. 4, (1978), 91–107.

Bentham, Jeremy (1787–1793), 'Notes on population', in William Stark (ed.) (1954), *Jeremy Bentham's Economic Writings*, vol. 1, London: Unwin, pp. 272–274.

Bentham, Jeremy (1782), *Principles of Penal Law*, in Jeremy Bentham, *Works*, vol. 1, pp. 365–580.

Bentham, Jeremy [1780] (1948), *An Introduction to the Principles of Morals and Legislation*, reprinted New York: Hafner Press, Macmillan.

Bentham, Jeremy (1791), *Essay on Political Tactics*, in Jeremy Bentham, *Works*, vol. 2, pp. 299–373.

Bentham, Jeremy [1793–1795], *Manual of Political Economy*, in William Stark (ed.) (1954), *Jeremy Bentham's Economic Writings*, vol. 1, London: Unwin, pp. 219–273.

Bentham, Jeremy (1793–1795), *Supply without Burthen; or Escheat vice Taxation,* in *Jeremy Bentham's Economic Writings*, edited by William Stark, London: Unwin, (1954), vol. 3, pp. 279–367.

Bentham, Jeremy (1797), *Outline of a Work entitled Pauper Management,* in Jeremy Bentham, *Works*, vol. 8, pp. 369–439.

Bentham, Jeremy (1801–1804), *Methods and Leading Features of an Institute of Political Economy (including finance), considered not only as a science but as an art,* in William Stark (ed.) (1954), *Jeremy Bentham's Economic Writings*, vol. 3, London: Unwin, pp. 305–380.

Bentham, Jeremy (1802), *Principles of the Civil Code*, in Jeremy Bentham, *Works*, vol. 1, pp. 297-364.

Bentham, Jeremy (1809), *Catechism of Parliamentary Reform or Outline of a Plan of Parliamentary Reform*, in Jeremy Bentham, *Works*, vol. 3, pp. 538–557.

Bentham, Jeremy, *The Rationale of Reward,* in Jeremy Bentham, *Works*, vol. 2, p. 197.

Bentham, Jeremy (1816), *Chrestomathia*, in Jeremy Bentham, *Works*, vol. 8, pp. 1–192.

Bentham, Jeremy (1817), *Plan of a Parliamentary Reform in the Form of a Catechism*, in Jeremy Bentham, *Works*, vol. 3, pp. 433–537.

Bentham, Jeremy (1819), *Radical Reform Bill,* in Jeremy Bentham, *Works*, vol. 6, pp. 195–585 and vol. 7, pp. 1–600.

Bentham, Jeremy [1822] (1989), *First Principles Preparatory to Constitutional Code*, in Jeremy Bentham, *Complete Works* (edited by Philip Schofield), Oxford: Clarendon

Press.

Bentham, Jeremy (1826), *Constitutional Code,* in Jeremy Bentham, *Works,* vol. 9, p. 108.

Bentham, Jeremy (1827), *Rationale of Judiciale Evidence, specially applied to English Practice,* in Jeremy Bentham, *Works,* vol. 6, pp. 195–585 and vol. 7, pp. 1–600.

Bentham, Jeremy (1838–1843), *The Works of Jeremy Bentham,* (edited by John Bowring), Edinburgh: William Tait.

Bentham, Jeremy [1814–1816] (1931), *The Theory of Legislation,* (edited by C.K. Ogden), New-York: Harcourt and Brace.

Bentham, Jeremy (1983), *A Table of the Springs of Action,* in Jeremy Bentham, *Complete Works* (edited by A. Goldworth), Oxford: Clarendon Press.

Bentham, Jeremy (1995), *Colonies, Commerce and Constitutional Law: Rid Yourselves of Ultramaria and Other Writings on Spain and Spanish America* (edited by Philip Schofield), *The Collected Works of Jeremy Bentham,* Oxford: Clarendon Press.

Campos Boralevi, Lea (1980), 'In Defence of a Myth', *The Bentham Newsletter,* May, pp. 33–46a, reprinted in Bhikhu Parekh (ed.) (1993), *Jeremy Bentham. Critical Assessments,* vol. 4, *Economics and Miscellaneous Topics,* London: Routledge, pp. 239–254.

Campos Boralevi, Lea (1983), 'Jeremy Bentham's Writings on Sexual Non-Conformity: Utilitarianism, Neo-Malthusianism and Sexual Liberty', *Topoi. An International Review of Philosophy,* **2** (1), 123–148.

Campos Boralevi, Lea (1984), *Bentham and the Opressed,* Berlin: Walter de Gruyter.

Crompton, Louis (1978), 'Jeremy Bentham's Essay on "Paederasty": An Introduction', *Journal of Homosexuality,* **3** (4) 383-387, reprinted in Bhikhu Parekh, (ed.) (1993), *Jeremy Bentham. Critical Assessments,* vol. 4, *Economics and Miscellaneous Topics,* London: Routledge, pp. 258–262.

Fukagai, Yasunori (2001), 'Bentham and Malthus on Wealth, Population and Pauperism', History of Economics Society, Wake Forest University, Winston-Salem, NC, June 29–July 2.

Folbre, Nancy (1992), '"The Improper Arts": Sex in Classical Political Economy', *Population and Development Review,* **18** (1), 105–121.

Groenewegen, Peter (ed.) (1994), *Feminism and Political Economy in Victorian England,* Aldershot: Edward Elgar.

Halévy, Elie (1972), *The Growth of Philosophic Radicalism* (with a preface by John Plamenatz), London: Faber and Faber (first English edition 1928).

Himes, Norman E. (1936), 'Jeremy Bentham and the Genesis of English Neo-Malthusianism', *Economic History,* 3 (2), 267–276.

Mill, James [1820] (1977), *An Essay on Government,* supplement to the *Encyclopaedia Britannica,* reprinted by C.V. Shields, Indianapolis: Indianapolis University Press.

Mill, James [1817] (1997), *The History of British India* (reprinted with notes and continuation by Horace Wayman Wilson), London: Routledge/Thoemmes.

Mill, James (1828), 'Essay in Government', in James Mill, *Essays,* London.

Mill, John Stuart [1873] (1940), *Autobiography,* London: Oxford University Press.

Mill, John Stuart and Harriet Taylor Mill [1832] (1970), *Early Essays on Marriage and Divorce,* reprinted in John Stuart Mill and Harriet Taylor Mill, *Essays on Sex Equality* (edited by Alice S. Rossi), Chicago: The University of Chicago Press, pp. 65–88.

Mill, John Stuart [1869] (1970), *The Subjection of Women,* reprinted in John Stuart Mill and Harriet Taylor Mill, *Essays on Sex Equality* (edited by Alice S. Rossi), Chicago: The University of Chicago Press, (1970), pp. 123–242.

Place, Francis [1822] (1930), *Illustrations and Proofs of the Principle of Population: including an Examination of the Proposed Remedies of Mr. Malthus, and a Reply to* the Objection of Mr. Godwin and others*, London, (1822), reprinted by Norman E. Himes, London.

Pujol, Michèle A. (1992), *Feminism and Anti-Feminism in Early Economic Thought*, Cheltenham: Edward Elgar.

Semple, Janet (1993), *Bentham's Prison. A Study of the Panopticon Penitentiary*, Oxford: Clarendon Press.

Stephen, Leslie (1900), *The English Utilitarians*, London: Duckworth.

Taylor, Harriet [1851] (1970), *The Enfranchisement of Women*, Westminster Review, vol. 55 (1851), pp. 284–301, reprinted in John Stuart Mill and Harriet Taylor Mill, *Essays on Sex Equality* (edited by Alice S. Rossi), Chicago: The University of Chicago Press, pp. 89–122.

Wheeler, Anna and William Thompson (1825), *Appeal to One Half of the Human Race, Women Against the Pretensions of the Other Half, Men, to retain them in political and hence in civil and domestic slavery*, London: Longman, Hurst, Rees, Orme, Brown and Green (1825), reprinted, London: Routledge, (1993).

Williford, Miriam (1975), 'Bentham on the Rights of Women', *Journal of the History of Ideas*, **36** (1), 167–176.

Wollstonecraft, Mary [1792] (1989), *Vindication of the Rights of Women, with strictures on political and moral subjects*, London, reprinted in *The Works of Mary Wollstonecraft* (edited by Janet Todd and Marilyn Butler), London: W. Pickering, vol. 5.

NOTES

1. This while he harshly criticized Montesquieu and Helvétius for their lack of disapproval
    regarding the custom, in some nations, of rewarding warriors with 'the favours of women' – a
    practice 'which supposes the slavery of the best half of the human species': see Bentham, *The
    Rationale of Reward,* in *Works,* vol. 2, p. 197.
2. Bentham, 'Offences Against Taste', in Bentham [1931], Appendix: 'Bentham on Sex', p. 493.
3. Bentham to George Wilson, December 19–30 1786, in Bentham, *Works,* vol. 10, p. 167.
4. Bentham, 'Offences Against Taste', in Bentham [1931], Appendix: 'Bentham on Sex', p. 476.
5. Ibid., p. 477.
6. Bentham, 'Sexual Eccentricities, Appendix to the Penal Code', Mss, LXVIII, p. 14, edited by
    Lea Campos Boralevi [1984], Appendix, p. 217.
7. Bentham's writings include fragments on 'Non-Conformity', written in the early 1770s,
    'Offences of Impurity', written around 1780, the chapter of the Penal Code on 'Paederasty' and
    an 'Introduction', written in French, to a text on 'Non-conformity', in 1785. In 1814, a chapter
    of the Penal Code was devoted to 'Sex' and in 1816, he had the project of using it as a basis for
    a treatise entitled 'Sex'. Finally, the 'Appendix on Sexual Eccentricities' was written between
    1824 and 1828: see Crompton 1978 and Campos Boralevi 1984, pp. 37–38, and Appendix, pp.
    205–218.
8. Bentham, 'Population', in Bentham [1793–1795], p. 272.
9. *Annals of Agriculture,* vol. 39, 1797, pp. 393–426. The tract was reprinted under the title:
    *Situation and Relief of the Poor. By Jeremy Bentham, Esq. Addressed to the Editor of the
    Annals of Agriculture* (see Himes 1936, p. 267).
10. Ibid., pp. 422–423, cited in Himes 1936, pp. 267–268, according to which the Reverend
    mentioned by Bentham was Joseph Townsend (1739–1816), utilitarian physician, whose
    Dissertation on the Poor Laws (1786), and *Observations on Various Plans for the Relief of the
    Poor* (1788) were well known by Bentham. Himes was the first author, in 1936, to underline
    the full implication of this 'significant passage': contraception as a means for controlling
    reproduction – and, thus, according to Bentham, for lowering the poor rates.
11. Bentham, 'Offences Against Taste', in Bentham [1931], *Appendix:* 'Bentham on Sex', p. 476.
12. 'I too have my spunge', adds Bentham, 'but that a slow one, and not quite so rough a one'
    (cited in Himes 1936, p. 267). See also Charles Bahmueller's arguments against Himes's
    interpretation of the word 'spunge', in Bahmueller 1981, pp. 238–239.
13. Himes 1936, p. 275. See on the same subject James Mill's *Elements of Political Economy,*
    John Stuart Mill's articles in the *Black Dwarf,* Francis Place's *Handbills on different methods
    of contraception in the 1820s,* or his *Illustrations and Proofs of the Principle of Population:
    including an Examination of the Proposed Remedies of Mr. Malthus, and a Reply to the
    Objection of Mr. Godwin and others,* in 1822. In the same years, inspired by Place, Richard
    Carlile published a pamphlet on birth control methods in the *Republican* ('What Is Love?',
    Republican, vol. 11, n. 18, May 6, 1825), reprinted in 1826 as *Every Woman's Book: or What
    Is Love?*
14. On this general question, see Yasunori Fukagai [2001].
15. Bentham, 'Population', in Bentham [1793–1795], p. 272. The importance of these notes render
    William Stark's opinion very outdated: according to him, '[t]he economist need not give them
    more than a passing glance: Bentham speaks here, not as a social theorist, but as a teacher of
    morals (or, as some would say with equal justification, as a teacher of immorality)'.
16. Bentham, 'Population', in Bentham [1793–1795], p. 272.
17. Ibid., p. 273.
18. Bentham, 'Offences Against Taste', in Bentham [1931], *Appendix:* 'Bentham on Sex', p. 479.
19. Ibid.
20. Ibid.
21. Bentham, University College Mss., LXXIV, p. 134, published by Ogden in his edition of
    Bentham, *The Theory of Legislation* [1931], *Appendix,* p. 437, cited by Campos Boralevi

[1984], p. 13.

22. As Campos Boralevi reminds us; see Campos Boralevi 1984, p. 13 ff.
23. Bentham, University College Mss., LXX, p. 270, edited by Campos Boralevi 1984, *Appendix*, p. 200.
24. Bentham, University College Mss., LXX, p. 270, quoted by Campos Boralevi 1984, pp. 13–14.
25. Bentham, University College Mss., LXXII, p. 182, edited by Campos Boralevi 1984, *Appendix*, p. 201. In her book on the *Panopticon*, Janet Semple gives useful information on the abortive practices in London at the end of the XVIIIth century, quoting advertisements for 'advise and friendship if early sought for [which] may be productive of unexpected benefit, and the means of preserving reputation unsullied', or for 'Pill Benedicta', at £1.1 a box, decribed as 'an effective remedy to remove all obstructions and irregularities' (see Jeremy Bentham, University College Mss., CVIII, p. 101, quoted by Janet Semple [1993], pp. 290–291). To summarize, writes Janet Semple, 'It seems a reasonable inference that the rate for abortion in London was a guinea and that it was widely available' (ibid., p. 291). Under the Common Law, abortion was not a crime before 'quickening' at 4-6 months of pregnancy. In 1803 Lord Ellenborough's Act made procuring abortion before quickening a crime, to be punished by fine or transportation – death remaining the penalty after quickening (ibid., p. 291 n).
26. Bentham, University College Mss., LXXII, p. 182, edited by Campos Boralevi 1984, *Appendix*, p. 201.
27. Ibid., p. 201.
28. Ibid., p. 201.
29. 'Political economy is at once a science and an art. The value of the science has for its efficient cause and measure its subserviency to the art' (Bentham [1801–1804], p. 319), hence the epistemological status of the relation between population and wealth, being both object of science and prescription of art.
30. Bentham distinguishes among four 'classes' of poor: 1. The industrious poor, 'those who are willing to work that they may live'; 2. Idle mendicants, 'those who prefer rather to depend upon the precarious charity of passengers for subsistence, than to labour for their subsistence'; 3. Suspected persons: 'those who, having been arrrested on account of a crime, and set at liberty because of the insufficiency of proof, have remained with a stain upon their reputation, which hinders their obtaining employment'; and 4. Criminals, 'who have been confined for a time in prison, and have been set at liberty'. (Bentham, *Principles of Penal Law, Works*, vol. 1, p. 543).
31. Bentham, University College Mss., LXXXVII, p. 80, cited in Bahmueller 1981, p. 16.
32. Ibid., p. 16.
33. Bentham, 'Offences Against Taste', in Bentham 1931, *Appendix*: 'Bentham on Sex', p. 493.
34. This when Bentham compares female prositution to 'paederasty': the manuscripts are here abbreviated by Ogden. Bentham, 'Offences Against Taste', in Bentham 1931, *Appendix*: 'Bentham on Sex', p. 494.
35. The project of the 'National Charity Company' was part of the *Panopticon* global system, here applied to the management of the poor.
36. Also named *Timoioterim*. Both institutions were to be built 'after the Panopticon Estate was secured'. University College Mss., CXVII, p.103, cited in Williford 1975, p. 173.
37. An example: 'next to prostitutes, and other loose women, place aged women': see Bentham, *Outline of a Work entitled Pauper Management Improved, Works*, vol. 8, p. 372. In these buildings, the 'aggregation-separation principle' joined with the 'inspection principle' was to be applied, leading Bentham to discuss the opportunity of a separate establishment as not necessary against moral corruption, since, in an industry-house of the proposed form, separation may ... be as perfect in the same establishment, as between two establishments ever so widely distant' (ibid., pp. 372–373).
38. Bentham, University College Mss., CXVII, p. 103, cited in Semple 1993, p. 290.
39. Ibid., p. 290.
40. See Williford 1975, p. 173. Bentham also adapts to the *Sotimion* the main principle of the *Panopticon*: a plan designed so as the residents could see their visitors without being seen.

41. See Semple 1993, p. 290 ff., or Williford 1975, pp. 172–174. The transaction was also to be profitable – a principle which underlay the whole project of the 'National Charity Company'. The children of prostitutes or unmarried mothers were to be placed to work in the *Paedotrophium* until they had earned enough to pay back the expenses of their upbringing – the effect of which was supposed to raise the value of the child's life, measured in the following terms: 'According to the calculations which had then been ... made, the pecuniary value of a child at his birth – that value which at present is nor merely equal 0, but equal to an oppressively large negative quantity, would, under that system of maintenance and education which I had prepared for ... have been a positive quantity to no inconsiderable amount'. (Bentham, *Works*, XI, pp. 103–104, cited in Semple 1993, p. 294).
42. Bentham, *Treatise on Judicial Evidence*, Edinburgh, 1825, p. 210, cited in Campos Boralevi 1984, p. 12.
43. Bentham, *Principles of Judicial Procedure, Works*, vol. 2, p. 114.
44. Bentham, *Specimen of a Penal Code, Works*, vol. 1, p. 167.
45. This is the reason why Bentham denounces the danger of the quest for total equality in an unequal society, sought by '[t]hose who, from a vague notion of justice and of generosity, would bestow upon females an absolute equality [and who] would only spread a dangerous snare for them. To set them free, as much as it is possible for the laws so to do, from the necessity of pleasing their husbands, would be, in a moral point of view, to weaken instead of strengthen their empire', Bentham, *Principles of the Civil Code, Works*, vol. 1, p. 335.
46. Bentham 1983, 'Marginals', p. 54.
47. Bentham, *Specimen of a Penal Code, Works*, vol. 1, p. 167.
48. 'Women ... are more alive to, and susceptible of shame than men. From their earliest infancy, and even before they are capable of understanding the object of it, one of the most important branches of their education is to instil into them principles of modesty and reserve' Bentham, *Principles of Penal Law, Works*, vol. 1, p. 457.
49. See the brilliant lines on women's education in Helvetius's *De l'Esprit*.
50. Bentham, University College Mss., CLXX, p.145, cited in Campos Boralevi 1984, p. 16.
51. These parts include 'those which concern *Domestic Economy*, and the care of health', Bentham, *Chrestomathia, Works*, vol. 8, p. 56.
52. Bentham, University College Mss., CLXX, p. 144, edited by Campos Boralevi 1984, *Appendix*, p. 201. According to Elie Halévy, the demand for universal suffrage for men was first expressed in England by Lord Stanhope in 1774, followed by John Cartwright in 1776 (see Halévy 1972, p. 122 ff.
53. Bentham, University College Mss., CLXX, p. 151, cited in Campos Boralevi 1980, p. 247.
54. The rule was: one deputy for 70,000 souls – that is to say for 70,000 men.
55. Bentham, *Rid Yourselves of Ultramaria*, in Bentham 1995, Letter 7, 'Under the Code, no Ultramarian Deputation can be formed, thence nor the supposed security afforded. Ultramarian Deputation none', p. 173.
56. Bentham, University College Mss., CLVIII, p. 118, cited in Campos Boralevi [1984], p. 8.
57. Bentham, University College Mss., CLXX, p. 144, edited by Campos Boralevi 1984, *Appendix*, p. 202. The same argument can be found many years later in the Constitutional Code, where Bentham gives examples of such royalty: England, Russia, Austria, Sweden and the Directory of the East India Company. See Bentham, *Constitutional Code, Works*, vol. 9, p. 108.
58. This, according to John Bowring. See Bentham, *Works*, vol. 10, p. 450. Like Campos Boralevi, who developed her arguments in Campos Boralevi 1980, I disagree with Terence Ball's position, who considers that, '[i]n his proposals for depriving women of any distinctive political rights and roles, Bentham considerably outdistances James Mill' (Ball 1980a, p. 103).
59. Bentham, University College Mss., XXXIV, pp. 302–303, cited in Ball 1980a, p. 97
60. Bentham, *Works*, vol. 3, p. 463.
61. 'If a man who calls for the right of suffrage to be given to any one human being, calls fo its being refused to any other human being, it lies upon him to give a particular reason for such refusal' (Bentham, *Constitutional Code, Works*, vol. 9, p. 107).
62. Bentham, 'Economy as applied to Office', in Bentham [1822], 1989, p. 99.

63. Ibid., p. 97.
64. Bentham, *Essay on Political Tactics, Works,* vol. 2, p. 327.
65. Ibid., p. 327.
66. Ibid., p. 327.
67. 'All the functions of law may be referred to these four heads: to maintain security; to provide subsistence; to produce abundance; to favour equality'. The two first are primary ends, and the two others 'subordinate' ends. Without security, equality could not exist; without subsistence, abundance is impossible.
68. 'Aristotle', writes Bentham in *An Introduction to the Principles of Morals and Legislation,* fascinated by the prejudice of the times, 'divides mankind into two distinct species, that of freemen, and that of slaves. Certain men were born to be slaves, and ought to be slaves. — Why? Because they are so' (Bentham, *An Introduction to the Principles of Morals and Legislation,* [1780] 1948, p. 268 n.).
69. Ibid., p. 9.

10. An Eighteenth-Century English Feminist Response To Political Economy: Priscilla Wakefield's *Reflections* (1798)

Robert Dimand

The case for women's ability to participate in the emerging discipline of political economy was stated with characteristic vigour by Lady Mary Wortley Montagu in 1760, when she wrote to Sir James Steuart about her re-reading of the manuscript of his *Inquiry into the Principles of Political Oeconomy* (Steuart 1767) that

> I confess I cannot help being a little vain of comprehending a system that is calculated only for a thinking mind and cannot be tasted without a willingness to lay aside many prejudices which arise from education and the conversation of people no wiser than ourselves. I do not only mean my own sex when I speak of our confined way of reasoning; there are very many of yours as incapable of judging otherwise than they have been early taught, as the most ignorant milkmaid. Nay, I believe a girl out of a village or a nursery more capable of receiving instruction than a lad just set free from the university (Halsband 1970, p. 294).[1]

While it is only in the nineteenth century that women began to publish expository works of political economy (beginning in England with Jane Haldimand Marcet in 1816 and Harriet Martineau in 1832, and in France with the English-born Mary Meynieu in 1839), women began to respond critically in print to political economy near the end of the preceding century. Kathryn Sutherland (1995, pp. 104–105) has drawn attention to a striking early instance of a feminist critique of the economic and social role of women that was presented as a response to Smithian political economy: the Quaker philanthropist Priscilla Wakefield's *Reflections on the Present Condition of the Female Sex; with Suggestions for its Improvement* (1798).

Priscilla Wakefield (née Bell, 1751–1832) is familiar to historians of economics, if at all, as the mother of Edward Wakefield, whose *Account of Ireland, Statistical and Political*, appeared in 1812, and as the grandmother and anxious guardian of Edward Gibbon Wakefield, the theorist of colonization who was closely involved with the Durham Report in Canada and the colonization of New Zealand, and whose writings drew Marx's close attention.[2] Palgrave's *Dictionary* (1894–1899) published articles on two of her sons and on her grandson without mentioning her. M.F. Lloyd Prichard (1968, p. 9), after quoting from Priscilla Wakefield's diary her concern about her grandson's obstinacy, identifies her only as 'a prominent Quaker, author of several books, including *A Family Tour through the British Empire* (1814), and an active social worker. She was founder of the first savings bank at Tottenham, where she also founded a maternity home and interested herself in the establishment of schools for the poor.' Like Jane Marcet a generation later, Priscilla Wakefield was a successful author of educational works for children: her *Introduction to Botany* appeared in eleven editions and was translated into French; *A Family Tour through the British Empire* reached a fifteenth edition; and *Mental Improvement, or the Beauties and Wonders of Nature and Art* an eleventh edition (E.I.C. in *Dictionary of National Biography*). *The Juvenile Travellers*, recounting an imaginary tour of Europe, was published in nineteen editions over fifty years.

Reflections on the Present Condition of the Female Sex was written in a more serious tone. Although stressing the responsibilities of women rather than their freedoms, Wakefield's book advocated a sweeping extension of the economic opportunities open to women. The opening words linked the book to the literature of political economy:

> It is asserted by Doctor Adam Smith that every individual is a burthen upon the society to which he belongs, who does not contribute his share of productive labour for the good of the whole. The Doctor, when he lays down this principle, speaks in general terms of man, as being capable of forming a social compact for mutual defence, and the advantage of the community at large. He does not absolutely specify, that both sexes, in order to render themselves beneficial members of society, are equally required to comply with these terms; but since the female sex is included in the idea of the species, and as women possess the same qualities as men, though perhaps in a different degree, their sex cannot free them from the claim of the public for their proportion of usefulness.

The use that Wakefield made of Smith's concept of productive labour is noteworthy. Smith did not identify productive labour with useful labour as closely as did Wakefield, for he accepted that some forms of unproductive labour such as national defence and the administration of justice were useful and necessary. Smith (1776, Book 2, Chapter 3) treated productive labour as labour that is hired out of capital rather than revenue (that is, labour that results in a sale that replenishes the capital advanced plus a profit) or, alternatively, as labour that produces a good rather than a service that vanishes at the moment of its performance. From either of these two rather different standpoints, reproductive labour in the household (the bulk of it performed by women) would not be productive labour, as it produced services rather than goods and was not sold outside the household (even though wage work outside the household might be impossible without someone carrying out the household production). Implicitly, Smith treated such household work of women as comparable to the role of domestic servants, which he declared unproductive. He made only passing mention of the sphere of household production and reproductive labour in *The Wealth of Nations*, but had more to say about the legal status of women in successive stages of development in his unpublished *Lectures on Jurisprudence,* where he acknowledged that 'the laws of most countries being made by men generally are very severe on the women, who can have no remedy for this oppression' (Smith 1978; Rendall 1987; Pujol 1992, pp. 16–22; Clark 1993; Nyland 1993). Wakefield, in contrast, took for granted that all useful labour was productive labour, and that the labour of women, whether within the household or in the market sphere, was useful and productive.[3]

Smith was not the only political economist whose authority was invoked by Wakefield, for she also noted that 'a century ago, as we are told by Sir Josiah Child, in his discourse concerning trade, ... that the education of the Dutch women prepared them to receive instruction from their husbands, in the different species of commerce in which they were engaged: He recommends the imitation of this example to the English, as one of the means that promoted the riches and prosperity of Holland' (P. Wakefield 1798, pp. 74–75).

Referring to the theoretical debate over women's social role centring around Macaulay (1790) and Wollstonecraft (1792), subsequently collected by Luria (1974), Wakefield (1798, p. 8) emphasized her greater attention to the practical matter of economic opportunity: 'Their rights and their duties have lately occupied the pens of writers of eminence; the employments which may properly exercise their faculties, and fill up their time in a useful manner, without encroaching upon those professions, which are appropriate to men, remain to be defined'.

Wakefield's *Reflections* (1798) were issued by the same publisher, Joseph Johnson, who had published Mary Wollstonecraft's *Vindication of the Rights of Woman* in 1792 and who had supported the radical Wollstonecraft with translation and reviewing work (such as her 1790 review of Macaulay in Johnson's *Analytical Review*) and introduced her to her future husband William Godwin. Johnson was the friend and publisher of the radicals Godwin, Tom Paine, and Joseph Priestly and of the poets Blake, Coleridge, and Wordsworth, and in 1798 spent six months in jail for selling a radical pamphlet (Holmes 1987, pp. 10, 298). In contrast to Wollstonecraft's assertion of the rights of women as citizens, Hannah More argued in several works,[4] notably in 1799 in her *Strictures on the Modern System of Education,* that women had obligations, not rights, and that if women were given a proper moral upbringing, no reform of their social or legal status was needed (Wardle 1951, p. 203; Hufton 1995, p. 453; More 1799; Luria 1974). Wakefield (1798) gave that argument a novel twist. While joining More in stressing women's obligations, Wakefield's analysis of how to enable women to fulfil those obligations to society made a powerful case for new educational and employment opportunities for women and against gender inequality in wages. The summary of the contents of the first chapter of her *Reflections* characterizes the chapter as 'Introductory Observations, shewing the claim which Society has on Women to employ their time usefully; pointing out the characteristic perfection of the mental qualifications of both Sexes, and the necessity which there is for the talents of Women being directed towards procuring an independent support' (Wakefield 1798, p. 1). By grounding her argument on obligations rather than on Wollstonecraft's vindication of women's rights, Wakefield distanced her reform proposals from any association with the enthusiasm of Wollstonecraft for the French Revolution or of the historian Catherine Macaulay for republicanism.[5] Wakefield's analysis accepted a division of society into four distinct social classes, so that her sweeping proposals for altering the social status of women were made more acceptable to the anti-Jacobin political climate of England in the late 1790s by being separated from any challenge to existing political institutions and class structure.

Wakefield's chapter summaries indicate the economic theme of her argument, and its adherence to class distinctions: 'The necessity of Women being educated for the exercise of lucrative employments shewn, and the absurdity of a Woman honourably earning a support, being excluded from Society, exposed' (P. Wakefield 1798, Chapter 3, p. 29). Wakefield (1798, p. 63) defined the first class as the nobility and those who rivalled them in power, the second class as those with 'a respectable subsistence approaching to opulence,' while the 'honest and useful industry' of the third class 'raises them above want, without procuring for them the means of splendid or luxurious gratification.' Chapters Four and Five were 'On the Duties, Studies, and Amusements' of women of the first and second classes of society, leading to Chapter Six on 'Lucrative Employments for the first and second classes suggested, recommending as agreeable means of procuring a respectable support, – Literature. – Painting; Historic, Portrait, and Miniature. – Engraving. – Statuary. – Modelling. – Music. – Landscape Gardening. – With Strictures on a Theatrical Life' (1798, p. 123).

In contrast to the 'duties, studies, and amusements' of the two highest social classes, Chapter Seven was

> On the duties, attainments, and employments of Women of the third class. – Censuring the giving of greater rewards to Men than Women, for similar exertions of time, labour, and ingenuity; and the necessity there is for Ladies of rank encouraging

their own Sex. – Recommending the teaching of Girls; the serving of retail shops; the undertaking for the female sex; turnery, and farming, as eligible means of support: with an extract from Sir F.M. Eden, of an account of a Female Farmer (1797, p. 140).

For the labouring poor, there were neither amusements nor attainments, nor even much scope for employments, for Chapter Eight offered only 'Observations on the condition of the fourth class of Women, suggesting a discrimination in distributing Charity, and an encouragement of Marriage, as means for its improvement: with remarks on Schools of Industry, and the Houses of the Poor' (1798, p. 176).

While Hannah More viewed women's obligations as self-denial and acceptance of their limited and subordinate role, Priscilla Wakefield viewed women as obligated to be useful members of society (in the sense she attributed to Adam Smith of engaging in productive labour) and to make proper use of their capacities (without upsetting the established hierarchy of social classes). 'The indolent indulgence and trifling pursuits in which those who are distinguished by the appellation of gentlewomen, often pass their lives, may be attributed, with a greater probability', declared Wakefield (1798, p. 3) 'to a contracted education, custom, false pride, and idolizing adulation, than to any defect in their intellectual capacities'. Admitting the possibility that the intellectual and physical capacities of men and women might differ, she held that

> this concession by no means proves, that even in this enlightened age and country, the talents of women have ever been generally exerted to the utmost extent of their capacity, nor that they have been turned to the most useful subjects; nor does it imply, that the cultivation they receive, is adequate to bring into action the full strength of those powers, which have been bestowed on them by nature (Wakefield 1798, p. 5).

History recorded 'memorable instances of female capacity in all the various branches of human excellence' and only mis-directed education of women had 'concealed, not only from others, but from themselves, the energies of which they are capable' (Wakefield 1798, p. 5).

In her second chapter, Wakefield invoked the Spartan example and urged a hardier rearing of girls, more like that given to boys, but, in a lightly ironic tone, reassured readers that

> No apprehension need be entertained of women becoming too robust; their natural inferiority in strength, and the indispositions incident to child-bearing, will too often secure the feminine delicacy of their persons and constitutions, and prevent them from acquiring more vigour than is requisite to the performance of the active duties of the mother and the mistress of the family (Wakefield 1798, p. 14).

Wakefield's third chapter, on education and the duties of women in marriage and in single life, used acceptance of a traditional goal to argue for a radical reformation of women's education and opportunities. She noted that 'In the education of females, the same view actuates every rank: an advantageous settlement in marriage is the universal prize, for which parents of all classes enter their daughters upon the lists; and partiality or self complacency assures to every competitor the most flattering prospect of success' (Wakefield 1798, p. 29). While accepting the goal of a happy marriage as laudable, she held that the prevailing education of women was geared to attracting a mate rather than to a lifetime of companionship and partnership. Besides, 'widowhood and a single life are the allotment of many ... Adversity often places both sexes in situations wholly unexpected; against such transitions, the voice of wisdom admonishes each to be prepared' (Wakefield 1798, p. 33). Married women should be educated so that they were capable of discharging the duty of educating in turn their own children 'at least, as far as respects principles, morals, and the cultivation of the heart' (1798, p. 40) instead of hiring a governess, while both single woman and, in case of widowhood, married women even of the more affluent classes needed to be capable of earning their own livelihood in a dignified and respectable manner.

Wakefield held that:

> There is scarcely a more helpless object in the wide circle of misery which the vicissitudes of civilized society display, than a woman genteelly educated, whether single or married, who is deprived, by any unfortunate accident, of the protection and support of male relations; unaccustomed to struggle with difficulty, unacquainted with any resource to supply an independent maintenance, she is reduced to the depths of wretchedness, and not unfrequently, if she be young and handsome, is driven by despair to those paths which lead to infamy ... our streets teem with multitudes of unhappy women, many of whom might have been rescued from their present degradation, or who would perhaps never have fallen into it, had they been instructed in the exercise of some art or profession, which would have enabled them to procure for themselves a respectable support by their own industry (Wakefield 1798, pp. 66–67).

Beyond such precautionary training, Wakefield decried the prejudice against women of 'any degree above the vulgar' spending their time usefully, employing their time and abilities to contribute to the support of themselves and their families:

> that which is a moral excellence in one rational being, deserves the same estimation in another; therefore, if it be really honourable in a man, to exert the utmost of his abilities, whether mental or corporal, in the acquisition of a competent support for himself, and for those who have a natural claim upon his protection; it must be equally so in a woman' (Wakefield 1798, p. 68).

While she strongly preferred having children taught at home by their mothers, Wakefield (1798, pp. 43, 47–48) accepted that it was not always practicable but lamented that 'few of the candidates for the important office of educating youth, are fitted for it; nay, very few have even an idea of the severe sacrifices which the undertaking requires, if it is properly performed'. For too many of the subordinate teachers in boarding schools, 'a smattering of the French language, and skill in the ornamental works which are in vogue, constitute their chief knowledge' although the misfortunes of individuals in the French Revolution had lately furnished a supply of better-qualified instructors. Accordingly, Wakefield called for the establishment of seminaries to train 'young women, of small expectations' as teachers, educating these future teachers 'not only by a regular course of study, but also by a thorough initiation into the philosophical principles of education, founded upon the opinions of the most eminent writers upon the subject'. Such training of women as teachers would have the advantage of

> affording a respectable subsistence to great numbers of young women, who are reduced to misery through want of employment, by enabling them to teach those sciences, which are exclusively taught by masters, an evil that calls loudly for redress … Women only … should be permitted to instruct their sex in these seductive arts [dancing and music]. It ought to be their privilege to do so in every other. Nature has imposed no invincible barrier to their acquisition and communication of languages, arithmetic, writing, drawing, geography, or any science which is proper for girls to learn (Wakefield 1798, p. 50–52).

The teaching positions in the proposed seminaries for female teachers should be taken over by women as soon as possible, so the proposal involved also higher education for women (as Mary Astell had advocated a century before) to provide the female faculty for the seminaries. A great extension of the role of women in education was thus derived from the need to protect 'the persons of girls advancing towards maturity' from being 'exposed to the wanton eye of a dancing-master' (Wakefield 1798, p. 51).

Wakefield protested that:

> Men monopolize not only the most advantageous employments, and such as exclude women from exercise of them, by the publicity of their nature, or the extensive knowledge they require, but even many of those, which are consistent with the female character. Another heavy discouragement to the industry of women, is the inequality of the reward of their labour, compared with that of men, an injustice which pervades every species of employment performed by both sexes ... Male stay-makers, mantua-makers, and hair-dressers are better paid than female artists of the same professions; but surely it will never be urged as an apology for this disproportion, that women are not as capable of making stays, gowns, dressing hair, and similar arts, as men (Wakefield 1798, pp. 150–153).

If women are not superior it was only because their lower rewards would not repay them for learning the trade. Accordingly, women of the upper two classes should resolve to employ only women, buy only clothes made by women, and frequent only shops where they would be served by women, whenever feasible. For example, 'The serving of retail shops, which deal in articles of female consumption, should be exclusively appropriated to women' (Wakefield 1798, p. 164). 'Every undertaker should employ women, for the express purpose of supplying the female dead, with those things which are requisite. How shocking is the idea of our persons being exposed, even after death, to the observation of a parcel of undertaker's men' (Wakefield 1798, p. 165). The business of a stationer, the compounding of medicines in an apothecary's shop, pastry and confectionery, toy making, and, for the widows of publicans and 'other women of a certain age', the keeping of respectable public houses, were all suitable occupations for women as well as men. So was farming, as documented by a lengthy extract from Sir Frederic Morton Eden (1797) (Wakefield 1798, pp. 171–175).

At the close of her *Reflections*, Wakefield (1798, pp. 194–195) considered how environmental influences, such as the improvement of the housing of the working poor, could 'gradually remove those obstacles that have hitherto impeded their progress in morals and civilization.' The design of the houses of the poor 'affects not only their enjoyment, but has a material influence upon their civilization.' In the overcrowded homes of the urban working poor, 'many indigent families are cooped up in one house, in obscure corners, concealed from the observation of those, to whom they look up with respect, on account of their superior rank', a situation risking the corruption of the 'health of body, and purity of mind, of a vast number of persons' (Wakefield 1798, p. 194). For all the social condescension in this passage, and a wish for surveillance that brings to mind Jeremy Bentham's Panopticon prison design, Wakefield's discussion recognized that social practice, including sexual morality and gender relations, evolves over time, and can be shaped by such environmental changes as improved housing.

Priscilla Wakefield advocated a sweeping expansion of educational and employment opportunities for women, not on the basis of their inherent equal rights as citizens (as the republican and revolutionary sympathizers Macaulay and Wollstonecraft had done), but on the grounds of enabling them to realize their capacities to discharge their responsibilities to society. Wakefield used the conservative language of the duties and obligations of women to argue for a radical alteration of women's education and opportunities. As a rhetorical strategy, this approach was not a success. Unlike her writings intended 'For the Amusement and Instruction of the Young', Wakefield's *Reflections* appeared in only two editions, with the second nineteen years later in 1817. In contrast, the more conservative Hannah More's *Strictures on the Modern System of*

Education (1799), which was published a year after Wakefield's *Reflections*, sold nineteen thousand copies in thirteen editions (Hufton 1995, p. 453). More's *Cheap Repository Tracts* (1795–1798) 'designed to keep the English poor from revolting like the French and priced to be within their reach ... sold two million copies in their first three years, a publishing feat unparalleled in the period' (Anderson and Zinsser 2000, p. 126). The more radical Wollstonecraft's *Vindication of the Rights of Woman* continues to be reprinted and attracted the interest of later women's suffrage activists (such as the economist Millicent Garrett Fawcett, who wrote an introduction to the centenary edition). No trace of an influence of Wakefield's *Reflections* can be discerned in one work of political economy where it might be expected, the extensive commentary in her grandson's four volume edition of *The Wealth of Nations* (E.G. Wakefield 1843). What sets Wakefield's *Reflections* apart from the better-known works of her contemporaries Macaulay, Wollstonecraft and More is Wakefield's concern with practical economic issues of women's ability to be self-supporting, her linkage of women's obligations to Adam Smith's distinction in *The Wealth of Nations* between productive and unproductive labour, and the way in which her writing was informed by acquaintance with *The Wealth of Nations*, Sir Frederic Morton Eden's *Condition of the Poor* (1797), and Sir Josiah Child's *Discourse about Trade*. Wollstonecraft (1792, pp. 58, 90, 133–134, 188) referred repeatedly to *The Theory of Moral Sentiments*, but not to *The Wealth of Nations*, and wrote little about trades that women could follow. Among English writers on women's rights and duties in the 1790s, Priscilla Wakefield stands out for her concern with possible employments and her contact with the literature of political economy.

REFERENCES

Anderson, Bonnie S. and Judith P. Zinsser (2000), *A History of Their Own: Women in Europe from Prehistory to the Present*, vol. 2, revised ed., New York: Oxford University Press.

E.I.C. (1899), 'Wakefield, Mrs. Priscilla (1751–1832)', in Sir Leslie Stephen and Sir Sidney Lee (eds), *Dictionary of National Biography*, vol. 20, Oxford: Oxford University Press, pp. 455–456.

Child, J. (1690), *A Discourse About Trade*, London: BART.

Clark, Henry C. (1993), 'Women and Humanity in Scottish Enlightenment Social Thought: The Case of Adam Smith', *Historical Reflections/Reflexions Historiques*, **19**, 335–361.

Eden, Sir Frederick Morton [1797] (1928), *The State of the Poor*, London B. and J. White (abridged and edited by A.G.L. Rogers), London: G. Routledge & Sons.

Gatens, Moira (1991). '"The Oppressed State of My Sex": Wollstonecraft on Reason, Feeling and Equality', in Mary Lyndon Shanley and Carole Pateman (eds), *Feminist Interpretations and Political Theory*, University Park, PA: Pennsylvania State University Press.

Halsband, Robert (ed.) (1970), *The Selected Letters of Lady Mary Wortley Montagu*, New York: St. Martin's, reprinted Harmondsworth, Middlesex: Penguin, 1986.

Holmes, Richard (1987), 'Introduction' and notes to Mary Wollstonecraft, *A Short Residence in Sweden*, and William Godwin, *Memoirs of the Author of 'The Rights of Woman'*, London: Penguin.

Hufton, Olwen (1995), *The Prospect Before Her: A History of Women in Western Europe 1500–1800*, London: Harper Collins and New York: Alfred A. Knopf.

Prichard, Muriel F. Lloyd (1968), 'Introduction' to *The Collected Works of Edward Gibbon Wakefield*, Glasgow and London: Collins.

Luria, Gina (ed.) (1974), *The Feminist Controversy in England 1788–1810*, New York: Garland Publishing.

Macaulay, Catherine (1790), *Letters on Education*, London, reprinted in Luria (1974).

More, Hannah (1799), *Strictures on the Modern System of Education*, London: T. Caddell, Jr, and W. Davies, in the Strand. Reprinted in Luria (1974).

Nyland, Chris (1993), 'Adam Smith, Stage Theory and the Status of Women,' *History of Political Economy*, **25** (4), 617–640.

Palgrave, R.H. Inglis (ed.) (1894–1899), *Dictionary of Political Economy*, London: Macmillan.

Pujol, Michèle (1992), *Feminism and Anti-Feminism in Early Economic Thought*, Aldershot, UK, and Brookfield, VT: Edward Elgar Publishing.

Rendall, Jane (1987), 'Virtue and Commerce: Women in the Making of Adam Smith's Political Economy,' in Ellen Kennedy and Susan Mendus (eds), *Women in Western Political Philosophy, Kant to Nietzsche*, Brighton: Wheatsheaf Books.

Smith, Adam (1759), *The Theory of Moral Sentiments* (edited by D.D. Raphael and A.L. Macfie, Glasgow Edition of the Works and Correspondence of Adam Smith), Oxford: Clarendon Press, 1976, reprinted Indianapolis: Liberty Fund (1982).

Smith, Adam (1776), *An Inquiry into the Nature and Causes of the Wealth of Nations*, (edited by R.H. Campbell and A.S. Skinner, textual editor W.B. Todd), Glasgow Edition of the Works and Correspondence of Adam Smith, Oxford: Clarendon Press, 1976, reprinted Indianapolis: Liberty Fund (1981).

Smith, Adam (1978), *Lectures on Jurisprudence* (edited by R.L. Meek, D.D. Raphael and

P.G. Stein), Glasgow Edition of the Works and Correspondence of Adam Smith, Oxford: Clarendon Press, reprinted Indianapolis: Liberty Fund (1982).

Spender, Dale (1982), *Women of Ideas and What Men Have Done to Them,* London: Routledge & Kegan Paul.

Steuart, Sir James (1767), *Inquiry into the Principles of Political Oeconomy* (edited Andrew S. Skinner), Chicago: University of Chicago Press (1966).

Sutherland, Kathryn (1995), 'Adam Smith's Master Narrative: Women and the Wealth of Nations', in Stephen Copley and Kathryn Sutherland (eds), *Adam Smith's Wealth of Nations: New Interdisciplinary Essays*, Manchester, UK: Manchester University Press, pp. 97–121.

Wakefield, Edward Gibbon (ed.) (1843), *An Inquiry into the Nature and Causes of the Wealth of Nations, by Adam Smith, LL. D* (with Notes from Ricardo, M'Culloch, Chalmers and Other Eminent Political Economists. With Life of the Author by Dugald Stewart), London: C. Knight & Co.

Wakefield, Priscilla (1798), *Reflections on the Present Condition of the Female Sex, with Suggestions for its Improvement*, London: J. Johnson, and Darton and Harvey.

Wardle, Ralph M. (1951), *Mary Wollstonecraft*, Lawrence: University of Kansas Press, as excerpted in the Norton Critical Edition of Wollstonecraft [1792] (1975).

Wollstonecraft, Mary (1790), Review of Catherine Macaulay's *Letters on Education, Analytical Review*, vol. 8, pp. 241–254.

Wollstonecraft, Mary (1792), *A Vindication of the Rights of Woman*, London: Joseph Johnson; Norton Critical Edition (edited by Carol H. Poston), New York: W. W. Norton (1975).

NOTES

1. Her enthusiasm for the book and its author, and her influence with her son-in-law the Earl of Bute (tutor and, briefly, prime minister to George III) contributed to the eventual publication of the book, despite Steuart's Jacobite past.
2. She was also the aunt of the prison reformer Elizabeth Fry.
3. Palgrave (1894–1899, vol. 3, p. 647) reports that her son Daniel Wakefield (1776–1846) 'Wrote An Essay upon Political Œconomy, being an inquiry into the truth of the two positions of the French Œconomists that labour employed in manufactures is unproductive, and that all taxes ultimately fall upon or settle in the surplus produce of land, 1st ed. 1799; 2nd, 1804, [and] was a follower of Sir J. Steuart' so the concept of productive labour was presumably a topic of discussion in the Wakefield family around 1798.
4. Wakefield (1798, p. 143) included 'Hannah More's Repository' in a suggested library for young women of the third class.
5. Wakefield also escaped the vituperation aimed at Catherine Macaulay for her marriage to a man twenty-six years younger than her, and at the memory of Mary Wollstonecraft after her widower, the radical philosopher William Godwin, published an indiscreet memoir of her (Hufton 1995, pp. 454-455; Spender 1982, pp. 127-156; Holmes 1987; Gatens 1991).

11. The Market for Virtue: Jean-Baptiste Say on Women in the Economy and Society

Evelyn L. Forget[1]

One of the most striking features of popular political rhetoric is the conflation of the mythology of 'virtue' with that of 'market'. It seems obvious to some that a well-functioning market economy flourishes in a society in which civic virtue is nurtured in the bosom of a well-functioning family, and that a well-functioning family is dependent upon the widespread acceptance of a particular set of social and economic roles for women. Similarly, a dynamic and productive economy, it is often claimed, allows women to specialize in their 'natural' (and unpaid) careers as wife and mother. 'Family' and 'economy' are mutually sustaining. Proponents of this position often present the argument in historical dress, recalling the Eisenhower era (or *Deuteronomy,* or the *Qur'an,* or Plato) in order to demonstrate the persistence of their particular vision and, therefore, its consistency with 'nature'.

This essay attempts to place the connection between gender and economy into a different historical context, by demonstrating how a patriarchal analysis of gender and a popular justification for a market economy co-existed and reinforced one another in the writing of Jean-Bapiste Say. Say's work is important because his *Traité d'économie politique* (1803)[2] became a standard textbook of economic analysis, both in France and (through its many translations) in the United States, Central and South America and throughout Europe. Say was one of the first, and certainly the most influential, of modern economists to both write a textbook of economics and in *Olbie,* his clearest and earliest statement of sympathy with *Idéologie,*[3] construct an analysis of the social role of women in an ideal society that would find its way into his economic analysis. His gender analysis is not particularly original or unique, but it is explicit, and it is through Say's economic writing that this vision of the place of women in society and the economy began to be naturalized into nineteenth-century economic analysis. The slowness with which feminist analysis has made inroads into economic theory suggests the power of that vision.

The importance of Say in the development of nineteenth-century economic analysis in France is well documented (see Gilbert Faccarello and Philippe Steiner 1990), and one can take John Stuart Mill's word for his intellectual debt to Say's economic writings (see, for example: John Stuart Mill 1923, p. 446). Say's economic analysis was widely read in Britain during his own lifetime, and had a subsequent influence through Ricardo and Mill. The rich relationship between American and French political and economic analysis during the revolutionary period is very well known and, in this connection, it is worth remembering that Thomas Jefferson had intellectual ties to *Idéologie* and was certainly acquainted with Say's economics. My claim is that, at the same time that Say's economics was being lauded by French, American, and English economists, his gender analysis was making similar inroads without fanfare and without recognition. By the time the social context that generated Say's analysis of gender changed, the analysis itself had become so much a part of the way in which economists think that it disappeared from conscious consideration and exerted its influence behind the scenes. Gender is, for many economists, simply not a matter of economic analysis.

The next section of this essay illustrates, with a very broad brush, the political context of feminist agitation to which Say reacted by constructing his analysis of the appropriate roles for women in the economy. Then, I examine Jean-Bapiste Say's analysis of the family as the fundamental unit of political economy, within which the subsistence of individuals is provided and moral virtues inculcated. It is upon these moral virtues that a market economy and a civil society must be based, according to Say. The analogy between the first and the family in Say's economics is documented. Finally, I suggest that this vision of social interaction, constructed in the chaos of the revolutionary decade, has echoes in contemporary economic analysis and in popular political rhetoric.

WOMEN IN THE FRENCH REVOLUTION

In popular histories of the French Revolution, the representations of women range from docile 'sisters' nursing the wounded revolutionaries, to 'Amazons' storming the Paris Council dressed in red caps and pantaloons (Doris Kadish 1991). The images and sympathies differ significantly, but the one point upon which all are in agreement is that women were not invisible during that conflagration. Revolutionary feminism was a significant political force, attracted both supporters and detractors, and influenced the women's movement in France throughout the nineteenth century (Claire Moses 1984;

Joan Rendall 1984; Renate Bridenthal and Claudia Koonz 1977).

The 1789 *Declaration of the Rights of Man* became the preamble to the *Constitution* of 1791. Olympe de Gouges, eager to ensure that the Revolution bring women 'political rights' in addition to the 'political voice' they had already obtained, wrote and published a *Declaration of the Rights of Women*.[4] Drawing its inspiration and style from the earlier document, her *Declaration* demanded equal rights for women before the law and in all aspects of public and private life. This decidedly political document was a contribution to an ongoing debate, throughout the revolutionary decade, about the natural roles of women and men in society. Mary Wollstonecraft's *A Vindication of the Rights of Woman* (1792), among other works, emerged out of this tempest. No intellectual actively involved, as was Jean-Bapiste Say, in the construction and legitimation of the social sciences could be unaware of the tumult, even if, as is much more likely, he was not aware of the many strains and details of women's activism during the decade.

The controversy wells up in distinct places: in May of 1793, Clare Lacombe (a former actress) and Pauline Léon (a former chocolate-maker) founded the *Société Républicaines-Révolutionnaires,* the most infamous women's revolutionary club of the time. With Léon as president, the Club established itself in the library of the Jacobins Club and took up the battle against 'enemies of the republic'. Strong supporters of the Jacobins, these Club members took their battle to the streets where, in revolutionary bonnets and pantaloons, they harassed the Girondins and silenced them in the galleries of the National Convention.

In June, the Jacobins took over the National Convention and expelled the Girondins with the support of the *Société*. In July and August, women were accepted on the councils of the Parisian sections. But later that year, the deputies to the Convention outlawed women's political clubs with only one dissenting vote. A delegation of women, wearing their infamous red bonnets, was led by Claire Lacombe to protest the betrayal before the Paris Council. Pierre Chaumette, president of the Council, responded:

> It is horrible – unnatural – for a woman to want to become a man ... since when has it been decent for women to abandon their pious household tasks and their children's cradles, to meet in public places yelling from the galleries? Impudent women who want to turn themselves into men, don't you have enough already? What more do you want? Your despotism is the only force we cannot resist, for it is the despotism of love, thus the work of nature. In the name of nature itself, stay as you are. Instead of envying our perilous, busy lives, you should be content to help us forget all this at home in our families, where we can rest our eyes with the enchanting sight of our children made happy through your cares (quoted in Bessières and Niedzwiecki 1991, p. 8).

The rhetoric had its effect. Olympe de Gouges was already dead, a victim of the guillotine, and Lacombe effectively silenced. The Terror or Robespierre's 'virtuous republic' sent women back into their homes, except for the few chosen to personify the 'goddesses of Reason', dressed in white with blue capes and bonnets of liberty as they were carried into the transformed cathedrals to the strains of *Ça ira* and the *Marseillaise* – priestesses for the newly established 'Cult of the Supreme Being'.

The debate about gender roles was similarly the inspiration for some of the more extreme revolutionary fiction. The Marquis de Sade played the controversy out at length in several novels, and Apollinaire saw over fifty years ago how 'public morals' were outraged by *Juliette*.

> The Marquis de Sade, that freest of spirits to have lived so far, had ideas of his own on the subject of woman: he wanted her to be as free as man. Out of these ideas – they will come though some day – grew a dual novel, *Justine* and *Juliette*. It was not by accident the Marquis chose heroines and not heroes. Justine is woman as she has been hitherto, enslaved, miserable and less than human; her opposite, Juliette represents the woman whose advent he anticipated, a figure of whom minds have as yet no conception, who is arising out of mankind, who shall have wings, and who shall renew the world (quoted in Sade 1988, p. ix).

If Juliette represents 'the woman whose advent [Sade] anticipated', she also represents the woman who is dreaded by many of his contemporaries.

Revolutionary stories present tales of 'Amazons' and 'Furies' alongside heroines of unfathomable courage. It was a romantic era, and the histories of the period capture the spirit. Well-dressed gentlewomen carrying hunting knives and half-sabres alongside their skirts jostle for position in the old histories with Burke's 'unspeakable abomination of the furies of Hell incarnated in the fallen form of the most debased women' (quoted in Bessières and Niedzwiecki 1991, p. 5). It was, and we must not forget this, the women of *Les Halles* – the market district – who made up the greatest portion of the crowd which stormed Versailles, who formed the mobs in the street riots, and who challenged the revolutionaries to make sure the revolution began for women as well. No one living through the revolution or the revolutionary decade could be ignorant of either the actions of crowds of women, the even more colourful legends of unspeakable behaviours ostensibly perpetrated by women, or demands (reasonable and measured, alongside strident and aggressive) for political suffrage. Robespierre went far in suppressing those demands, which he conceived dangerous to the republic, and Bonaparte, coming to power in 1799, ensured that women would be effectively muzzled for much longer via the infamous Napoleonic Code. But the period between 1789 and 1799 saw many individual women raise their voices in demands that had not been heard so clearly before, and certainly not at such insistent volume.

It is in this context that I want to present the gender analysis articulated by J.-B. Say. Say belonged (if one can belong to such an amorphous group) to that collection of individuals who were called *Idéologistes* by Destutt de Tracy (who was one of the founders of the movement) and *Idéologues* by Napoleon (who rejected their analyses and their political aspirations after having risen to political power with their help). The social and intellectual relationships in this milieu were very complex, and this essay is not the place to attempt to untangle them.[5] But it is important to read the labels carefully: in this pre-Marxian world, *Idéologie* meant the science of ideas. It was based on a sensualist philosophy which argued that human beings can only have reliable knowledge if they gather 'facts' by means of their own senses, and upon a behaviourist psychology. It was, according to its proponents, a science independent of 'men' and history. That is, it was not an articulation of class interests (a concept with which its proponents had great difficulty), nor was it imagined to be socially mediated. It was 'scientific', according to its disciples, in the same way that Newtonian physics was scientific.

The *Idéologistes,* however, were not a uniform intellectual group and the disparity of their positions on various matters related to the social sciences is well illustrated by the different analyses of women's economic and social roles that various members produced. I focus on Say's analysis because it is explicit and because Say's economic analysis had such a profound impact on nineteenth-century economics. Social and intellectual historians not primarily interested in the development of economic analysis may find, and indeed have found, the feminism of the circles surrounding Condorcet, who was also associated with this group, more compelling. There is no way to reconcile the two approaches represented by Say and Condorcet in order to produce a homogeneous analysis that could be attributed to the *Idéologistes*, and it would take another essay at least as long as this one to deal adquately with the differences.

This essay is primarily concerned with how J.-B. Say, an economist of significant historical import, was prepared to purchase social and political stability at the cost of denying women an independent existence as economic and social beings. But one must have a certain sympathy for an intellectual struggling to come to terms with many currents of political and philosophical inquiry in order to better understand 'the nature of things', while balancing the intellectual goal of understanding with the political goal of stabilization. And Say did consider the question of women's employment, which was not a matter that captured the attention of his contemporaries in any significant way. It is never easy, and seldom worthwhile, to praise or blame historical figures for having particular goals and attitudes, but if our goal is to understand the development of theory we must recognize the competing pressures to which Say was responding and respect, if not share, the resulting analysis.

THE STRUCTURE AND ROLE OF THE FAMILY IN AN IDEAL STATE

There is a danger involved in trying to discuss the analyses of gender offered by social commentators of earlier periods, because it is difficult to answer the charge that one is implicitly holding these individuals responsible to the sensibilities of our own time. These men, it is argued, are simply mouthing the wisdom that was the common currency of their own age; they cannot be expected to anticipate the social controversies of our own. In the case of Say, the problem evaporates. One need only attempt to understand his position in the context offered by the social debate of the revolutionary decade – a debate of which no aware, conscious and thinking individual could be ignorant. And it is surely superfluous to note that one need not judge, but should rather attempt to understand what may have induced an individual to develop his position and what may have been the consequences of that position.

The primary source of Say's writing on women in society and the economy is a little work entitled *Olbie, ou essai sur les moyens de réformer les moeurs d'une nation.* *Olbie* was written by Say as an entry in a contest sponsored in Years 5 through 8 by the Class of Moral and Political Sciences (an *Idéologiste* stronghold) of the *Institut National.* The topic in Year 5 was: 'What are the means of transforming the morals of a nation?', and transformed to 'What are the institutions which can transform the morals of a nation?' The prize was never awarded and the question was retired. Say's entry, in Year 8, was a portrait of an imaginary nation named 'Olbie' (from the Greek 'olbios', meaning 'happiness') which has just survived a revolution; that is, it was an explicitly utopian work describing the ideal future of a republican society. Say published his essay in Year 8, or 1800.

The most striking passage concerning women in *Olbie* sounds rather unsympathetic: [6]

> They are neither women or men these beings in petticoats, with hardened eyes and raucous voices, who amidst the population of our cities, push ahead of men, either to insult them or to lead them by the hand. This is a third sex (Say 1800, p. 48).

The heady mixture of violence, of intellectual possibility, and of social upheaval characterized by the destruction of church and monarchy (which had given a semblance of order to the *ancién regime*) may have gone just a bit too far for an economist who was really concerned with eliminating tariff barriers and reforming taxes. It is easy to imagine how someone might cling to the family as the last bastion of stability in a world turned inside out, as his friends and acquaintances were being led to the guillotine during the Terror. It is not surprising that attitudes engendered by the Terror would persist, and would appear in the form of poetry extolling the feminine virtues which Say published in *La Décade* during his tenure as editor, or in the guise of references to a pushy and raucous 'third sex' in *Olbie*.

Statements like this are, however, no more than an immediate reaction to the political turmoil of the period; they do not constitute an analysis. Nevertheless, Say does offer an analysis of gender roles in *Olbie*, where he maintained that the family is the fundamental unit of society, responsible for the maintenance of social order, and that women find their pivotal economic role in the context of household production where they share responsibility for the maintenance of the patriarchal family.

Say argued that the family serves two purposes: it provides the nurturing and subsistence of all of its members; and it is the school in which the civic virtues are learned. He observed that in *Olbie*, a community that had just weathered a revolution and was now in the process of setting up institutions to stabilize the republic, women play a key role in socializing other family members:

> The Olbians would have been weak moralists if they had no appreciation of the extent to which women influence morals. We owe to women our first memories and our last consolations. As children, we are the work of their hands; we are still when we reach adulthood. Their destiny is to dominate us without cessation, by the authority of their kindness, or by that of pleasure; and where women are not virtuous, it is vain for us to aspire to virtue. It is by the education of women that we begin that of men (Say 1800, p. 44).

This sounds strikingly similar to Chaumette's earlier chastisement of the women who appealed to the Paris Council and did not value the power of their 'despotism of love'.

The role that the father plays in training the children in the morals of a civilization should not be underestimated in Say's analysis. In *Olbie*, Say explicitly recognized the educational functions of the family and noted that the very principles that preserve order in the family are those that ensure social stability:

> The fathers of the families follow, little by little, the example offered by public authority; and the example that, in the beginning, is followed a little, is that which is unfailingly imitated more over time. In their houses one can read phrases applicable to order inside the family, and children nourished on these maxims, which experience shows them to be valid, regulate their conduct on the basis of

them, and transmit them to their own children. One is happy because one is wise; men and nations will not be happy otherwise (Say 1800, p. 80).

Moreover, the 'natural' attraction between men and women was to form the basis for marriage, which seems an unnecessary statement until we remember that some of the individuals writing during the revolutionary decade were imagining all kinds of alternatives to traditional (and less traditional) marriages (cf. Condorcet 1795):

> The Olbians do not, as is done in some sects, attack the inclination which attracts men to women. It is an instrument as powerful as it is gentle: is it necessary to break it rather than to use it? Neither do they follow the counsel of Plato who, in his imaginary Republic, wanted a lottery to determine once and for all, in an entire class of citizens, an exchange that reduces us to the level of brutes, if it is not ennobled by faithfulness and the delicate preferences of the soul. On the contrary, the Olbians blend honest love with all of their institutions that can admit it; and, one must acknowledge, they have taken some advice from our centuries of chivalry (Say 1800, pp. 45–46).

For Say, the family unit was not to be tampered with lightly.

WOMEN'S WORK AND THE ECONOMIC ROLE OF THE FAMILY

The economic role of the family in providing subsistence to its members is inseparable from the question of women's work, and Say addresses both issues in *Olbie*. The 'natural' division of labour between the sexes (*Olbie*, pp. 45–48), is economically beneficial; if women are not forced by poverty to work outside the home they will receive their subsistence in exchange for household labour which benefits the entire family 'even among the working class':

> The sexes mixed less in society, even among the working class. Good principles of political economy having spread a little comfort in that class, the women were no longer forced by indigence to share with men those difficult and disgusting occupations which one cannot watch them undertake without shuddering. They were able to give their time and their effort to the care of their households and their families which were much better tended, and they lost those masculine aspects which, in their sex, are something hideous: Woman and gentleness are two ideas that I do not know how to separate. The power of women is that of gentleness against strength: the moment that they try to obtain something by violence, they are no more than a monstrosity (Say 1800, p. 48).

It is, perhaps, redundant to note that Say's construction of femininity is influenced by his very sympathetic attitude towards the 'virtuous middle' classes of society. He believed that the happiness of any society, and particularly contemporary French society, would be measurably increased by expanding that part of society which lived in moderate comfort, and eliminating great extremes of wealth and poverty.

The 'natural' career of women is to be reinforced by social institutions, including good legislation regarding marriage and divorce.[7] Say noted that in *Olbie*, 'the law had been adjusted to the popular will insofar as the changes were compatible with social order' (*Olbie*, p. 49). Say's idealization of the patriarchal family and traditional marriage had its limits; the fundamental innovation of which he approved was the right to divorce. This argument was offered as clear support for the changes that had already occurred in France with respect to the divorce law. On 1 April 1792, a red-bonnetted delegation of women appeared before the Legislative Assembly demanding the right to divorce by mutual consent. On 20 September 1792, a law was passed which allowed divorce not only by mutual consent, but also at the request of one spouse on claims of incompatibility and in cases where one spouse was abandoned for more than two years. The right to divorce persisted until the Napoleonic Code killed it in 1804. This freedom to divorce effectively gave women the right to end forced marriages and domestic slavery, and was solidly supported by the *Idéologistes* with whom Say identified.[8]

Nevertheless, Say did not approve of legislation supporting divorce in order to give women the opportunity to reject their 'natural' career:

> [Olbians] recognize the necessity of encouraging in women the two virtues that become them more than any others, and without which the charm and ascendancy of their sex will vanish soon enough: I mean to say gentleness and chastity. Among this people the gentleness of women is encouraged by general morality which is, itself, the fruit of all the other institutions. Domestic and private virtues are esteemed and revered because they are useful. Poor household management, the cause of both scorn and poverty, is discouraged by paying attention to those habits which sweeten the morals and which, if I can express it thus, smooth the path of life (Say 1800, p. 47).

Thus women are still to find their primary occupation within the house.

While Say viewed household labour as a natural and valuable occupation, he recognized that working for wages was an inevitable fate for many women. In *Olbie*, his chief concern was to limit the mixing of the sexes in the workplace (Say 1800, p. 48). Certain professions, having the effect 'of hardening the heart or making bitter the character' (Say 1800, p. 47) would be closed to women, while others, including dressmaking, hairdressing and cooking, would be reserved exclusively for them (Say 1800, p. 55). Say noted that this would allow even the poorest woman to earn an 'honest' living. He advanced a utilitarian argument that the restriction this imposed upon men (that is, a law preventing them for engaging in the economic activities reserved for women) was justified because of the social benefit derived from limiting prostitution, which he regarded as the common result of indigence among women (Say 1800, p. 50):

> Poverty, a cruel scourge for anyone, is frightful for the most interesting half of the human race. It not only deprives women of the common sweetness of life, it pushes them to the most shameful corruption, the most destitute to the attraction which sometimes disguises the ugliness of vice. One must be hungry to sell her favours! What other motive than imperious need could make so many of the unfortunate overcome the disgust of prostitution. The unfortunate women! without choice, without desire, often the victim of depression, almost always shame in their souls, they solicit with the gracious smile of the outcast. Who would not prefer to be other than this? (Say 1800, pp. 50–51).

In any case, the cost of the policy of reserving some occupations solely for women, Say argued, was small because men have the whole world in which to exercise their industry, and can always count on the armed forces to provide subsistence (Say 1800, p. 55).

THE 'PROBLEM' OF INDEPENDENT WOMEN

Say's most original suggestion to combat indigence among women also appears in *Olbie* (Say 1800, pp. 52–54). A community of women was to be established in a house provided by the state. The work of the 'sisters' would provide for a modest but adequate lifestyle. The sole demand made by the state is that the sisters train a certain number of students to perform women's work, and care for a certain number of old women. No vows were exacted, and sisters retained the right to leave at any time. While living in the community, sisters were required to submit to a code of behaviour (designed, apparently, to safeguard their chastity and thereby protect their value on the marriage market). They could, for example, choose their friends, but could not entertain them unless they were in the presence of two other sisters. The consequence of breaking the rules was banishment.

This quasi-convent introduces several issues worth noting. The first is the very considerable restriction imposed upon individual behaviour by this institution. Say seems to have satisfied himself that the incursions upon liberty are minor – 'a liberty adequate to know the pleasures of society' (Say 1800, p. 54) – and are in any case justified because the sisters choose to enter into a voluntary contract (Say 1800, p. 53). And the liberty would, undoubtedly, be greater than young, unmarried women enjoyed during the *ancien régime*, although somewhat less than was enjoyed by the red-bonetted partisans of political debate before they were silenced.   Moreover, the restrictions on liberty are necessary, Say argued, if the women are to have the possibility of leaving the institution for 'the arms of a husband' (Say 1800, p. 54).   The second issue of note is that this institution reproduces the lineaments of the patriarchal family.   It solves the problem of female poverty by creating an institution which recognizes the 'natural dependence' of women.

It is worth remembering that one of the consequences of the revolution was the abolition of the existing religious orders.   This specific proposal does not show great imagination on the part of Say, but rather an adaptation of one of the features of the *ancien régime* which he found useful: an organized way of providing social services by regimenting unmarried women.   In his proposal, the state would replace the church as the authority to regiment and police the 'sisters'.   The pragmatism of the approach can, perhaps, be validated by noting that industrial convents were indeed adopted in France during the nineteenth century, and by all accounts flourished.

ECONOMIC THEORY AND GENDER ANALYSIS

That economic theory is not independent of the assumptions one makes about the roles of men and women in the private and public spheres is very clear from Say's analysis.   Women are poor, he argues, because they are unfortunate enough to live outside families and not because seamstresses (the occupation by means of which most independent women tried to support themselves) earn a wage below subsistence.   They turn to prostitution because they are poor.   This increases social instability, and more women find themselves alone and impoverished.   Therefore, the solution to female poverty is to eliminate prostitution (one of the few occupations open to unskilled women in urban centres), strengthen 'natural' families and recreate the social role of the family in the guise of his women's establishments for those women who would otherwise live independently.   These reforms would strengthen efforts to reduce the mixing of the sexes in the workplace, thereby encouraging virtue, social stability and strong families in which women are supported.   Because Say defined the problem to be solved as the poverty of independent women rather than the low wages earned by women who are restricted by social and institutional barriers to particular employments, he derived a rather different solution to that problem of female poverty than one might expect.   Moreover, his solution was 'natural'!   Say always argued that he opposed building elaborate systems of thought; he found that understanding economics simply involves the art of asking good questions and deducing those responses which flow, as a consequence, from the 'nature of things' (Say 1803, p. xxxv).

An obvious question is whether Say maintained this analysis of women and the family all his life, or whether *Olbie,* and in particular the analysis of gender it contains, was simply a reaction to the red bonnets and pantaloons, and raucous voices in the galleries – a temporary phenomenon. In fact the concerns which preoccupied Say about the sexual division of labour and the related issue of impoverished women in *Olbie* are consistent with his economic analyses in the *Traité d'économie politique* (1803) and the *Cours complet d'économie politique pratique* (1829). In the *Traité*, Say claimed that women's wages are lower than men's because a man's salary must be sufficient to provide subsistence at the socially required level for himself and his wife, and to raise and educate two children to working age, whereas a woman's wage need provide no more than what is necessary to keep one woman in working order. If there are too many unattached women without access to employment, even this minimum will be bid down (Say 1803, Book 2, Chapter 7, Section 4, p. 82).

In the *Cours complet*, Say does suggest that a partial solution to the problem of women's poverty may be to increase access to alternative employment, as long as the alternatives are 'appropriate'. He castigates government regulations that exclude women from trades such as embroidery and lace making: 'a portion of humanity that already has so little is owed this resource; and they are given instead seduction and debauchery' (Say 1968, p. 257). The desire to separate the sexes in employment is, however, a strong undercurrent throughout all of Say's work. The solution, as he see it, is to create separate spheres, rather than to let men and women work alongside one another; given the natural laws which determine the different wages for men and women, it would seem that separation would not solve the problem by bidding wages up. But it would, Say believed, strengthen the family – which was the best solution for poor women.

HOW REPRESENTATIVE WAS SAY'S GENDER ANALYSIS?

The positions Say adopted on the role of the family and on women's work were shared by many, but not all, people both inside and outside his intellectual milieu. There were many people, not all *Idéologistes*, who saw the aggressive demands made by very organized and vocal groups of women as both dangerous to the stability of the republic and unnatural. This fear echoes the concern expressed by moderate republicans when the *sans culottes* began to adopt the slogans of the 'Rights of Man' to gain political power for the unpropertied, slogans that they had designed to garner a larger share of political power for themselves – the propertied members of the third estate. It is true that the *Idéologistes* counted themselves, by and large, among this group of moderate republicans.

Yet, as we noted above, it is impossible to delineate a single gender analysis among the *Idéologistes*, despite the marked similarity between those of Say and Tracy, for three reasons. First, because the *Idéologistes* were never an organized sect, there are differences between individuals on many topics that were only tangentially related to their primary concerns. Second, the *Idéologistes* drew their inspiration from many sources, including Condorcet, Rousseau and Voltaire, all of whom had very different things to say about women despite the fact that elements of their works were later used to develop various feminist analyses. Third, and most importantly, there is a tension in the work of the *Idéologistes* between the rights of the individual and the needs of the collectivity. This shows up in various ways. The fundamental political concern of *Idéologie* was to encourage political and social stability in the new republic, but the fundamental analytical unit of *Idéologie* was the (male) individual and his psychology (using that word in the contemporary sense). Individual rights, pursued far enough, lead to social instability. Each *Idéologiste* had to negotiate that trade-off, and not surprisingly these different people drew the line between individual rights and social needs in slightly different places. Women's rights in the private and public spheres were perceived to be at the point where individual rights needed to be sacrificed for the collective good. Say dealt with this sacrifice by claiming that it was in the 'nature' of women not to desire the same rights as men, and in their interests to recognize their role as 'natural dependents'. But it was still a sacrifice of individual rights for social stability. This tension in Say's analysis concerning the concept of the individual was not unique to the *Idéologistes*; indeed it permeated the political theory of the revolution, and a great deal of feminist analysis has been devoted to the issue (Zerilli 1991, 1994; Brodribb 1992; Okin 1994).

In an era that offered many alternative versions of the way in which families and societies ought to be organized, Jean-Baptiste Say opted wholeheartedly for a 'natural' family-based system. Families were the most effective way of providing subsistence for women and children. The only modification he was prepared to make was that a divorce law seemed to him an improvement in social organization 'insofar as the change is compatible with social order'.

The family, dominated by the father, was to be the fundamental unit of civil society, because social stability required well-regulated families. This was not a self-evident position in the revolutionary decade.

FAMILIES AND FIRMS AS UNITS OF ECONOMIC ANALYSIS

If there was no self-evident way to treat the appropriate roles of women in the private and public spheres in 1800, there was similarly no self-evident way to model the operation of firms. Say intentionally adopted the analogy between firms and families, and between captains of industry (*chefs d'entreprise*) and fathers. He explicitly developed the notion that it is the family (directed by the father) and firms (directed by the entrepreneur) which were the fundamental units of economic analysis.

In the *Cours complet*, Say discusses the family in a manner reminiscent of the economic organization of the firm:

> In the family, all the means of subsistence come from the father; it is in his head that all useful thoughts are born; it is he that procures capital; it is he that works and directs the work of his children, who raises them, who sees to their establishment (1968, p. 561).

Say sees an analogy between the family and the firm, where individual workers relate to the entrepreneur as do children to their father (1968, p. 328). But he condemned as false and pernicious widespread notions to the effect that the economy needs to be directed by a central authority just as the family needs to be directed by the father (1968, p. 561). Rather, individual entrepreneurs require exactly the same freedom as do the governed in a civil society:

> In the state [as opposed to the family] it is an entirely different matter: the ideas that procure the support of the social body, the capital, the direction, are found among the governed. It is there that thought and action rest; it is there that the laws of nature are studied and productive enterprises are born from which are derived the revenues of society. Closer to all sorts of truths, it is the governed who analyze most successfully the moral and physical constitution of man, as well as the social economy (1968, p. 561).

And it is, of course, the case that individual workers employed within a firm recognize that their own interests are served by a division of labour in which the entrepreneur directs and they obey, just as it is in the interests of all members of the family to recognize that the direction and financial support of the father serve their own interests.

CONCLUSION

I have argued that the gender analysis that Jean-Baptiste Say developed in the revolutionary decade was not unique to his *Idéologiste* colleagues. Nevertheless, these analyses were consciously constructed in a period when a journalist, as was Say, and a scholar could not help but be aware of many suggested alternatives. The analysis of gender that Say articulated in *Olbie* persisted as the foundation of the nineteenth-century analyses that argued, for example, that the 'natural wage' of women is lower than that of men because men must support a family while women need only support themselves. Similarly, this analysis allowed economic theory to be used to support the 'separate spheres' argument that justified the impoverishment of so many independent women by closing the professions to them. And because women were so resolutely relegated to the private sphere, this allowed economic theory to develop without explicitly considering the roles of men and women in society, or the role that unpaid household production plays in allowing the market economy to function.

The most apparent conclusion that we can draw from Say's consideration of the economic and social roles of women is that social and political events have their counterparts in economic analysis. But the analysis survives and develops, even when its social context changes. When we lose sight of the precipitating events and the historical period in which theory developed, we also lose awareness of the implicit assumptions upon which that analysis rests. When we recover the history, it becomes easier to expose the assumptions and to challenge the theory.

It is useful to remember that economics, politics and 'family values' have a rather long relationship, and not necessarily the 'natural' one that dominates popular discourse. It is not helpful to approach current debates about the social roles of men and women and the place of the family in the political economy as though they were new issues. The concern does have a history, and it is perhaps in the context of current political debates that economic analysis might integrate a new vision of the ways in which gender is constructed.

REFERENCES

Azouvi, François (ed.) (1992), *L'institution de la raison. La révolution culturelle des idéologues*, Paris: Vrin.

Bessières, Yves and Patricia Niedzwiecki (1991), 'Women in the French Revolution (1789), Bibliography', *Women of Europe Supplements, 33*, Brussels: Women's Information Service, Commission of the European Communities.

Bridenthal, Renate and Claudia Koonz (1977), *Becoming Visible: Women in European History*, Boston: Houghton-Mifflin.

Brodribb, Somer (1992, 'Critical response to "Machiavelli's Sisters"', *Political Theory*, **20** (May), 332–336.

Condorect, Marie Jean de (1795), *Esquisse d'un tableau historique des progrès de l'esprit humain*, Paris.

Coole, Diana (1993), 'Constructing and Deconstructing Liberty: A Feminist and Post structuralist Analysis,' *Political Studies, 41* (March), 83–95.

Faccarello, Gilbert and Philippe Steiner (eds) (1990), *La pensée économique pendant la Révolution Française*, Grenoble: Presses Universitaires de Grenoble.

Hertz, Neil (1983), 'Medusa's Head: Male Hysteria under Political Pressure,' *Representations, 4*, 27–54.

Kadish, Doris Y. (1991), *Politicizing Gender: Narrative Strategies in the Aftermath of the French Revolution*, New Brunswick, NJ: Rutgers University Press.

Mill, John Stuart [1848] (1923), in W.J. Ashley (ed.), *Principles of Political Economy, With Some of Their Applications to Social Philosophy*, New York: Longmans, Green & Co.

Moravia, Sergio (1968), *Il pensiero degli Idéologues: scienza e filosofia in Francia (1789–1815)*, Firenze: La Nuova Italia.

Moses, Claire Goldberg (1984), *French Feminism in the 19th Century*, Albany: State Univesity of New York.

Okin, Susan Moller (1994), 'Political Liberalism, Justice and Gender (Review Article),' *Ethics,* **105** (October), 23–43.

Rendall, Joan (1984), *The Origins of Modern Feminism: Women in Britain, France and the United States, 1780–1860*, New York: Schocken Books.

Sade, Marquis de (1988), *Juliette* (translated by Austryn Wainhouse), New York: New Evergreen Edition

Say, Jean-Baptiste (1800), *Olbie, ou essai sur les moyens de réformer les moeurs d'une nation*, Paris: Deterville.

Say, Jean-Baptiste (1803), *Traité d'économie politique*, Paris: Deterville.

Say, Jean-Baptiste (1968), *Cours complet d'économie politique pratiqude*, Rome: Edizioni Bizzarri (reprint of the 1845 edition, edited and annotated by Horace Say), Brussels: Société Typographique Belge.

Steinbrügge, Lieselotte (1995), *The Moral Sex. Woman's Nature in the French Enlightenment* (translated from the 1992 German edition by Pamela E. Selwyn), Oxford: Oxford University Press

Steiner, Philippe (1990), 'Comment stabiliser l'ordre social moderne? J.-B. Say, l'économic politique et la Révolution française', in G. Faccarello and P. Steiner (eds), pp. 173–194.

Tracy, Destutt de (1926), *De L'amour*, Paris: Société d'édition les belles lettres.

Wollstonecraft, Mary (1792), *A Vindication of the Rights of Woman*, London: J.J. Johnson.

Zerilli, Linda M.G. (1991), 'Machiavelli's Sisters: Women and "The Conversation"

of Political Theory', *Political Theory*, **19**, 252–276.
Zerilli, Linda M.G. (1994), *Signifying Woman: Culture and Chaos in Rousseau, Burke and Mill*, Ithaca: Cornell University Press.

NOTES

1. I am very grateful to the referees who made important and helpful comments on the first draft of this essay, and to SSHRCC which subsidized the research that made this essay possible.
2. This volume went through five French editions in Say's lifetime, and yet was simply one component of a very effective popularization program that comprised many pamphlets, newspaper articles, books and a prolific correspondence.
3. 'Idéologie' and 'Idéologiste' were introduced by Destutt de Tracy in a paper read to the section of the Moral and Political Sciences Class of the *Institut National* concerned with the analysis of sensations and ideas to describe the science of ideas which concerns itself with 'ideas' or 'perceptions' and 'thinking or perceiving'. It was neither class-based nor socially constructed, according to Tracy, but rather a scientific analysis of the way in which human intellect worked. 'Idéologue' was Bonaparte's word for the same group.
4. For a complete translation of *Declaration of the Rights of Women*, and an excellent (if now somewhat dated, but still very useful) bibliographic essay on the many roles of women in the Revolution, see: Yves Bessières and Patricia Niedzwiecki, 'Women in the French Revolution (1789), Bibliography', *Women of Europe Supplements,* No. 33 Brussels: Women's Information Service, Commission of the European Communities, 1991, pp. 14–16.
5. Much has been written on *Idéologie* and the *Idéologistes.* Interested readers may want to consult Sergio Moravia (1968) and François Azouvi (1992).
6. All of the translations from Say's work are my own.
7. 'Let us make easy the path of virtue and not imitate those moralist-legislators who place their temple at the peak of a high mountain that one can reach only by a narrow path. That condemns the entire world to the abyss!' (Say 1800, p. 49).
8. Tracy's *De l'amour* (1926) strongly supported the right to divorce on the grounds cited.

12. Women in Nassau Senior's Economic Thought

Robert Dimand

INTRODUCTION: NASSAU SENIOR AS AN APPLIED CLASSICAL ECONOMIST

If perhaps not 'The Prophet of Modern Capitalism' (the subtitle of S. Leon Levy's 1949 biography), Nassau William Senior (1790–1864) was certainly a 'Critical Essayist, Classical Economist and Advisor to Governments' (the subtitle of Levy's 1970 second edition). Senior was the first professor of political economy in a British university, serving as Drummond Professor of Political Economy at Oxford from 1825 to 1830[1] and again from 1847 to 1852. He was elected the first Professor of Political Economy at King's College, London, in 1831, and was Examiner in Political Economy (1840–1857) and Law (1847–1860) at the University of London, with a seat in the University Senate (Levy 1970, pp. 106, 159). His views on reducing the revenues of the established Protestant church in Ireland forced him to give up the chair in London and led to his defeat for the Drummond chair at Oxford in 1841 (for which he was also defeated in 1857, see Levy 1970, p. 319).

As an applied economist who was a fervent Whig and enjoyed the prestige of an Oxford chair, Senior could exercise a stronger and more direct influence on public policy than was possible for such great figures in pure economic theory as David Ricardo, Robert Torrens, James Mill, or John Stuart Mill (despite the brief Parliamentary careers of Ricardo, Torrens, and the younger Mill) because these were Philosophical Radicals rather than Whigs. In addition to his academic and legal careers (the latter culminating in service as a Master of Chancery from 1836 until the position was abolished in 1853), Senior acted as an economic adviser to the Whigs, serving on Royal Commissions on the Poor Laws (1832–1834), on the Condition of the Unemployed Hand-loom Weavers (1837–1841), and on Popular Education (1858–1861). Senior reported privately to Lord Althorp (leader of the House of Commons in Earl Grey's government) in 1831 on a commission for a commercial treaty with France (Levy 1970, Appendix IX), to Lord John Russell in 1836 on the Irish Poor Law (Bowley

1937, Appendix I), and to Russell (then Prime Minister) on the reorganization of the English Poor Law Commission (Levy 1970, Appendix XIV). Asked in 1830–1831 by the Home Secretary, Lord Melbourne, to advise on reform of the law of trade combinations, Senior, in the words of Marian Bowley (1937, p. 242), 'recommended the most intolerant measures which, if they had been enforced, and provided they had not provoked a revolution, would have effectively hampered the Trade Union Movement ... recommendations which in practice would have undone the work of the Philosophical Radicals in achieving the repeal of the Combinations Laws in 1824–1825'. All picketing and all solicitation to join a union were to be illegal; employers or their assistants would be authorized to arrest anyone picketing or soliciting; and employers who countenanced combinations and strikes were also to be severely punished (Levy 1970, Appendix VII).

Another source of Senior's influence has been largely overlooked, mentioned by his biographer only in a single sentence listing newspapers to which Senior contributed (Levy 1970, p. 129). According to *The Economist 1843–1943, A Centenary Volume* (1943, pp. 20, 79, 82, 83), Senior, with his 'unrivalled European contacts' and 'his private intelligence from Paris', 'was responsible for the paper's news and views on foreign affairs'. The leading articles on domestic politics and financial policy were reserved for the editor, first James Wilson (who continued to edit the newspaper while serving as Financial Secretary to the Treasury) and then his son-in-law, Walter Bagehot. H. Scott Gordon (1955) finds that while the romantic critics of classical political economy were mistaken in attributing to most classical economists a doctrinaire commitment to laissez-faire, such a commitment was displayed by *The Economist* in its first decades, the era when Nassau Senior wrote many of its leading articles.

The Drummond Professorship at Oxford, Lincoln's Inn, the Chancery Court, *The Economist*, and Royal Commissions combined to integrate Nassau Senior into the world of public policy and university teaching, of applied economics and the teaching of political economy, far more closely than other classical economists who loom larger in histories of economic theory. His view of the social and economic role of women was revealed in passing remarks rather than developed systematically, but, shared by Senior with other Whig policy-makers (rather than radicals, philosophical or otherwise), it had direct, immediate implications for public policy, notably in the shaping of the New Poor Law. In the Poor Law Report of 1834, Senior and Edwin Chadwick strove to eliminate the dependence of unwed mothers on public relief and on compulsory child support, while strengthening ties of dependence within traditional families. Senior took for granted the restricted property rights of women. He considered the possibility and desirability of historical change in the social and economic status of women only in the course of criticizing Egyptian and Turkish society for the lack of such change. In contrast, John Stuart Mill's more systematic (and much more feminist) analysis of the 'woman question' exerted a more gradual influence on advanced opinion.

OXFORD LECTURES

The terms of the Drummond Professorship required the incumbent to publish at least one lecture each year.[2] Addressing all-male audiences at Oxford, Senior took little notice of the existence of women, even when discussing determinants of the birth rate. In *Two Lectures on Population*, Senior (1829, p. 5) illustrated the concept of decencies, goods that must be consumed to maintain one's standing in society, by stating that 'A carriage is a decency to a woman of fashion, a necessary to a physician, and a luxury to a tradesman.' In his second term as Drummond Professor, Senior (1852, p. 70) remarked that 'When Miss Linley became Mrs. Sheridan, her powers of action and song ceased to be wealth; they remained the delight of private societies, but were no longer objects of sale. If Sheridan had condescended to accept an income on such terms, his wife's accomplishments would have enriched him.' His only reference in the published lectures collected in his *Selected Writings on Economics* (Senior 1966) to paid employment of women was to the singing of the daughter of a fashionable Bath family before her marriage to a famous playwright and Parliamentarian.[3]   Senior accepted, without remark or objection, that her husband would decide whether or not she would continue to sing in public, and that any income she earned would belong to him. Unlike such younger classical economists as John Stuart Mill, Henry Fawcett, and Leonard Courtney, Senior took no part in the campaigns to establish married women's property rights (see Shanley 1989 on the role of Mill and Fawcett).

Apart from the higher classes in Otaheite (Tahiti) and West Indian Negroes,[4] Senior (1829, p. 24) held that 'there are scarcely any females whose fecundity is prevented or dismissed by promiscuous intercourse, except those unhappy individuals whose only trade is prostitution.   And they form so small a proportion of the population of the whole world, that the check to population occasioned by their unfruitfulness may safely be disregarded.' Therefore, the only effective preventive check (that is, a force restraining the birth rate) was abstinence from marriage, or at least from early marriage. Senior (1829, p. 25) told his audience that, for the purposes of expounding the principle of population, he would use the term 'marriage' to mean 'any agreement between a man and woman to cohabit exclusively for a period, and under circumstances likely to occasion the birth of progeny.' This sentence was the only one in those lectures in which Senior acknowledged that a woman shared in a decision to marry. All his subsequent references (e.g. Senior 1829, pp. 25, 26, 27) are exclusively to men deciding whether to marry, based on the standard of living they would be able to support. The correspondence between Senior and Malthus appended to the published lectures (Senior 1829, pp. 55–90) reveals that Senior's divergence from orthodox Malthusianism rested on his belief that the desire for a higher social standing had been a sufficiently strong preventive check for history to show a tendency for the available means of subsistence to increase more rapidly than the population. According to Brian Inglis (1971, pp. 279–283), the future archbishop Richard Whately (formerly Senior's tutor and soon to be his successor in the Drummond Chair) persuaded Senior to be conciliatory to Malthus, lest he give he give comfort to such common enemies as the popular radical William Cobbett (cf. Winch 1996, pp. 373–376, on the controversy between Senior and Malthus). Gertrude Himmelfarb (1983, p. 158n) remarks on the limited space devoted to population in the Poor Law Report, and on the Report's inconsistency about whether overpopulation was a serious problem.

A.W. Coats (1967, p. 160) notes that 'Senior went beyond his fellow economists in extolling the benefits of hard work, even though he himself defined employment as "toil, trouble, exposure, and fatigue", all of which are evils *per se'*. This attitude coloured Senior's jaundiced view of English labourers: he asserted in his Oxford lectures that

> When wages are high, they work fewer hours and inhabit better houses; and, if there still remain a superfluity the women and girls waste in dress, and the men in drink or luxurious living ... When their earnings become insufficient for a maintenance, they throw themselves on the parish. The virtue of which they possess the least is providence (quoted by Coats 1967, p. 161).

Rather than viewing the lower orders (identified by Senior 1827, p. 12, as nine-tenths or more of the whole population) as rational agents who could judge what was in their own best interests, Senior considered them improvident and disapproved of their consuming more leisure, better housing, or better clothing when they could afford it. E.G. West (1964) similarly noted that Senior, as a member of the Royal Commission on Popular Education in 1861 and as President of the Education Section of the National Association for the Promotion of Social Science, held that the labouring classes were unable to make rational, informed educational choices, but had no comparable concerns about the educational choices of the middle and upper classes.

Women appear rarely in Senior's lectures, and primarily as extravagant consumers, impulsively squandering potential saving on fancy clothing, if they belonged to the lower orders, or bowing to social pressure by keeping a carriage, if women of fashion. They had some connection with marriage and the birth rate, but, in contrast to *The Poor Law Report of 1834*, did not make decisions about these matters. Contrary to what Senior's *Letters on the Factory Act* (1837) revealed in passing, his lectures treated paid employment of women as a whim of a young lady of fashion with a pretty voice. Although Senior had intimate, daily involvement with the law of property as a Lincoln's Inn conveyancer and a Master in Chancery, his lectures show that he took for granted married women's lack of property rights in England – yet when he travelled outside the familiar world of Europe to Egypt and Turkey, he ascribed sweeping and deleterious social consequences to women's lack of rights there. Only there, deploring the lack of change in women's social and economic status in societies he considered alien and backward, did Senior (1859, 1882) acknowledge that gender relations are not immutable, but rather evolve and are interwoven with other social changes.

LETTERS ON THE FACTORY ACT

In his Oxford lectures, Nassau Senior stressed that he was developing political economy as a science, with universal principles, rather than expounding it as an art, a set of useful rules for practical application. For Karl Marx ([1867] 1977, p. 333), rather than Senior being an economic scientist, 'The manufacturers chose [Senior] as their prize-fighter, not only against the newly passed Factory Act but against the Ten Hours' agitation which aimed to go beyond it.' Perhaps a better analogy for the tone of Senior's *Letters on the Factory Act* (1837) would be a lawyer arguing his client's case from a prepared brief, which after all was how Senior primarily earned his living. Marx ([1867] 1977, pp. 333–338) ridiculed Senior's argument that profit was earned only in the 'last hour' of labour, so that a reduction in the length of the working day would eliminate all profit from the factories affected. Orace Johnson (1969) examined the analysis of the Factory Act by Senior and Marx, to the discredit of both, criticizing Senior for 'including stock figures ... in his flow numerator.' J. Bradford DeLong (1986), however, argued that Senior's mistake resulted not from ideological bias (as charged by Marx) or from inept, sloppy reasoning (as implied by Johnson), but rather from the inappropriate and implicit assumption that the turnover period of capital is invariant to the length of the working day.

Apart from opposing any possible legislative reduction in the length of the working day for children[5] (and hence for adults), Senior and the manufacturers who brought him to Manchester were more immediately concerned with the threat of two proposed amendments to the Factory Act, which would have kept textile factory owners from sitting as magistrates on Factory Act cases and allowed factory inspectors to visit the mills whenever they chose. Senior (1837,

p. 19) was critical of the Factory Act's requirement of schooling for child labourers: 'Instead of the vast and airy apartments of a well-regulated factory, they are kept in a small, low, close room; and instead of the light work, or rather attendance, of a factory, which really is not more exercise than a child voluntarily takes, they have to sit on a form, supposed to be studying a spelling-book.' In his 'Advertisement' to the *Letters*, Senior (1837, p. 4), referred to a letter to him by factory inspector Leonard Horner that he included as an appendix, asserting that 'He agrees with me, that the labour of children and young persons in factories, is comparatively light.' What Horner actually wrote was:

> I admit that the labour of children and young persons in Cotton Factories is comparatively light, in so far as muscular exertions are concerned; but there cannot be a question that, on the average, children who work eight hours only, and get fresh air and exercise for two hours daily *and in day-light*, must grow up more healthy and strong than those confined to the factory for twelve hours; and who, for a great part of the year, go to and leave the mill in the dark (Senior 1837, p. 31).

Senior's *Letters on the Factory* included a few passing recognitions of the gender of many of the young workers in the cotton factories. Senior (1837, p. 15) reported that, with the exception of the small number of mule spinners, work in cotton factories consisted only of 'watching the machinery, and piecing the threads that break. I have seen the girls who thus attend standing with their arms folded during the whole time that I stayed in the room – others sewing a handkerchief or sitting down.' Thanks to the salubriousness of factory labour,

> The factory work-people in the country districts are the plumpest, best clothed, and healthiest looking persons of the labouring class that I have ever seen. The girls, especially, are far more good-looking (and good looks are fair evidence of health and spirits) than the daughters of agricultural labourers' (Senior 1837, p. 23). 'We tried, indeed, an experiment as to the comparative appearance of different classes of the Manchester population. We went last Sunday to the great Sunday-school in Bennett-street, where we found about 300 girls in one large room. We desired first all the carders to stand up alone, then all the piecers, then all the reelers, and so on through the various departments. Then we desired all those not employed in factories to stand up; then all those employed in factories; and on each of these trials not one of us could perceive the least difference between the apparent health of the different classes of factory children, or between the children employed in factories and those not so employed (Senior 1837, p. 25).

In Senior's Oxford lectures, the only employed woman mentioned was Miss Linley of one of the first families of Bath, singing and acting before her marriage to the playwright Sheridan. Senior's *Letters on the Factory Act*, in contrast, show his awareness that many young women worked in cotton textile factories.

In contrast to Senior's passing recognition that many of the factory workers were female, other economists debated whether the Factory Acts should treat men and women differently. Harriet Martineau, writing as an equal-rights feminist (as distinct from a difference feminist), issued *The Factory Controversy: A Warning Against Meddling Legislation* (1855) to warn that legislation supposedly protecting females would actually take away their power of making decisions about their lives and earning their own support. Harriet Taylor Mill, in her 1851 essay 'Enfranchisement of Women,' and John Stuart Mill, in his *Principles of Political Economy*, insisted that everyone who had attained 'the age of self-government,' male or female, should be free to decide on their employment, that all professions and occupations should be open to both sexes, and that opening paid employment to women was needed to secure their economic independence – which was not a goal of Senior (Robson and Robson 1994, Pujol 1992). William Stanley Jevons, on the other hand, advocated legislation to exclude married women of childbearing age from factory work, which did not seem as easy and healthful to him as it did to Senior (see White 1994).

POOR LAW REPORT

Although nine Royal Commissioners, including the Bishop of London, signed the Poor Law Report of 1834, it was largely written by Nassau Senior and by his fellow-commissioner Edwin Chadwick, the public health reformer and disciple of Jeremy Bentham (see Finer 1952). According to Mark Blaug,

> the *Report of 1834*, with its strictures on 'the old system', was revered for three generations as a canonical book, teaching that all forms of dole, charity, and relief to the unemployed are suspect, because they only induce him [sic] to breed in idleness; that least relief is best relief; and that voluntary charity is always preferable to public aid because it is somehow capable of discriminating the 'deserving' poor from the 'undeserving'. Without the continued influence of 'the principles of 1834', Mrs. Jellyby is unthinkable (Blaug 1963, p. 124).

Quoting R. H. Tawney's description of the report as a 'brilliant, influential, and wildly unhistorical document', Blaug (1963) labelled it also wildly unstatistical. Seven of the thirteen imposing, but little read, volumes of appendices to the report printed thousand of pages of replies to parish questionnaires, without any statistical analysis or even summary (which would have been difficult, since different questions were posed to different parishes). The sheer bulk of the appendices added figurative as well as literal weight to the conclusions of the report, but the conclusions rested on the impressions that the Commissioners (especially Chadwick and Senior) formed of the impressions formed in turn by the Assistant Commissioners, with no counting of replies to questions. Even the industrious Sidney and Beatrice Webb, when researching their monumental history of English local government and the Minority Report of another Royal Commission on the Poor Laws three quarters of a century later, flinched from systematically tackling those appendices. Blaug (1963, 1964) argues that the questions were posed as to elicit responses agreeing with the preconceptions of the Commissioners (perhaps inevitably in an era before much thought was given to problems of survey design) and that statistical analysis of the raw data in the appendices fails to support the report's conclusions. The questions asked, for instance, when family allowances and wage subsidies were introduced in a parish, but not whether or not the parish had subsequently abandoned them. Although McCloskey (1973) dissents from Blaug's analysis of the economic effects of the Old Poor Law, Blaug's condemnation of the report's unhelpful and misleading presentation of evidence still stands.[6]

The Poor Law Report of 1834 (Checkland and Checkland 1974, pp. 64, 335) propounded a single, overriding 'Principle of Administering relief to the Indigent: That the condition of the paupers shall in no case be so eligible as the condition of persons of the lowest class subsisting on the fruits of their own industry'. Achievement of the twin goals of 'Conversion of paupers into independent labourers, and reduction of the rates' (pp. 64, 341), as well as 'Diminution of improvident marriages' (pp. 65, 349), depended on 'Drawing the requisite line of distinction between the class of paupers and the class of independent labourers, and thereby checking the tendency to the indefinite extension of pauperism' and on 'Removing from the distributors all discretionary powers, and thereby diminishing abusive administration' (pp. 66, 392). The able-bodied were not to receive relief, and 'outdoor relief' (family allowances, wage subsidies, or other payments in cash or kind to paupers living in the community) was to be avoided in favour of 'indoor relief', support of paupers living in the parish workhouse (with separate workhouses for adult male and adult female paupers, as well as another for children with access to schooling). Paupers on parish relief were to wear uniforms identifying them as such. Splitting up pauper families among sexually-segregated workhouses would discourage resort to parish relief as well as preventing further improvident procreation. For all the hostility of Senior and Chadwick to the Old Poor Law, and their concern that the New Poor Law should not be attractive to potential paupers, it should be kept in mind that they differed from Malthus[7] and Ricardo in not urging the eventual complete abolition of the Poor Law, recognizing that some people became indigent through no improvidence or other fault of their own (see Poynter 1969, especially Chapter 9, 'From Abolition to Amendment'; Cowherd 1978; Persky 1997; and, for a synthesis of recent research on the Old and New Poor Laws, Keen 2000). Senior was in the minority when a majority of the Political Economy Club endorsed the introduction of public relief in Ireland, but his opposition was based on Irish conditions rather than universal principles: how could the living conditions of publicly assisted Irish paupers, even in workhouses, be made less appealing than those of Irish peasants? (Poynter 1969, p. 308).

The *Poor Law Report of 1834* (Checkland and Checkland 1974, pp. 113–144) noted that

> In all the cases which have been mentioned, relief is professed to be afforded on the ground of want of employment, or of insufficient wages; but a class of persons have, in many places, established a right to public support, independently of either of these claims. These are widows, who, in many places, receive what are called pensions, of from 1s. to 3s. a week on their own account, without any reference to their age or strength, or powers of obtaining an independent subsistence, but simply as widows. In such places, they receive an additional allowance if they have children. The allowance for each child is generally about 1s. 6d. a week in rural districts unless the child be illegitimate, in which case it is more frequently 2s. or more.

'In many places' remained unquantified. The sharp tone of the last throwaway remark underlines the concern of the Poor Law Commissioners with 'the support of illegitimate children, the relief afforded to their mothers, and the attempts to obtain the repayment of the expense from their supposed fathers' (Checkland and Checkland 1974, pp. 258–274, 472–483, at p. 258). Women appeared in the *Poor Law Report* primarily as potential mothers of bastards (widowhood, not being a matter of choice, received much briefer discussion), although testimony about the idle and demoralized female inmates of the parish poorhouse at Gravesend, and the successful breaking of their spirit by the ladies' committee of the poorhouse, was quoted at length (pp. 432–436).[8] In contrast to Senior's *Two Lectures on Population*, the *Poor Law Report of 1834* viewed the unmarried women of the labouring classes as deplorable but active and rational decision-makers, who responded to economic incentives. The Report argued that illegitimacy would be greatly reduced if the burden of supporting an illegitimate child fell on the mother, without conferring any right to parish assistance or any charge upon the alleged father (apart from private legal actions for breach of promise or for loss of a daughter's services): 'We recommend that the mother of an illegitimate child born after the passing of the Act, be required to support it, and that any relief occasioned by the wants of the child be considered relief afforded to the parent' (p. 479) and 'We recommend, therefore that the second section of the 18 Eliz., cap. 3, and all other Acts which punish or charge the putative father of a bastard, shall, as to all bastards born after the passing of the intended act, be repealed' (p. 483). Such repeal would also reduce the number of improvident marriages and subsequent legitimate births to impoverished parents, because the Commissioners held that such marriages were often induced by the woman's threat of a court order for financial support of an illegitimate child: 'a marriage of which we may estimate the consequences, when we consider that it is founded, not on affection, not on esteem, not on the prospect of providing for a family, but on fear on one side, and vice on both' (p. 261). The Report quoted a vestry clerk in Cornwall as being 'satisfied from long and serious observation and all facts occurring that continued illicit intercourse has, in almost all cases, originated with the females; many of whom ... do resort to it as a source of support ... and thus receive the fixed weekly allowances from the parish officers' (p. 263). The Commissioners viewed the financial responsibility of the putative fathers, especially when the amount to be paid varied with the father's circumstances, as an invitation to perjury and extortion. Under the Old Poor Law, the entitlements of poor women were fluctuating and uncertain (Connors 1997). The New Poor Law resolved the uncertainty by limiting or eliminating the entitlements. Persky (1997, p. 186) observes that the Commissioners might with equal logic have argued that enforcing child support would reduce the number of illegitimate births by making men more careful. Instead, the Report viewed the mothers as the active decision-makers, contrary to the image of women in Senior's Oxford lectures.

In 1871, 'The Committee to Amend the Law in Points wherein it is Injurious to Women' (CALPIW, formed by Elizabeth Wolstenholme, Josephine Butler and Lydia Becker) protested particularly against the provisions of the New Poor Law regarding the responsibility of fathers of children born outside marriage. The father could be made to contribute only if named within twelve months of the child's birth (or if he was proved to have contributed to its support in that time), with the contribution limited to half a crown (2s. 6d.) per week (up to five shillings a week for the first six weeks of the infant's life) until the child turned thirteen or the mother remarried. A maximum of thirteen weeks of arrears could be collected and (a particular point of the Poor Law Report) parish officers were forbidden to help the mother obtain a support order against the father unless the child had become a charge on the parish. CALPIW advocated instead joint responsibility of both parents until the child reached the age of sixteen. The committee argued that infant mortality was promoted not by the irresponsibility of mothers but by their poverty. The committee also protested against the class distinction that made it a felony to seduce (or marry without parental consent) an heiress below the age of twenty-one or any other girl below the age of ten, arguing that the existing law protected property rather than children's welfare (Shanley 1989, pp. 89–92). The provisions of the Poor Law protested by CALPIW had been crafted by Senior and Chadwick in the 1834 Report.

TRAVELS IN THE MIDDLE EAST

Nassau Senior was an avid conversationalist and, especially after the end of his second Drummond Professorship and the abolition of the position of Master in Chancery, a peripatetic traveller. In 1859 he published *A Journal Kept in Turkey and Greece in the Autumn of 1857 and the Beginning of 1858*, 'written with no view to publication; but, as it throws light on questions of political importance, I think that I ought not, under the present circumstances, to withhold it' (Senior 1859, p. v). Another twelve volumes of his journals and conversations outside Britain were edited posthumously[9] by his daughter, Mary Charlotte Mair (Minnie) Simpson,[10] and selections from his conversations in Britain were published in her memoirs. Senior's journals circulated in manuscript among his friends while he was alive:

> six copies were made of [Senior's journal of his 1855 visit to] Algeria, four each of Rome in 1851 and of Ireland in 1852, eleven of Athens in 1857, seventeen of Cairo in 1856, and twenty-five of Paris in 1854 ... The Prince Consort, for instance, read 'every word of them' and often talked to his intimate friends about them. They were a source of inspiration for a number of leading articles by the author himself as well as other eminent critics, and certain portions of them were used in the revised lectures on political economy (Levy 1970, pp. 161–162).

The care that Senior devoted to preparing and circulating his journals was remarked by Count Cavour, who regretted in 1860 that 'since he [Senior] has taken to keeping a kind of journal, he has neglected more serious things' (Levy 1970, p. 160). Consequently, Senior's conversations and travels are exceptionally thoroughly documented.

In 1855–1856, Senior and his wife travelled to Egypt with an international commission invited by Ferdinand de Lesseps, the French consul-general in Egypt, to investigate the feasibility of his proposal for a Suez canal. The Table of Contents that Senior's daughter provided for Senior's *Conversations and Journals in Egypt and Malta* (1882) concisely expounded his conviction that the status of women in Islamic society was at the root of what he felt was wrong with Middle Eastern society and government. One of the headings for 3 February 1856 was 'Mahometanism Incompatible with Good Government,' while the headings for a 5 February conversation with Hekekyan Bey[11] (Senior 1882, vol. 2) read 'Hatred and Contempt of Turks for Christians' (p. 64), 'They think all Christians Merchants' (p. 65), 'No Peace between a Turk and an Unbeliever' (p. 66), 'The Turk abhors Restraint' (p. 66) with, for a 15 February conversation with Hekekyan, 'Mahometan Government a vast System of Bribery' (p. 114), leading up to a 9 March conversation with Clot Bey and Hekekyan: 'Incompatibility of Islamism with Good Government' (p. 198), 'Inferiority attributable to Polygamy' (p. 198), 'Seclusion produces Divorce'

(p. 199), 'Facility of Divorce produces Early Marriages' (p. 199), 'Evils of Fatalism' (p. 200), 'An Excuse for Inactivity and Carelessness' (p. 201). In the words of Clot Bey, with whom Senior concurred, 'Every hareem is a little despotism in which the vices of a despotism – its lawlessness, its cruelty, its intrigues, the pride and selfishness of its master, and the degradation of its subjects – are reproduced on a smaller scale, but not with less intensity' (Senior 1882, vol. 2, p. 198). For Senior, the failure of Islamic societies to develop socially and politically in ways of which Senior would approve stemmed from the institutional framework of gender relations: polygyny, easy divorce for men, and the seclusion of women in harems and behind the veil. Despotism in the state would not disappear as long as there was despotism in the household. Recording that 'The more I see of Cairo the more I am inclined to hate all its living inhabitants except my own friends and acquaintances,' Senior (1882, vol. 1, p. 162, cf. p. 166) particularly objected to 'the black or white veiled female spectres that jostle and dirty you in the muddy passages called streets' (and, for all his confidence in market forces, also remarked that 'I hate the shopkeepers, with whom every transaction is a negotiation in which you lose your time or your money'). Senior recorded the visits of Mrs. Senior to various harems: to the wife of the Khedive (Senior 1882, vol. 1, p. 20); to the wife of the heir (vol. 1, p. 57); and especially to Mehmet Ali's daughter Nasli Hanem (vol. 1, pp. 234–239) – Mrs. Senior 'was rather unwilling to do so, but I begged her to go, as she would to see a tigress at the Zoological Gardens' (vol. 1, p. 237). Veiling and seclusion in the harem were sufficiently exotic to Senior that he could safely use them as the basis for a critique of the status of women in Egypt and Turkey, and of despotism in the state as a projection of despotism in the patriarchal household, without raising any disturbing questions in his mind about the legal, political, and economic status of women in European society (see Dimand 1998 on Senior's journals of his travels in Egypt and Turkey as exemplars of the Orientalism examined by Said 1995; see also the warning of Brown 1999 against imposing anachronistic demands on nineteenth-century European writers encountering other cultures).

CONCLUSION

Senior's views on the social and economic status of women are scattered through his lectures, pamphlets, journals, and government reports. As an Oxford professor and as a key adviser to Whig ministries, Senior's views (especially as expressed in the Poor Law Report and subsequent Poor Law Amendment Act of 1834) had more immediate relevance to what was taught to university students and to the making of public policy than did the views of other eminent classical economists who, as Nonconformists or Philosophical Radicals or both, were excluded from England's ancient universities and the inner circles of policy-making. His celebration in his *Letters on the Factory Act* of the easy and healthy conditions of the young women employed in cotton factories contrasts with the disregard of female employment in his lectures, while the absence of women's agency in *Two Lectures on Population*, where with a single exception the decision whether to marry was ascribed exclusively to men, contrasts with the *Poor Law Report*, in which women were portrayed as amoral but rational decision-makers, responsive to economic incentives. Senior perceived adverse social and political consequences of patriarchal domination within the household when it was presented to his attention with the exotic trappings of the veil and the harem that excluded any parallels to his own society. In the context of Egypt and Turkey, safely distanced from Western European society, Senior saw gender relations as variable across societies, rather than universally fixed, and blamed the survival of the isolated patriarchal household for what he considered the failure of social, cultural, and political progress in Islamic societies. Senior's views on gender issues were notably less systematic and enlightened than those of such 'advanced Liberals' (or 'Philosophic Radicals') as John Stuart Mill or Henry Fawcett, but reflected views embodied in public policy at the time of the New Poor Law. Through his published Oxford lectures, his journalism in *The Economist* and elsewhere, his participation in Royal Commissions, and his advice to Whig governments, Nassau Senior's applied economic analysis figured prominently in British policy discussion from the 1830s to the 1860s.

REFERENCES

Blaug, Mark (1963), 'The Myth of the Old Poor Law and the Making of the New', *Journal of Economic History,* 23, 151–184, reprinted in M.W. Flinn and T.C. Smout (eds), *Essays in Social History,* Oxford: Oxford University Press, 1974, pp. 123– 153.

Blaug, Mark (1964), 'The Poor Law Report Re-examined,' *Journal of Economic History,* 24, 229–245.

Bowley, Marian (1937), *Nassau Senior and Classical Economics,* London: George Allen and Unwin.

Brown, James (1999), 'The Solitude of Edward Said: The Fate of Gibb, Lane and Massignon in Orientalism,' *Economy and Society,* 28, 550–569.

Caine, Barbara (1994), 'Feminism and Political Economy in Victorian England – or John Stuart Mill, Henry Fawcett and Henry Sidgwick Ponder the "Woman Question"', in Groenewegen (ed.), pp. 24–45.

Checkland, S.G., and E.O.A. Checkland (eds) (1974), *The Poor Law Report of 1834,* Harmondsworth, UK: Pelican Classics.

Coats, A.W. (1967), 'The Classical Economists and the Labourer,' in E.L. Jones and G.E. Mingay (eds), *Land, Labour and Population in the Industrial Revolution,* London: Arnold, reprinted in Coats (1971), pp. 144–179.

Coats, A.W. (ed.) (1971), *The Classical Economists and Economic Policy,* London: Methuen.

Connors, R. (1997), 'Poor Women, the Parish, and the Politics of Poverty', in H. Barker and E. Chalus (eds), *Gender in Eighteenth Century England: Roles, Representations, and Responsibilities,* London: Longman, pp. 126–147.

Cowherd, Raymond G. (1978), *Political Economists and the English Poor Laws,* Athens, OH: Ohio University Press.

DeLong, J. Bradford (1986), 'Senior's "Last Hour": Suggested Explanation of a Famous Blunder', *History of Political Economy,* 18 (2), 325–334.

Digby, A. (1987), 'Malthus and Reform of the English Poor Law', in M. Turner (ed.), *Malthus and his Time,* Basingstoke: Macmillan, pp. 157–169.

Dimand, Mary Ann, Robert W. Dimand, and Evelyn L. Forget (eds) (1995), *Women of Value: Feminist Essays on the History of Women in Economics,* Aldershot, UK, and Brookfield, VT: Edward Elgar Publishing.

Dimand, Robert W. (1998), 'Classical Political Economy and Orientalism: Nassau Senior's Eastern Tours', presented to History of Economics Society session 'On the Road Again: Political Economy and Travel', Allied Social Science Associations, Chicago.

The Economist 1843–1943, *A Centenary Volume* (1943), London: Oxford University Press.

Finer, S. E. (1952), *The Life and Times of Sir Edwin Chadwick,* London: Methuen.

Frank, Robert H. and Philip J. Cook (1995), *The Winner-Take-All Society,* New York: Penguin.

Gordon, H. Scott (1955), 'The London *Economist* and the High Tide of Laissez-Faire', *Journal of Political Economy,* 63 (4), 461–488.

Groenewegen, Peter (ed.) (1994), *Feminism and Political Economy in Victorian England.* Aldershot, UK, and Brookfield, VT: Edward Elgar Publishing.

Himmelfarb, Gertrude (1983), *The Idea of Poverty: England in the Early Industrial Age,* New York: Random House.

Hollander, Samuel (1997), *The Economics of Thomas Robert Malthus,* Toronto: University of Toronto Press.

Inglis, Brian (1971), *Poverty and the Industrial Revolution,* London: Hodder and Stoughton.

Johnson, Orace (1969), 'The "Last Hour" of Senior and Marx', *History of Political Economy,* **1** (2) 359–369.

King, Steven (2000), *Poverty and Welfare in England 1700–1850: A Regional Perspective*, Manchester: Manchester University Press.

Levy, S. Leon (1949), *Nassau W. Senior, the Prophet of Modern Capitalism,* Boston: Humphries.

Levy, S. Leon (1970), *Nassau W. Senior 1790–1864: Critical Essayist, Classical Economist and Adviser of Governments,* Newton Abbott, UK: David & Charles.

Martineau, Harriet (1855), *The Factory Controversy: A Warming Against Meddling Legislation,* Manchester: Ireland and Company and the National Association of Factory Operators.

Marx, Karl [1867] (1977), *Capital,* vol. 1. (translated by Ben Fowkes), New York: Viking.

McCloskey, D.N. (1973), 'New Perspectives on the Old Poor Law,' *Explorations in Economic History,* **10** (4) 419–436.

Oslington, Paul (2001), 'John Henry Newman, Nassau Senior, and the Separation of Political Economy from Theology in the Nineteenth Century', *History of Political Economy,* **33** (4), 825–842.

Persky, Joseph (1997), 'Retrospectives: Classical Family Values: Ending the Poor Laws as They Knew Them', *Journal of Economic Perspectives,* **11** (1), 179–190.

Poynter, J.R. (1969), *Society and Pauperism: English Ideas on Poor Relief, 1795–1834,* London: Routledge & Kegan Paul, Toronto: University of Toronto Press.

Pujol, Michèle (1992), *Feminism and Anti-Feminism in Early Economic Thought,* Aldershot, UK, and Brookfield, VT: Edward Elgar Publishing; paperback edition, with introduction by Janet A. Seiz, Cheltenham, UK, and Northampton, MA: Edward Elgar Publishing, 1998.

Robson, Ann P. and John M. Robson (eds) (1994), *Sexual Equality: Writings by John Stuart Mill, Harriet Taylor Mill, and Helen Taylor,* Toronto: University of Toronto Press.

Said, Edward (1995), *Orientalism,* revised edition, Harmondsworth, UK: Penguin.

Senior, Nassau W. (1827), *An Introductory Lecture on Political Economy, Delivered Before the University of Oxford, on the 6ᵗʰ of December, 1826,* London: J. Mawman. Reprinted in Senior (1966).

Senior, Nassau W. (1829), *Two Lectures on Population, Delivered Before the University of Oxford in Easter Term, 1828, to Which is Added, a Correspondence Between the Author and the Rev. T.R. Mathus,* London: Saunders and Otley. Reprinted in Senior (1966).

Senior, Nassau W. (1837), *Letters on the Factory Act, As it affects the Cotton Manufacture, Addressed to the Right Honourable the President of the Board of Trade.* London: B. Fellowes. Reprinted in Senior (1966).

Senior, Nassau W. (1852), *Four Introductory Lectures on Political Economy, Delivered Before the University of Oxford,* London: Longman, Brown, Green, and Longmans. Reprinted in Senior (1966).

Senior, Nassau W. (1859), *A Journal Kept in Turkey and Greece in the Autumn of 1857 and the Beginning of 1858,* London: Longman, Brown, Green, Longmans, and Roberts.

Senior, Nassau W. (1882), *Conversations and Journals in Egypt and Malta (1855–1856)*, (edited by M.C.M. Simpson), London: Sampson Low, Marston, Scarle & Rivington.

Senior, Nassau W. (1966), *Selected Writings on Economics: A Volume of Pamphlets 1827-1852*, New York: Augustus M. Kelley, Reprints of Economic Classics.

Shanley, Mary Lyndon (1989), *Feminism, Marriage, and the Law in Victorian England*, Princeton, NJ: Princeton University Press.

Stigler, George J. (1949), *Five Lectures on Economic Problems,* London: London School of Economics and Political Science.

West, E.G. (1964), 'Private versus Public Education: A Classical Economic Dispute', *Journal of Political Economy,* **72**, as reprinted in Coats (1971), pp. 123–143.

White, Michael V. (1994), 'Following Strange Gods: Women in Jevons's Political Economy,' in Groenewegen (1994), pp. 46–78.

Winch, Donald (1996), *Riches and Poverty: An Intellectual History of Political Economy in Britain, 1750–1834,* Cambridge, UK: Cambridge University Press.

NOTES

1. Originally, the statutes of the Drummond Professorship did not allow the incumbent to serve consecutive five-year terms.
2. The audience at Senior's inaugural lecture (Senior 1827), the first lecture by an economics professor at an English university, 'walked out one by one, leaving him only with the Vice-Chancellor,' perhaps because Senior's 'weak voice' made him difficult to hear (Levy 1970, pp. 52–53, cf. Oslington 2001, p. 828).
3. Senior did not appear to consider Miss Linley's singing as a serious career, but Frank and Cook (1995, p.45) report that the British soprano Elizabeth Billington earned between ten and fifteen thousand pounds sterling for the 1801 London season.
4. Senior (1829, p. 24) added that 'where the other forms of moral and physical evil are accumulated as they are among the West Indian slaves, it is probable that the removal of this obstacle [promiscuity] alone would do little to facilitate their increase.' He did not indicate the source of his information or of his family's wealth: his grandfather Nassau Thomas Senior was a slaveholder as owner of two plantations in Barbados (as of 1786) and others in Dominica and Tobago, as well as a slave-trader and monopolist as Governor of the Company of Merchants Trading to Africa from 1757 (Levy 1970, pp. 10–21). Britain banned the slave trade in 1807, and abolished slavery in the British Empire in 1834, with compensation to the slave-owners.
5. Senior argued that it would not be possible to operate a factory with both adult and child workers for eight hours a day and just adults for another four hours, or to keep track of two shifts of children, so that none worked more than the allowed time.
6. In contrast to Blaug's critique of the Poor Law Report, a more conservative commentator, George Stigler (1949, pp. 25–36), took Senior's Report of the Handloom Weavers as his text to argue that the most talented classical economists (such as Senior) displayed more sophistication and insight in their applied analyses than in their treatises and programmatic statements. 'On the side of formal analysis, it is abundantly clear that the demand curve is subject to detailed study, income effects are recognized, the firm household is the unit of analysis, the law of substitution enters, imperfections of competition are duly examined. On the substantive side, the report ignores no important questions. Modern economists at their best can write somewhat better reports, and usually write inferior ones. Even if this high estimate of the report be accepted, it may be said that Senior was, after all, an economist of unusual attainments, hardly to be taken as typical of the economists of his time. I should enthusiastically agree' (Stigler 1949, p. 34).
7. Malthus was, however, a cautious advocate of public works as a response to unemployment. See Poynter (1969, pp. 225–227), Digby (1987), and Hollander (1997).
8. Chadwick's daughter Marion (1844–1928) 'became a leading figure in the Women's Rights Movement' (Finer 1952, p. 5). In a character sketch of her father written in 1928, she held that 'He had a great respect for the intellectual powers of women and was one of the earliest supporters of their professional and educational rights, and also Women's Suffrage' (Finer 1952, p. 514). Perhaps his view of the intellectual powers of women changed after his alliance with Florence Nightingale over public health and sanitation.
9. Senior had intended at least some of these for eventual publication, and had written prefaces to his conversations with Alexis Tocqueville and to his collected journals, conversations and articles about Ireland.
10. Named for her mother, the former Mary Charlotte Mair.
11. Hekekyan Bey was one of five or six Armenians brought to Egypt by Mehmet Ali, the Turkish Khedive (Viceroy), and sent to France to be educated for official positions. He was embittered by his dismissal after the death of Mehmet Ali. The British Museum holds seven letters from Senior to Kekekyan from 1856 to 1862.

13. William Thompson and Anna Doyle Wheeler: A Marriage of Minds on Jeremy Bentham's Doorstep

Chris Nyland and Tom Heenan

On Jeremy Bentham's doorstep ideas met and mingled. Pessimistic political economists and the odd industrialist called, as did Jacobins, the occasional feminist, Utilitarians and other levellers. In the autumn of 1822, a middle-aged Irishman stepped over the doorstep and into Bentham's Westminster home. It was a short stroll to the Commons and the Lords. But the Irishman's parliament was on the other side of Bentham's doorstep, where progressives and pessimists argued and speculated about mankind's – and occasionally womankind's – future. Amidst this heady atmosphere the Irishman William Thompson worked away on his germinal study of political economy and met Anna Doyle Wheeler.

For those who crossed Bentham's doorstep, two great events had invariably shaped their views – the French and Industrial Revolutions – and Thompson was no exception. In the months preceding his arrival in London, Thompson had journeyed through the British Midlands, a fact noted but not explored by his biographers, Richard K.P Pankhurst and Dolores Dooley. For a reformer who sympathized with the dispossessed this was an important experience, for it made him much more aware of the industrialization process and the near-pauperized labourers who spent their waking hours toiling for pittances in the mills, foundries and sweatshops. As an informed observer, Thompson was aware that an employer's market existed in England. The passing of the *Combination Acts* (1799–1800) and the rescindment of the 1563 *Statute of Artificers* (1814) had restricted the activities of trade unions and deregulated the labour market. Coupled with a depressed economy – a hangover from Britain's war with France – these legislative measures produced a reservoir of cheap, legally marginalized labour from whom employers could pick and choose. Consequently, working conditions and wages were appalling, and an industrial proletariat was in the process of being forged and so was still highly vulnerable.

But Thompson was also a child of the French Revolution, which not only sparked his belief in progress, but also sharpened his Irish sense of grievance. As a youth he was remembered by his Irish contemporaries for wearing the symbol of the French Revolution, the tricolour (Dooley 1996, p. 7). Nonetheless, he was not an obvious candidate to jump on the Revolution's bandwagon, and certainly not one likely to lend his support to the emerging socialist movement. By the standards of the Irishman of his day, Thompson was born – in 1775 – with the most silver of spoons in his mouth. A native of County Cork, he was a scion of Ireland's Protestant Ascendency and a member of Wesley's Irish Establishment Church. His family was landed gentry with substantial mercantile interests in Cork City. Amid its prosperous port, Thompson's father, John, had acquired wealth and standing as a merchant and owner of a fleet of trading vessels. Furthermore, at Glandore on the city's periphery, he resided on a 1400-acre estate. With wealth came political power, and John Thompson served terms as the Mayor of Cork City and the High Sheriff of the county. On his father's death in 1814 William inherited the family fortune, including the Glandore estate.

But the influences that had shaped his father's world were too narrow for William. Thus he employed the trappings inherited from his father as an instrument to step beyond the constraints of his class and culture, to envisage what he deemed to be a better world. In so doing, he was motivated by an acute awareness of the other Ireland beyond the doorstep of Cork's establishment. Like a small number of his class and creed – most notably the nationalists, Wolfe Tone and Henry Gratten – Thompson was attracted to, though appalled by, this other Ireland. There, as Woodham-Smith later noted:

> No Catholic could vote, hold any office under the Crown, or purchase land, and Catholic estates were dismembered by an enactment directing that at the death of a Catholic owner his land was to be divided among all his sons, unless the eldest became a Protestant, when he could inherit the whole. Education was made impossible, since Catholics might not attend schools, not keep schools, nor send their children to be educated abroad. The practice of the Catholic faith was proscribed (Woodham-Smith 1962, p. 20).

As a consequence of these statutes, three-quarters of Cork was disenfranchised, impoverished, and denied the solace of their God. With the echoes of the Revolution in France reverberating throughout Ireland, a nationalist and mostly Protestant-led body of dissidents – which included Thompson – seized on this discontent to campaign for parliamentary reform, Catholic emancipation and improved conditions for Ireland's impoverished peasantry.

These events blended in Thompson's mind a potent cocktail of politics, economics and social science, from which emerged one of the most original and far-reaching socialist economic thought systems of the pre-Marx period. Thompson would attempt to rescue political economy from the liberal grips of Smith and Ricardo, and lace it with a leftist reading of Bentham's more hopeful Utilitarianism. In so doing, the Irishman would call into question the morality of the prevailing individualism which had premised Smith and Ricardo's works, formulating instead his own co-operative form of political economy.

But arguably his greater contribution was in the campaign that he and his collaborator, Anna Wheeler, waged to liberate women from the social and economic yoke imposed on them by the prevailing patriarchy. Drawing on Bentham's Utilitarianism, Thompson and Wheeler argued that men and women alike had a right to their heavens on earth. This would not come from the traditional male bastions of the pulpit and parliament, but through the growth of reason and the establishment of a co-operative form of political economy. Unlike the parliament and pulpit, reason, they believed, was available to men and women alike, and would eventually be employed to equalize society, levelling disparities in wealth and power between the sexes.

As Asa Briggs has noted, England entered the nineteenth century concerned – amongst other things – for 'the state of the poor and the provision of education' (Briggs 1959, pp. 15–17). Thompson was well aware of these concerns, and in the years prior to his arrival in London had attempted to alleviate the plight of the poor in Cork, through the promotion of a broadly based liberal education for all, regardless of class or creed. Thompson was a proprietor of the Cork Institute, a role he inherited from his father, and a member of the local Philosophical, Scientific and Literary Society, hence he was particularly well situated to express his views on the need to liberate reason from the traditional restraints imposed by the pulpit, parliament and those intent on protecting their entrenched privileges. Both the Institute and the Society housed the intellectual capital of Cork City's establishment, which was Protestant, male and seemingly keen to keep its privileges intact. Nonetheless, Thompson doggedly pushed his dissenting agenda. During the 1812 election, for example, he lent his support to the Catholic emancipist candidate, Christopher Hely-Hutchinson, to the consternation of Cork's conservative powerbrokers. Not surprisingly, Thompson was disparagingly dubbed 'the red republican' (Pankhurst 1954, p. 4).

But it was his push for universal education which brought him into the most conflict with Cork's establishment. Thompson held that universal education should not only engender reason, but also provide the necessary instruments for human progress. It should raise the moral tone, increase the general happiness, and improve social values. More particularly, it should not dwell on the study of 'dead languages' or the classics. Riddled with rarefied prose about moribund regimes, these served no 'useful purpose' for a practical man like Thompson or the poorer classes. As a farmer by trade, Thompson was first and foremost a practical man, and dismissed the classics as indulgences of the idle classes. The new emerging society, he argued, must be versed in agriculture and politics, and the principles, processes and effects of manufactures and commerce. To achieve this, education must endeavour to improve the material lot – and hence the general happiness – of all, including women.

Thompson was determined to ensure that his views were prominently placed on the Cork Institute's agenda. Originally, the Institute had been established in 1806 to provide a liberal education to all Cork's children, particularly those from the city's poorer quarters. For Thompson, this entailed developing 'useful citizens for active life, ... benevolent tradesmen and merchants and country gentlemen, and mak[ing] their wives and daughters equally intelligent, respectable and useful'.[1] Under a Royal Charter of 1807, the Institute received an annual Parliamentary allowance of 2000 pounds to assist in the fulfilment of its mission. However, by 1818, Thompson had grown concerned that the allowance was not being used for its intended purpose, but was being frittered away on courses that were of interest only to the educated and upper classes, and unnecessary renovations to the Institute's premises. Furthermore, Thompson had grown increasingly frustrated at the Institute's refusal to allow women to attend its classes. In a debate that raged in the pages of Cork's *Southern Reporter,* Thompson sternly reminded the Institute's management of its obligations to educate the poor and middling classes regardless of their gender. In May he published a pamphlet, *Practical Education for the South of Ireland*, which contained an open letter to the Chief Secretary for Ireland, Sir Robert Peel. Listed amongst Thompson's complaints against the Institute's management was its continued exclusion of women.

Though Thompson lost his battle with the Institute's management, it prompted him to explore the possibilities for establishing a school that would provide educational opportunities for all. Aware that in 1815–1816, Jeremy Bentham had published *Chrestomathia*, in which he had advocated a secular education based on understanding rather than rote learning, Thompson sought out his advice in October 1818. By April 1819, Bentham had supplied Thompson with a list of schools on which the latter might base his own.[2] In the following October, Bentham related to a colleague that Thompson was progressing with the school, and 'lectur[ing] on my principles, for which he has written for my assistance'.[3]

Thompson's attraction to Bentham's ideas was understandable. Like Thompson, Bentham thought that 'knowledge' – channelled through education – fuelled human progress's advancement towards 'perfection'. Of course, Bentham had a reformer's and not a revolutionary's idea of 'perfection'. Once society had been raised to Bentham's reasonable standards, 'law and government' could be structured on 'independent principles', and not the old order's adherence to precedent and tradition. 'All virtue', Bentham suggested, particularly those virtues that underpinned the law and government, would then be based on 'utility'; in other words, on the principle that 'the greatest happiness of the greatest number ... is the measure of the right and wrong' (Bentham 1977, p. 3). All legal and political disputes would be deferred 'explicitly and constantly' to this principle (Bentham 1977, p. 104). It was naturally and scientifically ordained, and far more acceptable than the rule of kings, or other so-called higher reasons. Utility, Bentham declared, was 'the sole and all-sufficient reason for every point ... whatsoever', and the ideal basis for government (Bentham 1977, p. 56). For too long, power had resided with the lawyers, politicians and clergy, all of whom 'elaborately organised, and anxiously cherished' their own 'sinister interest[s] and artifice[s]'. They produced fictions, devoid of reason, to protect their interests, entrench their power, and cloud public opinion. Only by extending the franchise to all educated adults capable of making reasonable decisions could this elite be challenged. It was such views that lured Thompson to Bentham's doorstep.

But Thompson had brought with him some ideological baggage of his own. Like Bentham, he admired Turgot, Condorcet and Saint-Simon's endeavours to develop a rational science of society and government. Turgot, too, had believed that ideas would propel humanity towards a state of 'higher perfection'. History was not finished, but motoring onwards and upwards fuelled by reason. All that was required was to 'discover the springs and mechanisms'. Once located, the mind – through education – would 'destroy all artificial evils of mankind and enable men to enjoy all the good offered by nature' (Pollard 1971, p. 85).

Condorcet too thought that history would progress onwards according to preordained natural laws. Such was his certainty that he developed a 10-stage theory of history, commencing with primitivism and concluding at what he saw as the pinnacle, the founding of the French Republic. Underpinning this development were increases in agricultural and industrial production, which in turn fuelled the arts, sciences and philosophical enquiry. But at its core was reason. Condorcet, like Thompson, believed that reason had freed men from the superstitions and miseries, and the pains and privations, that had plagued less developed historical stages. As Pollard has observed, Condorcet's writing contained the 'essentials' of 'liberal-democratic western society[:] ... universal education, universal suffrage, equality before the law, freedom of thought and expression, freedom and self-determination for colonial peoples, national insurance and pensions and equal rights for women' (Pollard 1971, p. 93). All of these 'essentials' would have been applauded by Thompson. For Condorcet was the dreamer in Thompson's baggage. While Bentham had come to seek limited reform within the existing social structure, Condorcet had envisaged another society, in which humanity would achieve all of which it was truly capable. It was this possibility that fuelled Thompson's belief that reason would eventually establish economic and social equality for all, regardless of gender.

As with John Stuart Mill, it was Saint-Simon who gave Thompson's dreams a collectivist scope. Thompson was well-versed in Saint-Simon's work. The former had travelled extensively through France and the Low Countries, where he had met with, and been influenced by, Saint-Simon's supporters. As with Condorcet, Saint-Simon believed history was driven by '[t]he supreme laws of progress of the human spirit [which] ... dominate everything'. 'Men are but its instruments' and must 'obey the law, by accounting for the course which it lays ... instead of being blindly pushed along by it' (Pollard 1971, p. 85). Humanity's only recourse was to discover the principles that determined progress, and establish a social system upon these principles. Saint-Simon's government would not be of the people, but would be drawn from those sufficiently educated to locate the principles underpinning progress. Nonetheless, his government would be elected by the people. It would exclude generals, politicians and others blinkered by their association with the old order, but include untainted intellectuals, artists and the professional classes; that is those mandated to develop a scientifically ordained society. As he objected to *laissez-faire* political economy, with its individualistic bent, Saint-Simon's elect would institute state socialism, ridding society of the miseries wrought by capitalism. Unlike Turgot, whose history stalled at the bourgeois stage, Saint-Simon dreamed beyond it, to a collectivist epoch governed, on behalf of the people, by an enlightened few. Though his dream influenced Thompson, the latter attempted to place Saint-Simon's principles on firmer, more practical footings. To do so, Thompson turned to the Scottish co-operativist, Robert Owen.

The two men appear to have become acquainted during Thompson's stay with Bentham from 10 October 1822 to 24 February 1823. According to both Pankhurst and Dooley, Thompson was unimpressed by Owen's attempts to have the aristocracy and ruling elites fund his co-operative ventures on behalf of the labouring class. Such overtures, Thompson contented, compromised Owen's support for bettering the labourers' lot. Being self-contained, a disciplinarian and not predisposed to placing his interests above those of the collective good, Thompson was also disturbed by Owen's charisma, which he considered dangerous (Dooley 1996, p. 24; Pankhurst 1954, p. 21). But they did hold a common view of England's emergent industrial capitalism. Like Thompson, Owen considered it as 'quite unfavourable to the individual and general happiness', and likely to 'produce the most lamentable and permanent evils unless its tendency [was] counteracted by legislative interference and direction'. Both men were disturbed by the capitalist's propensity to accumulate wealth regardless of the consequences for the greater social good, and thought capitalists should be obliged to use some of their profits to ensure that their labourers' bodies and souls remained intact. But unlike Thompson, Owen was not prepared to reject the right of capitalists to profit from their investments. Owen was a moral straightener, not a revolutionary. As E.P. Thompson noted, Owen was a 'paternalist' who sought to 'remoralize', not liberate, the unruly Scottish labouring classes, whom he felt 'had almost all the vices and very few of the virtues of a social community' (Thompson 1968, p. 859). They were the source of Owen's and the common wealth and had to be refined – or constrained. They were also cogs in the production process, whose job was 'to produce the greatest pecuniary gain to the proprietors'. In short Owen, as a seeker of patronage from the privileged, was too far entrenched in the system to challenge it. William Thompson, by contrast, was made of sterner stuff, and would push Owen's collectivism to what he saw as its logical end – socialism.

Despite being philosophically poles apart, David Ricardo was another who helped shape Thompson's thoughts on political economy and, in turn, the 'woman question'. Ricardo's work focused Thompson's thoughts on the cogs of capitalism. Though he was not a supporter of Utilitarianism, Ricardo was another frequenter of Bentham's doorstep. A self-made man, Ricardo had little time for the poor, whom he held in Malthusian contempt. They should fend for themselves, he argued, and certainly not be encouraged to procreate on the proceeds of charity or 'hand-outs' from the Poor Laws. Despite their obvious philosophical differences, Ricardo and Thompson corresponded. It was Ricardo who in May 1822 told Bentham of Thompson's imminent arrival in England and work on the 'distribution of wealth' (Pankhurst 1954, p.16).[4] Undoubtedly, Thompson had read Ricardo's 1817 work, *Principles of Political Economy*. By the time Thompson arrived in London in mid-July, *Principles* was in its third edition. Ferociously deductive, it was, according to Rolls, the work of 'an economic man always striving to achieve his maximum advantage' (Rolls 1992, p. 157). *Principles* reinforced the right of capitalists to accumulate wealth at the expense of those who shouldered the labour. They were to be recompensed at a rate necessary 'to enable [them] ... to subsist and to perpetuate their race, without either increase or diminution'. But Ricardo acknowledged that it was the 'comparative quantity of labour expended on [commodities], and not the price commodities brought in the market place' that determined value (cited in Rolls 1992, pp. 159, 161). It was on this point that Thompson based his argument in opposition to Ricardo and other advocates of *laissez-faire* political economy.

In 1824, Thompson's response, *An Inquiry into the Principles of the Distribution of Wealth Most Conducive to Human Happiness Applied to the Newly Proposed System of Voluntary Equality of Wealth,* was published. Bentham had read *Inquiry* prior to its publication. Thompson had sent the manuscript to him in May 1822, and during his stay with Bentham had continued refining the work. In the tradition of Saint-Simon, Condorcet and Turgot, *Inquiry* was premised on the notion that ideas – or 'the diffusion by individual knowledge' – fuelled 'human improvement and happiness' (Thompson 1824, p. 317). Thus, through broadening the dissemination of knowledge, humankind's collective capacity to reason would be increased which, to paraphrase Bentham, would add to the greater happiness of all. Indeed, Thompson forthrightly declared, 'no regulation, no institution, ought to be for one moment substituted for [the Utilitarian] principle of the greatest happiness'. It must 'accept no parley, no compromise with any other interest', and 'must reign untroubled and suffer no divided empire'. But before the principle could prosper, humankind had to be sufficiently fed. If not, Thompson declared, then 'mind and morals ... and the regulatory principle of Utility suffered'. Hence he formulated his rationally ordained system of political economy, based on the 'principle of the greatest happiness'. In keeping with Saint-Simon, it would 'make the noble discoveries of political economy ... useful to [the] social science'; and, furthermore, it would be solidly based on Ricardo's theory of value (Thompson 1824, pp. viii, 37).

Thompson, like Ricardo, believed that human labour determined the measure of wealth. But whereas Ricardo suggested that labourers, like other cogs in the production machine, were to be bought and sold by capitalists, Thompson proffered a less draconian alternative. He argued that nature's elements, which provided the essentials for life, were not wealth, as they were untouched by 'human labour' (Thompson 1824, p. 6). Consequently, as the act of labour produced wealth, Thompson contended that labourers had a moral right to their finished products. Under capitalism, however, the labourer sold that right – through necessity – to the capitalist who owned the means of production. This arrangement inevitably wrought vast inequalities in wealth between the labouring and capitalist classes. According to Thompson, the labourer was reduced to 'feed[ing], ... cloth[ing] and pamper[ing] the rich'. Rather than producing socially useful products, labourers toiled to meet the capricious demands of the rich. The latter, in turn, exchanged the labourers' products at speculative prices in the market place, leading to what Thompson eloquently termed the 'artificial value of caprice' (Thompson 1824, pp. 195–196).

Furthermore, labourers were compelled by 'immediate want' to sell their labour for subsistence wages. According to Thompson, employers 'calculated that whatever could be saved from the labourers would go to enrich themselves'. As a result, labourers could either withhold their labour and face starvation, or sell their skills for pittances determined by the capitalists' bottom line. Thompson damningly suggested, '[t]he constant effort of ... society [was] to deceive and induce, to terrify and compel, the productive labourer to work for the smallest possible portion of the produce of his own labour'. Drawing again on Bentham, Thompson declared that 'the greatest happiness of the whole human race [was being] sacrificed ... in the estimation of the capitalists, to produce an additional quarter per cent profit'. As Thompson saw it, the crassness of the bottom line had triumphed over Bentham's more enlightened Utilitarian principles (Thompson 1824, pp. 36, 176).

Thompson's solution was to remove the capitalist from the production process, enabling labourers to keep the fruits of their labour. Under capitalism, coercive industrial relations and the resultant 'unnatural distribution of wealth', offered labourers little incentive to increase their productivity (Thompson 1824, pp. 168–170). To rectify this, Thompson suggested the institution of an economy based on voluntary exchange. As each labourer and his community were entitled to the fruits of their labour, they were free to exchange those fruits with like-minded labourers and communities. The value of each commodity available for exchange would be determined by the labour expended in its production. As labourers now had a stake in the economy, Thompson argued, they would inevitably increase their production, adding to the general wealth and happiness. According to Thompson, this arrangement would emanate from an exercise of reasoned benevolence, and herald the next stage in history's upward and onward progression. It would be premised on the enlightenment ideals of Turgot and Condorcet, incorporate Saint-Simon and Owen's collectivism, and most importantly achieve its Utilitarian purpose, all on a humanist twist of Ricardo's *Principles*.

As Thompson was refining *Inquiry* in the winter of 1822–1823, another visitor arrived on Bentham's doorstep, who turned the Irishman's attention onto humankind's most neglected members; women. Anna Doyle, like Thompson, had been born into Ireland's Protestant Ascendancy, though in 1785. Little is known of her mother, Ann, but her father, Nicholas, was a Dean in the Church of Ireland, while her godfather was the Irish nationalist, Henry Gratten. When Anna was two years old her father died, and so she was raised by her mother, assisted by Anna's uncle, Sir John Doyle. Anna grew into a headstrong girl, and by the age of 15 had met and married Francis Massy Wheeler, in 1800, against her family's advice. Though Francis was financially well-heeled and socially well-situated, he was a drunkard, wastrel and abusive, with seemingly a greater love for his racehorses than his wife. Largely confined to Wheeler's Ballywire estate in County Limerick, Anna, by the time she was 28, had given birth to six children, of whom only two – Henrietta (1801) and Rosina (1802) – lived beyond infancy.

But while Anna seemed bound bodily by her marriage contract, she refused to subject her mind to the will of her husband. Both Pankhurst and Dooley comment that Wheeler read widely, most notably the works of the French rationalists and Wollstonecraft's *Vindication of the Rights of Woman* (Pankhurst 1954, p. 71; Dooley 1996, p. 33). Aided by her brother, John Milley, and uncle, Sir John, Anna and her daughters finally fled Ballywire for the Channel Island of Guernsey in August 1812. Sir John was the island's governor, and though he supported Anna financially, her flight from Ballywire was nonetheless a brave but desperate move, because women who fled their husbands forfeited all legal rights to be maintained. Over the next four years, Anna developed her social skills amidst the diplomatic niceties of Guernsey's government house and society. But the experience did not dull her intellectual curiosity or rebellious streak. On Sir John's recall to London in 1816, Anna packed her daughters off to boarding school, and established a salon in the northern French city of Caen, where she mixed with, and was influenced by, the followers of Saint-Simon. With the death of her husband in 1820, Anna returned to Limerick for the funeral, after which she settled in London, and became involved with Owen's co-operative movement. She returned to France in 1823, this time living in Paris, where she met the French socialist, Charles Fourier. As with Owen, Fourier was interested in establishing co-operative communities, and so Anna sought in vain to bring the two together. She had also begun contributing to Owen's journal under the pseudonym, 'Vlasta' – adopted in honour of a legendary Bohemian warrior woman who had fought to end male subordination – and translating Owen's works into French. According to Pankhurst, she and Owen frequently corresponded. In one of her letters, Anna remarked that women had to 'pretend to an overwhelming degree of admiration for their respective masters whether wise or foolish or cruel'. She airily asked, 'Shall man be free and woman a slave?' and replying to her own question, she declared defiantly, 'Never, say I' (cited in Pankhurst 1954, p. 72).

It was a combination of this defiance, the sorry story of her marriage, and her radical predisposition that drew Thompson to Wheeler. There is no record of their first meeting. Perhaps they met through Owen, but more than likely it was on Bentham's doorstep. As Dooley has established, by 1824 Wheeler was a regular caller on Bentham, and had come to see the common ground that existed between the French socialists, Owen's Co-operativism and Bentham's Utilitarianism (Dooley 1996, pp. 67, 71). Though Wheeler agreed with these movements' common call for equality, she thought that they too often disregarded women's subordinate social, political and economic status. Consequently, as Dooley emphasizes, Wheeler and Thompson sought to test Utilitarianism's boast of seeking to promote the greatest happiness of the greatest number, by highlighting the fact that women had not yet been extended the political franchise, and by demanding to know how the Utilitarians intended to rectify this situation (see Dooley 1996, pp. 126–128, 131, 134).

Thompson was no stranger to the gender issue, having already noted women's subordinate status in *Inquiry*. Perhaps Wheeler swayed Thompson to include gender inequality in the work. Nevertheless, as *Inquiry* dealt with all major aspects of social, political and economic oppression regardless of sex, mention of gender inequality was not out of place. Thompson felt that the subordination of women resulted from their incapacity to compete on equal terms with men in the workplace. Because labour's productive capacity was primarily determined by muscular strength, women, having less muscular capacity, were not capable of competing on equal terms with men. Hence they were less capable of producing items of value, and so sold their labour for less in the marketplace and, as a result, accumulated less than their male counterparts. Furthermore, women were the bearers and nurturers of children. Though 'necessary to human existence and happiness', these activities were unproductive in that they did not generate profit or greatly assist wealth accumulation (Thompson 1824, p. 289). Moreover, as these activities removed women from the production process, they were rendered financially dependent on their male spouses or fathers. Thus, though women 'form[ed] one-half of human society', they performed significantly less than 'one-half of [the] useful human operations' involved in the production process (Thompson 1824, p. 289). According to Thompson, this discrepancy has meant that '[h]owever equal men have ... proposed to be made to each other, the relative inferiority of all women to all men has been ever insisted on; [and the] old association and the brute right of superior strength have everywhere prevailed'. As a result, '[t]he weaker sex, as [with] the weaker men, have been universally the prey of the stronger' (Thompson 1824, p. 314).

Thompson mooted in *Inquiry* that 'the present aids of machinery' might provide women with 'more strength than they possess', thereby equalizing the respective productive capacities of the sexes. But this was only a partial solution. Real equality would only be achieved with a change in the political economy from competitive individualism to co-operativist socialism. But this posed a moral dilemma to Thompson, which he failed to adequately address in *Inquiry*. In maintaining that labourers were morally entitled to the fruits of their labours, Thompson implicitly asserted that this applied to both men and women. However, because women's lesser physical strength meant that they were unable to produce at the same capacity as men, their entitlement would always be less. Thus if Thompson's moral obligation to the rights of labourers was to be fulfilled, it would merely reinforce gender inequality (Thompson 1824, p. 36). It was not until *Labor Rewarded* (1827) that he reconciled this dilemma. In detailing his blueprint for a co-operativist society, Thompson recommended that stronger labourers were morally obliged to share the fruits of their labour with all members of society. Furthermore, all work within the society should be shared in common by its members – regardless of gender – whether it be work in the home or workplace. According to Thompson, these measures would 'produce the most favourable results for human happiness', thereby achieving the greater happiness of the greater number (Thompson 1827, p. 13).

The impetus for Thompson's clear focus on gender issues – as well as his collaboration with Wheeler – was provided by the notable Utilitarian, James Mill. In 1820 Mill had written his *Article on Government*, which appeared as a supplement to the 1824 edition of the *Encyclopaedia Britannica*. In *Government* Mill put forward a view of representative government based on Utilitarian grounds, which did not include women. He maintained that '[a]lmost all women find their interest involved either in that of their fathers, or in that of their husbands; [and] therefore ... should be excluded from political rights' (cited in Thompson 1825, p. 28). Foot and Mulvey Roberts have suggested that Thompson and Wheeler assumed that Utilitarians and radicals would unite to condemn Mill's position on women. But this did not eventuate. Foot and Mulvey Roberts consider this response particularly surprising as Bentham was considering speaking out against the persecution of homosexuals (Foot and Mulvey Roberts 1994). But Bentham did not challenge Mill. Instead, the Utilitarians pontificated in private, were absent when challenged to publicly defend the principle of the greater happiness of the greater number.

Disappointed with Bentham, in 1825 Thompson and Wheeler published their own defiant response to Mill, convolutedly entitled *Appeal of One Half of the Human Race, Women, Against the Pretensions of the Other Half, Men, to Retain Them in Political, and Thence in Civil and Domestic Slavery.* Though the work appeared only under Thompson's name, he insisted that it was his and Wheeler's 'joint property', and that he had simply sought to capture on paper Wheeler's thoughts (cited in Pankhurst 1954, p. 76; see also Thompson 1825, p. vii). Given Wheeler's flight to Guernsey and associated social disgrace – not forgetting the public vilification that surrounded Wollstonecraft's life and politics – it was perhaps not too surprising that even a determined woman like Wheeler would allow a man to peddle her opinions in public. For as Thompson noted repeatedly in *Appeal*, public opinion was in reality male opinion. Women lent little more than muffled voices to the public discourse. In tackling Mill's *Article*, one of *Appeal's* aims was to rectify this situation.

Using Mill as their springboard, Thompson and Wheeler forthrightly challenged the male rooted patriarchy's right to rule and appropriate the fruits of production. They dismissed Mill's contention that women's interests were involved with those of men as 'palpable and self-evident false reasoning' (Thompson 1825, p. 32). For Mill to claim that the interests of 'almost' all women were 'involved' with either those of their fathers or husbands was demonstrably false. For starters, Thompson and Wheeler noted, women with neither a husband nor father, and those marked with the social blot of illegitimacy, were 'without anyone to represent their interests' (Thompson 1825, p. 30). This, they estimated, was not a trifling number to be airily dismissed by Mill's use of the word, 'almost', but amounted to between one-sixth and one-quarter of all women. With this number excluded from the political process – along with the majority of the male population who failed to meet the property qualification of the franchise – Thompson and Wheeler rightfully challenged Mill's boast to support the greatest happiness of the greatest number. They declared that Mill, in promoting 'the greatest quantity of human happiness[,] ... [had] put aside one half of the human race ... as unentitled to consideration' (Thompson 1825, p. 34).

Furthermore, Thompson and Wheeler argued that it was 'impossible that the happiness of any individual should be involved in that of another'. This was particularly so with women, given their 'dissimilarit[ies] of constitutions' and 'organisation'. Women had 'totally different objects and occupations in life', experienced 'differences in pleasure, pains and privations', and held contrary 'views for the future'. Hence the interests of fathers or husbands were far more likely to correspond with those of their sons than their daughters or wives. While fathers and sons shared 'manly pleasures', daughters were more inclined to follow in their mothers' footsteps. Sons inevitably inherited their fathers' mantles, which included the family property and control of the purse-strings, while daughters were bequeathed their mothers' 'upper servant' status. Thus Thompson and Wheeler stressed that it was 'an absolute contradiction in terms to speak of an identity of interest'. Instead, a 'contrariety of interest [wa]s the general rule' (Thompson 1825, pp. 38, 47–48, 52–53).

The pair also thought Mill's argument was illogically premised. All agreed that man – as distinct from woman – was not a beneficent being by nature. Mill acknowledged that men are necessarily inclined to use for their own exclusive advantage whatever power they can acquire over the actions of their followers[,] and that the more knowledge they happen to possess, ... the more skill they use their power to promote such exclusive interest, at the expense of those over whom their power extends.

This, Mill stressed, was 'a governing law of human nature'. Thompson and Wheeler, too, noted man's 'propensity' to chase 'object[s] of desire' and unfettered power at others' expense. Yet, as they indicated, Mill's so-called identity of interest assumed that men were capable of beneficently acting in the interests of all. Given Mill's 'governing law', this was evidently not the case, as men's nature compelled them to bolster their own wealth and power at the expense of women and other so-called lesser mortals (Thompson 1825, pp. 4–8).

According to Thompson and Wheeler, men's compulsion to dominate was a throwback to less enlightened times, when the physically stronger survived and prospered. '[M]uscular strength' was an essential attribute in the contest between men and their fellow animals for life's material necessities. Thompson reiterated in *Appeal* that women's 'permanent inferiority of strength and occasional loss of time in gestation and rearing infants[,] eternally render[ed] the[ir] average exertions ... in ... the competition of wealth less successful than those of men'. Consequently men, because of their greater productive capacity, accumulated the bulk of wealth and, hence, the greater share of happiness. Brawn was valued over brain, and so 'want of strength' equated to 'want of wealth' (Thompson 1825, pp. 33, 155). Thus women were not only the weaker but also the poorer sex.

Little had changed in the interim, according to Thompson and Wheeler. Though society had acquired the trappings of civilization, it was still ruled by brutish male force. Despite his civilized pretensions, the nineteenth-century British man of means was not too far removed from his barbarous forebears. He still governed by might, with 'disdain to reason', satisfying his 'pleasures of mere animal appetite' and his lust to command. It was not in his nature to be magnanimous. On the contrary, Thompson and Wheeler suggested, the British man of means was inclined to 'boundless misuses of uncontrolled power'. This power was employed 'without knowledge or benevolence ... for [his] own apparent exclusive benefit at the expense of all other sentient beings, children, women or other men, whose interests may appear to them incompatible with their own' (Thompson 1825, pp. 55–57). Thompson and Wheeler considered that any measure promoted by men on behalf of women merely reflected the position, and further entrenched the power, of the former over the latter. The pair acknowledged, albeit grudgingly, that legally and materialistically the position of women had marginally improved.

Theoretically, for example, they were men's equal before the law. In practice, however, women were largely excluded from decisions on finances and politics, and on marriage forfeited property rights and the 'liberty of acting' independently from their husbands. Though women, by nature, had been equally apportioned the same 'knowledge, talent and virtues' as males, they were still socially and – in practice – legally inferior (Thompson 1825, p. 51). As a consequence, male power extended unencumbered from the Parliament to the family purse.

With male power still the predominant force, Thompson and Wheeler suggested that society had evolved into a free-for-all,

> where the effort of all [wa]s to outwit, supplant and snatch from each other; where interest [wa]s systematically opposed to duty; where the so-called system of morals [wa]s little more than a mass of hypocrisy preached by knaves, unpracticed by them, to keep their slaves ... in blind uninquiring obedience; and where the whole motley fabric [wa]s kept together by fear and blood.

Society's 'master key', or 'moving principle', was the unfettered desire to acquire 'individual wealth' (Thompson 1825, pp. ix–x). With the lurch towards *laissez-faire* capitalism and its rampant individualism, men had tightened their grip on the production process and the accumulation of wealth, thereby cornering 'all objects of desire [and] the supposed means of happiness'. Without the wherewithal to compete successfully, women lapsed into 'a [near] state of absolute slavery'. With little earning capacity of their own, they were subjected to exploitative 'power without restraint[,] ... sufficient to confound knowledge [and] ... eradicate sympathy' between the sexes. Indeed, they were 'entitled to no physical, intellectual or sympathetic enjoyment on their own account'. Instead, they became the 'ignorant slaves of man's animal propensities', the most notable of which was his lust for 'sexual gratification' (Thompson 1825, pp. ix–x, 54–55, 156).

Lust was symptomatic of men's desire to dominate women. More ominously, it had been sanctified in the 'yoke' of the marriage 'contract'. Not surprisingly, Thompson and Wheeler branded the so-called 'contact' an 'audacious falsehood'. A contract, they explained, 'impli[ed] the voluntary assent of both contracting parties', a prerequisite not apparent in the matrimonial arrangements of their day, in which women 'submit[ed] their minds as well as their bodies ... to the yoke'. As Wheeler's plight suggested, women suffered 'all of [marriage's] pains and privation[s]', while men, through arbitrarily abusing their power and position, secured 'unbridled enjoyment'. Marriage merely rendered respectable the 'law of the stronger ... on the weaker, in *contempt* of the interests and wishes of the weaker'. It was an 'ancient barbarism', respectably masked under turns of phrase like Mill's 'identity of interest' (Thompson 1825, pp. 53, 55–57, 167).

Thompson and Wheeler considered such remarks to be convenient twists of the truth, proffered by male pontificators, to keep women subserviently placed. Though pre-Orwellian, Thompson and Wheeler were mindful that public opinion could be dexterously manipulated to reinforce the establishment's position. As the establishment of their day was all male, men inevitably controlled the public discourse and, consequently, dictated society's morals and values, and drafted its '[c]ivil and criminal laws'. Under the auspices of this establishment, 'education, custom and public opinion' engendered in women fears of 'moral and physical persecution' if – like the free-spirited Wollstonecraft – they were found to have transgressed against the male-ordained order (Thompson 1825, pp. 43, 189). Indeed, perhaps the pair wrote with Wollstonecraft's life in mind – her failed marriage and subsequent affair with Godwin, her child born out of wedlock, and the vicious public attacks on her reputation. For Thompson and Wheeler, the attacks on Wollstonecraft and on the reputations of other women who had flagrantly defied the prevailing male-orchestrated 'morality', were intended to keep women, in general, subserviently situated.

But as Thompson and Wheeler repeatedly emphasized, this so-called 'morality' reeked of 'hypocrisy' and lauded the vice of male dominance as a virtue (Thompson 1825, p. 180). Given men's adulterous predilections, not to mention their other abuses of power, Thompson and Wheeler branded such criticisms of women who dared to defy the *status quo* as 'hypocritical and pernicious'. Indeed, Thompson admired defiant women like Wheeler, who had no time for women's traditional roles, which had enslaved them and stunted their intellectual growth. Unlike sons, daughters were not allowed to cultivate 'reason and foresight', and so lapsed into 'imbecility'. By contrast, he noted, men generally liked their women helpless, feeble-minded and housebound. They were mere 'chattels' or 'breeding stock', to be traded – hopefully on 'good terms' – by their families (Thompson 1825, pp. 41–42). Those like Wollstonecraft who broke the mould were publicly damned and destined for destitution.

Through *Appeal*, Thompson and Wheeler sought to champion the cause of women's political and economic rights. Of course, this entailed rebutting Mill's claim that politics were not women's business. Thompson and Wheeler countered that to exclude women from politics was to deny them their fair share of happiness. Drawing on the Utilitarian tradition, the pair considered that it was in the 'general interest' for 'the articles of wealth and all other happiness', as well as their 'means' of acquisition, to be extended 'to every individual of every family'. Unlike some Utilitarians, Thompson and Wheeler felt that for this to be achieved, all – including women – must be accorded their 'share of the power of self-government'. Without this 'ingredient', they added, 'neither intelligence, morality nor happiness can exist' (Thompson 1825, pp. 46–47).

But for those two socialists the franchise was not enough. What was also required was a fundamental shift in political economy that would allow a real – as distinct from Mill's assumed – identity of interest to flourish between the sexes. Because the prevailing individualistic free-for-all overly advantaged men, Thompson and Wheeler recommended that it be replaced by collectivism. In a collectivist society, Thompson and Wheeler argued, 'benevolence and reason' would finally triumph over brute force, and both men and women would 'perceive that it [wa]s in their mutual interest to promote ... the happiness of each other'. Consequently, a true Utilitarian-oriented identity of interest would emerge, based on an 'equality of happiness' between the sexes (Thompson 1825, p. 48).

However, this was still very much in the formative stage. For collectivism to materialize, Thompson and Wheeler felt that initially the legal and political constraints on women's rights must be removed. The male establishment, which dictated the public discourse and wielded political power, must rule for all, and not merely their class and gender. Legislators had to be convinced that women were entitled to the same rights as men. In this regard, *Appeal* was well ahead of its time. For example, it championed women's rights to divorce 'worthless and vicious husbands', and to retain any property that they had brought into their marriages. It argued that daughters should be afforded the same educational opportunities as sons, enabling them to enter the trades and professions. This would stop the rot that afflicted female intellect, allowing women to 'be the cultivated and equal sharers of the most mingled pleasures ... of which human nature is susceptible' (Thompson 1825, pp. 163–164). Most importantly, it urged that women should become full and functioning sharers in the political process. Thompson and Wheeler passionately believed that all members of society – both male and female – were entitled to a political voice. It was an essential tenet of their brand of Utilitarianism. Only through full political representation, 'under the shield of free inquiry', would 'the real interests ... of all ... be discovered', and the 'baneful prejudices' of the old muscular-ridden order be removed (Thompson 1825, p. 182).

But this was only a step towards the righting of ancient wrongs, rather than a blueprint for change. As a materialist, Thompson considered that real advances in women's rights were dependent on changes in labour relations between the sexes. It was his appreciation of what was occurring in the factories of the Midlands that enabled Thompson to perceive the vehicle that could change these relations in women's favour. In short, his awareness of the industrialization process made him aware that mechanization could significantly impact on the respective roles of men and women in industry. Thompson predicted that labour relations would alter in women's favour as increases in mechanization lessened the demand for, and the 'inefficienc[ies]' of, muscular male labour. Expanding on *Inquiry*, Thompson and Wheeler estimated that increased mechanization would render redundant three-quarters of the professions and trades currently fuelled by physical force, enabling more women to enter the workforce and secure livelihoods (Thompson 1825, pp. 183–184). This, of course, would be dependent upon raising the educational standards of women. In *Inquiry*, Thompson had recommended that women's 'faculties' should be developed, enabling them to undertake the same employment as men (Thompson 1824, p. 158). Once women were ensconced as equal participants in the production process, Thompson envisaged that the material grounds for their political ostracism would become superfluous; hence they would be able to win their fair share of the happiness quotient. But, as Thompson and Wheeler lamented, 'ages of ignorance' would have to be overcome before this would be achieved (Thompson 1825, p 188).

Increased mechanization, however, would not address the root of the problem – the status that accrues to those who accumulate wealth in a system of individualistic competition. As mechanization would not overcome the disadvantage women experienced in seeking to accumulate wealth, because of the fact that they gave birth, Thompson and Wheeler emphasized that real equality would only be achieved when individualism was replaced by 'Mutual Co-operation'. Under the latter, '[a]ll talents, all faculties, whether from nature or education, whether of the mind or muscle, [would be] ... equally appreciated'. Furthermore, all who 'contribut[ed] their exertions, muscular or mental, to the common good' would be rewarded (Thompson 1825, pp. 199–200). In having to give birth, women would not be required to achieve the same productive levels as men, 'but to contribute what they c[ould] ... to the common happiness' (Thompson 1825, pp. 205–206). On the other hand, men would be taught to acknowledge 'the peculiar pains, privations and cares which women suffer[ed] in nourishing and rearing the infancy of the whole race'. All would be aware that they were equal sharers in life's continuum, thereby engendering a new respect between the sexes. Hence, sexual exploitation of women would disappear, Thompson and Wheeler mooted, as men learnt the value of 'voluntary affection'. More importantly, mutual co-operation 'w[ould] complete and for ever insure the perfect equality and entire reciprocity of happiness between men and women' (Thompson 1825, p. 199). Though it was still a distant goal, Thompson and Wheeler held that mutual co-operation marked the final stage in progressive history's onward and upward spiral.

After the publication of *Appeal* Thompson wrote *Labor Rewarded* and continued campaigning for a co-operative political economy until his death in 1833. But the tide of capitalism was too strong. Nonetheless, his work – particularly *Appeal* – deserves greater attention. As Pankhurst, and Foot and Mulvey Roberts indicate, *Appeal* was the 'most significant work' on women's rights between the 1792 publication Wollstonecraft's *Vindication* and John Stuart Mill's *Subjection of Women* in 1869 (Pankhurst 1954, p. 94; Foot and Mulvey Roberts 1994, p. ix). *Appeal's* achievement was in its marrying of women's rights with Bentham's Utilitarianism and radical political economy, and its appreciation of the significance of both production and reproduction. In supporting the greater happiness of the greater number, Thompson and Wheeler placed women's rights on the socio-economic agenda. The prevailing system of individualistic competition, they argued, in being premised on physical strength, discriminated against women. With social status dependent on one's capacity to generate wealth, women, because of their inferior strength, were considered lesser beings. Forced into depending on men for sustenance, women were not only denied their independence and rights, but also suffered sexual and economic exploitation. Thus, to raise women's social and economic prospects, Thompson advocated his co-operativist alternative, in which the labours of all, relative to the strengths nature had accorded them, would be equally rewarded. Arguably, *Appeal* was Thompson's and certainly Wheeler's most notable triumph. But Thompson and *Appeal's* tragedy was the coming of Marx. Both would be swamped in Marx's formidable wake.

REFERENCES

Bentham, Jeremy [1817-1820], *The Correspondence of Jeremy Bentham, Volume 9, January 1817 to June 1820,* (edited by Stephen Conway), Oxford: Clarendon Press.

Bentham, Jeremy (1977), *A Comment on the Commentaries and A Fragment on Government* (edited by J.H. Burns and H.L.A. Hart), New York: Cambridge University Press.

Briggs, Asa (1959), *The Age Of Improvement 1783–1867,* London: Longman.

Cork *Southern Reporter*, 19 May 1818.

Foot, Michael and Mulvey Roberts, Marie (1994), 'Introduction', in *Appeal of One Half of the Human Race, Women, Against the Pretensions of the Other Half, Men, to Retain Them in Political, and Thence in Civil and Domestic Slavery,* Bristol: Thoemmes Press.

Pankhurst, Richard K.P. (1954), *William Thompson (1775–1833) Britain's Pioneer Socialist, Feminist, and Co-operator,* London: Watts & Co.

Pollard, Sidney, (1971) *The Idea of Progress: History & Society,* Hammondsworth: Penguin Books.

Rolls, Eric (1992), *A History of Economic Thought,* London: Faber & Faber.

Thompson, E.P. (1968), *The Making of the English Working Class,* London: Penguin Books.

Thompson, William (1824), *An Inquiry into the Principles of the Distribution of Wealth Most Conducive to Human Happiness Applied to the Newly Proposed System of Voluntary Equality of Wealth,* London.

Thompson, William (1825), *Appeal of One Half of the Human Race, Women, Against the Pretensions of the Other Half, to Retain Them in Political, and Thence in Civil and Domestic Slavery,* London.

Thompson, William (1827), *Labor Rewarded: The Claims of Labor and Capital Conciliated: Or How to Secure Labor the Whole Products of its Exertions,* London: Hunt & Clarke.

Woodham-Smith, Cecil (1963), *The Great Hunger: Ireland, 1845–1849,* London: Hamish Hamilton.

NOTES

1. Cork *Southern Reporter*, 19 May 1818. Cited in Dooley 1996, p. 18; see also Pankhurst 1954, p.12.
2. For Bentham's recommendations see his letter to Thompson of 7 April 1819 in *The Correspondence of Jeremy Bentham, Volume 9, January 1817 to June 1820,* (edited by Stephen Conway), Oxford: Clarendon Press, 1989, pp. 329–330.
3. Letter from Jeremy to Sir Samuel Bentham, 16 October 1819, ibid., p. 358.
4. See also the letter from Bentham to Ricardo, 28 October 1819, in which Bentham refers to Thompson as 'our ... Hibernian friend'. Ibid, p. 364.

14. Taking Harriet Martineau's Economics Seriously

David M. Levy

'There will one day be a resurrection of names and reputations, as certainly as of bodies.'   John Milton quoted in Wallbridge (1848)

I propose to take Harriet Martineau seriously as an economist. I am aware that this flies in the face of professional practice.[1] The reasons I have for this are two-fold. One is historical: she was taken seriously by her contemporaries. Another is textual: there are interesting and important economics in her writing. I shall focus on a cluster of issues related to a specific problem,[2] American racial slavery, to which she was a potent, avowed opponent.[3] Against this I must confront her *avowed* unoriginality[4] and her *avowed* bias.

Her avowed unoriginality seems to be the important reason for historians of economic theory not to pay attention to her novels. Her novel of slavery stands out in this regard. While she claims to have made it out of standard components, she asserts that it is not 'copied' from the authorities and, in particular, she writes that she 'recast' the arguments.[5] In the world in which I live, many a fine reputation has been won by 'recasting' arguments. We shall read this novel carefully. By this I mean that we must compare the implications she develops from her account with the cliometric evidence when it exists.

Her bias seems to be the interesting reason for recent economic historians not to pay attention to Martineau's field-report on slavery.[6] In spite of their vast command of the literature, Robert Fogel and Stanley Engerman explicitly ignore Martineau's analysis of slavery because of their methodological principle of not consulting any travellers' reports. The travellers had biases and they did not work with hard data. Indeed, Fogel and Engerman claim that the bias which results from appealing to traveller's reports explains the discord between their results and what previous scholars have found.[7]

The question of hard and soft data is neither here nor there. The same selection over statistical estimation would reproduce the bias in the analysis of 'hard data' which Fogel and Engerman find in the 'soft data'. Just as biased observers could pick and choose which evidence they found most pleasing, so too statistical workers with 'preferences over outcomes' can pick and choose which estimate they find most pleasing (Feigenbaum-Levy 1996).

Now suppose that travellers and scholars have preferences which lead to biased research. What conclusion do we draw from this? Listening only to unbiased experts is an odd principle. Consider a jury composed of naive spectators who are addressed by expert witnesses. The jury, not being stupid, is aware that the expert witnesses are biased, yet they surely will not ignore the testimony but rather strike some sort of balance between the contending experts.[8] If contending experts are in agreement, then while they may both be wrong, their common error surely cannot result from simple bias. Thus, supposing Martineau is an expert witness against slavery, we who evaluate her argument will find it edifying to read the pro-slavery writers as experts who are opposed to Martineau's client. This will be particularly important when she considers an issue which has not been the subject of cliometric examination.

It is important to note that Martineau's bias is *avowed* and that she visits the American South as an open enemy of the slave system. Martineau (1837b) spoke explicitly to the issue of bias when she pointed out that her views on slavery were exceedingly well known before she went to the South. Without her open expression of her views, she believed that she would have imposed upon her hosts as a spy rather than a guest. One of the principles of modern thinking on statistical ethics is that transparency is of critical importance. There are many biased estimators in routine use in modern statistical practice. Some of these are Bayesian but two stage least squares is one which is not immediately identified as such. These openly biased estimators raise no ethical issues because the bias is transparent.

Transparency is an important norm for Martineau in more than her analytical life. She offers a remarkably deep criticism of slavery vis-á-vis markets in terms of a life of transparency which men and women live. We shall close this essay with this criticism.

PERSONAL ABUSE AS A RATIONAL CHOICE

The abuse which Martineau received in British periodicals for her Malthusianism has been widely and carefully studied.[9] The pen and ink drawing of Martineau by Daniel Maclise (1834) was printed first in the 'progressive-conservative' [= anti-antislavery] press[10] to accompany one notorious attack (Maginn 1834).[11] The fact that her contemporaries saw in her something which transgressed gender boundaries is deeply suggestive that she has accomplished something out of the ordinary.[12] The first step in taking Martineau seriously as an economist is to consider the possibility that she knows more about the economics of sex than those who evaluate her performance as an economist.[13] Martineau's novel of slavery, *Demerara,* was published in 1833,[14] the same year as the great act abolishing slavery in the British empire was passed. On the strength of her reputation as an opponent of slavery, Martineau was invited to visit the American South to observe slavery up close and personal. Here she found the compelling piece of evidence against the argument of 'paternalistic' slavery.[15]

The key was the fact that in a world in which the incest taboo is honoured, fathers do not use their daughters sexually.[16] But slave owners did not view the young women they owned as their daughters. The sexual use of slaves, Martineau argued from the pro-slavery commonplace, was sufficiently important to affect the demand for irregular sex. As a Malthusian, Martineau attended to the trade-off between sex and material income. Unlike Adam Smith and T.R. Malthus, who confined themselves to contexts where the Christian convention of one man–one family is generally enforced, she finds in America an instance where a man can have more of both sex and material income by acquiring additional families, only one of which will be white:

> Every man who resides on his plantation may have his harem, and has every inducement of custom, and of pecuniary gain,* [*The law declares that the children of slaves are to follow the fortunes of the mother. Hence the practice of planters selling and bequeathing their own children.] to tempt him to the common practice.[17]

Then she proposes a test for moral motivation: 'Those who, notwithstanding, keep their homes undefiled may be considered as of incorruptible purity' (Martineau 1837b, vol. 2, p. 223).

Martineau is here responding to the claim that the morality of slavery can be judged by the relative infrequency of prostitution in Southern cities. So it can, Martineau argues, but not the way the slavery apologists thought. Why, she asked, would a man rent a woman for an hour when he can buy her and keep the children to sell? Thus the relative infrequency of prostitution in slave cities can provide evidence that slaves were used sexually in sufficient numbers to affect the market demand for irregular sex.[18]

The Pro-Slavery Experts

Are the data speaking or is this Martineau's bias? Let us consider what the contending experts have to say. It is, I take it, no coincidence that in 1852 and 1853, in the midst of the debate over *Uncle Tom's Cabin* and its stories of sexual usage, three massive American attacks on Martineau's claims on slavery and sexual exploitation, published over various times and places, were collected together with an unrelated essay into a volume called *The Pro-Slavery Argument*. From the words in these attacks, we can evaluate Martineau's bias.

The first line of argument from William Harper tacitly assumes that the sex is uncoerced. On the basis of this clever postulate, he gives a cogent cost–benefit explanation for why Martineau's account is true:

> In such communities, the unmarried woman who becomes a mother, is an outcast from society - and though sentimentalists lament the hardship of the case, it is justly and necessarily so. She is cut off from the hope of useful and profitable employment, and driven by necessity to further vice. Her misery, and the hopelessness of retrieving, render her desperate, until she sinks into every depth of depravity, and is prepared for every crime that can contaminate and infest society. She has given birth to a human being, who, if it be so unfortunate as to survive its miserable infancy, is commonly educated to a like course of vice, depravity, and crime.
>
> Compare with this the female slave under similar circumstances. She is not a less useful member of society than before. If shame be attached to her conduct, it is such shame as would be elsewhere felt for a venial impropriety. She has not impaired her means of support, nor materially impaired her character, or lowered her station in society; she has done no great injury to herself, or any other human being. Her offspring is not a burden but an acquisition to her owner; his support is provided for, and he is brought up to usefulness; if the fruit of intercourse with a freeman, his condition is, perhaps, raised somewhat above that of his mother. Under these circumstances, with imperfect knowledge, tempted by the strongest of human passions - unrestrained by the motives which operate to restrain, but are so often found insufficient to restrain the conduct of females elsewhere, can it be matter of surprise that she should so often yield to the temptation? (Harper 1853, pp. 42–43).

Harper attempts to make the case that it is better to have a black concubine than engage a white prostitute (1853, pp. 43–45) which is, of course, Martineau's point – although she would say 'more profitable' not 'better'. Harper is not content to respond to – or ratify – Martineau's model. He draws on Coleridge to attack the motives of utilitarians concerned with distant people:

> Are we not justified then in regarding as criminals, the fanatical agitators whose efforts are intended to bring about the evils I have described? It is sometimes said that their zeal is generous and disinterested, and that their motives may be praised, though their conduct be condemned. But I have little faith in the good motives of those who pursue bad ends. It is not for us to scrutinize the hearts of men, and we can only judge of them by the tendency of their actions. There is much truth in what was said by Coleridge. 'I have never known a trader in philanthropy who was not wrong in heart somehow or other. Individuals so distinguished, are usually unhappy in their family relations - men not benevolent or beneficent to individuals, but almost hostile to them, yet lavishing money and labor and time on the race - the abstract notion'. The prurient love of notoriety actuates some (Harper 1853, p. 93).

John Henry Hammond levels the charge of sexual hysteria against Martineau:

> But your grand charge is, that licentiousness in intercourse between the sexes, is a prominent trial of our social system, and that it necessarily arises from Slavery. This

is a favorite theme with the abolitionists, male and female. Folios have been written on it. It is a common observation, that there is no subject on which ladies of eminent virtue so much delight to dwell, and on which in especial learned old maids, like Miss Martineau, linger with such an insatiable relish. They expose it in the slave States with the most minute observance and endless iteration. Miss Martineau, with peculiar gusto, relates a series of scandalous stories, which would have made Boccacio jealous of her pen, but which are so ridiculously false as to leave no doubt, that some wicked wag, knowing she would write a book, has furnished her materials – a game too often played on tourists in this country. The constant recurrence of the female abolitionists to this topic, and their bitterness in regard to it, cannot fail to suggest to even the most charitable mind, that 'Such rage without betrays the fires within' (Hammond 1853, p. 117).

To quiet concerns with the truth of her model, Hammond asks what it is edifying to believe:

But I do not intend to admit that this charge is just or true. Without meaning to profess uncommon modesty, I will say that I wish the topic could be avoided. I am of opinion, and I doubt not every right-minded man will concur, that the public exposure and discussion of this vice, even to rebuke, invariably does more harm than good; and that if it cannot be checked by instilling pure and virtuous sentiments, it is far worse than useless to attempt to do it, by exhibiting its deformities (Hammond 1853, p. 118).

But he does respond to the sharp implication of the model. It is true. And as such, it provides evidence of the love of slave owners for their slaves; hence, slaves really aren't thought of as cattle. Lucky slaves:

One of your heavy charges against us has been, that we regard and treat these people as brutes; you now charge us with habitually taking them to our bosoms. I will not comment on the inconsistency of these accusations. I will not deny that some intercourse of the sort does take place (Hammond 1853, p. 119).

What is 'ridiculous' is *avowedly* buying a slave for sexual use from a woman.

What Miss Martineau relates of a young man's purchasing a colored concubine from a lady, and avowing his designs, is too absurd even for contradiction. No person would dare to allude to such a subject, in such a manner, to any decent female in this country (Hammond 1853, p. 120).

With arguments like this, one can certainly appreciate why attacking Martineau's motivation was an attractive use of time. But possibly the high point of personal attacks comes from a Dr W. Gilmore Simms, Esq. of South Carolina, who opens his essay by attacking Martineau's motives on the basis that although she is deaf, she makes light of her difficulty, pointing to the beneficial silence in which to think. In this Simms finds her denial of the providential order.[19]

Simms charges her with intellectual dishonesty, forcing the evidence to fit her preconceptions. How so? Carlyle's opinion of slavery is different from hers; and if Carlyle says so, who is she to disagree?

> Had it not been for this name of odium, and that Slavery had been assimilated with those features of government policy which it is her cue to obliterate, we should have seen her, as we have in latter days seen Carlyle, boldly looking through all the mists and mystifications of the subject, and probing it with an independent analysis, with which neither prescription, nor prejudices, nor selfish policy, could be permitted to interfere. Her self-relying nature would have sufficed for this, had she not determined against Slavery, before acquiring any just knowledge of that condition which has received this name (Simms 1853, p. 198).

The example where this dishonesty shows is as follows:

> Alleged rapes, by negroes upon white girls, are frequently stated by Northern journalists. We refer to Mr. Tappan for such particulars as resulted from the examination of the Commissioners of the Magdalen Asylum into the morals of New-York; and we regret that Miss Martineau had not looked more closely into the negro quarters, and into the various police trials of negro offenders in the different cities of the free States. Had she done this, she would have spared us the entire chapter on the morals of Slavery (Simms 1853, pp. 210-211).

The reason it would have been good if Martineau had not included this chapter on the morals of slavery is explained a little while later. Her charges are true:

> There is one painful chapter in these two volumes, under the head of 'Morals of Slavery'. It is painful, because it is full of truth. It is devoted to the abuses, among slaveholders, of the institution of slavery; and it gives a collection of statements which are, no doubt, in too many cases, founded upon fact, of the illicit and foul conduct of some among us, who make their slaves the victims and instruments, alike, of the most licentious passions. Regarding our slaves as a dependent and inferior people, we are their natural and only guardians; and to treat them brutally, whether by wanton physical injuries, by a neglect, or perversion of their morals, is not more impolitic than it is dishonorable. We do not quarrel with Miss Martineau for this chapter. The truth – though it is not all truth – is quite enough to sustain her and it; and we trust that its utterance may have that beneficial effect upon the relations of master and slave in our country, which the truth is, at all times, most likely to have every where (Simms 1853, pp. 228–229).

Think of the burden of an expert testifying for slavery.[20] One can defend slavery, but this is tricky if one must avow such practices as slave concubinage and rape as a punishment.[21] If slavery is the status quo it is perhaps a more prudent use of one's time to argue that one should not pay attention to the expert testifying for markets. Preservation of slavery can be maintained if the pro-market voices are ignored. Thus anti-antislavery can be seen as a low-cost substitute for pro-slavery. Here the question is not whether the allegation which supports the anti-antislavery argument is true but whether it is effective. An example of this might be best seen in the attacks on William Wilberforce. By the time emancipation was picking up political momentum, Wilberforce's reputation for austerity was set in stone.[22] Mid to late nineteenth-century evangelicals, Wilberforce's co-religionists, were invariably characterized as 'anti-fun' (Levy-Peart 2001). However, in the eighteenth century when his crusade against slavery was just beginning, Wilberforce's opposition to slavery was given a rational choice explanation in an insufficiently studied cartoon by the famous Paul Gillray.[23] Perhaps Wilberforce opposes slavery because emancipation will reduce the price of sex with black girls? Or perhaps he is being bribed? The Gillary rational-choice explanation for Wilberforce's views has at least the charm of being coherent.

Why Payment in Leisure?

In *Demerara* Martineau makes the conventional case that slavery reduces the incentive to diligence:

> Then it is surely best for all parties to make the connexion between labour and its reward as clear as possible. I doubt whether any slave believes that his comfort depends on the value of his work. At any rate, it often sees that it does not. An this difficulty will for ever attend the practice of holding labourers as fixed capital ....
> Our slaves never invent or improve ... Why should they? No invention would shorten their toil, for they do no task work. No improvement does them any good, for they have no share in the profits of their labour (Martineau 1832–1834, vol. 2, pp. 71–72).

She repeats Adam Smith's claim that the slave is more expensive than free labour because the slave has less incentive to take care of his/her maintenance.[24] And like Smith she quotes the proverb that it is better to play for nothing than to work for nothing. In a way the entire Carlyle–Mill debate is whether that piece of proverbial wisdom is controlling! But slave owners also had access to the *Wealth of Nations*, or if that was too hard going, to Martineau's *Illustrations.* A diligent slave-owning student of Smith, who as a result of this study understands the incentive issues, might be able to do something about them. Thus, the slave-owning student of economics may behave differently – and more profitably – than an ignorant slave owner. To illustrate the incentive effect, Martineau introduces a character, Alfred, who seems to have studied political economy in Britain. Alfred, who not coincidentally acquired a moral aversion to treating people as if they were horses,[25] upon his and his sister's return to their parents' slave plantation persuades his father to try something Smithian. Since this is an economic tale which ignores transactions costs, *voilà!* – strong incentives to economic tale which ignores transactions costs, *voilà!* – strong incentives to diligence within pages:

> Mr. Bruce meanwhile was looking alternatively at two gangs of slaves at work after a rather different manner. He was standing on the confines of two different estates; and, in a field at a little distance, a company of slaves was occupied as usual; that is, bending over the ground, but to all appearances scarcely moving, silent, listless, and dull. At hand, the whole gang, from Cassius down to the youngest and weakest, were as busy as bees, and from them came as cheerful a hum, though the nature of their work rather resembled the occupation of beavers.

> 'Task-work with wages,' said Alfred, pointing to his own gang; 'eternal labor, without wages,' pointing to the other. 'It is not often that we have an example of the two systems before our eyes at the same moment. I need not put it to you which plan works the best' (Martineau 1832–1834, 2: pp. 70-71).

In *Society in America* Martineau finds an example of her thought experiment and encounters the same nasty sort of moral issue with which Fogel would grapple – would we really want *efficient* slavery?[26]

A kind-hearted gentleman in the south, finding that the laws of his State precluded his teaching his legacy of slaves according to the usual methods of education, bethought himself, at length, of the moral training of task-work. It succeeded admirably. His negroes soon began to work as slaves are never under any other arrangement seen to work. Their day's task was finished by eleven o'clock. Next they began to care for one another: the strong began to help the weak: first, husbands helped their wives, then parents helped their children; and, at length, the young began to help the old. Here was seen the awakening of natural affections which had lain in a dark sleep.

> Of the few methods of education which have been tried, none have succeeded so well as this task-work. As its general adoption might have the effect of enabling slavery to subsist longer than it otherwise could, perhaps it is well that it can be employed only to a very small extent (Martineau 1837a, vol. 2, pp. 157-158).

It is clear that Martineau doesn't think that task work can be generalized. Perhaps she didn't see the induced technology which might be forthcoming. This possibility we will consider later.

The bonus payment for extra effort is in terms of leisure; consequently, we must consider the classical discussion of the 'backward bending' supply of labour. For our purposes the most interesting statement is by David Ricardo who made the vital point that while leisure and durable goods are both luxuries, the worker may be more certain of getting the leisure than the durable good.[27] In

Demerara Martineau makes the point that slaves cannot constrain their owners to honour promises. She has a slave-owing character explain this: 'Promises to slaves are nothing, you know, if circumstances alter, as they have done in this case' (Martineau 1833, p. 131). Therefore, if an owner promised a 'neat cottage' or freedom for extra work, what reason does the slave have to believe the promise will be honoured?

A Pro-slavery Expert

I find less interest among pro-slavery writers in the incentive issues than in sex with slaves. Nonetheless, on one incentive issue which she raised I have found a speaker on the other side. One of Martineau's vigorous American critics agreed that the inability to offer a slave freedom as a reward for years of hard work was a problem:

> Of late years, some arbitrary laws have been passed in Carolina, which forbid the citizens to free their slaves. I do not approve of these laws myself ... I am persuaded that it would be a wholesome policy to revoke these laws. It would, in the first place, prevent their frequent evasion. A more important consideration is, that it would give to the owner a power now denied, of doing full justice to the claims of the faithful and the intellectual, without compelling him to banish them from their native homes, while bestowing upon them their own mastery (Simms 1853, pp. 238–239).

To the extent that under slavery the uncertainty of long-term contracts relative to short-term contracts is greater than in a free market, then vis-à-vis the free worker, the rational slave would be more willing to accept in exchange for extra effort goods which can be immediately consumed (that is leisure) rather than durable goods which can be confiscated. If this is so, then it immediately follows that the optimal leisure of slaves will be higher than the optimal leisure of free labour and consequently the optimal time inputs will be respectively lower and higher.[28] If we were to compare two firms with the same size labour force, the same capital stock and the same production function, then from the neoclassical property of diminishing marginal products of factor inputs, the lower labour input of the slave firm will increase the marginal product of the slave labour relative to that of the free labour.

Hence, two of Fogel and Engerman's dramatic results – the relative high marginal product of slave labour and the relatively low time input – are immediate neoclassical implications from Martineau's classical observations. Needless to say, the higher leisure does not mean the slave is necessarily better off, because the slave cannot make a contract to buy freedom with extra labour input.

Slaves as 'Lemons'

Martineau has identified a characteristic of the legal system of slavery. While sensible short-term contracts can be made in such a way that they are self-enforcing – the task-work example is particularly elegant – long-term contracts cannot be so easily designed. But this is not the only flaw she finds in the slave system. Here it is important to consider *Society in America* as an expansion of *Demerara*. In *Demerara* she claims that the legal system in slavery won't work efficiently because in the case of crime the slave is too valuable to punish optimally. Let me quote at length:

> The government and the holders of the property are the parties to the maintenance of the law. The infringers of the law are the third party, whom it is the mutual interest of the other two to punish. So the matter stands in England, where the law works comparatively well. Here the case is wholly changed by the second and third parties being identical, while the first treats them as being opposed to each other. The infringer of the law, that is, the rebellious slave, being the property of – that is, the same party with, his owner, the benefits of the compact are destroyed to all. If the slave is not to be punished, the owner's property (his plantation) is not safe. If he is punished, the owner's property (the slave) is injured. No wonder the master complains of the double risk to his property; but such risk is the necessary consequence of holding a subject of law in property (Martineau 1832–1834, 2: pp. 23–24).

The initial reaction of a modern economist will surely be that she has it backwards. Under slavery all the external economies associated with slave crime will be internalized. Here's a test. Is Martineau right? Ask an economist whether a problem with slavery is that the slaves are not punished severely enough.

Society in America she illustrates her claim with a little story. Let a professional tell the tale:

> One night, when the girl was undressing her, the lady expressed her fondness for her, and said, among other things: 'When I die you shall be free'; – a dangerous thing to say to a slave only two years younger than herself. In a short time the lady was taken ill, – with a strange, mysterious illness, which no doctor could alleviate. One of her friends, who suspected foul play, took the sufferer entirely under her own charge, when she seemed to be dying. She revived; and as soon as she was well enough to have a will of her own again, would be waited on by no one but her favourite slave. She grew worse. She alternated thus, for some time, according as she was under the care of this slave or her friend. At last, the friend excluded from her chamber every one but the physicians: took in the medicines at the room door from the hands of the slave, and locked them up. They were all analyzed by a physician, and arsenic found in everyone one of them. The lady partially recovered; but I was shocked at the traces of suffering in her whole appearances. The girl's guilt was brought clearly home to her. There was never a case of more cruel, deliberate intention to murder (1837a,

vol. 2, pp. 318-319).

Now, what to do?

> If ever slave deserved the gallows, (which ought to be questionable to the most
> decided minds,) this girl did. What was done? The lady was tender-hearted, and
> could not bear to have her hanged. This was natural enough; but what did she
> therefore do? Keep her under her own eye, that she might at least poison nobody else,
> and perhaps be touched and reclaimed by the clemency of the person she would have
> murdered? No. The lady sold her (1837a, 2: pp. 318–319).

This is of course exactly the case which George Akerlof (1970) analyzed in
his celebrated market for lemons. Martineau does not draw the implication that
the rational slave owner would be leery of the single resold slave. However, if
they hadn't figured this out before, then surely Martineau's book would be
illuminating.[29]

Now, consider Fogel and Engerman's results that slaves were rarely resold
except in groups in the case of an estate sale. The first is indeed what we would
expect from the Akerlof model. The exception seems to be an interesting case
where the condition of asymmetric information does not hold: the current owner
may not have the information which the previous owner had; thus there is no
possibility to sell the 'lemon' and keep the 'cream puff' which makes the
Martineau–Akerlof model tick.

The Pro-Slavery Experts on 'Lemons'

Martineau writes from an anti-slavery vantage from which it is taken for
granted that slave owners, as maximizing agents, would exploit whatever
opportunities come their way. The pro-slavery experts claimed that slavery
would allow the caring master to elevate the character of his charges.[30] In a
system of slavery, then, according to its expert defenders, perhaps the nasty sort
of maximizing which characterizes the 'lemons' market would not exist?
Consider the opinion of E.J. Stearns, who asserts that slavery in its own
mysterious way brings the best of mankind to the top:

> ... the slave-holders generally are the *elite* of society, – the picked men ... far, in
> advance of 'the majority in our world', in both 'consideration' and 'self-control'. As
> to 'an enlightened regard to their own interest', if by that is meant, minding the main
> chance, i.e., looking out for the greatest good of the greatest number, meaning
> thereby, as Thelwell has it, 'number one', I am very much afraid that they would have
> to yield the palm to us Yankees (Stearns 1853, p. 47).

And how does this speak to the 'lemon' problem? Consider Harriet Beecher
Stowe's *Uncle Tom's Cabin*, Stearn's target, in which an old, trustworthy slave

is sold to pay debts. This Stearns finds to be incredible:

> I challenge Mrs. Stowe to bring forward a *single instance* in which such a slave as
> Uncle Tom is here represented to have been, was *ever* sold by his master to a slave-
> dealer. Servants like Uncle Tom are known throughout the community ... and valued,
> too; or rather they are justly considered invaluable; and Mr. Shelby had only to let it
> be known that he was obliged to part with Tom, to have had a dozen of his neighbors
> in competition for the purchase, and at a higher price, too, than any prudent dealer
> would be willing to offer; for they would know what they are purchasing, and the
> dealer, whatever his own knowledge, would find it no easy matter to transfer that
> knowledge to his customer (Stearns 1853, p. 146).

So Stearns, after his denial of sharp dealing among the civilized slave owners,
finds so much of it as to deny all plausibility of Stowe's naive story of honest
dealing.

A more detailed account, and one lacking Stearns' amusingly incoherent
homily, is provided by A. Woodward:

> ... Shelby had a number of slaves from whom he could select; I know from personal
> observation, that it is a universal practice among slaveholders to sell the most
> worthless and vicious slaves to negro traders. If they are forced sell such a negro as
> she represents Tom to be, some neighbor who is acquainted with the slave, will give a
> higher price for him than a negro trader will. A negro trader will give as much for a
> negro who is a rogue, as he will for one who is an honest man. The negro trader pays
> no attention to the character of a negro; for the very good reason that the character of
> the negro is unknown to those to whom he expects to sell. No representation or
> recommendation whatever, can have any influence with those to whom they sell.
> They know nothing about the character of the negro whom they purchase, and they
> have no reliable means of learning any thing about them (Woodward 1853, p. 83).

The supply may very well be sensitive to the incentives. *Uncle Tom's Cabin*
surely provided the pro-slavery experts with an occasion to think very hard about
the logic of re-selling slaves.

Evaluating Institutions: What Does 'Inefficient' Imply?

For an economist in the modern neoclassical tradition, showing that an
institution is 'inefficient' is tantamount to showing that the relative prices under
this institution do not equal relative marginal social costs. From Martineau's
tales we can see two interesting source of such divergence. The 'lemons'
problem is self-evident, post Akerlof. It bears on slavery because under slavery
there is one more type of capital to be sold. The stories Martineau tells suggest
also that slavery will change the exchange value of such immediately
consumable goods as leisure relative to consumer durables. This seems a rather
intriguing source of 'inefficiency' of slavery.

When an economist proves an institution is 'inefficient', what does this mean? Buchanan (1959) gives an interesting answer: the proof can be tested by looking to see whether the institution is changed. Thus, a Smithian proof that command slavery is inefficient, when widely known, will change the nature of slavery to something perhaps akin to market slavery. Piece work or task work incentives may be straightforward to implement: Martineau saw them in the field, Fogel and Engerman documented them in the data. The inability to make long-term creditable contracts cannot be so easily changed without slavery ending; nor can the lemons problem. As long as slavery exists these should leave their tracks in the data.

A related way to think about 'inefficiency' is that the firms inside the institution have different input prices than those outside; hence innovations should be focused to conserve the relatively more expensive input. If it is relatively cheaper to get slaves to work harder for briefer periods – as Martineau's tales suggest – then we have a way of making sense of Fogel-Engerman's claim that the gang system was the not-so-secret centre of the South's survival.[31] But this raises a serious conceptual issue. If a divergence between relative prices and relative social marginal costs induces innovation, then how do we do efficiency comparisons? Slave capitalism and liberal capitalism will have non-comparable levels of technology. It has been suggested by a generation of Chicago economists that efficiency, after all is said and done, is what exists for a long time. This claim, of course, depends upon the modern notion of efficiency.

But our exercise was to take Martineau seriously as an economist. How would she evaluate the institutions? Let us consider her words on this which begin her first novel in which she compares Domestic to Political Economy:

> Political Economy treats of the Production, Distribution and Consumption of Wealth: by which terms is meant whatever material objects contribute to the support and enjoyment of life. Domestic economy is an interesting subject to those who view it as a whole; who observe how, by good management in every department, all the members of a family have their proper business appointed them, their portion of leisure secured to them, their wants supplied, their comforts promoted, their pleasures cared for; how harmony is preserved within doors by the absence of all causes of jealousy; how good will prevail toward all abroad through the absence of all causes of quarrel. It is interesting to observe by what regulations all are temperately fed with wholesome food, instead of some being pampered above-stairs while others are starving below; how all are clad as becomes their several stations, instead of some being brilliant in jewels and purple and fine linen, while others are shivering in nakedness; how all have something, be it much or little, in their purses ... Such extremes as these are seldom or never to be met with under the same roof in the present day, when domestic economy is so much better understood than in the times when such sights were actually seen in rich men's castles: but in that larger family, – the nation, – every one of these abuses still exists, and many more (Martineau 1832–1834, pp. 1, v–vi).

Martineau is obviously concerned with distributional issues. Where did this come from? It is hardly her fault if her twentieth-century readers did not catch the consequences of her avowed unoriginality. The working normative metric in Adam Smith and T.R. Malthus is the happiness of the *majority* of the people, the *median* well-being (Levy 1995, Hollander 1997). The fact that the working normative metric of modern neoclassical economics is the *mean* income – where differences between the income that goes to the slave and to her master do not matter – means that Martineau's arguments are original to us. Hence, taking Harriet Martineau seriously as an economist is tantamount to taking the past of economics seriously. Her texts are a good place to begin this exercise.

Transparency, Sympathy and the Condition of Women

Martineau's chapter on the 'Morals of Economy' are of such importance that they are included in a modern abridged edition of *Society in America*. She asks what effect the existence of the hidden harem economy has upon the condition of free women. She considers a particularly famous example of inter-racial sexuality:

> The Quadroon connexions in New Orleans are all but universal, as I was assured on the spot by ladies who cannot be mistaken. The history of such connexions is a melancholy one: but it ought to be made known while there are any who boast of the superior morals of New Orleans, on account of the decent quietness of the streets and theaters (Martineau 1981, p. 225).

Here's the context:

> The Quadroon girls of New Orleans are brought up by their mothers to be what they have been; the mistresses of white gentlemen ... The girls are highly educated, externally, and are, probably, as beautiful and accomplished a set of women as can be found. Every young man early selects one, and establishes her in one of those pretty and peculiar houses, whole rows of which may be seen in the Ramparts. The connexion now and then lasts for life; usually for several years. In the latter case, when the time comes for the gentleman to take a white wife, the dreadful news reaches his Quadroon partner, either by a letter entitling her to call the house and furniture her own, or when the newspaper announces marriage (Martineau 1981, p. 225).

It perhaps did not escape Martineau's readers that the boasted courage of Southern gentlemen did not extend to giving their significant other the news in person. It is easily imagined that the second-hand market is not particularly thick:

> The Quadroon ladies are rarely or never known to form a second connexion. Many

commit suicide: more die broken-hearted. Some men continue the connexion after marriage. Every Quadroon woman believes that her partner will prove an exception to the rule of desertion (Martineau 1981, p. 225).

Martineau then asks what are the consequences for white women:

Every white lady believes that her husband has been an exception to the rule of seduction. What security for domestic purity and peace there can be where every man has had two connexions, one of which must be concealed; and two families, whose existence must be not known to each other; where the conjugal relation begins in treachery, and must be carried on with a heavy secret in the husband's breast, no words are needed to explain (Martineau 1981, pp. 225–226).

This is her answer. The degradation is not the predictable European one of late marriage and temptation to extra-marital sexuality:

The degradation of the women is so obvious a consequence of the evils disclosed above, that the painful subject need not be enlarged upon. By the degradation of women, I do not mean to imply any doubt of the purity of their manners. There are reasons, plain enough to the observer, why their manners should be even peculiarly pure. They are all married young, from their being out-numbered by the other sex: and there is ever present an unfortunate servile class to their own sex to serve the purpose of licentiousness, as to leave them untempted (Martineau 1981, pp. 230–231).

The problem is the result of the non-transparency of domestic life, the consequence of living a lie. This non-transparency destroys sympathy:

Where the generality of men carry secrets which their wives must be the last to know; where the busiest and more engrossing concerns of life must wear one aspect to the one sex, and another to the other, there is an end to all wholesome confidence and sympathy, and woman sinks to be the ornament of her husband's house, the domestic manager of his establishment, instead of being his all-sufficient friend (Martineau 1981, p. 231).

Martineau here offers her own witness as testimony:

I am speaking not only of what I suppose must necessarily be; but of what I have actually seen. I have seen, with heart sorrow, the kind politeness, the gallantry, so insufficient to a loving heart, with which the wives of the south are treated by their husbands (Martineau 1981, p. 231).

Is this non-transparency a characteristic of non-market societies in general? Did the hidden economy of the late Soviet Union induce the sort of non-transparency which Martineau describes in the domestic economy of a slave society? Here might be the best reason to take Harriet Martineau seriously. She proposes a problem and sketches a solution. And we have no good reason to doubt her solution, in part because we have not thought about the problem as much as she has. There is much she has to teach us.

REFERENCES

Abbott, Edith (1906), 'Harriet Martineau and the Employment of Women in 1836', *Journal of Political Economy,* **14**, 614–626.

Abbott, Edith (1908), 'History of the Employment of Women in the American Cotton Mills: II', *Journal of Political Economy,* **16**, 680–692.

Abbott, Edith (1911), 'English Poor-Law Reform', *Journal of Political Economy,* **19**, 45–59.

Akerlof, George A. (1970), 'The Market for "Lemons"', *Quarterly Journal of Economics,* **84**, 88–500.

American Statistical Association (2000), *Ethical Guidelines for Statistical Practice,* Arlington, VA.: American Statistical Association.

Arbuckle, Elisabeth Sanders (1994), *Harriet Martineau in the London Daily News,* New York & London: Garland.

Arnstein, Walter (1983), *The Bradlaugh Case,* Columbia: University of Missouri Press.

Bates, William (1883), *The Maclise Portrait-Gallery of 'Illustrious Literary Characters',* New York: Scribner and Welford.

Berger, Max (1945), 'American Slavery as Seen by British Visitors, 1836–1860', *Journal of Negro History,* **30**, 181–202.

Blaug, Mark (1958), *Ricardian Economics,* New Haven.

Buchanan, James M. (1959), 'Positive Economics, Welfare Economics, and Political Economy', *Journal of Law and Economics,* **2**, 124–138.

Craft, William (1860), Running a Thousand Miles for Freedom; or, The Escape of William and Ellen Craft from Slavery, London.

Craft, William (1863), 'Anthropology at the British Association', *Anthropological Review,* **1**, 388–389.

David, Deirdre (1987), *Intellectual Women and Victorian Patriarchy,* Ithaca: Cornell University Press.

Feigenbaum, Susan and David M. Levy (1996), 'The Technological Obsolescence of Scientific Fraud', *Rationality and Society,* **8** (3), 261–276.

Fogel, Robert William (1989), *Without Consent or Contract,* New York: W.W. Norton & Company.

Fogel, Robert William and Stanley L. Engerman ([1974] 1989), *Time on the Cross,* New York: W.W. Norton & Company.

Fogel, Robert William and Stanley L. Engerman (1992), *Without Consent or Contract. Markets and Production: Technical Papers,* New York: W.W. Norton & Company.

Foster, Eugene A. *et al. (*1998), 'Jefferson Fathered Slave's Last Child', *Nature,* **396** (5 November) 27–28.

Froeb, Luke M. and Bruce H. Kobayashi (1996), 'Naive, Biased, yet Bayesian: Can Juries Interpret Selectively Produced Evidence?' *The Journal of Law, Economics and Organization,* **12**, 257–276.

Froude, James Anthony (1885), *Thomas Carlyle: A History of His Life in London 1834-1881,* New York.

Gillray, James (4 April 1796), *Philanthropic Consolations, After the Loss of the Slave-Bill,* Library of Congress Holdings Prints and Photographs. PC-1-8793.

Gordon, Scott (1955), 'The London *Economist* and the High Tide of Laissez Faire', *Journal of Political Economy,* **63**, 461–488.

Hammond, James Henry (1853), 'Hammond's Letters on Slavery', *The Pro-Slavery Argument,* Philadelphia.

Harper, William (1853), 'Harper on Slavery', *The Pro-Slavery Argument,* Philadelphia.

Hollander, Samuel (1997), *The Economics of Thomas Robert Malthus,* Toronto: University of Toronto Press.

Hunter, Shelagh (1995), *Harriet Martineau: The Poetics of Moralism,* London: Scolar Press.

Levy, David M. (1978), 'Some Normative Aspects of the Malthusian Controversy', *History of Political Economy,* **10**, 271–285.

Levy, David M. (1995), 'The Partial Spectator in the *Wealth of Nations*: A Robust Utilitarianism', *European Journal of the History of Economic Thought,* **2**, 299–326.

Levy, David M. (1999), 'Malthusianism and Christianity: The Invisibility of a Successful Radical'. *Historical Reflections/Réflexions Historiques,* **25**, 61–93.

Levy, David M. (2001a), 'Economics Texts as Apocrypha', in Evelyn Forget and Sandra Peart (eds), *Reflections on the Classical Canon: Essays in Honor of Samuel Hollander,* London: Routledge.

Levy, David M. (2001b), 'How the Dismal Science Got Its Name: Debating Victorian Racial Quacks'. *Journal of the History of Economic Thought,* **28**, 5–35.

Levy, David M. (2001c), How the Dismal Science Got Its Name: Classical Economics & the Ur-Text of Racial Politics, Ann Arbor: University of Michigan Press.

Levy, David M. and Sandra J. Peart (2001-2002), 'Secret History of the Dismal Science', <www.econlib.org.>

Levy, David M. and Sandra J. Peart (2001), 'Who are the Canters: The Evangelical-Economics Anti-Slavery Coalition', Presented at the History of Economics Society, Winston-Salem.

Maclise, Daniel (1834), Pen & ink drawing, 'Miss Harriet Martineau', *Fraser's Magazine of Town and Country,* **8**, 576.

Maginn, William (1832), 'On National Economy', *Fraser's Magazine of Town and Country,* **6**, 403–413,

Maginn, William (1834), 'The Gallery of Literary Characters. No. XLII. Miss Harriet Martineau', *Fraser's Magazine of Town and Country,* **8**, 576.

Maginn, William (1833), 'Miss Harriet Martineau', *Fraser's Magazine for Town and Country,* (8 November), 576.

Marks, Patricia (1986), 'Harriet Martineau: *Fraser's* 'Maid of Dishonour', *Victorian Periodicals Review,* **19**, 28–33.

Marshall, Alfred (1964), *Principles of Economics,* eighth edition, London: Macmillan.

Martineau, Harriet (1832–1834), *Illustrations of Political Economy,* London: Charles Fox.

Martineau, Harriet (1837a), *Society in America,* London.

Martineau, Harriet (1837b), *Views of Slavery and Emancipation,* New York.

Martineau, Harriet (1981), *Society in America* (edited by Seymour Martin Lipset), New Brunswick and London: Transaction Books.

Persky, Joseph (1990), 'Retrospectives: A Dismal Romantic', *The Journal of Economic Perspectives,* **4**, 165–172.

Posner, Richard A. (1999), 'An Economic Approach to Legal Evidence', *Stanford Law Review,* **51**, 1477–1546.

Quarles, Benjamin (1954), 'Ministers Without Portfolio', *Journal of Negro History,* **39**, 27–42.

Ricardo, David (1951), *Works and Correspondence of David Ricardo* (edited by Piero Sraffa), Cambridge: Cambridge University Press.

Sanders, Valerie (1986), *Reason Over Passion: Harriet Martineau and the Victorian Novel,* Sussex: Harvester Press.

Scrope, G. Poulette (1833), 'Miss Martineau's *Monthly Novels',* *Quarterly Review,* **49**,

136–152.

Simms, William Gilmore (1853), 'The Morals of Slavery', *The Pro-Slavery Argument*, Philadelphia.

Slavery: A Treatise, Showing that Slavery is neither a Moral, Political, nor Social Evil (1844), Penfield, GA.

Smith, Adam (1976), *An Inquiry into the Nature and Causes of the Wealth of Nations* (edited by W.B. Todd), Oxford: Clarendon Press.

Stearns, Edward Josiah (1853), *Notes on Uncle Tom's Cabin: Being a Logical Answer to Its Allegations and Inferences against Slavery as an Institution*, Philadelphia: Lippincott, Grambo & Co.

Stein, Bruno and Peter S. Albin (1967), 'The Demand for General Assistance Payments: Comment', *American Economic Review*, **57**, 575–585.

Stigler, George J. (1949), *Five Lectures on Economic Problems*, London.

Stigler, George J. (1969), 'Does Economics Have a Useful Past?', *History of Economics*, **1**, 217–230.

Thrall, Miriam (1934), *Rebellious Fraser's: Nol Yorke's Magazine in the Days of Maginn, Thackeray and Carlyle*, New York: Columbia University Press.

Trevelyan, George Otto (1961), *The Life and Letters of Lord Macaulay*, Oxford: Oxford University Press.

Wallbridge, Edwin Angel (1848), *The Demerara Martyr: Memoirs of the Rev. John Smith, Missionary to Demerara*, London.

Webb. R.K. (1960), *Harriet Martineau: A Radical Victorian*, New York: Columbia University Press.

Whately, E. Jane (1868), *Life and Correspondence of Richard Whately, D.D.*, New edition, London.

Wheatley, Vera (1957), *Life and Work of Harriet Martineau*, London.

Woodson, Carter G. (1918), 'The Beginnings of the Miscegenation of the Whites and Blacks', *Journal of Negro History*, **3**, 335–353.

Woodward, A. (1853), *A Review of Uncle Tom's Cabin; or, An Essay on Slavery*, Cincinnati: Applegate & Co.

NOTES

1. To the extent that modern economists have heard of Harriet Martineau, it is as the pre-eminent popularizer of classical economics (Blaug 1958, pp. 129–138). Blaug suggests she should be judged as a journalist and not as an economist because she bears some responsibility for our discipline becoming the 'dismal science' (Blaug 1958, pp. 138-139). Blaug neither considers Martineau's novel of slavery nor reveals any awareness of the anti-slavery origin of the 'dismal science' (Persky 1990; Levy 2001b, c). Blaug gives evidence for his position with which one can argue. Martineau seems not to bring out the best in scholars. My candidate for the sentence which maximizes abuse but with zero substance with which to disagree is provided by a scholar usually above such silliness, (Scott Gordon 1955, p. 463), who states that: 'Professor Webb dates the effort to disseminate the principles of political economy among the working classes from about 1820 and links this mainly with the discussion of the poor law and the growing trade-union movement of the thirties. But, as he freely admits, these efforts were largely unsuccessful. Harriet Martineau and her ilk "wrote down" as far as they could, goodness knows, but they were unable to achieve the levels of such journals as *Twopenny Trash* and *Pigs' Meat'*.
2. George Stigler (1950) suggests that the classical economists did their best work analysing specific problems. He considers Nassau Senior on the handloom weavers. In an early twentieth-century series of papers in the *Journal of Political Economy,* Edith Abbott considers Martineau as analytical witness to the employment of women in America (Abbott 1906, 1908). Martineau's discussion of the poor law has always been taken seriously (Abbott 1911; Stein-Albin 1967). There are many useful discussions of Martineau in the *Journal of Negro History.* If we are not interested in Martineau's problems it behooves us to find scholars who were. JSTOR is a magical device by which such contributions can be found. The gender/racial aspects of our concern with a problem is too obvious to belabour.
3. Arbuckle (1994, p. xii) quotes a contemporary judgment: 'Harriet Martineau alone … kept [British] public opinion on the right side'. Quarles (1954, p. 41) notes, 'With the birth in 1862 of these two influential emancipation societies, there was less need for American Negroes to journey to England to bolster anti-slavery sentiment and thus forestall diplomatic recognition of the Confederacy. Dating from the Emancipation Proclamation the Union trumpet no longer gave forth an uncertain sound. Thenceforth anti-Confederate sentiment in England could be left safely in the hands of native reformers such as Harriet Martineau'.
4. 'It must be perfectly needless to explain what I owe to preceding writers on the science of which I have treated. Such an acknowledgement could only accompany a pretension of my own to have added something to the science – a pretension which I have never made. By dwelling, as I have been led to do, on their discoveries, I have become too much awakened to the glory to dream of sharing the honour. Great men must have their hewers of wood and drawers of water; and scientific discoverers must be followed by those who will popularize their discoveries' (Martineau 1834, vol. 9, p. vi). This is widely quoted (see for example Wheatley 1957, p. 98).
5. 'I leave it to those who may be amused by the employment to point out whence I derived this argument, or that anecdote, or those elements of scenery. At the same time, I cannot admit that I have *copied.* The characters are intended to be original, the arguments are recast, the descriptions recomposed ...' (Martineau 1833–1834, vol. 2, p. v).
6. An older literature attends to her discussions most carefully see for examples (Berger 1945).
7. 'Lacking *hard* data, travellers with prior beliefs about slavery imposed these views on what they "observed". Later scholars, with kindred prior beliefs could pick and choose among these biased accounts to "discover" in the soft data of traveller's reports, just what they would like to believe' (Fogel and Engerman [1974] 1989, p. 51). 'The prevailing view of the slave trade has been fashioned by historians primarily from the accounts of firsthand observers of the slave South. Since such observers lacked the hard data needed to actually determine the scope and nature of this trade, they could only convey their impressions. Unfortunately these impressions are far from uniform. There were not many detached and objective observers of slavery after 1830. Most so-called observations or travel accounts were actually polemics against or for slavery. In choosing between these conflicting and contradictory tracts, the historians who fashioned the conventional view of the slave trade uniformly rejected the impressions of southern writers as

apologetics and accepted the views of northern European critics as accurate. It is, of course, tempting to believe that truth must be on the side of justice, and that conviction may have guided these scholars, since no objective criteria for the decisions that led them to reject some accounts and accept others is apparent'. In the 1989 'Afterword' Fogel and Engerman (1989, p. 286–287) stand by their disparagement of traveller's reports.

8. Froeb and Kobayashi (1996), followed by Posner (1999), consider a 'split the difference' rule. The assertion in the text is an obvious inference from this idea.

9. I commend Marks (1986) to the reader. Here are specimens. (Scrope 1833, p. 151): 'We should be loth to bring a blush unnecessarily upon the cheek of any woman; but may we venture to ask their maiden sage the meaning of the following passage: – "A parent has a considerable influence over the subsistence-fund of his family, and *an absolute control over the numbers to be supported by that fund*". Has the young lady picked up this piece of information in her conferences with the Lord Chancellor? or has she been entering into high and lofty communion on such subjects with certain gentlemen of her sect, famous for dropping their gratuitous advice on these matters into areas, for the benefit of the London kitchen-maids? ... *a female Malthusian.* A *woman* who thinks child-bearing a crime *against society*! An *unmarried woman* who declaims against *marriage*!! A *young woman* who depreciates charity and a provision for the *poor*!!!'. Maginn (1834, p. 576): 'We wish that Miss Martineau would sit down in her study, and calmly endeavour to depict to herself what is the precise and physical meaning of the words used by her school – what is preventive check – what is moral check – what it is they are intended to check – and then ask herself, if she is or is not properly qualified to write a commentary on the most celebrated numbers of Mr. Carlile's *Republican* ...' Scrope refers to John Stuart Mill's arrest for distributing Francis Place's neo-Malthusian tracts. Maginn's reference to Richard Carlile is this. His newspaper *Republican* had the first version of *Every Woman's Book* which other neo-Malthusians judged far too explicit for contemporary standards. Moreover, the link between neo-Malthusianism and atheism begins with Carlile (Arnstein 1983, p. 343). The conflict between Malthusianism and Christianity is discussed in Levy ([1978] 1997).

10. *Fraser's* ought to be a household word among economists as it is the magazine in which Carlyle's 'Occasional Discourse on the Negro Question' was published in 1849. This racist screed is the locus of the 'dismal science' label.

11. 'The sketch of Maclise is, of course, a caricature; but an innocent one. Crocker's article in the *Quarterly*, bearing on Miss Martineau's adoption of the principles of Malthus, is coarse and ungenerous. Tom Moore address her in a parody, "Come live with me and be my Blue". Maginn ungallantly hints that no one who inspects her portrait can wonder at her celibate proclivities, or is likely to attempt the seduction of the "fair philosopher" from her doctrines of the population question' (Bates 1883, p. 211). Miriam Thrall regards Maginn 1834 as 'one of the most contemptible attacks ...' Thrall (1934, p. 311).

12. 'Of the personal appearance of the strong-minded lady, William Howitt enables us to form an amusing conception by giving us the words of an old woman who met her at Ambleside:–"Is it a woman, or a man, or what sort of an animal is it?" said I to myself; there she came, stride, stride, stride,– great heavy shoes, stout leather leggings on, and a knapsack on her back' (Bates 1883, p. 211) goes on to compose a 'verse' in which each stanza ends with the name of 'Harry Martineau' Bates (1883, pp. 211–212). Not surprisingly, Martineau's gender-breaking performance has been the subject of much modern interest among specialists (for example Sanders 1986; David 1987).

13. This perhaps serves as a counter example to Stigler's claim that the modern literature is efficient, taking into account all that is valuable in the past (Stigler 1969).

14. The American equivalent would be a book titled *Harper's Ferry* just after John Brown's raid. In the words of Trevelyan (1961, vol. 1, pp. 103-104), 'death in prison, of Smith, the Demerara missionary: an event which was fatal to Slavery in the West Indies in the same degree as the execution of John Brown was its deathblow in the United States'. Wallbridge (1848) has been frequently reprinted. (The lovely John Milton passage above I quote via Wallbridge as I am in ignorance of the original).

15. The importance of Foster *et al.* (1998) is precisely for the demonstration of how flimsy have been the defences of Jefferson's conduct.

16. The discussion of sexual usage is taken from Levy (2001a).
17. The importance of this line of argument is stressed by Carter Woodson (1918, p. 349): 'Persons who professed seriously to consider the future of slavery, therefore, saw that miscegenation and especially the general connection of white men with their female slaves introduced a mulatto race whose numbers would become dangerous, if the affections of their white parents were permitted to render them free. [Harriet Martineau, *Views of Slavery and Emancipation*, p. 10.] The Americans of the future would thereby become a race of mixed breeds rather than a white and a black population'.
18. Martineau (1837a, vol. 2, p. 325): 'It is a common boast in the south that there is less vice in their cities than in those of the north'. She then goes on to develop the argument that owning a sexual object as slave is a good substitute for renting one in a brothel. The argument to which Martineau refers can be found in the anonymous 1844 *Slavery* together with an added homosexual twist (1844, p. 27): '... who, on entering any large Northern city, is not made painfully aware of the low state of moral feelings, in noting the innumerable evidences of prostitution that meet his eye on every side? What visitor of New York city, has failed to notice with what unblushing effrontery prostitutes of both sexes make Broadway their place of assignation?' Responding to *Uncle Tom's Cabin*, Stearns (1853, pp. 82–83) discusses prostitution and concubinage as substitutes.
19. Simms (1853, pp. 188–189): 'What person beside herself would undertake to argue for the advantages of being deaf? To prove that the ears are but surplusage, is certainly to suggest to the deity a process of improvement, by which the curtailment of a sense will help the endowments of a philosopher'.
20. The remaining paragraphs in this section are drawn from Levy and Peart 2001–2002.
21. Martineau's friend William Craft makes this case on the basis of his observation. 'For instance, it is a common practice in the slave States for ladies, when angry with their maids, to send them to the calybuce sugar-house, or to some other place established for the purpose of punishing slaves, and have them severely flogged; and I am sorry it is a fact, that the villains to whom those defenceless creatures are sent, not only flog them as they are ordered, but frequently compel them to submit to the greatest indignity. Oh! If there is any one thing under the wide canopy of heaven, horrible enough to stir a man's soul, and to make his very blood boil, it is the thought of his dear wife, his unprotected sister, or his young and virtuous daughters, struggling to save themselves from falling a prey to such demons!' (Craft 1860, p. 8). Craft's role as abolitionist speaker is discussed in Quarles (1954); his role in establishing the fundamental quackery of the British anthropologists (Craft 1863) is discussed in Levy (2001b, c).
22. R.W. Webb quotes William Cobbett in 1829 on the advantages of America: 'No Wilberforces – think of that – NO WILBERFORCES' (Webb 1960, p. 135).
23. The etching from 4 April 1796 titled 'Philanthropic Consolations, after the loss of the Slave-Bill'. This is described in the Library of Congress catalogue as follows: 'William Wilberforce and Samuel Horsley, Bishop of Rochester, cavort with two black women in a well-furnished room. Wilberforce and a woman, wearing a print dress with her breasts exposed, sit on a couch smoking cheroots. Horsley, in his bishop's robes, embraces a woman sitting on his knee holding a wine glass. A black servant boy brings in a tray of filled glasses'. It is produced in Levy and Peart 2001 (visual CD).
24. Smith (1976): 'The wear and tear of a slave, it has been said, is at the expense of his master; but that of a free servant is at his own expense. The wear and tear of the latter, however, is, in reality, as much at the expense of his master as that of the former. The wages paid to journeymen and servants of every kind must be such as may enable them, one with another, to continue the race of journeymen and servants, according as the increasing, diminishing, or stationary demand of the society may happen to require. But though the wear and tear of a free servant be equally at the expense of his master, it generally costs him much less than that of a slave. The fund destined for replacing or repairing, if I may say so, the wear and tear of the slave, is commonly managed by a negligent master or careless overseer. That destined for performing the same office with regard to the free man, is managed by the free man himself'. This argument, with the quotation from Smith, is repeated in Marshall (1964, p. 466).
25. The pro-slavery side of the British debate continually used the argument that the profit-maximizing slave owners would not abuse their slaves for the same reason that profit-maximizing

horse owners would not. Levy (2001c) gives some texts. Here is a response to the argument in a letter from Whately to Senior about Senior's review of *Uncle Tom's Cabin*; 'Only t'other day I heard a man repeat the argument of the *Times* that self-interest is a sufficient security; as in the case of cattle, where, by-the-bye, it is so little a security that we have a law against cruelty to them. But even the most humane master of cattle treats them in manner which one could not approve towards men, *e.g.,* selling most of the calves that a cow bears; and knocking on the head a horse that is past work. I suggested that it would be an advantage to slaves if masters could acquire a taste for human flesh. When a negro grows too old to be worth keeping for work, instead of being killed by inches by starvation and over-work, he would be put up to fatten like an ox' (Whately 1868, p. 213).

26. Fogel (1989, pp. 391–392) reports how he grappled with the moral problem of slavery: 'I was also startled to discover the numerous ways in which masters relied on rewards to elicit labor – a device I had assumed was almost entirely absent since David Hume, Adam Smith, John E. Cairnes, and most the other classical writings had identified this lack as the fatal flaw in slavery as an economic system'. There is a cost in not taking Martineau's economics seriously.

27. 'Happiness is the object to be desired, and we cannot be quite sure that provided he is equally well fed, a man may not be happier in the enjoyment of the luxury of idleness than the enjoyment of the luxuries of a neat cottage, and good clothes. After all we do not know if these would fall to his share. His labour might only increase the employments of his employer' (Ricardo 1951, vol. 7, pp. 184-185). I owe this reference to Sam Hollander.

28. Smith (1976, pp. 99–100): 'Workmen, on the contrary, when they are liberally paid by the piece, are very apt to overwork themselves, and to ruin their health and constitution in a few years'.

29. American readers of the attack on slavery (Martineau 1837b) which was culled from *Society in America* would find this bit of information on page 6. Perhaps cliometrics might locate a 'Martineau effect' in the resale price of slaves?

30. Thus here J.A. Froude explains Thomas Carlyle's 'Negro question' and the proposal for re-enslavement: 'He did not mean that the "Niggers" should have been kept as cattle, and sold as cattle at their owners' pleasure. He did mean that they ought to have been treated as human beings, *for whose souls and bodies the whites were responsible*; that they should have been placed in a position suited to their capacity, like that of the English serfs under the Plantagenets ....' (Froude 1885, vol. 2, p.15) emphasis added.

31. Fogel and Engerman (1992, vol. 1, p. 257): 'The central focus of planters was the organization of the labor force into highly coordinated and precisely functioning gangs characterized by intensity of effort'.

15. John Stuart Mill, Harriet Taylor and French Social Theory

Evelyn L. Forget

Disentangling the relative contributions of Harriet Taylor and John Stuart Mill to their joint feminist writings has led to over a century of controversy. In the absence of definitive evidence, the claims of historians reveal more about the nature of the discipline than about Mill and Taylor. But there has been one tendency apparent throughout the debate: the independent and the joint works of Mill and Taylor are treated in splendid isolation from events and debates occurring elsewhere. Contrast this with the recent discussion of all the competing interests and varied contributions involved in the later parliamentary debate on the franchise for women (Kinzer, Robson and Robson 1992).

This essay enlarges the frame of reference within which we view the early essays of 1832, the *Enfranchisement of Women* (1851) and *The Subjection of Women* (1869) to include the influence of French thought on Mill. This allows us to better understand the nature of the team of Taylor and Mill and the intellectual environment in which they wrote. And, most importantly, it allows us to detect a shift in Mill's feminism that is likely caused by his debate with Auguste Comte, and marked by the publication of Taylor's *The Enfranchisement of Women*.[1] While in his earliest essay on marriage, Mill was prepared to make large claims about the 'nature' of women, the *Subjection* fully articulates the impossibility of pontificating about human nature without a clear understanding of the ways in which human character is formed. The *Subjection* also much more adequately recognizes the historical contingency of particular institutions, such as the marriage laws. The increased complexity that comes from attempting to understand a nineteenth-century debate in the context of nineteenth-century thought paints the usual conclusion of historians – that Harriet Taylor was clearly the more 'radical' of the two – as the anachronism it is.

This is not to say that Mill is a twenty-first century feminist. His *Subjection* was criticized, at the time and subsequently, for the absence of a clear recommendation on expanding the possibility of divorce. He maintained, in the early essay on marriage (1832) and in the *Principles of Political Economy* (1848) that he could not see the advantage in the large-scale entry of women into the labour force if the consequence were a reduction in the general wage rate. Taylor, by contrast, was much clearer and more consistent on both issues: all marriage laws must be eliminated, and women must enter the labour force with the same rights and responsibilities as men. But 'radical' is a unidimensional term, and the debate was not.

Throughout his writing on women, Mill linked co-operative production – socialism – and women's emancipation. He anticipated a future where new forms of economic society in which women would play a social, political, and economic role fully equal to men would supersede contemporary ideas concerning the laws of production and distribution. And he fully accepted, at least after the debate with Comte, that 'natural' gender roles were, in fact, socially constructed and that we have no basis in the past upon which to predict future behaviour and institutions. Mill's unwillingness to take a stronger position on contemporary policy debate has attracted criticism from feminist historians who see in it evidence of an individual unable to transcend the common gender stereotypes of his day. It seems much more reasonable, however, to attribute Mill's intellectual carefulness to too much imagination, rather than too little. He leaves himself open to a charge of utopianism. Taylor, who paid a good deal less attention to abstract theory, is not so problematic.

A CENTURY OF DEBATE ON THE TAYLOR–MILL TEAM

Intellectual historians have long been infected by the notion that ideas are the product of a 'great mind'. Consequently they tend to try to come to terms with complex writings by examining an author for consistency and also, perhaps, by tracing the evolution of an idea over a writer's lifetime. If others appear in the narrative, they appear in the guise of 'influences' – minor characters that either deflect the great one from his or her project, or supply a missing puzzle piece to the unfolding work. Mill, who more than most spent a good deal of energy observing and trying to understand the nature of his own thought, consistently portrayed the feminist writings as 'joint products' of his and Taylor's pens. These claims have confused us.

The earliest intellectual historians to attempt to disentangle the two contributions tended to undervalue Taylor's role. Alexander Bain, Mill's friend and biographer, claimed that Taylor encouraged Mill's intellect by 'intelligently controverting' his ideas (Bain 1882, p. 173). Harold Laski was even less impressed:

I believe that (Mill) was literally the only person who was in the least impressed by her. Mrs Grote said briefly that she was a stupid woman. Bain said she had a knack of repeating prettily what J.S.M. said and that he told her it was wonderful. Morley told me that Louis Blanc told him he once sat for an hour with her and that she repeated to him what afterwards turned out to be an article Mill had just finished for Edinburgh (Stillinger 1961, pp. 24–25).

Stillinger relied heavily on these early criticisms when he suggested that:

Harriet of the incomparable intellect ... was largely a product of life (that is Mill's) imagination, an idealisation, according to his peculiar needs, of a clever, domineering, in some ways perverse and selfish, invalid woman (Stillinger 1961, p. 27).

Rossi argues that these negative characterizations of Taylor find their ultimate source in the evaluations of individuals associated with the Philosophic Radicals, the social circle to which Mill belonged and the members of which tended to regard Taylor as evidence of Mill's 'defection' from their political aims (Rossi 1970, p. 37).

Not everyone has claimed that Taylor was entirely uninfluential. Some find her a useful source for 'errors' they discern in Mill's work. Hayek, for example, cautiously attributed Mill's sympathy for socialism to Taylor's influence, suggesting that, after her death, he recovered his senses (Hayek 1951; p. 266).[2] Basil Willey made similar claims about his writing on religion (1950, pp. 141–186).

Francis Mineka ressurects a much more sympathetic picture of Taylor, one that owes something to the warm appraisals of her character by William Fox and intimates from the circle of Unitarian Radicals:

However over coloured by emotion his estimate of her powers may have been, there can be no doubt that she was the saving grace of his inner life. Without her, John Mill might well have been a different person, but one can doubt that he would have been as fine, as understanding or as great a man (Mineka 1944, pp. 274–275).

Stefan Collini articulates both the importance of comprehending Harriet Taylor's intellectual influence on Mill, and the frustration imposed by their complex relationship, when he writes that:

any complete account of Mill's thinking on the subject of women would have to come to terms with the role of this very clever, imaginative, passionate, intense, imperious, paranoid, unpleasant woman (Mill, *Collected Works*, vol. XXI, p. xxx).

All of these characterizations portray Harriet Taylor as an 'influence' to be reckoned with by those who would understand the thinking of the great intellectual – John Stuart Mill.

A new wave of criticism began with Alice Rossi's 1970 essay, '*Sentiment and Intellect*'. She claimed that the 1851 essay, *The Enfranchisement of Women*, was primarily Taylor's work, citing a letter from Mill to Taylor in February 1849 referring to a pamphlet on the topic she had nearly completed, and noting that the content of the article paralleled Taylor's 1831 essay on the topic (Rossi 1970, p. 42). This attribution is accepted by J. Robson (Mill, *Collected Works*, vol. XXI, pp. lxxiii–lxxvii), who provides additional evidence, and forms the basis for a subsequent reappraisal by feminist writers such as Michèle Pujol ([1995] 2000, p. 307) and Barbara Caine (1994). Both echo Rossi's claim that Taylor 'was far more radical' than Mill had been either twenty years earlier or twenty years later.

As we shall see, radical is far too simple an adjective to capture the nature of the debate to which Taylor and Mill were contributing. Taylor certainly had far more sympathy for a radical rethinking of sex roles than did Mill, but she rethought those roles in the context of an otherwise unchanged social system. Mill, in 1831, contemplated the possibility of abolishing capitalist production and reconstituting the family, but he did not imagine that many women might question their assignment to the 'traditional' occupations of household production and childrearing.

'How much was hers?', 'How much his?' and 'Who is the more radical?' are questions that stem from a view of scholarship that sees it as primarily an individual undertaking. We are at a loss when it comes to understanding how two very strong-willed and unique characters came together, in the context of ongoing and competing social debates about social questions that crossed intellectual and national boundaries, to create a body of work that can truly be described as a 'joint production'. Mill's own description was far more sophisticated.

THE EARLY ESSAYS: THE SAINT-SIMONIAN INFLUENCE

In late 1832 or 1833,[3] Harriet Taylor and John Mill exchanged essays on marriage, which were essentially the formalizations of well-rehearsed positions. Both had been engaged with the subject from their earliest period of intellectual activity. Mill, for example, introduces his *Subjection of Women* by referring to the equality of the sexes as 'an opinion I have held from the very earliest period when I had formed any opinions at all on social and political matters' (Mill, *Collected Works*, vol. I, p. 125). An early published example of his criticism of common attitudes towards women appears in his 'Periodical Literature: Edinburgh Review' (1824), in Mill, *Collected Works*, vol. I, pp. 311–312 (see Mill, *Collected Works*, vol. XXI, p. xxx). His initial interest in gender equality, then, cannot be attributed to Taylor. Both the *Monthly Repository*, the journal dominated by the Unitarian Radicals (the social circle in which Harriet Taylor's thought was formed) and the Philosophic Radicals' *Westminster Review*, published articles sympathetic to women's education.

Similarly, *pace* Hayek, Mill's initial attraction to socialism cannot be simply attributed to Taylor. The Unitarian Radicals were sympathetic to both feminism and socialism. Nevertheless, for exposure to socialist ideas, he had to look beyond the Philosophic Radicals, and it was not to the Unitarian Radicals that he turned. Mill's early interest in gender equality was nourished by his exposure to contemporary French ideas, which also gradually exposed him to a well-articulated socialist system that he found attractive. That socialism and feminism are related is clear throughout his writing. In 1869, for example, he wrote to Parke Godwin that the 'emancipation of women, & cooperative production, are ... the two great changes that will regenerate society' (Mill, *Collected Works*, vol. XVII, p. 1535).

Mill's acquaintance with the Saint-Simonians began in 1829, three years before Taylor and Mill exchanged their early essays on marriage (Mill, *Collected Works*, vol. I, p. 171). The Saint-Simonians were then in the early stages of their development, and had not yet developed the socialism that would come to dominate their work, nor had they developed their philosophy into a religious cult. They were just beginning to question the premise of hereditary property. But Mill was 'greatly struck with the connected view which they for the first time presented ... of the natural order of human progress' (Mill, *Collected Works*, vol. I, p. 171). His chief contact was Gustave d'Eichthal, with whom he corresponded for many years. Mill met Saint-Amand Bazard and Barthelémy-Prosper Enfantin, the leaders of the movement in 1830, and set himself the task of reading virtually everything they and their disciples wrote. He was most impressed by one young St.-Simonian, Auguste Comte, whose *Système de politique positive* (1824) he found most clearly articulated. Comte soon left the movement, but Mill remained in touch and gradually came to understand 'the very limited and temporary value of the old political economy, which assumes private property and inheritance as indefeasible facts, and freedom of production and exchange as the *dernier mot* of social improvement' (Mill, *Collected Works*, vol. I, p. 175).

The scheme gradually developed and articulated by the Saint-Simonians called for the management of the labour and capital of the community in such a way that people, classed according to their ability, would be required to take a share of the work required, and would be paid in accordance with their work.   This, Mill wrote in his *Autobiography*, seemed 'a far superior description of Socialism to Owen's.   Their aim seemed ... desirable and rational, however their means might be inefficacious' (Mill, *Collected Works*, vol. I, p. 175).   But it was, in fact, another element of Saint-Simonian thought to which Mill was most attracted.   He 'honoured them most for what they have been most cried down for – the boldness and freedom from prejudice with which they treated the subject of family', which needed 'more fundamental alterations than remain to be made in any other great social institution' (Mill, *Collected Works*, vol. I, p. 175).

> In proclaiming the perfect equality of men and women, and an entirely new order of things in regard to their relations with one another, the St. Simonians in common with Owen and Fourier have entitled themselves to the grateful remembrance of future generations (Mill, *Collected Works*, vol. I, p. 175).

The *Autobiography*, of course, is a later reconstruction.   But it would have been impossible for anyone to follow the adventures of the Saint-Simonians in 1830 while remaining unaware of their gender analysis.[4]

Feminist issues steadily grew in importance in Saint-Simonian rhetoric until, by 1832, they were the most important concern of the movement. Hundreds of people regularly attended Saint-Simonian lectures in Paris and London, where they were presented with the argument that a new harmonious relation between the classes ought to replace conflict, and that inheritance ought to be eliminated.   The movement organized educational programmes and workshops in Paris, and set up communal living quarters for their adherents.   The revolution of July 1830 created a new freer atmosphere in Paris, and the Saint-Simonians took advantage of the opportunity to issue proclamations demanding ownership of goods in common, the abolition of inheritance and the franchise for women.   Contemporary marriage was condemned because the double standard of morality existing in society and the inability of most women to support themselves economically meant, they argued, that most marriages were little more than a form of prostitution.[5] Even supposing that marriages had been entered into freely, inequitable property rights[6] and the social and legal norms enforcing wifely obedience[7] were worthy of condemnation.   They argued that the institution of marriage needed reform, and among the direct necessities was permissive divorce legislation.

These very pragmatic reforms, however, began to recede in importance as the utopian project flourished.   The communal houses and educational projects became less and less important, while the analysis grew increasingly abstract.   Saint-Simonian writers began to argue that women would take a full political, economic and social role only after 'universal association' – that is, the new society – was achieved. Then the morality and sympathy that were seen as the natural characteristics of women would form a new social unit that included all of the qualities required to usher in the new age. The social system would be based on the marital couple, always seen as comprised of a female and a male, and each couple would perform a single social or economic task fitted to their unique set of characteristics, and be compensated by a single salary in accordance with their work. This would ensure the economic equality of men and women.[8] Husbands and wives both keeping their own names at marriage would symbolize this 'natural' equality, based on 'natural' differences.[9] But, when would women gain full partnership? When war and slavery are abolished, the conjugal union perfected, the condition of the poorest classes improved, and all human beings associated into a single family, women can expect to come into their own. Until that time, 'we declare,' writes Émile Barrault, 'woman is legitimately excluded from public life' (Barrault n.d., p. 74). This was Saint-Simonian feminism in 1831. Its key features were a strong rhetorical concern with the equality of women, an unshakeable belief that men and women are different and will naturally adopt different but equal social roles, and a lingering set of doubts about how quickly gender equality ought to be brought into being.

This digression on the Saint-Simonians is justified by the similarity between Mill's position, expressed in the early essay, and those of the Saint-Simonian movement. The chief differences between Mill and Taylor revolve around the appropriate social roles for women. Taylor argued that women should be admitted to all of the privileges and responsibilities of male adults, without exception, that women should take financial responsibility for their own children, and that all marriage laws should be abolished. Mill was, characteristically, more guarded, and he has been criticized for not considering the possibility that social roles, as they existed in England in 1832, were other than the necessary consequence of natural differences between the sexes. Specifically, he argues that, while every woman should be educated to support herself so that marriage is a voluntary contract,

> It does not follow that a woman should *actually* support herself because she should be *capable* of doing so: in the natural course of events she will *not* ... it will be for the happiness of both (husband and wife) that her occupation should rather to be to adorn and beautify (life). Except in the class of actual day-labourers, that will be her natural task, if task it can be called, which will in so great a measure be accomplished rather by *being* than by *doing* (Rossi 1970, pp. 74–75).

These specific female roles 'will naturally be the occupations of a woman who has fulfilled what seems to be considered as the end of her existence and attained what is really its happiest state, by uniting herself to a man whom she loves' (Rossi 1970, p. 77).

But the traditional gender roles that colour Mill's discussion are embedded in a larger discussion that lends further evidence to the claim that he benefited from a Saint-Simonian influence. Taylor argued that divorce would pose no problem with respect to the support of children if each woman took full responsibility for her own offspring. Mill demurred. He called for the existence of temporary, childless marriages until the partners were certain of the longevity of their connection (Rossi 1970, pp. 80–81). In those cases where 'deliberate reflexion' is not adequately united to 'loftiness and delicacy of feeling', however, these young marriages will often, Mill recognized, produce children who must be cared for. He could not:

> see how this difficulty can be entirely got over, until the habits of society allow of a regulated community of living, among persons intimately acquainted, which would prevent the necessity of a total separation between the parents even when they had ceased to be connected by any nearer tie than mutual goodwill, and a common interest in their children (Rossi 1970, p. 81).

That is, until 'full association' or a society conforming to the Saint-Simonian project, were attained.

As far as the indissolubility of marriage is concerned, both Mill and Taylor support permissive divorce in their earliest essays. In Mill's case, this is particularly interesting because he was not prepared to be so bold in his published work. The reference he makes is to a socialist writer, although not a Saint-Simonian:

> Robert Owen's definitions of chastity and prostitution, are quite as simple and take as firm a hold of the mind as the vulgar ones which connect the ideas of virtue and vice with the performance or non-performance of an arbitrary ceremonial (Rossi 1970, p. 83).

I have essentially argued that, notwithstanding the absence of any direct citation of Saint-Simonian literature in his 1832 essay and notwithstanding the fact that the only socialist writer he cites is not a Saint-Simonian, Mill's 1832 essay is strongly reminiscent of Saint-Simonian doctrine. In particular, his peculiar (from a twenty-first century perspective) linking of 'natural' gender roles with a demand for the equality of the sexes, is exactly parallel to the Saint-Simonian literature with which he was intimately familiar.

A crisis in the Saint-Simonian movement occurred on 19 November 1831, when the Saint-Simonian leader Enfantin unveiled a plan to emancipate women through 'the rehabilitation of the flesh' (Enfantin 1832). This was a complex new moral code that he denied was an invitation to promiscuity, although he alienated many members of his flock who thought otherwise. The greatest critic was his co-leader Saint-Amand Bazard, who resigned in protest. Enfantin subsequently declared himself the 'father of humanity', and on 21 November dismissed women from the Saint-Simonian hierarchy. He retracted his more extreme statements, and declared that it was simply wrong for men to make moral laws for women without their full participation. But he did not reinstate women into the hierarchy. Rather, he retreated to his country estate with a small number of followers and encouraged a breakaway group to head off to Egypt in search of the 'Female Messiah' who could serve, beside Enfantin, as the 'mother of humanity'.[10] A number of women who were not prepared to wait for the Messiah and a mite annoyed at their exclusion from the leadership of the movement weakened their ties with Saint-Simonianism. They attached themselves to Charles Fourier or to others, to pursue more pragmatic concerns such as female education and the right to enter the professions and trades, that had initially animated the Saint-Simonians. This crisis more or less brought about the trial of the Saint-Simonians, on a charge of 'forming a society for the discussion of political and religious subjects without leave of the government, and also a charge of preaching immoral doctrines, a charge founded on the theory of *la femme libre*' (Mill, *Collected Works*, vol. XII, p. 119).[11]

There is no direct evidence to determine whether Mill's position was derived from Saint-Simonian doctrine or whether he was attracted to the latter because of parallels between their thought and his own writing. Given what we know of Mill's method of analysis, the second possibility seems more convincing, especially when we recognize that there were some aspects of Saint-Simonian thought he found laughable if not repugnant. Writing to Carlyle of the Saint-Simonian trial, he notes that:

> There was much in the conduct of them all, which really one cannot help suspecting of quackery ... surely there is an *admixture* of charlatanerie in it, I mean on the part of the Supreme Father (that is, Enfantin) (Mill, *Collected Works*, vol. XII, p. 119).

Mill – like Comte, like d'Eichthal, like a number of early adherents – drifted away from Saint-Simonianism as mysticism crowded out social reform. But he remained intrigued by their work.

AUGUSTE COMTE, HARRIET TAYLOR, AND JOHN STUART MILL

While we have only indirect evidence and the reconstructed testimony of

Mill's *Autobiography* on which to posit an intellectual link to the Saint-Simonians, no such uncertainty surrounds Comte's role. In debate with Auguste Comte, Mill's feminism was transformed. He came to appreciate fully the extent to which we remain ignorant of the forces which create human character, and came to understand the extent to which social roles are more than the ultimate expression of 'natural' differences between the sexes. The Saint-Simonians awaited a New World based on love and sentiment; Comte should arrive at the New Jerusalem in a chariot of reason and science.

As we have seen, Mill's first brush with Auguste Comte occurred in the context of his Saint-Simonian explorations. But they lost contact for a number of years after Comte broke with the movement. Mill's correspondence with d'Eichthal refers to him fairly regularly, and the Saint-Simonians seemed to consider Comte a disciple until 1832 when he formally announced his resignation, although he had ceased contributing to the *Producteur* – the Saint-Simonian organ – in 1826.

In 1841, Mill again sought out Comte. Their subsequent correspondence provides ample testimony, in case we need more, of the almost electrical charge Mill derived from the analytical work of a logical mind – *'une véritable passion intellectuel'* (Mill, *Collected Works*, vol. XIII, p. 489). He is prepared to set aside all quarrels, all caution, in order to travel as far as he can with a presentation to which he is attracted. As Lévy-Bruhl has noticed, 'that which is most striking is the force of the attraction to which Mill abandoned himself in writing to Comte' (Lévy-Bruhl 1899, p. iv). Mill writes, in his first letter to Comte, 8 November 1841:

> It was in the year 1828, Monsieur, that I read for the first time your little *Traité de politique positive*; and that reading gave all my ideas a great jolt, which with other causes but to an even greater extent than them, caused my definitive break with the Benthamist section of the revolutionary school, in which I was raised, even which I can almost say, in which I was born. Although Benthamism undoubtedly rests very far from the true spirit of the positive method, that doctrine still seems to me the best preparation that exists today for true positivism applied to social doctrines (Mill, *Collected Works*, vol. XIII, p. 489).[12]

He flatters Comte shamelessly:

> I can say that I have already embarked upon a path very near to yours, ... but I have yet to learn from you many things of primary importance, and I hope to give you before long the proof that I have learned them well (Mill, *Collected Works*, vol. xii, p. 489).

On 18 December 1841, he refers to his forthcoming *Logic*, and dares hope that Comte will point out 'the questions on which there is no longer room for any discussions between us, and those where I might yet profit from the greater maturity of [Comte's] philosophical conceptions' (Mill, *Collected Works*, vol. xxi, p. 491).

To further the intellectual exchange, he is prepared to be conciliatory. In breaking with the Saint-Simonians, Comte dedicated himself to the development of a social science rather than to the reform of existing institutional arrangements. Mill responds:

> I am comfortable with the wise reserve with which you set aside as premature all immediate discussion on most political institutions ... at least in the temporal order (Mill 1965, *Collected Works*, vol. 13, p. 553).

Comte had made him aware that all social regeneration depended on the 'spiritual' – that is, positivist and not metaphysical – awakening of humanity, rather than the reform of existing institutions on the basis of the impotent social theory then current.

This attitude of acceptance also characterized Mill's first discussions with Comte about women. In fact, he was so accepting that Harriet Taylor wrote to him in 1844, after having seen the correspondence with Comte for the first time:

> I am surprised to find in your letters your opinion undetermined where I had thought it made up – I am disappointed at a tone more than half-apologetic with which you state your opinions... Do not think that I wish you had said *more* on the subject, I only wish that what was said was in a tone of conviction, not of suggestion (Hayek 1951, p. 114).

It may have been this comment that made Mill regret the concessions he had made to Comte, and resolve to keep the letters to himself (Bain 1882, p. 74).

The essence of the debate between the two men concerns the influence of environment on the formation of women's character. On 13 July 1843, Mill makes clear to Comte his fear that their inability to agree on the conclusion when it appeared that they agreed so much on method implied that the principles were not fully established. And it was, he feared, the principles concerning the influence of biology on human character that were lacking (Mill, *Collected Works*, vol. XIII, pp. 589–590). Comte, apparently believing that Mill's reticence was due to a personal prejudice, had suggested on 29 June that their differences would be overcome as soon as Mill began to think more clearly on the subject. Just as he had gone through a stage of believing men and women equal, so must Mill. He had overcome the belief; so would Mill (Lévy-Bruhl, pp. 217–218). On 16 July, Comte acknowledged that definitive proof was not available, but nevertheless argued that the hierarchy of the sexes in the animal world was sufficient evidence from which to conclude that the sexes were fundamentally different and unequal (Lévy-Bruhl, p. 231).

On 30 August, Mill wrote a very long and complex, and not entirely consistent, response. He acknowledged that physiology had shown women to be childlike in their muscular, cerebral and nervous systems, but denied that this was sufficient evidence of a natural inferiority of women. He argued that no one had yet demonstrated that the inferiority of children was due to anatomical differences from adults rather than a simple lack of exercise and experience. Mill pointed out that, although men started with greater mental and physical prowess than women, when women exercised their physical and mental organs, they showed greater improvement than did men. But he did acknowledge that physiologists had demonstrated that women were, because of the excitability of their nerves, more like young men than grown men. Then Mill shifted the debate, and suggested that the real issue was not whether women were equally as capable as men of governing, but whether, whatever differences may exist between the sexes, society would not be better governed by men and women together rather than by either alone (Mill, *Collected Works*, vol. XIII, pp. 592–595).

Comte began to suspect that the differences between himself and Mill were greater than he had supposed. On 5 October, he criticized Mill for putting far too much emphasis on the effect of education and habit on the formation of character. He reminded Mill that women had never excelled in any field, and concluded that this was because they were naturally inferior (Lévy-Bruhl, 245-50). Mill responded on 30 October (Mill, *Collected Works*, vol. XIII, p. 604ff.), replying that he was prepared to put this particular issue on hold until the sciences of biology, ethology[13] and social statics were better developed. Comte declared that it was useless to pursue the issue, that biology was sufficiently developed to justify the principles that Mill seemed incapable of understanding, and that if Mill understood the positivist philosophy, he would acknowledge that the female question was, indeed, settled (letter of 14 November 1843, in Lévy-Bruhl, pp. 273–279). On 8 December, Mill replied that he was prepared to end the discussion, but that he too was certain of his position (Mill 1965, *Collected Works*, vol. XIII, p. 615ff.).

This debate touched upon central issues of Mill's philosophy. In his *Autobiography*, he tells us that long before his debate with Comte and even before his relationship with Taylor, he was troubled by the idea that human character, and especially his own character, was formed by forces beyond the control of any individual. This doctrine of philosophical necessity weighed upon him 'like an incubus' (Mill 1965, *Collected Works*, vol. I, p. 175). Ultimately he resolved the matter to his own satisfaction, concluding, 'our will, by influencing some of our circumstances, can modify our future habits or capabilities of willing'.

The issue first surfaced very early in the debate with Comte. Comte argued that one could study the laws of the human mind *statically* through the science of physiology, or one could attempt to understand them *dynamically*, by examining the historical progress of the human spirit (Comte 1830-1842, pp. 769–794). Biology and sociology, then, are sufficient for an understanding of human beings in general. After sociology is fully developed, there would then be time to understand the individual human being, as determined by forces past and present. Meanwhile, if Mill felt the need to know more, Comte suggested he read about phrenology, as developed by Franz Joseph Gall.

Mill did read Gall, but he kept coming back to the idea of a science intermediate between biology and sociology, which he called ethology. Ethology would go far beyond the elementary laws of associationist psychology, as espoused by the Benthamites, and examine how an individual character emerges from the welter of physical and moral forces to which an individual is exposed. Moreover, he believed this science must be developed before sociology could be properly developed:

> You must suspect me of metaphysical tendencies, in that I believe in the possibility of a positive psychology, which would certainly not be that of Condillac nor of Cousin, nor even that of the Scottish school, and that I believe everything to do with our intellectual and affective faculties is part of that analysis, which would serve in your system to verify phrenological physiology and which has for an essential goal to separate the truly innate faculties from those others, produced by way of the combination and mutual action (18 December 1841 in Mill, *Collected Works*, p. 492).

This was a fundamental challenge to Comte. Mill was essentially arguing that one cannot understand sociology, or the science of the social behaviour of aggregates, until one had some idea of how an individual behaved. An aggregate is, after all, the sum of the individuals. Comte, by contrast, believed individual psychology to be the product of biological and social forces which are logically antecedent. One does not attempt to understand humanity by studying individuals, Comte believed, but rather must attempt to understand individuals by first studying society.

Mill did, however, enter into the spirit of debate with Comte. He reports on 9 June 1842 that he has read the six volumes of Gall and is a little more persuaded that there might be something to phrenology (Mill, *Collected Works*, p. 525). But he felt that phrenology could not furnish anything convincing in the way of evidence until many more details were provided. Moreover, he recognized that one of the difficulties he faced with this work is that it devalued many of the insights of Helvétius (and by extension,

Bentham) with respect to the role that education might play in the formation of the individual. He worried that phrenology would encourage people to dismiss individual differences as biological, and therefore to dismiss as futile attempts to reform political institutions and the environment. Comte responded on 19 June that Mill's criticisms were just: biology alone was insufficient, and that is why sociology was needed (Lévy-Bruhl, pp. 72–74, 75–76). He saw no need for ethology. And this, of course, is the very same debate that the two replayed in the discussion of Women. And, like the later debate, this one too ended without resolution.

It is important, though, to recognize that in debate with Comte, Mill was forced to examine the differences between the sexes, and he argued with vehemence that we simply do not have enough knowledge about the way individuals are formed by innate natural forces on the one hand and society on the other to justify existing social institutions as manifestations of natural differences. In the 1832 essay, he seemed to take it for granted that existing gender roles were the result of natural differences between the sexes, and that even if institutions such as the marriage laws were modified, these natural differences would reassert themselves. Now it was clear that all institutions could be modified, and indeed, the natural historical progress of humanity seemed to suggest to him that all institutions were contingent. And as we shall see below, Mill would never again make unqualified blanket statements about nature and the roles of women.

Mill's final opinion on Comte and women is expressed in his *Auguste Comte and Positivism* ([1865] Mill, *Collected Works*, vol. X, pp. 261–368):

> M. Comte takes this opportunity of declaring his opinions on the proper constitution of the family, and in particular of the marriage institution. They are of the most orthodox and conservative sort ... He ... strenuously maintains that the marriage institution has been, in various aspects, beneficially modified with the advance of society, and that we may not yet have reached the last of these modifications; but strenuously maintains that such changes cannot possibly affect what he regards as the essential principles of the institution – the irrevocability of the engagement, and the complete subordination of the wife to the husband, and of women generally to men; which are precisely the great vulnerable points of the existing constitution of society ... At a later period, ... his opinions and feelings respecting women were very much modified, without becoming more rational: in his final scheme of society, instead of being treated as grown children, they were exalted into goddesses: honours, privileges, and immunities, were lavished on them, only not simple justice (Mill, *Collected Works*, vol. X, pp. 310–311).

Comte opposed divorce because he believed that the possibility of liberal divorce would lead to social instability. Mill thought this unconvincing, and believed that liberal divorce:

would in general be used only for its legitimate purpose – for enabling those who, by a blameless or excusable mistake, have lost their first throw for domestic happiness, to free themselves (with due regard for all interests concerned) from the burthensome yoke, and try, under more favourable auspices, another chance (Mill, *Collected Works*, vol. X, p. 312).

Then he cut the matter short, declaring that 'any further discussion' would be 'incompatible with the nature and limits of the present paper'. This final evaluation is interesting because in it Mill was prepared to defend divorce four years before the publication of the *Subjection of Women*, which was less than clear on the issue. He had always been prepared to do so in his private and unpublished correspondence. And he recognized the inevitability of the transformation of social institutions and gender roles as society 'progressed'; all social analysis is historically contingent.

And what was Taylor's view of all this? One sentence from the penultimate paragraph of her *Emancipation of Women* (1851), published a few years after the conclusion of the Mill-Comte correspondence, is striking:

What is wanted for women is equal rights, equal admission to all social privileges; not a position apart, a sort of sentimental priesthood ([1951] Rossi 1970, p. 120).

If Mill was impatient with the mysticism of the Saint-Simonians and with the later Comte, Taylor was even less tolerant.

THE EMANCIPATION OF WOMEN (1851)

Shortly after Mill's correspondence with Comte came to an end, Taylor and Mill prepared to publish *The Emancipation of Women*. This is the one piece of writing that is undeniably attributed to Harriet Taylor. Rossi argued that the body of this piece must be attributed to Taylor, because it contains arguments similar to those she made in 1832, but that Mill had not made in the earlier essay and would not make in the later *Subjection of Women*. This has led later commentators, such as Barbara Caine and Michèle Pujol, to suggest that the arguments are ones that Mill did not support, even though he was prepared to allow the editor of the *Westminster Review*, which published the piece, to believe that he was the author.[14]

There is no question that feminist principles are more openly espoused in this article than they were in Mill's 1832 piece, or would be in his *Subjection* (1869). The piece is set up as a comment on the 'Women's Rights Convention' held in Worcester Massachusetts, and claims that the three principal demands – that of equal admission to education, the franchise and full political rights, and '*partnership* in the labours and gains, risks and remuneration, of productive industry' (Rossi 1970, p. 95) – are unobjectionable. The primary issue concerns whether or not women should enter into productive employment on an equal footing with men. It will be remembered that Mill had claimed otherwise in 1832.

Taylor addresses the issue of whether 'to give the same freedom of occupation to women as to men, would be an injurious addition to the crowd of competitors, by whom the avenues to almost all kinds of employment are choked up, and its remuneration depressed' (Rossi 1970, p. 104). She examines the worst possible case, that in which the wage would be so depressed that 'a man and a woman could not together earn more than is now earned by the man alone' (Rossi 1970, p. 104). And she concludes:

> Even if every woman, as matters now stand, had a claim on some man for support, how infinitely preferable is it that part of the income should be of the woman's earning, even if the aggregate sum were but little increased by it, rather than that she should be compelled to stand aside in order that men may be the sole earners, and the sole dispensers of what is earned (Rossi 1970, p. 105).

This is consistent with Taylor's 1832 paper, although infinitely better argued. Is this a statement with which Mill must have disagreed?

In the 1832 essay, he unquestioningly accepted existing gender roles as 'natural'. In his later writings, the issue is much more difficult to see quite so clearly. In the *Subjection of Women*, for example, he says:

> In any otherwise just state of things, it is not, therefore, I think, a desirable custom, that the wife should contribute by her labour to the income of the family. In an unjust state of things, her doing so may be useful to her, by making her of more value in the eyes of the man who is legally her master; but, on the other hand, it enables him still farther to abuse his power, by forcing her to work, and leaving the support of the family to her exertions, while he spends most of his time in drinking and idleness (Rossi 1970, p. 179).

It seems clear enough that Mill acknowledges that in the present, very imperfect state of society, Taylor's argument may be valid in some circumstances. And invalid in other circumstances. And almost certain to be superseded in the natural course of events, as history unfolds.

The *Principles of Political Economy* (which Mill claimed to be a joint production of his and Taylor's) is equally hedged. In a discussion of the Factory Acts, it is claimed that the much-vaunted 'protection' of women embodied in the legislation is little more than a device to ensure that women would be available for household production:

> If women had as absolute control as men have over their own persons and their own patrimony or acquisitions, there would be no plea for limiting their hours of

labouring for themselves, in order that they might have time to labour for the husband, in what is called, by the advocates of restriction, *his* home. Women employed in factories are the only women in the labouring rank of life whose position is not that of slaves and drudges (Mill, *Collected Works*, vol. III, p. 953).

So Mill was concerned about the exploitation of working class women. And, in their case at least, there is little question that freedom of employment is an essential solution to poverty. Nevertheless:

It cannot ... be considered as a *permanent* element in the condition of the labouring classes, that the mother of the family (the case of a single woman is totally different) should be under the necessity of working for subsistence, at least elsewhere than in their place of abode (Mill, *Collected Works*, vol. II, p. 394).

This particular passage is in the 1848 edition of the *Principles*, is absent from the 1852, 1857 and 1862 editions, and is reinserted in the 1865 and 1871 editions.

Mill is conflicted on the issue of married women working outside the home, and the reason for this is his adherence to some version of the wages fund theory.[15] He is concerned that wages will be driven down by the glut of workers, so that twice as much labour is required to earn the same living wage as before. If this were to happen, it would clearly be undesirable from a social perspective. From a personal point of view, the issue is far more complex. And to resolve matters, Mill fell back on the distinction he had learned from the Saint-Simonians and from Comte: he distinguished between the present, very imperfect, society in which personal matters must take precedence and a new, ideal society of the future. At present, it may indeed be desirable for married working women – and even for women of the middle classes – to work outside the home, even if the consequence is a depressed wage rate. Come the New Jerusalem, this will clearly be superseded by a better state of affairs. And the perfect state of affairs he anticipates is not a return to outmoded and rigid gender roles based on some idea of the unchanging 'nature of women'. It is rather an entirely new order of society in which gender relations, property relations, and production and distribution themselves have been reformed.

In the meantime, however, personal interest in particular cases must be left to decide matters. Mill was adamantly opposed to legislation restricting employment opportunities for women, because 'these things, once opinion were rightly directed on the subject, might with perfect safety be left to be regulated by opinion, without any interference of law' (Rossi 1970, p. 180). This is particularly the case in a situation where 'the utmost latitude ought to exist for the adaptation of general rules to individual suitabilities' (Rossi 1970, p. 179).

There is no reason to believe that Mill disapproved of the content of *The Enfranchisement of Women*. On 20 March 1854, he did, however, write to Taylor:

> I should not like any more than you that that paper should be supposed to be the best we could do, or the real expression of our mind on the subject. This is not supposed of a mere review article written on a special occasion as that was, but would perhaps be so if the same thing were put out, years after, under our own auspices as a pamphlet (Mill, *Collected Works*, vol. XIV, p. 189).

There is prickliness in Mill's reaction to this piece that suggests a certain amount of discomfort with it. His *Subjection of Women* was intended to be a better presentation of the Taylor–Mill position, and it is much more characteristically Mill's: it is qualified and hedged in a way that the very clean and polemical *Enfranchisement* is not. Taylor's focus and concern was always on the pragmatic; how should institutions be transformed here and now in order to improve the lot of women? Mill, despite his apparent rejection of the utopian elements of French thought, was always focused on an abstraction. He was a theorist.

THE SUBJECTION OF WOMEN

Mill's final statement on the roles of women in society draws together many of the ideas already mentioned. This was produced after Harriet Taylor's death, and can be seen as Mill unconstrained. Without Taylor's immediate presence and modifying effect, he indulged his taste for theory at the expense of the immediately practical. Therefore, the residual elements of his exposure to the Saint-Simonians and his debate with Comte are much more readily apparent than they were in the joint productions. On questions of suffrage and property rights, *Subjection* is unequivocal; both must be reformed to ensure full political, economic and social equality for women. On other issues – in particular divorce and ideal gender roles – Mill was more guarded.

First Mill, like Comte, accepted that 'family life (is) ... the principal source of the social feelings, and the only school open to mankind in general, in which unselfishness can be learnt, and the feelings and conduct demanded by social relations be made habitual' (Mill, *Collected Works*, vol. X, p. 310). The difference is that Mill believed:

> the moral regeneration of mankind will only really commence, when the most fundamental of the social relations is placed under the rule of equal justice, and when human beings learn to cultivate their strongest sympathy with an equal in

rights and in cultivation (Rossi 1970, p. 236).

Mill shied away from precise recommendation with respect to practical issues such as divorce legislation. This is a matter that he had dealt with in the past: in 1832 he wrote very clearly (in his unpublished essay on marriage) that individuals ought to be permitted to correct a mistake. This position is reiterated in his *Auguste Comte and Positivism*. In a letter to an unknown correspondent of 1855, he writes:

> My opinion on Divorce is that though any relaxation of the irrevocability of marriage would be an improvement, nothing ought to be ultimately rested in, short of entire freedom on both sides to dissolve this like any other partnership (Mill, *Collected Works*, vol. XIV, p. 500).

And yet, there is no clear recommendation in the *Subjection*.

The omission was deliberate, and in fact the reasoning recalls the best tradition of Père Enfantin. In a letter of 22 July 1870, to Henry Keylock Rusden, he writes:

> The purpose of that book [*Subjection*] was to maintain the claim of women, whether in marriage or out of it, to perfect equality in all rights with the male sex. The relaxation or alteration of the marriage laws ... is a question quite distinct from the object to which the book is devoted, and one which, in my own opinion, cannot be properly decided until that object has been attained. It is impossible, in my opinion, that a right marriage law can be made by men alone, or until women have an equal voice in making it (Mill, *Collected Works*, vol. XVII, p. 1751).

Yes, Mill supported a relaxation of the rules regarding the indissolubility of marriage. Yet all institutional arrangements are historically contingent. As society progresses, ideal arrangements change. And Mill was focused on principle.

A hint of the distinction between the present, very imperfect, world and the ideal world that would yet come, and the quite different policy recommendations for the two, is already present in the discussion of divorce in Mill's 1832 essay, written before he corresponded with Comte. Mill introduces the concept of divorce by recognizing that 'the indissolubility of marriage is the keystone of woman's present lot, and the whole comes down and must be reconstructed if that is removed' (Rossi 1970, p. 73).

Nevertheless, he argues in that essay that:

> In considering ... what is the best law of marriage, we are to suppose that women already are, what they would be in the best state of society; no less capable of existing independently and respectably without men, than men without women (Rossi 1970, p. 77).

This distinction between the present world and the ideal becomes much more apparent after Mill's debate with Comte, with the result that Mill was not prepared to deal with the issue of divorce in *Subjection*.

Gender roles, and the related issue of women's nature, are treated in a parallel manner. Here, again, the legacy of the debate with Comte is apparent. In the 1832 essay, Mill already recognized that 'there is no natural inequality between the sexes; except perhaps in bodily strength; even that admits of doubt' (Rossi 1970, p. 73). Moreover, 'every step in the progress of civilization has tended to diminish the deference paid to bodily strength (and) ... has similarly been marked by a nearer approach to equality in the condition of the sexes' (Rossi 1970, p. 73):

> If they (i.e. men and women) are still far from being equal, the hindrance is not now in the difference of physical strength, but in artificial feelings and prejudices (Rossi 1970, p. 73).

And yet, in 1832, Mill has no difficulty referring to the 'natural task' of women, which is to be accomplished by '*being* (rather) than by *doing*' (Rossi 1970, p. 75), or suggesting that

> The only difference between the employments of women and those of men will be, that those which partake most of the beautiful, or which require delicacy and taste rather than muscular exertion, will naturally fall to the share of women: all branches of the fine arts in particular (Rossi 1970, p. 77).

That is, all of the sources (including but not limited to the Saint-Simonians, who suggested to Mill that the nature of women is largely determined by education and habit) already left their trace in the 1832 essay.

The debate with Comte challenged and reinforced these ideas, so that by 1869 when Mill came to write *Subjection*, he declared that:

> It cannot now be known how much of the existing mental differences between men and women is natural, and how much artificial; whether there are any natural differences at all; or, supposing all artificial causes of difference to be withdrawn, what natural character would be revealed (Rossi 1970, p. 202).

This does not, of course, prevent him from speculating, and here the debate with Comte replays itself. For example, Mill acknowledges that physiologists have shown the brains of women to be smaller, on average, than those of men, but suggests that they might, as compensation, operate more quickly:

> It would not be surprising – it is indeed an hypothesis which accords well with the differences actually observed between the mental operations of the two sexes – if men on the average should have the advantage in the size of the brain, and women in activity of cerebral circulation (Rossi 1970, p. 200).

He considers whether women are, by nature, more prone to 'nervous susceptibility' (Rossi 1970, p. 194), less capable of sustained thought (Rossi p. 197), or more intuitive (Rossi 1970, p.193). But he concludes repeatedly:

I have before repudiated the notion of its being yet certainly known that there is any natural difference at all in the average strength or direction of the mental capacities of the two sexes, much less what that difference is. Nor is it possible that this should be known, so long as the psychological laws of the formation of character have been so little studied, even in a general way, and in particular case never scientifically applied at all; so long as the most obvious external causes of difference of character are habitually disregarded ... (Rossi 1970, p. 200).

That Mill is writing this with the memory of Comte in mind seems clear enough when he begins his diatribe on the habitual errors of the anonymous 'Englishman', who cannot imagine what is not observed, and the equally nameless 'Frenchman' who imagines that what he observes is evidence of 'nature' (Rossi 1970, p. 202). In fact, Mill dismisses outright any attempt to determine the character of women through simple induction, 'mere empirical generalizations, framed, without philosophy or analysis, upon the first instances which present themselves' (Rossi 1970, p. 201).

Mill's willingness to hold in abeyance any firm conclusions about the nature of women, which was somewhat ambiguous in his 1832 essay, clarifies itself in his analysis of gender roles in *Subjection*. He proposed to:

[give] to women the free use of their faculties, by leaving them the free choice of their employments, and opening to them the same field of occupation and the same prizes and encouragements as to other human beings (Rossi 1970, p. 221).

This he considers no more than a simple extension of the principles of freedom and competition.

There is no need for legislation to enforce 'natural' gender roles because 'what is contrary to women's nature to do, they will never be made to do by simply giving their nature free play' (Rossi 1970, p. 154):

What women by nature cannot do, it is quite superfluous to forbid them from doing. What they can do, but not so well as the men who are their competitors, competition suffices to exclude them from ... If women have a greater natural inclination for some things than for others, there is no need of laws or social inculcation to make the majority of them do the former in preference to the latter (Rossi 1970, p. 154).

This statement is quite markedly more sophisticated than Mill's 1832 discussion of 'natural' gender roles. This is the consequence of a fundamental theoretical and methodological debate on the nature of social theory.

Is there evidence in *Subjection*, as Michèle Pujol argues, of 'Mill's subscription to a bourgeois Victorian view of woman's nature' (Pujol 1992, p. 34) or that 'Mill's patriarchal views on sex roles represent the one instance of irreconcilable disagreement with Harriet Taylor' (Pujol 1992, p. 35)? Or Richard Krouse's argument that Mill demonstrated an undying attachment to a romantic ideal of womanhood (Krouse 1982, 1983)? Not a lot. Mill claims that 'the majority of women' will continue to pursue the one vocation where they face no competition – motherhood (Rossi 1970, p. 183). In a world where birth control is unreliable at best, it only requires a commitment to 'a natural attraction between the sexes' to generate that outcome. Will 'motherhood' continue to be defined and delimited in the same way after the elimination of unnatural restrictions on the participation of women in society? That remains, in Mill's analysis, an open question.

CONCLUSION

I have argued that the tendency of historians to treat the Mill–Taylor project of feminism in isolation from other intellectual currents – in particular, in isolation from Mill's deep attraction to French thought – has led to a set of unproductive issues in the secondary literature. In particular, the idea that one can characterize such a wide-ranging debate in the nineteenth century on the basis of whether Mill or Taylor was the 'more radical' is too simplistic. Taylor was a pragmatist, focused on the here and now. Mill was, in his heart, a theorist with very strong tendencies towards utopianism. It is, in fact, deeply ironic that Mill was so attracted to the Saint-Simonians at the start of his investigation into these issues, because the same split occurred in the Saint-Simonian movement between the 'pragmatic' women of the movement and the utopian 'Père Enfantin'. Mill may ultimately have dismissed the latter as a crank, but he showed a similar predilection.

The secondary literature has made much of one difference between the writings of Mill and Taylor. Taylor was adamant that women ought to be permitted access to employment on the same terms as men, while Mill hesitated, concerned that the flood of middle-class women into the workforce would push down the wage rate. There is little evidence that this was an 'irreconcilable difference'. Once one fully accounts for Mill's distinction between policies for the here and now – where Taylor's suggestion may have merit because of the very imperfect relations between men and women – and policies for the ideal state, much of the tension in Mill's thought disappears. Should married women work alongside men for subsistence? Mill cannot accept that this is an ideal permanent solution. Does that imply that an ideal permanent solution is a return to rigid gender roles, legislated into existence? Hardly. An ideal permanent solution is, as in the case of divorce legislation, to be worked out after the artificial restrictions on women's participation in the political, social and economic activities of the nation are eliminated.

This leaves the strong suggestion that Mill's characterization of the Mill-Taylor intellectual partnership has a good deal of merit. 'One can,' writes John Stuart Mill in *Subjection*, 'to an almost laughable degree, infer what a man's wife is like, from his opinions about women in general' (Rossi 1970, p. 151). The companionship and criticism of 'a really superior woman', he says, is the best antidote to the tendencies of the speculative thinker to 'overlook the contradiction which outward facts oppose to (his) theories', and 'to lose sight of the legitimate purpose of speculation altogether' (Rossi 1970, p. 192). Consequently, one is unsurprised by his claim in the *Autobiography* that from Harriet Taylor he learned much about 'the ultimate aims' of social theory, as well as 'the immediately useful and practically attainable', while his own 'strength lay wholly in the uncertain and slippery intermediate region, that of theory' (Mill, *Collected* Works, vol. I, p. 197).

Taylor, 'a superior woman', served the role of reminding Mill, 'a speculative mind', that utopian solutions are of limited usefulness in a political debate. *Subjection*, and especially Mill's animated debate with Auguste Comte, demonstrates the strength of that tendency in Mill's intellectual life.

REFERENCES

Bain, Alexander (1882), *John Stuart Mill: a criticism*, London.
Barrault, Emile (n.d.) 'Le mariage,' in Enfantin *Oeuvres*, **45**, 71–96.
Caine, Barbara (1994), 'Feminism and Political Economy in Victorian England – or John Stuart Mill, Henry Fawcett and Henry Sidgwick Ponder the '''Woman Question''', in Peter Groenewegen (ed.), *Feminism and Political Economy in Victorian England*, Aldershot: Edward Elgar Publishing.
Comte, Auguste (1830–1842), *Cours de Philosophie Positive*, 6 vols.
Comte, Auguste (1851–1854), *Système de Politique Positive*, 4 vols, Paris.
Comte, Auguste (1889), 'Traité de Politique Positive,' appearing originally in the third part of the *Catéchisme des Industriels* (see *Early Essays on Social Philosophy*, translated by J.D. Hutton, London).
Enfantin, Barthelémy-Prosper (1832), 'Enseignements fait par le Père Suprème', in *Réunion général de la famille, séances des 19 et 21 novembre 1831*, Paris: Bureau de Globe.
Enfantin, Barthelémy-Prosper (1865–1878), *Oeuvres de Saint-Simon et d'Enfantin*, 47 cols. Paris. (cited as *Oeuvres*)
Forget, Evelyn L. (1992), 'J.S. Mill and the Tory School: the rhetorical value of the recantation', *History of Political Economy*, **24** (1), 31–59.
Forget, Evelyn L. (2001), 'Saint-Simonian Feminism', *Feminist Economics*, **7** (1), 79–96.
Hayek, F.A. (1951), *John Stuart Mill and Harriet Taylor: Their Friendship and Subsequent Marriage*, Chicago: University of Chicago Press.
Kinzer, B.L., A.P. Robson and J.M. Robson (1992), *A Moralist in and out of Parliament. John Stuart Mill at Westminster, 1865–1868*, Toronto: Univeristy of Toronto Press.
Krouse, Richard (1982), 'Patriarchal Liberalism and Beyond: from John Stuart Mill to Harriet Taylor', in J. Bethke Elshtain (ed.), *The Family in Political Thought*, Amherst: University of Massachusetts Press, pp. 145–172.
Krouse, Richard (1983), 'Mill and Marx on Marriage, Divorce, and the Family', *Social Concept*, **1**(1), 36–76.
Lerner, Max (1961), *Essential Works of John Stuart Mill*, New York: Bantam.
Lévy-Bruhl, L. (1899), *Lettres Inédites de John Stuart Mill à Auguste Comte, Publiées Avec les Réponses de Comte et une Introduction*, Paris.
Mill, John Stuart (1965–), *The Collected Works of John Stuart Mill*, Toronto: University of Toronto Press.
Mill, John Stuart ([1832] 1970), 'Early Essay on Marriage and Divorce', in Rossi, pp. 65–84 (also published in Mill 1965, vol. 21, pp. 35–50).
Mill, John Stuart (1865), *Auguste Comte and Positivism*, in Mill 1965, vol. 10, pp. 261-368.
Mill, John Stuart ([1869] 1970), 'The Subjection of Women,' in Rossi, pp. 123–242 (also published in Mill 1965, vol. 21, pp. 259–340).
Mineka, Francis (1944), *The Dissidence of Dissent*, Chapel Hill: University of North Carolina Press.
Mueller, Iris Wessel (1956), *John Stuart Mill and French Thought*, Urbana: University of Illinois Press.
Owen, Robert ([1835] 1840), *Lectures on the Marriages of the Priesthood of the Old Immoral World ... with an Appendix containing the Marriage System of the new Moral World*, Leeds: Hobson.

Pujol, Michèle (1992), *Feminism and Anti-Feminism in Early Economic Thought,* Aldershot: Edward Elgar Publishing.

Pujol, Michèle (1995), 'The Feminist Economic Thought of Harriet Taylor (1807–1858)', in D.A. Dimand, R.W. Dimand and E.L. Forget (eds), *Women of Value,* Aldershot: Edward Elgar Publishing.

Pujol, Michèle (2000), 'Harriet Taylor Mill' in R. Dimand, M.A. Dimand and E.L. Forget (eds), *A Biographical Dictionary of Women Economists,* Aldershot: Edward Elgar Publishing.

Rossi, Alice, S. (ed.) (1961), *Essays on Sex Equality,* by John Stuart Mill and Harriet Taylor Mill, Chicago: University of Chicago Press.

Stillinger, Jack (ed.) (1961), *The Early Draft of John Stuart Mill's Autobiography,* Urbana: University of Illinois Press.

Taylor, Harriet ([1832] 1970) 'Early Essay on Marriage and Divorce', in Rossi, pp. 84–87 (also published in Mill 1965, vol. 21, pp. 375–377).

Vaysset-Boutbien, Raymonde (1941), *John Stuart Mill et la sociologie Française contemporaine,* Paris.

Wiley, Basil (1950), *Nineteenth Century Studies,* London: Chatto and Windus.

NOTES

1. Although this 1851 essay is credibly attributed to Harriet Taylor, Mill was pleased to allow the editor to believe it was his own. See John Robson's discussion in Mill, *Collected Works*, vol. XXI, pp. lxxiv–lxxvii.
2. The Fabian socialists likewise attributed Mill's socialism to Taylor, and therefore developed a much more sympathetic view of Taylor, as well as of the possibility of an intellectual partnership between men and women (see Rossi 1970, p. 38).
3. The evidence for dating is slight. Hayek postulated a date of 1832, which Rossi accepts. John Robson (Mill, *Collected Works*, vol. XXI, pp. lviii–lx; lxiii) suggests late 1832 or 1833, but characterizes the conclusion as a 'rather hollow certainty'.
4. For a fuller discussion of Saint-Simonian feminism, see Forget (2001).
5. *Oeuvre* XLV, Sermon 48, 'L'Affranchisement des femmes' (Abel Transom n.d.), 360–371.
6. *Oeuvre* XLV, Sermon 47, 'Le Prolétaire des femmes' (anon., n.d.), 354–360.
7. *Oeuvres* XLV, Sermon 23, 'Le mariage' (E. Barrault, n.d.), 80–81.
8   Oeuvres XLV, Sermon 23, 'Le mariage', 71–72.
9. Oeuvres XLV, Sermon 49, 'Aux railleurs' (n.d.), 381.
10. And, incidentally, they would build the Suez Canal while they were there.
11. See Mill's untitled article on the trial in the *Examiner,* 9 September 1832, p. 585. Enfantin, Duveyrier and Chevalier were sentenced to one year in prison, and Barrault and Rodrigues to a fine.
12. The Comte–Mill correspondence is in French. The translations here are mine.
13. That is, a science intermediate between biology and sociology that Mill hoped would explain the formation of human character.
14. See Mill 1965, *Collected Works*, vol. 21, pp. lxxiii–lxxvii for a discussion of this matter.
15. This notwithstanding his well-known recantation of the wage-fund doctrine in 1869, and despite the credible claim that he had never actually maintained the more rigid forms of the doctrine (see Forget 1992).

Index

absolutism 3–4, 25, 40–42, 52, 54, 56
Adam and Eve 43–4, 52, 57
agriculture 77, 244
Alexander, William 6, 110, 116, 119–20
  The History of Women, from the Earliest Antiquity to the Present Time 6, 119
Alembert, J. d' 12, 127–130
Aristotle 11, 22, 193
Astell, Mary 45, 200

Barre, Poulain de la *see* Poulain
Bazard, Saint-Amand 289, 293
Bentham, Jeremy 2, 10–11, 14–5, 165–86, 201, 230, 241, 243–51, 252, 259, 261
biology 3–4, 63, 65, 67, 71, 101, 108, 133, 296–7
Brown, John 110, 113

Cabanis, Pierre-Jean-Georges 143, 145, 159–60, 165
capital 12, 110, 169, 195, 270, 273, 289
capitalism 15, 108–10, 121, 246–9, 255, 259, 274
Carlyle, Thomas 267–8, 282, 284, 293
Chadwick, Edwin 14, 225, 230–31, 233
child care 17, 26, 119, 134, 258, 288
childbearing 15, 25–6, 30, 134, 258
children 46, 53, 56, 65, 124, 157, 166, 174, 179, 182–3, 185, 199, 218, 231–3, 291–2
church 97, 100, 110, 145, 211, 216
civil society 44, 52, 143–4, 152, 155, 207, 218–9
class 7–12, 18, 32, 88, 110, 197, 210, 231, 238
Comte, Auguste 138, 285, 289, 293–299, 301–306

Condorcet, Nicolas 6–8, 16, 110, 122–3, 125, 127–38, 141, 144, 165, 210, 218, 245–6, 248–9

Condorcet, Sophie *see* Grouchy, Sophie de
conjectural history 29, 35
consent theory 41–2, 50
conservatism 9, 14, 115–6, 121
contract 4, 48, 50, 53, 55, 57, 270–71, 274
  employment 51–3, 55
  marriage 52–7, 291
crime 157, 271

decadence 109–12, 114, 118,
deductivism 21, 25–6
  economic 29, 35
democracy 9–10, 89, 110
Descartes, René 4, 21–4, 30
determinism
  biological 5, 85, 101
  cultural 5, 31
  economic 5, 96, 101
  theological 4, 57
discrimination 3, 21, 25, 33, 167
  discrimination theory 22
  positive discrimination 172, 176
division of labour 14, 26, 32, 213, 217, 219, 220
divorce 79, 93, 95, 97, 166, 174, 177, 214, 218, 223, 235, 257, 285, 290, 292, 298–9, 303

education 8–9, 12, 44–6, 112, 124, 131–4, 136, 145, 152–5, 159–60, 166, 179, 197, 199–200, 243–5, 290, 296, 298, 304
Eichtal, Gustave d' 289, 293–4
Enfantin, Barthelémy-Prosper 289,

292–3, 303, 306
Enlightenment 9, 108, 121–2, 127, 142
environment 3–5, 65–7, 75, 79, 88, 121, 160, 179, 295, 298
equality 9, 40, 54, 57, 136, 175, 185, 245
    class 9, 15
ethology 296–8
exchange value 15, 273

Factory Acts 16–18, 230–31, 300
family 14, 17, 27–8, 57, 78, 88–90, 93, 117, 123, 134, 206, 211–4, 216–7, 218–9, 220, 231, 264, 288, 290, 302
Fawcett, Henry 226, 236
feminism 1, 5, 12, 15, 130, 207, 210, 285, 289, 291, 294
Filmer, Robert 41–3, 50, 56
Fourier, Charles 250, 293
franchise 8, 9, 121
freedom 166, 270, 305
French Revolution 7–8, 10–11, 13–14, 108–10, 121–3, 129, 131–2, 137, 164, 197, 200, 207, 241–2

gender
    analysis 2, 4, 7–8, 16, 65, 85, 206–7, 216–8, 220, 290
    behaviour 63, 65–6, 68, 71, 74–5, 78–80
    boundaries 263
    conservatism 6, 9, 13, 120
    debate 4, 8–9, 14, 18
    differences 2–3, 5, 21–23, 30–32, 39, 44, 46–7, 55–6, 64–5, 75, 80, 86, 88–9, 101, 116, 198, 251, 291, 294, 298
    economics 7–8, 21, 63, 75, 78
    emancipation 9
    equality 2–4, 7, 9, 14–15, 128–9, 132, 136–7, 251, 257, 288, 291–2, 294
    inequality 9, 135, 166, 171, 197, 251–2
    relations 4–7, 10, 14, 33, 40, 42, 53, 63, 65–6, 68–9, 71, 78–80, 87, 93, 113, 116, 118, 235, 255–8, 290, 301

roles 209, 212, 216, 220, 286–7, 292, 299–301, 304–7
    status 2–4, 7, 18, 65, 77
Godwin, William 110, 122–25, 141, 196, 256
goods 47, 49, 54, 269–70, 290
Gouges, Olympe de 208–9
government 9, 26, 67, 69, 85, 245–6
    covenant of 41
    despotic 69, 74–5
    monarchic 69, 71–5
    republican 69–71, 74–5, 78
Grotius, Hugo 4, 52, 65, 105
Grouchy, Sophie de 6–9, 11, 123–4, 142–61

Hume, David 79, 88, 284

ideologues (*Idéologues, Idéologistes*) 160, 207, 210, 214, 217–8, 220, 223
Industrial revolution 16, 241
inequality 120, 123, 134, 144, 156–8, 166
inheritance 93, 96, 100, 289–90
injustice 156–7, 159

Jevons, William Stanley 18, 230
justice 3, 21, 53, 87, 128–9, 143, 145, 149–53

labour 15, 72, 158, 169, 195, 248–9, 289
    force 134, 270
    capacity to 47, 50, 55
    freedom of 128
    market 8, 13, 17–18, 124, 175
    productivity 4, 33, 56, 95
    relations 257–8
Lacombe, Clare 208–9
law 9, 16, 47, 67, 74, 78, 151, 156–8, 173–5, 177–8, 245–6, 301, 305
    marriage law 285–6, 298
    natural law 48, 50, 65, 78, 124, 245
leisure 269–70, 273
liberalism 3, 16, 121
liberty 1, 8, 14, 47–8, 50, 63, 74, 127–8, 133, 136, 151, 156, 186, 215–6

Locke, John 4, 25, 40–58, 63–5, 67, 105, 110
luxury 70, 109–12, 115, 118

Macauley, Catherine 197, 201–202, 205
male domination 2, 4, 16, 25–6, 29–32, 39, 55, 236, 254–5, 256
Malthus, Thomas 10, 14, 110, 122–3, 125, 136–7, 168, 227, 231, 240, 264, 275
    Essay on Population 10, 136
Marcet, Jane Haldimard 194–5
marriage 9–10, 17, 44, 53–4, 68–9, 78–9, 91, 95, 98–9, 115, 122–4, 157, 166, 174, 176–7, 198–9, 213–4, 226–7, 233, 250, 255, 285–6, 288–90, 292, 303
Martineau, Harriet 16, 194, 230, 262–77, 281–4
Marx, Karl 18, 121, 195, 228, 259
Masham, Damaris 45
materialism 101–102, 105, 116
Meynieu, Harriet 194
militarism 98–9
Mill, Harriet *see* Taylor, Harriet Hardy
Mill, James 1, 11, 137, 168, 181–182, 224, 252–4, 256
Mill, John Stuart 1, 14, 16–17, 34, 137–38, 168, 177, 208, 224, 226, 230, 236, 246, 259, 285–307, 310
    Principles of Political Economy 17, 230, 286, 300–01
    On the subjection of women 1, 137–8, 259, 285, 288, 299–300, 302, 304, 305–307
Millar, John 6, 10, 87, 105, 110, 116, 118–121
    Observations Concerning the Distinction of Ranks in Society 6, 116, 118, 121
modes of subsistence 77–8, 85, 86–7, 89, 92, 101–102, 108, 116
    agricultural 77, 94–7, 100, 102, 117, 134
    commercial 86, 97, 99–100, 102, 108, 118
    hunting 77, 89–91, 102, 105, 134
    pastoral 77, 91–3, 97, 100, 102,

117, 134
monarchy 66, 110, 113, 145, 211
monetary theory 40
money 49, 156–7
Montagu, Mary Wortley 194
Montesquieu, Charles Secondat, Baron de 4–5, 7, 29, 35–6, 63–8, 85, 87–8, 101, 105, 110–11, 128, 190
    The Spirit of the laws 29, 63–4, 76, 78–9, 85, 88, 100
    Persian Letters 36, 79, 88
morality 143, 149, 153, 155
More, Hannah 13, 196–8, 201–2
    Strictures on the modern system of education 196, 201

Owen, Robert 15, 246–7, 249–51, 290, 292

parliament 41, 243, 255
patriarchal authority 4, 14, 41–2, 44, 52, 56, 64, 88, 90, 92–3, 218–9, 253, 255
physiology 41, 68, 296–7
political economy 25, 40, 67, 71, 76, 125, 194–5, 202, 220, 224–5, 228, 243, 246–8, 257, 259, 274
polygamy 68–69, 80, 235
poor laws 14, 231–34, 236–7, 241
population 1, 12, 14, 27–8, 31, 77, 122, 124, 136, 166, 169, 226–7
Poulain de la Barre 3, 4, 21–36, 63, 85 105
    Equality of the sexes 22, 25, 28, 35
    Dialogues on the Education of women 22, 35
    The Superiority of men 22, 25, 28
poverty 156, 158, 213–4, 233, 301
prejudice 3, 33, 35, 135, 165, 179–80, 182–4, 186, 199, 290, 294
Priestley, Joseph 130, 196
productive labour 12, 55–6, 98
productivity 57, 89, 117
progress 7–8, 15–6, 63, 80, 102, 110, 119–20, 128, 135–7, 177, 236, 242–3, 245–6, 298
property 4–5, 9, 27, 47–8, 50, 54, 63, 74, 89, 91–3, 96, 117–8, 128,

156–8, 253, 257, 289, 301
private property 41–2, 47, 50, 289
property rights 54, 56, 74, 255,
    290
property theory 40, 55
prostitution 171–3, 216, 226, 264–5,
    283, 290
public policy 14, 225
Pufendorf, Samuel 4, 52, 65, 105

queens 54, 132, 181
Quesnay 12, 76

race 18, 128, 132
rationalism 15, 30, 66, 87
relativism 29, 35, 63, 76, 79–80, 85,
    87–8, 101
religion 128, 132, 165, 186
Ricardo, David 14–15, 207, 224, 231,
    243, 247–9, 261, 269
rights 2, 4, 8, 10–11, 49, 54, 89, 243
    equal rights 15–18, 132, 180, 208,
        230
    human rights 9–10, 21, 110, 132,
        143, 145, 149–52
    individual rights 218
    natural rights 64, 75, 131, 134,
        159
    political rights 133, 144
    'rights of man' 3, 10, 21, 44, 132,
        135, 143, 218
Rousseau 35–36, 143, 149, 155, 165,
    218
Roussel, Pierre 145–6

Saint Simon 15, 245–6, 248–50,
    288–9
Saint-Simonians 288–95, 299, 301–
06
Say, Jean–Baptiste 13–14, 137, 160,
    206–220
    Treatise on Political Economy 137
scripture 22, 25, 41–3
Senior, Nassau 13–14, 225–36, 240
slavery 11, 16, 27, 48, 50, 90, 98,
    128, 178, 181, 185, 262–75, 281–
    4, 291
    women as slaves 6, 74, 95, 113,
        118, 134–5, 250, 255
    marriage as slavery 10, 98, 176,

178, 180, 214
Smith, Adam 1, 5–7, 9–10, 12, 16,
    63, 78–9, 86–102, 105–108, 116,
    118, 131, 142–6, 149, 159–60,
    195–6, 198, 202, 243, 264, 268,
    275, 284
    The Wealth of Nations 1, 197,
        202, 268
    Lectures in Jurisprudence 2, 5–6,
        9–10, 79, 196
    Theory of moral sentiments 7–8,
        131, 142–5, 201
social contract 40–41, 49
socialism 15, 17, 125, 160, 246–7,
    251, 286–7, 289–90
state socialism 246–7
sociology 16, 297, 298
stage theory 6, 10, 28, 63, 77–8, 80,
    85, 86–102, 105, 108–9, 116, 118,
    124

Taylor, Harriet Hardy 1, 11, 14, 16–
    17, 230, 283–307, 310
    On the enfranchisement of women
        17, 138, 230, 285, 288, 301–2
    The emancipation of women 299
Thomas, Antoine 6, 85, 110, 113–6,
    118, 120
Thompson, William 1, 15–16, 241–
    59, 261
Torrens, Robert 14, 224
Tracy, Destutt de 160, 218, 223
Turgot, A.R.J. 129–30, 138, 245–6,
    248–9

Uncle Tom's Cabin 264, 272–3
unemployment 158, 172, 240
use value 15–16, 47
Utilitarianism 11, 15, 155, 165, 167,
    175, 177, 185, 215, 241, 243,
    247–249, 251–2, 256–7, 259, 265
utility 57, 185, 245

Voltaire 127–8, 131, 156, 164, 218

wages fund theory 301
Wakefield, Priscilla 11–13, 194–202,
    205
    *Reflections on the present
        condition of the female sex:*

with suggestions for its improvement 11, 195–97, 201–2

wealth 4, 6–7, 15, 42, 49, 54, 70, 77, 91–2, 94, 98–9, 116, 123, 144, 156, 169, 171, 174, 214, 242, 247–9, 256
  accumulation of 15, 49, 109, 111–13, 115–8, 121–2, 124, 255, 258

Webb, Sidney and Beatrice 231

Wheeler, Anna Doyle 1, 15–16, 240, 249–59

Wilberforce, William 268, 283

Wollstonecraft, Mary 7, 10–11, 110, 121–125, 165, 196–7, 202, 205, 208, 250, 252, 256, 259
  A vindication of the rights of woman 10, 165, 196, 202, 208, 250, 259

women
  dependence of 26, 124, 216, 251
  discrimination against 159
  education of 45–6, 136, 257–8, 293, 299
  exclusion of 8, 244, 256
  emancipation of 58, 180, 286, 289
  exploitation of 258–9, 301
  protection of 175–7
  subjection of 177, 186, 302
  subordination of 25, 27–8, 35, 41, 44, 58, 122, 124, 128–9, 134, 251
  suppression of 136
  working-class women 7, 9, 16

women's
  abilities 31, 34, 113
  authority 97, 99–100, 102
  bodies 117
  employment 1, 12–14, 17, 210, 213, 217, 228, 236, 286, 293, 299, 301, 306
  equality 53, 97, 102, 109, 291
  freedoms 11, 52, 130, 183
  independence 13, 210, 230
  inequality 95–6, 296
  intelligence 45, 57, 87, 117
  labour 7, 89
  liberation 137, 243
  natural attributes 64, 89, 304–6
  natural rights 53, 57
  obligations 196–7
  participation 293, 306
  physiology 46
  place in society 87–8, 254
  poverty 216–7
  progress 14, 120
  qualities 132, 291
  rationality 57, 64
  responsibilities 11, 286, 291–2
  rights 10, 52, 57, 131–2, 137–8, 196–7, 208, 218, 225–7, 259, 286, 299
  roles 131, 134, 196, 206, 210, 212, 218, 219, 225, 227, 256, 286, 291, 298
  role in reproduction 31, 89
  sexuality 6, 70, 118, 166
  social position 3, 5, 6, 21, 31, 40, 42, 57, 86–7, 87–8, 100, 102, 105, 108, 110, 169
  spirituality 57
  status 1, 2, 6, 12, 21, 29, 33, 36, 85, 86, 94, 98, 102, 108–110, 116–119, 133, 157, 174, 179, 197, 227, 235
  subservience 4, 256
  suffrage 1, 11, 130, 180, 182–4, 251, 285, 290, 299
  'weakness' 64, 251, 254
  wealth 117, 119